A Midsummer Eve's Dream

A Midsummer Eve's Dream

VARIATIONS ON A THEME
BY WILLIAM DUNBAR

A. D. Hope

NEW YORK   THE VIKING PRESS

The Reason why the Women here continue longest un-married, is, first, because that they live a more free and pleasant life, than when married, being now at perfect liberty to admit the embraces of any or several Men, if they please. These sort of Women generally marry amongst the common People, and seldom content themselves with their Husbands alone . . . Nor are they therefore rudely accounted Whores; but on the contrary, are always thought as fitting to be chose for Wives as any other; and accordingly in their Turn get Husbands as well as the rest.

William Bosman, *A New and Accurate Description of the Coast of Guinea*, 1705

Contents

1	Introduction	1
2	The Setting of the Poem	7
3	Goddesses and Fairies	28
4	Fays and Goddesses	50
5	The Fairy Cult	71
6	Love and Ceremony	95
7	The Fairy Cult in Edinburgh	118
8	The Blest Bond	129
9	St Valentine's Day	148
10	Wae Worth Maryage!	165
11	The Ball o' Kirriemuir	179
12	The Thing That Women Most Desire	198
13	Mother to Daughter	219
14	Islands of Women	240
15	Lineaments of Gratified Desire	256
	Appendix: 'The Tretis of the Tua Mariit Wemen and the Wedo' with a translation	269
	References	301
	Glossary	319
	Index	329

A Midsummer Eve's Dream

1

Introduction

SOME poems seem designed to tease us out of thought. They lead us on to ask questions which we know cannot be answered, yet there is a delight in the search for an answer which is its own reward for the wild goose chase, and indeed may make the chase seem more attractive than more sober kinds of inquiry.

William Dunbar's poem, 'The Tretis of the Tua Mariit Wemen and the Wedo', has proved such a lure to me—the fascination of a puzzle to which there is perhaps no longer an answer. Written for recitation at the court of James IV of Scotland about the end of the fifteenth century, and chosen by the first printers in Scotland as one of the texts to display their art for their royal patron, it presents us with a whole nest of puzzles. It is almost certainly by Dunbar, yet no other poem of his survives in this, by then old-fashioned, alliterative metre, and the verse is handled by an obvious master of the form; there are no known sources or analogues, which is in itself an oddity in medieval poetry, and it fits into the conventions of no one known class of poem, which is even more so in an age when the poets largely confined themselves within the recognised 'kinds'; but more puzzling than all is its combination of two apparently incongruous modes, the romantic and the realistic, the courtly and the vulgar.

It begins and ends in the highest and most delicate style of courtly description. The narrator goes out on Midsummer Eve to observe the amusements of the season, comes to an enclosure of hawthorn trees, and there overhears and oversees the meeting of three beautiful and richly dressed ladies who are drinking wine together in an arbour. Two are married women and the third is a widow who asks the other two to give their opinions and experience of the state of marriage. At this point the tone of the poem changes almost completely. The two young wives in turn describe their misery. One has been married off by her kinsmen to an old man hideous in appearance, repulsive in person and character, and incapable of 'Venus works'. She describes his attempts at these works in considerable detail and in exuberantly coarse but poetically effective language. The second wife is in a similar plight, for she has been married to a man of pleasure who has made himself impotent by excessive sexual indulgence. She too describes her husband with a wealth of contemptuous and realistically frank detail, and her own plight with vigour and feeling. Both young women proclaim that, if they could choose their mates for a year as the birds are supposed to do on St Valentine's Day, they would dispense with marriage altogether. The widow then tells her story, beginning with a parody of a medieval preacher beginning his sermon:

> Than said the Weido, I wis ther is no way othir;
> Now tydis me for to talk; my taill it is nixt:
> God my spreit now inspir and my speche quykkin,
> And send me sentence to say, substantious and noble;
> Sa that my preching may pers your perverst hertis,
> And mak yow mekar to men in maneris and conditiounis.

(ll. 245-51)

It appears that she has had two husbands, one more or less corresponding to the first wife's, the other to the second wife's. She has managed both with superb hypocrisy, obtained their goods, and, she implies, helped them to their graves. Even while they lived she was unfaithful to them and now she is rich and leads a life of freedom and pleasure taking as many lovers as she pleases. This, she tells the other two, is the way for a wise woman to deal with men and with marriage. This is how they can attain their wishes to have a life of perfect sexual freedom. The two ladies approve the widow's sermon and promise to follow her example. Up to this point the tone has been coarsely realistic. Now the poem returns to the tone of elegant and elevated romantic description with which

2

it opened. The three ladies spend the rest of the night in drinking and dancing courtly dances. Then there is a beautiful description of the dawn. The ladies return home to sleep, and the narrator emerges from hiding and writes down their conversation in a pleasant arbour, presumably the one they have just left. The poem concludes with a sly question to the audience which has just heard the poem recited: which of the three wanton ladies would they choose for a wife if they had to wed one of them?

Critics of the poem have described it as 'coldly obscene';[1] 'representing a corrupt condition of society and a special depravity of the sex which in better times maintains standards of purity';[2] or as 'essentially coarse and corrupt' and its author as evincing 'the mind of a celibate warped by longing for forbidden fruit'.[3] Such views do more credit to the state of innocence among scholars than to their common sense, and such critics seem to me to have overlooked two things which are perhaps a key to the way the poem should be taken. The first is the fact that, of the three women, the first two at any rate really have something to complain about and something that was a common and serious grievance in an age when women of the upper classes were so often married off without their consent. To be married to a husband who is both impotent and disgusting is a real disaster for a woman. If Dunbar were seriously writing a satire on women, why did he give the first two ladies such very good cases and allow them to argue in such a way that we feel the full force of the frustration, misery, despair, and disgust their situations entail? In the second place, is the description of their married life really obscene? It is extremely vivid and detailed but one has to remember that the women are speaking, they think, in private, and it is only the most sheltered of scholars who is unaware that women in all ages and grades of society enjoy this sort of freemasonry on matters of sex, childbearing, and health and disease. In the circumstances of the poem and under the customs of the age in which Dunbar is writing there is, I believe, nothing obscene in the conversation; it is frank and coarse, if you like, but it is to import modern views into the fifteenth century to imagine that Dunbar intended his ladies to seem obscene, revolting, or

3

immoral because of the subjects they discuss and the way they discuss them. That he may have intended the substance of their arguments to seem wrong or perverse is another matter. He was a churchman and a perfectly orthodox moralist, who could not have approved of views which, if taken seriously, challenge the basis of Christian society. But how seriously did he intend his hearers to take these views? The final question he addresses to them is not indignant or even condemnatory but suggests rather a tone of sly amusement or of tolerant irony:

> Ye auditoris most honorable, that eris has gevin
> Oneto this uncouth aventur, quhilk airly me happinit
> Of thir thre wantoun wiffis, that I haif writtin heir,
> Quhilk wald ye waill to your wif, gif ye suld wed one?
>
> (ll. 527-31)

The purpose of the poem, in fact, need not be to reprobate lust and immorality or to condemn women, any more than the purpose of Shakespeare's Falstaff is in any serious sense to make cowardice and drunkenness odious. The picture may in either case be presented to us mainly for the fun of it.

Fun indeed seems to me to be the keynote of the whole poem, as it is of the spirit in which the three ladies conduct their discussion in spite of the very real causes of complaint that each of them has against marriage; for there is another side to their conversation. The description of cruel and unnatural aspects of marriage may indeed convey all the disgust and bitterness of the experience. But the ladies themselves have obviously another point of view. Their attitude to their husbands and to marriage is one of derision. The descriptions of the behaviour of these unfortunates in the marriage bed conveys not only the disgust of the past moment but the amusement of the present. Each lady describes her worthless husband with tremendous and conscious gusto, holds him up to witty and triumphant ridicule. In the widow's speech this ridicule is extended to the whole male sex considered as lovers. The element of complaint is a minor one. The women are primarily enjoying themselves. After each 'confession' they have another round of drinks and laugh

4

uproariously. The conversation in fact begins with a thesis: that marriage should be abolished except as a temporary arrangement, and that the law of nature should replace it. The first wife begins, not with a statement of her grievance, but with a statement that women should be freed from marriage and should be able to choose their sexual mates as birds do for a year and to change when they like. It is assumed that in a year a woman will exhaust a man sexually and she should then be free to choose another mate; the second wife agrees with this doctrine. The widow tells them how they can in fact achieve their ambitions without overthrowing the institution of matrimony, and indeed by using it to their purpose. The poem therefore goes far beyond a mere attack on women or on matrimony. Ironically or not it proposes a law of nature and a morality based on it which would not only free women but would reverse the role of the sexes, would overthrow not only the rules of the church but the customs of society.

Dunbar's purpose in presenting this picture may be more than ironical; it may, I suspect, have been intended to present to his audience, not a fantastic reversal of values for their amusement, but aspects of Scottish life which they would be so well able to recognise that comment on his part would have been needless. But if this is so, they were aspects of life which history has not preserved in any detail. Indeed, not a great deal has survived about daily life, manners, and conversation of the Scots before the Reformation. I have tried to piece out what has survived with evidence from earlier and from later ages and from other parts of the British Isles. My object has been to suggest what may possibly have been the poem's meaning for a contemporary audience, but I own frankly that I have more often yielded to the pleasure of following conjecture for its own sake. For this reason alone it would be a mistake to treat this as a work of scholarship. When it first became apparent that the possible explanations I have suggested could not be proved, my first thought was to abandon the whole project; but the byways and prospects into which my investigation had led me had overcome me with an interest and a charm of their own and quite apart from their possible bearing on Dunbar's poem. In the end I found myself using the poem itself more as a means of organising this material than the material as a means of illuminating the poem. It is, I hope, not unscholarly, but it aims at what I might call the poetry of scholarship rather than its practical use. It is the poetry of archaeology that makes us still enjoy Sir Thomas Browne's *Hydriotaphia*, and not the light it throws on the urns dug up in the field at Old Walsingham, about which he was in any case mistaken. Its fascination depends on the raising of speculations on 'what songs the Syrens sang, or what name Achilles assumed when he hid himself among women', on the evocation of things passing beyond the 'diuturnity of our memories'.

If I have no claim to the music of Browne's prose, I have at least come to think of my book as an essay in the poetry of things only half-remembered in the conversation of mankind. I offer it not as a work of scholarship or of literary criticism, but as a tribute of love and admiration to a brother poet, an imaginative commentary, or, if you like, a fantasy on one of his themes.

2

The Setting of the Poem

ONE thing at least seems clear: the poet meant to surprise his auditors. He meant them to think they were about to hear a courtly romance or a courtly dream allegory, perhaps something along the lines of his poem 'The Golden Targe'. This poem opens with a hundred ladies dressed in green and with long flowing hair landing from a ship on a May morning, while the poet in his dream observes them from hiding. It is equally clear that he intended to surprise the auditors by the sudden change of tone and manner when the ladies begin to converse. One might imagine that the device was a practical joke of the sort practised at the court in 1507 and again in 1508, when an elaborate tournament was held with one of the negress servants at the court in place of the usual queen of beauty. Dunbar took part in this travesty, with his mock love poem addressed to 'my ladye with the mekle lippis'. Yet 'The Two Married Women and the Widow' does not seem to be merely a practical joke. The audience was surely meant to be taken by surprise at the change of manner and style, but there seems no intention to make fun of the style itself. There is no hint of parody in the opening passage and the poet returns to the elevated and idealised treatment of the scene at the end as seriously and as enthusiastically as he began. If I am right in my conjecture, his purpose in this passage is not to ridicule a literary form, but to use it to suggest to the auditors that the three ladies are something very different indeed from the three citizens of Edinburgh they later turn out to be. The opening passage is in fact packed with ambiguous hints that would lead a contemporary audience to assume that they were not women of flesh and blood at all.

Apon the Midsummer evin, mirriest of nichtis,
I muvit furth allane, neir as midnicht wes past,
Besyd ane gudlie grein garth, full of gay flouris,
Hegeit, of ane huge hicht, with hawthorne treis;
Quhairon ane bird, on ane bransche, so birst out hir notis
That never ane blythfullar bird was on the beuche harde:
Quhat throw the sugarat sound of hir sang glaid,
And throw the savour sanative of the sueit flouris,
I drew in derne to the dyk to dirkin efter mirthis;
The dew donkit the daill and dynnit the feulis.
   I hard, under ane holyn hevinlie grein hewit,
Ane hie speiche, at my hand, with hautand wourdis;
With that in haist to the hege so hard I inthrang
That I was heildit with hawthorne and with heynd leveis:
Throw pykis of the plet thorne I presandlie luikit,
Gif ony persoun wald approche within that plesand garding.
   I saw thre gay ladeis sit in ane grene arbeir,
All grathit in to garlandis of fresche gudlie flouris;
So glitterit as the gold wer thair glorius gilt tressis,
Quhill all the gressis did gleme of the glaid hewis;
Kemmit was thair cleir hair, and curiouslie sched
Attour thair schulderis doun schyre, schyning full bricht;
With curches, cassin thair abone, of kirsp cleir and thin:
Thair mantillis grein war as the gress that grew in May sessoun,
Fetrit with thair quhyt fingaris about thair fair sydis:
Off ferliful fyne favour war thair faceis meik,
All full of flurist fairheid, as flouris in June;
Quhyt, seimlie, and soft, as the sweit lillies
New upspred upon spray, as new spynist rose;
Arrayit ryallie about with mony rich vardour,
That nature full nobillie annamalit with flouris
Off alkin hewis under hevin, that ony heynd knew,
Fragrant, all full of fresche odour fynest of smell.
Ane cumlie tabil coverit wes befoir tha cleir ladeis,
With ryalle cowpis apon rawis full of ryche wynis.
And of thir fair wlonkes, tua weddit war with lordis,
Ane wes ane wedow, I wis, wantoun of laitis.
And, as thai talk at the tabill of many taill sindry,
Thay wauchtit at the wicht wyne and waris out wourdis;
And syne thai spak more spedelie, and sparit no matiris.

(ll. 1-40)

The three ladies in this elaborate picture are, it is true, represented as their status in society would demand. They drink the richest wines, and wine was a drink of the upper classes at the time; they wear the curch and veil, the head-dress which Don Pedro de Ayala, the Spanish envoy to the court of James IV, thought the handsomest in the world and becoming to such handsome women as the Scots ladies seemed to him.[1] They are holding their Midsummer Eve frolic perhaps in one of the garden closes which, particularly on the south of the city at that time, were the site of new houses for gentlemen and wealthy merchants. The description of the garden with its arbour and table and the firm conviction of the ladies that they enjoy complete privacy:

> To speik, quoth scho, I sall nought spar; ther is no spy neir:
>
> (l. 161)

recalls the gardens described by Philip Stubbes as the ones employed by wanton ladies in London a generation or so later:

> In the Feeldes and Suburbes of the Cities thei haue Gardens, either palled or walled round about very high, with their Harbers and Bowers fit for the purpose. . . Then to these Gardens thei repaire when thei list, with a basket and a boy, where thei, meeting their sweete hartes, receiue their wished desires.[2]

They are dressed as befits their station and the occasion. In fifteenth-century Scotland the dress of all classes was strictly regulated, like their food, drink, and amusement, though the strictness of the regulations and their frequent repetition suggest that they were not as strictly observed.

> No one living in a burgh, except alderman, baillies and members of the Town Council and their wives, may wear silk, or costly scarlet gowns or furrings of martens. . . The costume thus regulated according to rank, seems in the later part of the fifteenth century to have been rather picturesque. . . Female dress consisted of the kirtle, a close fitting garment reaching from the neck to the feet and buttoned at the wrists, and the gown worn over it and open in front. A stomacher which covered the breast, a collar, and the kerchief or headdress completed a lady's attire. . . In quality and colour the dress of the higher classes

9

differed from that of the lower. The high-priced cloth used for the former was usually coloured in black, brown, green and scarlet. The cheaper sorts worn by the latter were grey, blue, and russet, blue being worn on holidays.[3]

It is clear, then, that the three ladies in the arbour are in most respects dressed in the height of fashion for their time and that their manners and their situation give no reason at first sight to doubt that they are not just what they seem: two married women and a widow of the upper classes of the city of Edinburgh.

Except, perhaps, for two things: they are all dressed alike and they wear their hair hanging down their backs.

> Kemmit was thair cleir hair, and curiouslie sched
> Attour thair schulderis doun schyre, schyning full bricht;
>
> (ll. 21-2)

To wear the hair combed out and hanging down the back was ordinarily the custom for unmarried girls in England, Ireland, and Scotland in the fifteenth and sixteenth centuries, and there were differences in the costume appropriate to maids, married women, and widows. Sir William Brereton, who visited Edinburgh in the early seventeenth century, noticed that it was still the case there:

> Touching the fashion of the citizens, the women wear and use upon festival days six or seven several habits and fashions; some for distinction of widows, wives and maids, others apparalled according to their own humour and fantasy. . . Young maids not married are all bareheaded.[4]

When the thirteen-year-old English Princess Margaret was married to James IV in 1503 she wore her hair hanging loose and full-length under a coif over which the crown was placed. The young wife in Clapperton's 'Wa wourth maryage', the *chanson à mal mariée* perhaps contemporary with Dunbar's poem, declares that her plan shall be, if ever she should be rid of her old and impotent husband, to dress like a maiden again in order to be seen by the lovers she wishes to attract:

I suld put on my russet gowne
My reid kirtill my hois of brown
and lat thame se my yallow hair
under my curche hingand doun
Way wourth maryage for evirmair.[5]

Married women usually wore their hair up or completely covered by an elaborate head-dress, though there were exceptions towards the end of the century and pictures of the times show a great variety of styles. What may be regarded as the respectable normal practice is shown on funeral brasses of the period. A married woman such as Joan, Lady Cromwell of Tattershall, Lincolnshire (1475) may wear her hair streaming down her back from a jewelled or ornamental fillet, but the conventions are well illustrated by the brass of the daughters of Sir Thomas Urswyk of Dagenham, Kent (1479): in front kneels a nun, behind are the two married daughters in elaborate head-dresses completely concealing the hair, while behind them again are five smaller kneeling figures, the unmarried daughters wearing conical hats over hair combed out and hanging free to their waists. This representation is the more convincing as showing a convention rather than individual taste and choice, since all the girls, married or unmarried, are wearing exactly the same dress. Hair and head-dress alone denote their state.

Although the widow expressly tells her companions that she wears the distinctive dress of widowhood in public, it is perhaps not surprising that, on a festive and private occasion, she should appear in her true colours, since, as she confesses, she wears widow's weeds in order to deceive people. But it is more surprising in view of the great variety of women's costumes among the upper classes, and the way they vied with one another as the fashionable always do, that these ladies should all in fact be dressed alike. It is almost as though they were wearing some kind of uniform, and this indeed may be the case: the uniform of elves and fairies.

Costumes and hair-styles like those worn by the three ladies appear in two other poems of Dunbar. In 'The Golden Targe' the dreamer describes the ladies who have just landed from the mysterious ship:

Ane hundreth ladyes, lusty in to wedis
Als fresch as flouris that in May up spredis,
  In kirtillis grene withoutyn kell or bandis;
    Thair brycht hairis hang gletering on the strandis
In tressis clere, wyppit with goldyn thredis;
  With pappis quhite, and mydlis small as wandis.

(ll. 59-63)

These elegant creatures, with their green clothing, their long hair hanging free and laced with gold thread, and their bare breasts, are not of course mortal women at all but goddesses from classical literature and allegorical personages. It is only when their companions, the gods, arrive on the scene clothed all in the same colour that we realise that Dunbar, in medieval fashion, sees them as denizens of Fairyland:

Thare was Pluto, the elrich incubus,
In cloke of grene, his court usit no sable.

(ll. 125-6)

Pluto here, as in the fourteenth-century romance *Sir Orfeo*, appears a king of Fairyland and wears the appropriate costume. Dunbar's goddesses wear green kirtles under their green mantles and with their long hair hanging loose they are also presented as fairies in their appearance.

Another of Dunbar's poems, 'To Aberdein', describes the entertainment that city gave to Queen Margaret in 1511. After a civic reception and a salute of cannon, the queen saw pageants presented in the streets: the Annunciation, the Three Kings at Bethlehem, the Expulsion from Eden, Robert the Bruce, and a symbolic representation of the origin of the house of Stewart. This rather mixed bag concluded with a choral item in which twenty-four girls welcomed the queen in song, accompanying themselves with timbrels:

Syne come thair four and tuentie madinis ying,
All claid in greine of mervelous bewtie,
With hair detressit, as threidis of gold did hing,
With quhyt hattis all browderit rycht bravelie,
Playand on timberallis and syngand rycht sweitlie;

(ll. 41-5)

But this costume was probably no more ordinary wear for the prettiest girls in Aberdeen than that described in 'The Golden Targe'. The queen, who herself was only twenty-one, visited the city in May and the green dresses and white hats over the long hair may be meant to indicate a costume appropriate for May Day celebrations, but are more likely to have been meant to present the girls as a choir of nymphs or fays in their traditional green dresses with flowing hair. To many of the auditors it may have represented rather more than a loyal compliment or a conventional entertainment: it may well have represented a welcome by local guardians of mounds and caves and springs in whose existence they had implicit belief and, indeed, whom they and their neighbours had often met or avoided meeting. About a century later the testimony at the Aberdeen witch trials shows that the belief in fairies and commerce with them was still very much alive.

The courtly audience for which Dunbar's poem was written was just as likely to have believed in the existence of fairies as the humbler citizens of Aberdeen. Even the learned and sophisticated John Major, illustrating a point in the exposition of the Gospel of St Matthew at Paris in 1518, refers seriously to the Scottish belief in 'Isti Fauni et vocati brobne [brownies] apud nos domi', and, in his scholarly reserve, he maintains what can at least be called a suspension of disbelief.[6] For the ordinary citizen the Wife of Bath's regretful retrospect on the vanished Fairyland of England would have seemed no more than a plain description of the present in fifteenth-century Scotland:

> In tholde dayes of the Kyng Arthour,
> Of which that Britons speken greet honour,
> Al was this land fulfild of fayerye.
> The elf-queene, with hir joly compaignye,
> Daunced ful ofte in many a grene mede.
> This was the olde opinioun, as I rede;
> I speke of manye hundred yeres ago.
> But now kan no man se none elves mo . . .

(ll. 857-64)

Whatever the case in England in the fourteenth century, and one suspects that the formidable Wife of Bath is simply being cautious in the presence of the clergy, elves were certainly to be seen in Scotland in Dunbar's day as they are in Ireland still. The belief was still strong, though its decline had begun in Lowland Scotland, at the end of the eighteenth century: in the Highlands, as in Ireland, it has persisted to the present day. *The Statistical Account of Scotland* records it in parish after parish, though in many others the minister who drew up the report affirms with satisfaction that superstitions current earlier in the century are now dying out. Yet in 1793 the minister of the parish of Kirkmichael in Banffshire described the local beliefs in terms which could very well apply to Dunbar's account of his experience at midnight on Midsummer Eve, three hundred years earlier.

> Notwithstanding the progressive increase of knowledge and proportional decay of superstition in the Highlands, these genii are still supposed by many people to exist in the woods and sequestered valleys of the mountains, where they frequently appear to the lonely traveller, clothed in green, with dishevelled hair floating over their shoulders and with faces more blooming than the vermeil blush of a summer morning. At night in particular, when fancy assimilates to its own preconceived ideas every appearance and every sound, the wandering enthusiast is frequently entertained by their musick, more melodious than he ever before heard.[7]

If Dunbar did not want his auditors to take his ladies, at any rate on first sight, as fays or fairies, it is curious that he should have chosen to dress them in green, since the association of this colour with the dress of fairies gave it a sinister reputation. It would be unlikely that three fashionable ladies, in an age when the upper classes vied with one another in variety of dress, should have chosen to wear what seems practically a uniform and that it should be of a colour supposed to bring bad luck both in love and war. In the Lowlands, in later times at any rate, no green might enter the dress or decorations for a wedding, in accordance with the popular rhyme

> They that marry in green
> Their sorrow is soon seen.

In the Highlands it was also thought disastrous to wear green in battle. Even at the end of the eighteenth century the fate of the Sinclairs at the battle of Flodden in 1513 was remembered as a warning to their descendants.

> No gentleman, however, of the name of Sinclair, either in Canisbay or throughout Caithness will put on green apparel, or think of crossing the Ord upon a *Monday*. They were all dressed in green, and they crossed the Ord upon a Monday, in their way to the battle of Flowden, where they . . . fell in the service of their country, almost without leaving a representative of the name behind them.[8]

Nearly two centuries later, the Highlanders attributed the death of Viscount Dundee at the battle of Killiecrankie, a battle that otherwise was all in his favour, to the fact that he had worn green on that day.

The prejudice against green clothing may not have been as strong in Dunbar's day. There is evidence that it was worn on occasions and it was one of the colours prescribed as suitable for the dress of the lower classes by the parliament in 1457. Yet it was an ill-omened colour for other reasons. In romantic colour symbolism, it stood for inconstancy, faithlessness, and triviality of mind as it does in the poem attributed to Chaucer, 'Against Women Inconstant', based on one by Machault. The poet recommends a changeable lady to wear green for this reason:

> Ye can but love ful half yeer in a place;
> To newe thing your lust is ever kene.
> Instede of blew, thus may ye were al grene.

It may well be, of course, that it is for this very reason that Dunbar chose to dress his wanton wives in this colour, but other details in the introduction and the conclusion to the poem reinforce the idea that they are actually presented in fairy costume.

The most obvious of these is the time of year and the time of night: just after midnight on Midsummer Eve or the Eve of the Nativity of St John the Baptist. This festival was celebrated on 23 June with similar customs all over Europe. It marks the point where the days begin to shorten and the sun begins to wane and sink lower in its course across the sky, so that it was natural for magical fire ceremonies to be held then as they were at Beltane in May at what was counted as the beginning of summer. Quite a number of ceremonies and customs were, in fact, common to the two festivals. But St John's Eve and Hallowe'en were also associated in the old Scottish calendar, one marking the end of the year and the other its mid-point. On both occasions all kinds of supernatural beings, witches, fairies, ghosts, and demons were abroad in particular power and force, and it was thought that at midnight they became visible, so that if the poet had wished to see denizens of the invisible world he could hardly have chosen a better moment. His audience, before learning that these ladies are three citizens of Edinburgh, would naturally conclude that, at the time and the season and appearing as they do, they are supernatural beings whom the poet is describing.

Several other details would reinforce this impression. Although it is midnight, the poet in approaching the 'gudlie grein garth' sees no lights and hears no voices such as he might expect if a party were in progress. When he has pierced the hedge he comes to a ditch or embankment which he can apparently see over and hears loud voices nearby. But the curious thing is that he sees no one. Then suddenly he sees the three ladies already seated and the feast already in progress. They appear suddenly in a blaze of light which appears to proceed from themselves:

> So glitterit as the gold wer thair glorius gilt tressis,
> Quhill all the gressis did gleme of the glaid hewis;
> Kemmit was thair cleir hair, and curiouslie sched
> Attour thair schulderis doun schyre, schyning full bricht;
>
> (ll. 19-22)

Dunbar's audience could hardly avoid the impression that this was the famous fairy light, so frequent in descriptions of the feasting and revels in fairy mounds or in encounters with fairies in the fields. The fourteenth-century fairy romance *Sir Orfeo* is one of the earliest descriptions of the light that shines in the underground world of Fairyland.

When he was in the roche ygo
Wele thre mile other mo,
He com into a fair cuntray,
As bricht so sonne on somers day, . . .
Al that lond was euer licht,
For when it schuld be therk and nicht,
The riche stones licht gonne,
As bricht as doth at none the sonne.

(ll. 349-52, 369-72)

King Orfeo has followed sixty fairy ladies whom he encounters when they are hunting and has ridden after them into a hillside to find his vanished queen. In the seventeenth century the scholarly author of *The Secret Commonwealth* recorded the belief as it was then current in Perthshire. Writing of a woman he knew who was said to have been taken from childbed to live among the fairy people, had been given up for dead, but had later returned to her husband and borne him several more children, he says of the fairy dwelling:

> Among other Reports she gave her Husband . . . She found the place full of light, without any Fountain or Lamp from whence it did spring.[9]

About a century and a half later an old woman of Nithsdale, sitting with a neighbour under a hawthorn bush at night, heard loud laughter and saw the fairies ride by accompanied by the fairy light:

> A beam o' light was dancing owre them mair bonnie than moonshine: they were a' wee wee fowk wi' green scarfs on, but ane that rade foremost, and that ane was a good deal larger than the lave wi' bonnie lang hair, bun' about wi' a strap whilk glinted like stars. . . Marion an' me was in a brade lea fiel' where they came by us; a high hedge o' haw-trees keepit them frae gaun through Johnnie Corrie's corn, but they lap a' owre it like sparrows and gallopt into a green know beyont it.[10]

Except that the fairies are now 'wee folk', whereas in the older tradition they were of ordinary human size, the Fairy Hunt or the Fairy Ride described here is in essence that which was obviously known to the composer of *Sir Orfeo*. There seems no reason to doubt that Dunbar's audience would have been acquainted with the tradition and would have recognised the fairy light that illuminates the feast in his poem.

The next items in the opening description that suggest a fairy scene are the hawthorn hedge of the 'garth' in which the meeting takes place, the holly, and the green arbour in which the ladies appear seated at their table. Hawthorn was in common use for hedging and holly was a common enough plant in gardens, but their mention here, their mention together, and the fact that no other trees are mentioned, could not fail to suggest to Dunbar's auditors that the meeting at least took place on fairy ground.

The hawthorns are said to be 'of a huge height', in other words they were ancient trees, and this immediately puts us in mind of the venerable trees which were to be found all over the British Isles, objects of superstitious dread or religious awe. Those mentioned in *The Statistical Account of Scotland* include oaks, planes, ashes, hawthorns, birches, hollies, yews, and elms; of these, hawthorns are most frequently mentioned as venerated in one particular locality or another. Such trees were protected by magic powers which would bring disaster on anyone who cut, removed, or injured them in any way. Irish folk tradition is full of stories such as that of the man who uprooted some fairy thorn trees and was found next morning paralysed in his bed. E. Estyn Evans wrote in 1945 of the prevalence of this belief in Ireland:

> These trees which must be counted by the thousand, are said 'never to have been planted but to have grown of their own accord'. They may be found on ancient monuments or alongside holy wells, but the great majority are scattered through the fields and it is worthy of note that the cult is at least as strong in the Protestant north-east as in other parts of the country. A venerable thorn, pink-flowering stands under my window as I write and casts its shadow into the Senate Room of the University [Queen's University, Belfast]. But no one will remove it or even lop its branches and the story goes that when the buildings were being erected the plans had to be changed in order that the thorn should not be interfered with. If a lone tree surrounded by half-a-dozen scientific departments has claimed such respect, it can be imagined in what awe the country thorns are held.[11]

Ireland preserves Celtic beliefs and customs which were formerly common in England, Scotland, Wales, and many parts of Europe. The trees that 'grow of their own accord' may be a survival of the once widespread belief that hawthorns originated from lightning and gave protection from being struck by it. Belief in the power residing in sacred trees is illustrated by James Howell's account of what happened to the impious puritan who cut down down one of the two stems of the great thorn at Glastonbury supposed to have been planted by Joseph of Arimathea:

> He was well serv'd for his *blind* Zeale, who going to cut doune an ancient white Hawthorne-tree, which, because she budded before others, might be an occasion of *Superstition*, had some of the *prickles* flew into his eye, and made him Monocular.[12]

The minister of New Parish in Perthshire noted in 1796:

> There is a quick-thorn of very antique appearance, for which the people have a superstitious veneration. They have a mortal dread to lop off or cut any part of it, and affirm, with a religious horror, that some persons, who had the temerity to hurt it, were afterwards severely punished for their sacrilege.[13]

Solitary sacred trees, or 'bell-trees' as they are known in Scotland, shared this superstitious awe with sacred groves, which at one time seem to have been a general feature of Celtic religion, as so many place names in various parts of Europe, including southern Scotland, still testify. Traces of the ancient *nemeton* or *sacred wood* are common in Scotland.

> About a century ago [wrote J. G. Dalyell in 1884] there stood a row of trees 'all of equall size, thick planted for about the length of a butt', near the chapel of St. Ninian, in the parish of Belly, then 'looked upon by the superstitious papists, as sacred trees from which they reckon it sacriledge to take so much as a branch, or any of the fruit'.[14]

Martin Martin, in his account of the Loch Siant Well in Skye about the end of the seventeenth century, remarks:

> There is a small coppice near it of which none of the natives dare venture to cut the least branch for fear of some signal judgement to follow upon it.[15]

What such judgment might be is well illustrated from an account by Giraldus Cambrensis of the impious troop of archers in the army of Henry II during his expedition to Ireland in 1171. The abbey of Finglass had a 'garth' of ash, yew, and other trees round its cemetery. The trees were reputed to have been planted by the saintly abbot Kennach and some of his successors, but the grove had obviously taken over the character of its pagan prototypes, if, indeed, it was not an original pagan grove put to Christian use. The archers, having no woods at hand, cut and lopped the holy trees and uprooted some of them and used them for their fires.

> But they were speedily smitten by God . . . by a sudden and singular pestilence; so that most of them miserably perished within a very few days . . . the rest endeavoured to save themselves by flight, but the ship in which they embarked being wrecked, they found in their extremity that He who rules the land, rules the sea also.[16]

The 'gudlie grein garth' in which the poet finds the three ladies has in fact the appearance of such a grove of ancient sacred trees. This is a subject to which I shall return in considering its location, but we may notice that, though it is called a 'garth' and a 'garding', it is not apparently the garden or close of a dwelling-house. No building is mentioned and the ladies at the end of the poem have to return home through what appears to be open meadow and woodland.

But hawthorn and hawthorn groves were not only holy in themselves. They were intimately connected with the fairies, and with the powers of healing and blasting attributed to the fairy folk. There would be no accident in the fact that the two old women of Nithsdale were sitting under a 'haw-buss' when they saw the Fairy Ride, for it was believed that to sit or sleep under a hawthorn was a protection from fairies and witches. Thomas Keightley recounts a story from eighteenth-century Scotland of two Lowland Scots lads ploughing a field in which was a fairy thorn believed to be a trysting place of the fairy people. One of them drew a circle round the tree within which it was not permissible to plough, and they were rewarded by a table heaped with a feast.[17] Similar accounts of the association of fairies with hawthorn could be multiplied indefinitely.

In the ballad of 'Sir Cawline' from the Percy Manuscript, the knight is bidden to meet the fairy king at midnight under the thorn tree that grows on the fairy hill.[18] There is every likelihood that Dunbar's audience would associate midnight on Midsummer Eve in a grove of ancient thorn trees with the apparition of fairies which everything in the appearance of these ladies would at first suggest. The poet's retreat into the 'plet thorn' would strike them as the correct procedure designed to protect him from their magic by which he might have been made a captive in Fairyland, from their resentment by which he might have been blasted, blinded, or deprived of health or wits, or even from their enticements should they decide to take him for a lover. All three were dangers described in legend and folk tale often enough, and protection rather than mere freedom from discovery would have been the watcher's first thought before he discovered the real nature of these midnight visitants. Sir John Mandevile describes the way in which hawthorn could afford such protection according to medieval belief, though the association with the crown of thorns worn by Christ was probably an accretion on the idea of powers residing in the sacred tree itself. The Jews, says Mandevile,

> maden him a Crowne of the Braunches of Albespyne, that is White Thorn, that grew in that same Gardyn, and setten it on his Heved, so faste and sore, that the Blood ran down be many places of his Visage, and of his Necke, and of his Schuldres. And therefore hathe White Thorn many Vertues: For he that berethe a Braunche on him thereoffe, no Thondre ne no maner of Tempest may dere him; ne in the Hows that it is inne may no evylle Gost entre ne come unto the place that it is inne.[19]

Mandevile's ghosts are, of course, spirits of any kind. The custom of hanging up hawthorn at the doors or within houses as protection against fairies and witches is known in a number of places, though, as often happens with popular beliefs, the opposite holds in other places. To sit or sleep under a hawthorn on May Day or on Midsummer Eve and Hallowe'en, on this other line of belief, could expose the unwary to enchantment or abduction by fairies.

Hawthorn, like the fairies themselves, is also associated with healing, rejuvenation, and the restoration and preservation of beauty. The association of hawthorn with holy wells is well known. The dew from the hawthorn that hung over the St Patrick's Stone in an island in the Shannon and filled the hollow in the stone was believed to have especial healing powers, like the water of Tober Breda, the holy well of St Bridget in Cork, which was similarly shadowed by an ancient fairy thorn.[20] The records of the Scottish witch trials show many instances in which those accused of witchcraft claimed that they had learned their healing art or obtained their medicines from the fairies. Midsummer Eve itself was particularly associated with healing charms and rites: laying the sufferer under a sacred tree, sprinkling him with flax-seed, wearing flowers which were afterwards cast into the fire, or going *deasil* round the bonfire and leaping through it. Similar ceremonies appear to have been common to most of Europe. Barnabe Googe's translation of Thomas Kirchmeyer's description of them in Germany is agreed to have fairly general application. The young men and women danced around the midsummer fires wearing garlands of flowers or with bunches of violets in their hands:

> When thus till night they daunced haue, they through the fire amaine
> With striving mindes doe runne, and all their hearbes they cast therin,
> And then with wordes devout and prayers, they solemnely begin,
> Desiring God that alle their illes may there consumed bee,
> Whereby they thinke through that yeare, from Agues to be free.[21]

Among the objects of such rites were of course those which ensured sexual vigour or the cure of impotence and sterility. The latter were frequently attributed to witchcraft or the malevolence of fairies. In view of these associations it is interesting to notice that they have a place in Dunbar's poem. What the two wives have to complain of is primarily that their husbands are impotent, the one through age and the other through debauchery. But they may not be the only ones in this condition. What causes the narrator in the first instance to draw near to the grove of ancient thorn trees surrounding a ditch or earthen bank similar to those so often found on or around fairy mounds or hills is the song of a night bird and the 'savour sanative of the sueit flouris' in a valley wet with dew.

It is the curative or restorative properties of the place that first attract him and it is interesting that at the end of the poem these qualities should be mentioned again with a specific reference to the restoring of sexual potency (curage):

> The soft sowch of the swyr and soune of the stremys,
> The sueit savour of the sward and singing of foulis,
> Myght confort any creatur of the kyn of Adam,
> And kindill agane his curage, thocht it wer cald sloknyt.
>
> (ll. 519-22)

It may be making too much of merely ornamental matter, but it fits in well with the idea that the setting of the poem is closely connected with the rites of midsummer and the beliefs in the habits and powers of fairies. This part of the setting could at least be expected to reinforce the audience's expectation of fairy adventure at the beginning of the poem.

The only other tree beside hawthorn mentioned in these opening lines is holly. The narrator is either under a holly bush when he first hears the voices of the ladies or the voices appear to come from under the holly; the verse can be interpreted either way. Holly, like hawthorn, is especially associated with fairies, with protection from lightning, with divination of love and marriage, and with the foreboding of death. But it is opposed to hawthorn in being connected with the winter festivals, hawthorn with those of spring and summer. Bercilak, the fairy knight who appears at Arthur's court at Christmas in the fourteenth-century romance *Sir Gawain and the Green Knight*, bears, as a sign of his peaceable intentions, a branch of holly in his hand. Throughout Scotland holly was formerly hung up in houses, especially over doors and windows, as a protection against fairies and witches at Hogmanay, and male holly was a lucky omen worn by 'first-footers' on New Year's Day. It may be accidental, but it is curious to find two of the trees especially connected with fairies associated with three green-clothed ladies appearing in a blaze of light a moment after midnight on Midsummer's Eve. Other ways in which they were associated with the fairy cult and with the subjects discussed by the three ladies will be discussed in due course.

It is remarkable as well that, although the poet seems to say that he set out to witness the midsummer festivities, he seems to have taken a curious course to find them. In the streets he could have seen fires with people dancing and leaping through the flames, on the tops of the hills he might have expected to find crowds engaged in rolling down bannocks or fiery wheels and rushing after them to learn their fortunes for the year in health and marriage. In the town, again, he might have had the opportunity to observe torch-light watch processions and vigils outside the churches on the chance of seeing the spectres of those foredoomed to die in the ensuing year. Among the farms near the city he could have seen the farmers and their families going *deasil* about the field and driving their cattle through the flames of bonfires. These were the ordinary 'mirths' associated with the season. Instead he makes for a solitary spot so far from all revels and ceremonies that the occupants of the grove feel themselves quite safe from intrusion. And what draws him to the spot? Not the sounds of voices or of merrymaking but the scent of flowers and the compelling fascination of a night bird's song from the hawthorns:

> Quhairon ane bird, on ane bransche, so birst out hir notis
> That never ane blythfullar bird was on the beuche harde:
> Quhat throw the sugarat sound of hir sang glaid,
> And throw the savour sanative of the sueit flouris,
> I drew in derne to the dyk to dirkin efter mirthis;

(ll. 5-10)

One can hardly avoid the conclusion that it was 'mirths' of a very special kind that the poet set out to find. Spying on private supper parties can hardly have been his intention, but if he were looking for celebrations of a fairy cult, or for fairies themselves at their revels, dances, and banquets, he was taking just the right course to find them and it is likely that this would be obvious to the auditors of the poem.

It would be tempting to see in this fascinating bird a creature of the other world like the fairy birds that occur in Celtic legend and romance leading the hero who pursues them into the power of the fays. There is a Welsh folk tale of a young man leaving the farm house and sitting down to listen to a little bird which sang so sweetly that he was quite enchanted. He imagined that he had been listening only a few minutes, but when he rose he found the farm house in ruins and the tree under which he had been sitting dry and dead. He learned later that he had been under the power of the fairies for more than a generation of human time.[22] This is reminiscent of the story of Pryderi and his companions in the *Mabinogion* who sit listening at a feast in Harlech to the magic birds of the fay Rhiannon and sit for seven years without knowing what time has passed. It is clear from the Mabinogi of Pwyll, prince of Dyved, a tale which probably goes back beyond the twelfth century in origin, that Rhiannon is one of those fays who lure mortal heroes to their underworld or magic island or castle or palace at the bottom of a lake. And these birds, which lure or charm, are obviously the fays themselves who are of course all shape-changers. In the story of 'Cuchulinn's Sick Bed' in the *Lebor-na-h'Uidre*, one of the earliest examples of this type of tale, two birds approach the place where the hero and his companions are and sing a song that causes all the men to fall asleep. Cuchulinn himself is lured away feeling sad and drowsy and meets two women who afterwards turn out to be fays, one of whom is in love with him. The spell they cast on him deprives him of his strength and he is then tempted to join them in their fairy paradise to be cured of his sickness.[23] It is clear here that the birds are the enchantresses themselves.

It would be tempting, as I say, to see in the bird that lures the poet in Dunbar's poem to the hawthorn enclosure a representative of the fairy birds of Celtic and romance tradition. The poem does not give much warrant for this, though taken with the other suggestions of a fairy scene, it could have helped to influence the audience towards such an impression.

If the poet's intention was to use conventional literary material to mislead his auditors into a no-man's-land of romance, they might of course have taken the bird for a nightingale, traditionally associated with temptation to illicit love. But as the twelfth-century

English poem, *The Owl and the Nightingale*, reminds us, there are no nightingales in Scotland, and since the scene of Dunbar's poem is firmly set there, the enchanting bird, if it is only a bird, is probably the native woodlark. The Reverend William Osburn, minister of Tillicoultry, about thirty miles from Edinburgh, wrote of this bird in 1795:

> The woodlark ought to be particularly mentioned, as one of our sweetest warblers. He begins to sing early in the spring, and continues till late in harvest. Like the nightingale, he is frequently heard singing in the most melodious, enchanting manner, in the clear, still summer evenings. On these occasions he commonly prolongs his song till midnight, and sometimes till morning.[24]

This is almost sure to have been the actual bird that Dunbar's poem would have suggested to his hearers, whether or not they associated it with magic or supernatural enticements.

To conclude, if Dunbar's intention in the opening part of his poem was not merely to suggest a general literary and romantic scene, but one in which the narrator set out to find and succeeded in finding, or even one in which he was lured to a fairy revel, we have still to ask: what could have been his purpose in presenting something so apparently incongruous with the facts of the case which appear as soon as the three ladies begin to talk? If the poem was not merely a rather pointless practical joke, it may be worth while to look for a possible purpose. It is of course easy to find what one wants to look for and what follows must be taken as an alternative to the simpler explanation. Most practical jokes are apt to seem pointless looked at from another age and from what is now almost another civilisation. Dunbar may have wished to do no more than give his audience the momentary amusing shock of pulling their legs as relief to the general course of court entertainments. But, as I have already said, I think the poem itself hardly supports this explanation. It is worth while to ask why, if these ladies are presented as fays, are they also presented as ladies of Edinburgh? What possible connection can there be between the Fairyland of popular tradition or the great fays of the literary tradition and the apparently practical and realistic views of three

Edinburgh housewives on the estate of marriage? I think there is at least a possible answer. But it leads us first of all to ask and answer several other questions. The first of these is simply: what did the nature and name of *fairy* imply in Scotland in the fifteenth century?

Goddesses and Fairies

THE poet may have meant to present his three ladies as fays or as fairies or as impersonating either. In Scotland or elsewhere in Europe in the Middle Ages we can distinguish two clear though interrelated traditions, one traced through folklore and popular customs, the other through literature in which the most important element is that of the Arthurian romances. The fairies of popular superstition live in mounds and hills, caves and springs; they are of both sexes and appear in considerable companies; they lure mortals into their underground dwellings where they spend their time in feasting and dancing; they bewitch cattle and human beings, cure and blast by spells, steal babies and replace them by elfin children, and make love to their mortal neighbours. Their appearance as described in the Scottish witch trials is homely and human enough to justify the common name they had of the Good Neighbours. They have a government of a human type and a king and queen whose relations are those of ordinary husband and wife. The high fairies, as C. S. Lewis calls them,[1] the great fays of the romances, live royally in castles or palaces beneath lakes or the sea or on magic islands. They are mistresses of their own domains, living in splendour, able to change themselves and others into what shapes they please, powerful magicians, and avid for love. They offer themselves freely to knights whom they encounter and often lure them to their dwellings. They are princely in their behaviour, ravishingly beautiful (though they may also appear as hags for their own purposes), and imperious, ruthless, and jealous in temperament. They rarely have male counterparts but are often surrounded by maidens or minor fays and often appear in triple form or as three sisters. Their world is courtly and martial as that of the lower fairies is humble and rustic.

Behind both traditions lies the same medley of old cults and religions, some aboriginal to prehistoric Europe, some peculiar to the Celtic peoples, and some perhaps compounded and confused from more than one source.

With the coming of Christianity the religions and cults which it displaced did not simply disappear. The divine beings were sometimes euhemerised into kings, queens, and heroes of legendary history as happened in the sagas of pre-Christian Ireland. In other cases they were assimilated to historical or semi-historical persons, as some scholars suppose was the case with King Arthur and a Celtic god of the same name in Welsh tradition; or legends and powers attributed to a local deity were transferred to a local saint. In many cases the cult persisted more or less secretly alongside the Christian practices and in others, though the cult died out, folk-lore and legend preserved the mythology and, usually, with the passage of time, confused and transformed it. These legends were later taken over into literature where they were often elaborated and manipulated almost out of recognition. It is in this way that the fairy lore and the fays of the literary tradition have come down to us. Tracing them back to their originals is a tangled and uncertain business, even when the indications are clearer than in the case of Dunbar's poem.

This is particularly true of any attempt to deal with such beliefs in Scotland which, unlike Wales and Ireland, has preserved little of its heroic literature or its medieval folklore and legend. More-over, there is probably no part of the British Isles where what might have been preserved could possibly have given us a wider choice. The population of Scotland in Dunbar's day was an amalgam of peoples and languages which could in theory, and probably did in fact, preserve elements of ancient beliefs from all these sources and had not only preserved but combined and altered and added to the original elements in the most confusing ways. In prehistoric times the land had been occupied by various non-Indo-European peoples.

It is thought that the Picts, probably a Celtic people, intermarried with some of these aborigines and preserved some of their traditions and beliefs as well as their practice of succession in the female line. Who the Picts were, what admixture of aboriginal races they contained, what language they spoke, and what their affinities with the other Celtic peoples may have been are all matters of great uncertainty and dispute. But it seems fairly certain that the Celtic tribes of Britain and Ireland migrated a great deal in the period extending from about 500 B.C. onwards. Ptolemy records the Cornovii, the tribe which gave its name to Cornwall, as also settled in the far north of Scotland; the Dumnonii appear in southern Scotland, Devonshire, and the west of Ireland; the Picts themselves are the Cruithne found in early medieval Ireland and probably the Coritani whom Ptolemy placed in the north-east midlands of England, the area round Leicester and Lincoln. It is likely that, even before the Roman invasion and settlement of Britain, what is now Scotland contained a considerable admixture of the various Celtic groups who had peopled the British Isles. Some scholars even find evidence for a Gaulish element among them.[2] During the Roman occupation the legions who guarded the border brought their gods with them, as numerous altars and inscriptions in the north of England and southern Scotland testify. Civil communities were attached to the military posts, and gods from the Mediterranean, from the East, from Germany and Gaul are found in association with local British deities. Even a Celtic tribal divinity like Brigantia is pictured with oriental and Roman attributes.[3] What happened to these civil populations when the troops were withdrawn is not known, but during and after the Roman occupation the area between the line of the Forth and Clyde and the wall of Hadrian seems to have been occupied by British tribes who later took over the defence of the northern borders against the Picts and the Scots who were pushing into the west from Ireland; these Britons, apparently allied to the Welsh, were the Strathclyde British in the west and the Votadini whom the Welsh called Gododdin in the east. Within a century or so southern Scotland had been overrun by the Scots and by the Angles from Northumbria. For a time the Picts reasserted their power and then gave way to Irish Scots who seem to have wiped out their organisation, their church, and their language. About the same time Scandinavian raids began and ultimately led to considerable Norse settlement in the north and round the coasts. It is clear that elements of faiths, rites, and myths from many sources might have been found in the popular superstitions of medieval Scotland. In Pictish art, for example, pagan and Christian, sacred and secular, native and foreign scenes and symbols appear side by side. Scenes of pagan sacrifice such as those on the cross at St Vigeans, Angus, or the female rider who possibly represents the Celtic goddess Epona on the cross at Hilton of Cadboll in Ross-shire may suggest that pagan rites and deities sometimes survived fairly openly.[4] At any rate there is plenty of evidence that beliefs connected with them did.

Celtic goddesses and female tutelary spirits seem to have been particularly numerous. This is natural since they tended on the whole to be attached to particular areas and to the earth itself, its fields, forests, wells and rivers, wild and domestic animals, or else to be protectors of the fertility and the well-being of a particular tribal group. Thus they appear as goddesses of war, of magic, of agriculture, of arts and festivals or of love and motherhood, according to circumstances.[5] They are almost always local divinities, and because of their intimate connection with the life of the land and the prosperity of crops and cattle they tended to resist extinction and extirpation among a peasantry which clung to local cults, rites, and festivals in spite of all the church could do to discourage or destroy the old beliefs. They might compromise by turning their old deities into saints or fairies, but the practices remained and often reveal the ancient goddess under this protective colouring. In the Celtic areas and in western Germany these local goddesses are apt to appear in threes or as a triple divinity, and sometimes in multiples of three. It is among such divine triplets that we should look for candidates for divine beings whom later times transformed into a trio of fairies.

Among the first that would naturally occur to anyone are the *Matres* or *Matronae* whose altars and dedicatory inscriptions occur all over France and Britain, in many parts of Germany, and in northern Italy. In Britain the majority of their shrines appear in two regions, that of Hadrian's Wall and southern Scotland and that of Gloucestershire and Wiltshire, but they are to be found throughout the Roman province.[6] They are sometimes single, in pairs, or represented with a companion god, but they usually appear as three female figures in mantles and long flowing robes, seated, in a recess or series of recesses, under archways. They are often seated in separate chairs. They often have children or babies with them sometimes at the breast, or they hold baskets of fruit or loaves in their laps; they sometimes hold a small dog, a fish, a knife or a flower or objects which may be cups. They sometimes wear head-dresses; sometimes their hair is dressed or hangs free to their shoulders. The inscriptions refer to them as *Deae Matres, Matres, Matres Campestres, Matres Parcae, Matres Nemetiales,* or as guardians of individual households, tribes, and localities. J. A. MacCulloch says of them:

> Popular superstition has preserved the memory of these three goddesses in the three *bonnes dames, dames blanches* and white women, met by wayfarers in forests or in the three fairies or wise women of folk-tales who appear at the birth of children. But sometimes they have become hateful hags. . . A Welsh name for fairies *Y Mamau*, 'The Mothers' and the phrase 'the blessing of the Mothers' used of a fairy benediction may be reminiscent of such goddesses.[7]

Points of likeness between the three fairies in Dunbar's poem—even if they are meant only to look like fairies—and the *Matres* is that the latter are three in number; they are fertility goddesses and the three ladies are certainly concerned with one aspect of fertility; they appear seated in what often looks like a grotto or a bower; in some instances they appear as goddesses of groves (*Nemetiales*), and there is some evidence to suggest that they became fairies or fates in later tradition, or fays in legend and the romances.

It is characteristic of a dethroned and suppressed religion or mythology that its traditions tend to become confused. One group of divine beings is apt to be assimilated to others and this was particularly likely to happen in the Celtic world where gods were both local and their attributes were generalised.[8] Another group of divinities, if, indeed, they *are* quite separate, are the so-called water-nymphs, who may appear in art like the mother-goddesses, in threes and often enclosed in a grotto or grottoes covered by arches. Unlike the mothers, who are always fully clad, these tutelary deities of wells and springs are usually wholly or partly naked, their hair is long, and they are represented holding or sitting by a pitcher or urn from which water is flowing. In a group found in the sacred well of Coventina at Carrawburgh on Hadrian's Wall, and dating from the second or third century A.D., they are represented in a reclining posture, each bearing in one hand a jar or beaker, while the other hand supports the urn from which the source flows. As in a relief of three water-nymphs from Unterheimbach in Germany, there are sometimes indications of a grove of trees around the spring. Throughout Scotland and Ireland in later times a sacred well was often, as we have seen, associated with a sacred tree or sacred grove. At the end of Dunbar's poem he mentions the sound of a stream or streams nearby the grove where he is watching the end of the ladies' revel. There is, perhaps, not much point in trying to distinguish too precisely between tutelary deities of woods, caves, hills, mounds, wells or springs even in pagan times in Celtic countries. But in later times they all became fairies, hags, and witches, were euhemerised into fictive saints, or replaced by actual saints. A character they all share is one common to fertility cults: concern with childbirth and barrenness and with luring mortal men to be their lovers. The six hundred or so sacred wells in Scotland were sometimes devoted to the cure of specific ills, but more often, like St Fillan's Well at Comrie in Perthshire, generally beneficent. It was, however, especially visited by women wishing for children, and the fact that they made their visits at Beltane and Samain and went *deasil* round the well suggests that St Fillan had replaced an original pagan goddess or goddesses as St Bridget did in many other cases.[9] The fays of literature are nearly always amorous, but this is also a characteristic of the fairies of popular legend. The fairy queen who lures Thomas the Rhymer to Fairyland is a case in point. A folk tale from Sutherlandshire which has obviously an ancient line

33

of descent, though recorded in the nineteenth century, illustrates the amorous and the perilous nature of these encounters. Three young men, who lived at the foot of Ben Mohr and were engaged to marry three sisters, the daughters of a neighbour, were out hunting, became lost and were benighted. After some hours of wandering they discovered a hut with a blazing fire where they warmed themselves and roasted some of the venison they had taken. Then one of the brothers, who was a piper, played for them various marches and reels and the eldest of the three expressed a wish to dance, if only their three sweethearts were there.

> Hardly had he spoken than three beautiful maidens, all dressed in green, appeared, who held out their hands to them and led off a merry reel. But the piper was the first to see that these girls were all web-footed. He guessed their real nature and contrived to escape by cutting the green ribbons the girls had given them to hold. After many adventures in the night he returned to the 'bothy' in the morning to find it burned to the ground and the bones of his brothers among the ashes.[10]

Though the story is modern it has an obviously ancient derivation. The three maidens are fairies who in older versions would have lured the lost hunters to their cave or house in a hill and kept them there as lovers. But, as the dead were reputed to live in fairy mounds or an underwater paradise, the distinction between the two fates is a hazy one in folklore. This story represents the triple goddess in her dangerous aspect. The web-feet may indicate that in the original version they were fairies of wells or lakes. Stories of sea, river, or lake maidens who lure men to their death or to become their lovers in an underwater home, as in the story of Hylas, are not specifically Celtic but common to folklore of many peoples. Yet it is a frequent theme in Celtic areas. A Maiden Well at Dollar in Clackmannanshire preserved the legend of a beautiful spirit who haunted it and was wooed by many men whom she resisted; but in the fourteenth century she dragged one of her would-be lovers into the well and drowned him.[11] The romances and the Irish folk legends contain many similar instances. The susceptibility of fairies to music is also well known and, in the tale of the three hunters, it is the music of the pipes as well as the wish expressed by the eldest brother which causes them to appear. In the twelfth-century Irish story, *The Tale of Bricriu*, the three daughters of Airitech live in a cave and, in the shape of wolves, destroy the flocks in the surrounding countryside. They are lured out and persuaded to assume human shape by the power of fairy music, which allows the hero to kill them as they sit side by side.[12] The use of music as a lure by the fairies themselves is too well known to need illustration.

Another group of divine beings which occur singly, in threes, or multiples of three, and are particularly common in Scotland, are the Maidens. There is a very large number of them and the fact that they are all called by the same name does not, of course, mean that they are all necessarily of the same nature or the same origin. Among the most primitive are the Maidens associated with the corn harvest. In many parts of Scotland, England, and Wales and indeed throughout Europe, the last sheaf cut at the harvest was taken to incorporate the spirit of the corn, and, according to its treatment in local custom, to ensure a good or a bad harvest for the ensuing year. The Scottish customs, as described by Sir James Frazer, are particularly interesting since they show that the last sheaf was in some places known as the Cailleach or Old Woman, in others as the Maiden, and in others again the two reapers who came first and last in the reaping were awarded the Maiden bringing good luck and the Cailleach bringing bad luck. The festival customs recorded for these events in various districts make it probable that originally it was a period of sexual licence like the spring and midsummer festivals and that actual marriage to the 'Maiden' or the 'Auld Wife' was once a feature of it. When one learns that in other parts of Europe, in almost precisely similar customs, the last sheaf is known as the Harvest Child (eastern Europe) or as the Bride (southern Germany),[13] it becomes possible that here we have fragmentary variants of an ancient cult of a triad of fertility goddesses, representing the maiden, the bride or mother, and the widow respectively, as was the case with the group Kore, Demeter, and Hecate in classical mythology. It may be worth notice that of the three ladies in Dunbar's poem one, if we are to believe her, is still a virgin—though much against her will—one is married, and the third a widow.

There were also Maidens, Cailleachs or Old Wives, and less specific Women or Ladies associated with castles, chapels, stones, hills, mounds, rivers, wells, caves, trees, and glens. Maidens are found particularly in those parts of Scotland which had formed the core of the old Pictish kingdom. Old Wives were more common in the central west and north-western Highlands and Islands, Maidens in the east and north-east. They are so common as to lead one to suspect that it was a specific cult and that the rock or mound or well was the residence of, and in some cases identified with, one or more of these female spirits. Their numbers are usually nine but may be one, three, five, or seven. The predominance of the number nine would suggest that it is the original number, though this may represent a separate cult which was later combined or confused with the triad mentioned above. The modern names and legends suggest that in many cases the original nature and use of an earthwork, castle, mound, or cave had been forgotten when the cult was extended to them. Most of the Maiden Castles, for example, which abound in England and Scotland, are Iron Age Celtic or Roman fortifications which were originally actual forts or fortified settlements. The Maiden Ways are usually short stretches of Roman road. Another common name for these, the Devil's Causeway, suggests that the ascription took place long after the Romans left Britain and that the Devil and the Maidens were the powerful supernatural parties thought capable of constructing these great works in an age which had forgotten the technique. Most of the Maiden Castles, the Maiden Bowers, and Maiden Chapels or similar sites are probably, as Sir Mortimer Wheeler argues, post-Norman names.[14] But the cult is obviously much older. In Roman Gaul and Roman Britain there are inscriptions to the *Virgines* or Maidens. The older associations of the name are with wells, hills, and standing stones and other natural sites. There were Nine Maidens' Wells at Auchindoir, Aberdeen and Newburgh, Fifeshire, while the Nine Wells at Ochils in Perthshire, the hamlet of Nine Wells near Dundee, the nine white stones laid out annually at St Bride's Well at Sanquhar in Dumfries-shire on May Day, are probably all connected with the same cult. With these we may include perhaps the Maiden Well at

Dollar in Clackmannanshire, Maidwell in Northumbria, and Maiden-well in Lincolnshire, and some at least of the Lady Wells and Bride Wells which occur in various places.

Standing stones were sometimes the abode of these spirits, either natural rocks, monumental stones, or megalithic circles. A single standing stone at Strathmartin, Angus, had a legend about nine maidens attached to it. Another Maiden Stone is recorded at St Andrews. Lomond Hills had a Maiden Bore Rock, Dumfries a Maiden Bower Crag, and one of the latest examples of Pictish sculpture is the Maiden Stone of the Chapel of Garioch, Aberdeen-shire. The Clach-bhan or Woman Stone at Kirkmichael, Banff, may belong to the same group though, like the Cailleach Vear in Argyll and the Clach na Gruagach in Skye, it may be associated with a giantess or goddess of the type of the Old Wife. There are other examples of single or multiple Maiden Stones. A circle of monoliths in Cornwall is known as the Nine Maidens, another group in Derby-shire is known as Nine Ladies. Long Meg and her Daughters in Cumberland and the Nine Stone Ridge in Roxburghshire, among others, are probably to be associated with the same cult as are trees and hills with similar names associating them with women. An ancient ash tree in Kincardineshire was known in the eighteenth century as the Maiden of Midstrath;[15] the *Tripartite Life of St. Patrick* mentions a Maidens' Hazel in Armagh associated with a legend of nine Lombard princesses who came to visit the saint.[16] The three isolated stacks off the shore near Dunvegan Castle in Skye are known as Macleod's Maidens. The shapes of certain hills may by themselves suggest such names as the Maiden-pap in Perthshire or the Hill with the Paps (Bennochie) in Aberdeenshire. But the Paps of Anu or Danu in Kerry remind us that not only were such hills sometimes named for their likeness to breasts but because they were thought to be the breasts of a goddess. The other name of the Maiden-pap, Schiehallion, is said to mean the 'magical or supernatural hill of the Caledonians'.[17] It was a fairy hill, as was the Binny-craig near Linlithgow in West Lothian, and it is possible that these as well as the Lady Hill at Grange in Morayshire, the Banhill at Kilsyth, Stirlingshire, the 'Woman Hill' near Aberdeen,[18] and other hills of similar name preserve traces of the same beliefs. We shall have occasion to consider Maiden Castles again in discussing Edinburgh and the romances. But we may notice here that besides the numerous sites in England, there were Maiden Castles at St Vigeans, Angus, Collessie and Markinch, Fife, Campsie near Glasgow, Falkirk, Stirlingshire, and elsewhere. The most famous of course was Edinburgh itself, which was known as *Castellum Puellarum* or Maiden Castle at least from the early twelfth century. The occurrence of the name in three documents of 1142, 1174, and 1175 disposes of the theory that Geoffrey of Monmouth was responsible because of his use of it in the *Historia Regum Britanniae* which was completed between 1136 and 1139. Geoffrey's work became immensely popular and is the prime source of the Arthurian romances which usually refer to Edinburgh in this way. But it is highly unlikely that the name had become so well accepted by 1142, or even thirty years later, as to be used as a matter of course in the *Registrum de Neubotle*, the Treaty of Falaise and in official pipe-rolls. It was obviously already current when Geoffrey adopted it for his romantic history.[19]

It is not only likely that many 'maiden' sites have been lost but that most of these beings later became saints or fairies where any memory of their rites or legends survived. Two local tales of the eighteenth century show the sort of thing that was remembered and suggest how much had by then been forgotten. The Reverend James Reid of Auchindoir, Aberdeenshire, wrote of what must once have been a sacred well:

> In the south-east corner of the parish, there is a spring called 'the Nine Maidens' Well', near which, tradition says, nine young women were slain by a boar that infested the neighbouring country. A stone with some rude figures on it marks the spot where the tragical event is said to have happened. The boar was slain by a young man of the name of Forbes, the lover of one of the young women, and a stone with a boar's head cut on it was set up to preserve the rememberance [*sic*] of his gallantry and courage. The stone was removed by Lord Forbes to his house of Putachie and it is from this circumstance that a boar's head is quartered in the arms of that family.[20]

About the same time what is obviously a version of the same legend was recorded at Strathmartin near Forfar in Angus:

> In the north end of the parish is a large stone, called Martin's stone, of which Gordon takes notice in his Itinerary. . . Tradition says, that at the place where the stone is erected, a dragon, which had devoured nine maidens (who had gone out on a Sunday evening, one after another, to fetch spring water to their father) was killed by a person called Martin, and that hence it was named Martin's Stone. There is also a stone on the west gate of the churchyard which has the figures of 2 serpents upon it.[21]

The nine maidens connected with a well and a standing stone in each case are clearly vestigial memories of older divinities whom the legend has changed into human inhabitants of the district in question. The carvings suggest that these were Pictish standing stones, as in fact they are, and the beast that attacked the maidens in each case may have been suggested by the carvings. Both the boar and the serpents occur on Pictish monuments. But either or both may be part of the original legend. The boar was a sacred animal among the Celtic peoples. In the Welsh tale of Kulhwch and Olwen in the *Mabinogion*, a boar, which is really a knight changed to this shape for his sins, is hunted by Mabon son of Modron, and Arthur and his knights. Some scholars identify Mabon with the Celtic god Maponus and Modron with the *Matronae* who seem to be the same as the *Matres*.[22] One version of our story, therefore, may be a late form of a legend in which the Maidens had a conflict with the divine boar and were defended by a male god or hero associated with them. But there is also evidence that connects the Maidens with serpents or dragons. Nine Maidens are frequently associated with St Bride and it seems clear that St Bride and her train in turn were often assimilated to the cult of the Nine Maidens or used to euhemerise it. It was believed in parts of Scotland that serpents came out of their holes on St Bride's Day, 1 February, and a serpent was known in some places as 'an ribhinn'— the damsel (Skye) and 'an righinn'—the nymph or the princess or as 'the daughter of Ivor or Edward', or 'the queen'.[23] Geoffrey of Monmouth in the early twelfth century tells the fabulous story of a certain King Ebraucus, founder of Edinburgh, 'the castle of Mount Agned, which is now called Maidens' Castle and the Dolorous Mountain'.[24] In the Welsh romance of *Peredur Son of Efrawg*, the hero, who is said to be the son of this same Ebraucus, in one of his many adventures comes to a hall where he finds three maidens who welcome him. Their father, a one-eyed man who rejoices in the name of the Black Oppressor, is overcome by Peredur who learns that he has lost his eye in combat with a great serpent which lives in a neighbouring mound called the Dolorous Mound. By pledging his love to another maiden whom he finds sitting on top of another mound, Peredur is enabled to overcome the monster.[25] The fact that Peredur is the son of the supposed founder of Edinburgh, ruler of the Castle of Maidens, makes it at least possible that the Dolorous Mount and the Dolorous Mound are one and the same and that if we could trace the story back to its original, we might find that the cult of the Maidens at Edinburgh included the legend of a dragon and perhaps of a divine hero who overcame it.

Another association or possible association of the Maidens with a guardian serpent occurs in a tale 'in the manner of Ossian' and handed down from age to age, according to the minister of the parish of Glenorchy and Inishail in Argyll. It concerns a small island in Loch Awe not far from Kilchurn Castle. It was known as Fraoch-Elan, and the legend related how a woman called Mego longed for the fruit of a tree on the island which was guarded by a serpent and asked her lover Fraoch to get some for her. He crossed to the island and was killed in his encounter with the monster.[26] This of course is the eighteenth-century remains of a story that must have been brought from Ireland centuries earlier. The old Irish saga of the *Táin Bo Fraich* tells how Fraoch, who was the son of the goddess Bébind (White Lady), was loved by Findabair, daughter of King Aillil and Queen Medb. Fraoch, whose mother was one of the *síde*, was extremely beautiful but the king and queen did not approve of the match, since they feared it might cause resentment among other suitors whose support they wished to retain. So they asked Fraoch to fetch them a branch of a rowan tree which grew on the bank of the river where he was swimming. The tree was

guarded by a *peist* or monster, and though he killed it he was so
savaged that he seemed to be mortally wounded. He was laid on a
bed and immediately there appeared three fifties of women in crimson
with green head-dresses, all young and beautiful and uttering loud
laments. They were women of the *side* who adored the beautiful
Fraoch, took him away and cured him of his wound. In another
version of the story Queen Medb herself sent him for the magic
berries of the rowan which grew on an island in a loch and had
the dragon or serpent coiled around its roots. In this version Fraoch
killed the serpent but died of his wounds. The queen had sent him
to his death for spurning her love.[27] The second version from *The
Dean of Lismore's Book* is clearly closer to the Scottish version,
but the other suggests the connection of the tale with triple groups
of fairies or maidens. Stories like those of Herakles who slays or
outwits a dragon on the island of the three nymphs called Hesperides,
daughters of Atlas, and that of the viper-maiden whom he encoun-
tered in Scythia and who took him for her lover in her grove,
indicate that these beliefs are very ancient and extended beyond the
Celtic area. Herakles, like Fraoch, is a demigod, Fraoch like Herakles
in the latter tale is in search of a stolen herd. The paths of folklore
branch and recross as they lead us further and further into the
jungle of past faiths and half-remembered myths. Adonis who
spurns the love of Venus is killed by a boar, Fraoch who spurns
the divine Medb is killed by a dragon. At St Vigeans, Angus, the
Maidens had a 'castle' with a cave and spring below it. On Mid-
summer Day there were processions to the cave. But the parishioners
of the church at St Vigeans believed that it had been built by a
water kelpie who would destroy it if the sacraments were administered
there.[28] Was the kelpie connected with the Maidens of St Vigeans
as the boar and the dragon were elsewhere? In May 1580 the
Kirk Sessions of Perth forbade the annual procession of young men
and women to the Dragon's Hole, a cave in the side of the hill
of Kinnoul with 'piping and drums striking before them'; there they
celebrated 'superstitious games', 'not without suspicion of filthiness
after to follow'.[29] Was this dragon associated with the cult of the
Maidens so common in this part of Scotland? Folklore specialists

may piece such myths together in a tentative fashion, but there are usually more ways than one in which it can be done. In research, as in the folk tales themselves, the inhabitants of the other world are elusive and tantalise us with glimpses only, and this is perhaps part of their charm.

Often the Maidens can only be suspected behind well-established saints by the similarity of the offerings made at sacred wells, the rites performed there, the number of holy ladies involved, or by some discrepancy between the local cult and Christian belief. A great number of saints occurring in threes have been identified in these ways as former triple goddesses in Germany.[30] The celebrated St Triduana or Tredwall had a well and a chapel at Restalrig, a mile or so from Edinburgh. The water of her well, like many others associated with the Maidens, was especially propitious for afflictions of the eye. Her legend records that she was importuned by a Pictish chieftain called Nectaneuis, who sent a messenger to say he could not live unless he enjoyed the beauty of her eyes. The reply of this alarming saint was to remove her eyes, stick them on a spike and hand them to the messenger with the words: 'take what your chief desires'.[31] When one learns that Triduana was not a personal name but that of a three-days' fast practised by the old Celtic Church, and that the person behind it was one of three maidens, the others with the only slightly less curious names of Potencia and Emeria, it becomes likely that the well was originally presided over by a trio of pagan divinities. Of the same sort is the belief held in Dunbar's day and recorded at the end of the sixteenth century by Bishop Leslie, in St Donewald. The saint was, it appears, of noble descent and was renowned for his piety, living with his nine equally pious daughters near Dundee in continual fasting and prayer. Gartnait, King of the Picts, built a church and convent at Abernethy, the old Pictish capital, and endowed it for the support of the daughters when their father died. But a Nine Maidens' Well at Newburgh a few miles from Abernethy continued to draw crowds on 14 September, Holyrood Day, until modern times. The nine maidens in question were the daughters of St Donewald,[32] but it would seem probable that originally they represented the Maidens and he the attendant god or divine hero associated with harvest festivals.

There are some signs that Christianity was not the first religion to which these cults of trios of female spirits had to assimilate themselves. The Mothers and the Maidens, the later hags, witches, and fairies, appear to belong to an older stratum of religious beliefs which had a much wider range, then, and were later displaced by a pantheon of great gods. The older stratum is female and for the most part nameless. The latter have names and form a predominantly male society. The former are local rural and peasant divinities; the latter tribal, national and aristocratic. This is particularly true of Ireland where there are only few and faint traces of the *Matres*, and the Maidens seem, in general, to have got themselves attached to or absorbed by great goddesses like Aine, Morrigan, and Brigit. But Máire MacNeill records what seems an extraordinarily archaic survival of the older type of cult in the district round Cullen Well in a remote part of south Kerry:

> Cullen is in the foothills below the twin mountains called Dhá Chioch Annan, the Paps of Anu, mother of the gods. The region of South Kerry and West Cork . . . has had no tradition whatever of Crom Dubh. So here the mother goddess and her sisters, the Irish representatives of the Gaulish Matronae may have reigned supreme . . . The surrounding region was since time immemorial a refuge land, and not until the nineteenth century were modern roads driven through it.[33]

The cult is that of St Latiaran, a saint not mentioned in old records of Irish saints, and her two sisters Lasair (Flame) and Ingean Bhuidhe (the Yellow-haired girl). They are patrons of neighbouring parishes and each originally had a sacred well, but tradition says that they once all lived together and that they had a brother, St John of Mushera. His feast was celebrated, like that of St John the Baptist, on Midsummer Eve and those of the three sisters at the beginning of spring, summer, and harvest, so that the saints probably replace the familiar three fertility goddesses and the attendant god. A legend of Latiaran carrying live coals in her apron from a forge near her cell would seem to connect her with St Brigid, about whom a similar legend is told and whose sacred fire at Kildare is thought to preserve a pre-Christian cult. Another tale from the same district relates that each of the three sisters went down into the ground and disappeared and that a well sprang up on the spot. This would suggest that they were nymphs, or Maidens of the types already mentioned, before they were saints. Other names they bear in stories about them in the region suggest their assimilation to or identity with the three Irish war goddesses. Three wells at Donaghmoyne dedicated to St Ceir, St Lasair, and St Brigid may be connected with the same or with a related trio of goddesses.[34]

St Brigid of Kildare was closely associated in Scotland with the cult of the Maidens, as we have seen. In Ireland she seems to have taken over the attributes and rites of the triple goddess Brigid, about whose cult I shall have more to say in a later chapter. The ancestors of the Scots must have brought this cult in its Irish form to Scotland and Irish missionaries would have contributed to its spread. It was, at any rate, immensely popular. The older Scottish historians preserve a legend that it was a Pictish cult in the first place and that St Brigid herself introduced it. Bishop Leslie writing in 1578 says:

> The Scottis, Peychtes, Britanis, Inglismen and Irishmen with sik veneratione in ilk place haue honouret S. Brigida, that innumerable Kirkes erected to God, amang thame al, to her, ye sal se; yie and mae to her than to ony of the rest; the Irland men contendes that her haly body thay haue wt, thame in that house quhilke thay cal Dun, in quhilke place the body of thair Apostle S. Patrick is keipet. Our cuntrey men ascryues the same Glore vnto thame, quha thinkes, that hitherto thay haue honouret it, in the Chantrie of Abernethie, and rychtlie haue done thay think.[35]

The Aberdeen Breviary, a sixteenth-century compilation of saints' lives, but based on much older traditions, records that Domnath, King of the Picts, while at war with the Britons, was warned divinely to summon Brigid from Ireland. When he did she founded the church at Abernethy, the old Pictish capital. One version of the Chronicle of the Kings of the Picts which may go back to the twelfth century says that the church at Abernethy was founded by Dairlugdach, an abbess of Kildare, in the reign of Nechtan Morbet, son of Erip or Wirp. An insertion in the text adds that he 'offered to St. Bridget, till the day of judgement, Abernethy, with its territories, which are situated from the stone in Apurfeirt to the stone beside Ceirfuill, that is, Lethfoss, and thence upwards to Athan'.[36] John of Fordun's chronicle written in the fourteenth century contains a statement by his fifteenth-century redactor, Bower, to the effect that Garnad (Gartnait), the son of Dompnach, built the collegiate church at Abernethy, and that afterwards St Patrick sent St Brigid to Scotland 'as we have learned from a certain chronicle of the church of Abernethy, with her nine virgins'. The king offered to God and the blessed Mary and the blessed Brigid and to her virgins, all the lands still held by the prior and canons of the church from of old. The nine virgins died within five years and were buried in the church.[37]

These legends are not evidence for Brigid's actual presence in Scotland, but for a tradition that her cult had preceded the later Irish missions and had existed among the Picts as an independent one. If the pagan goddess who is represented by Brigid in Ireland and Brigantia in the north of England and southern Scotland are the same, or at least related, we might expect such a separate tradition. Brigid in Ireland is associated with nineteen virgins, in Scotland with nine, and there might well be other differences based on British and Pictish beliefs. The maidens' festival on St Bride's Eve in which the unmarried girls carried a sheaf of corn, dressed like a woman, from house to house and solicited presents, suggests that in Scotland the saint's nine virgins had become confused with or identified with the harvest maidens already mentioned. The 'Maiden' was commonly hung in the house and kept till the next spring, and St Bride's Day (1 February) was the first day of spring.[38] It is interesting to notice that in the legends both St Bride and her nine maidens and St Donewald and his nine virgin daughters are associated with religious foundations at Abernethy by a Pictish king called Gartnait. It is true that these kings lived about a century apart but one could easily be confused with the other in this sort of tradition by the time it reached the fourteenth or fifteenth century. If these are in fact variants of a single legend, it would be additional evidence for separate and local cults of Brigid in Scotland.

Any survey of supernatural trios of female beings likely to have been recognised in Scotland in the fifteenth century should, of course, include the Weird Sisters familiar to us from Shakespeare's *Macbeth*. In Shakespeare they are simply three witches; but Holinshed from whom he took the story describes them as appearing suddenly 'in the middest of a laund',

> three women in strange and wild apparell, resembling creatures of elder world . . . But afterwards the common opinion was, that these women were either the weird sisters, that is (as ye would say) the goddesses of destinie, or else some nymphs or feiries, indued with knowledge of prophesie by their necromanticall science bicause euerie thing came to passe as they had spoken.[39]

Holinshed appears to distinguish between nymphs and fairies on the one hand and the Weird Sisters on the other. His original, Hector Boece, in Bellenden's Scottish translation calls them 'three weird sisters or wiches, quhilk come to thame with elrege [elvish] clothing'. Another version mentions the fairy dress and adds 'The pepill traistit thame to be werd sisteris'.[40] The metrical version of Boece simply says that their clothing was of 'elritche hew', that is it was green. In this version Macbeth and Banquo meet them in a forest, the usual resort of fairies.[41] The early fifteenth-century chronicle of Andrew of Wyntoun, a careful and responsible historian, records the incident as a dream of 'Fynlow Makbeth' at the court of King Duncan. One version says it occurred when Macbeth was young. In his dream he was out hunting with the king when he saw three women passing by,

> And thai thre women than thocht he
> Thre werd sisteris like to be.[42]

It is clear that the weird sisters were associated with, but distinguished from, the fairies, as they were in the sixteenth century flyting between Alexander Montgomerie and Sir Patrick Hume of Polwarth. After a burlesque description of the Fairy Ride on Allhallows Eve and the

46

birth of a monster begotten by an elf upon an ape (who is, of course, Hume of Polwarth), Montgomerie continues:

> The Weird Sisters wandring, as they were wont then
> Saw reavans rugand at that ratton be a ron ruit.—

that is they saw the infant under a thorn tree being torn by ravens. From its hideous appearance they surmised that it was destined to mischief and laid on it all the diseases possible and prophesied its misfortunes, miserable death and damnation.

When they withdrew Nicneven and her nymphs appeared in the guise of witches—

> Some backward raid on brod sows
> and some on black bitches.
> Some, on steid of a staig, ouer a starke monke straide.

They rode nine times widdershins about the thorn under which the infant was lying, dismounted and, barefoot and barelegged, some of them took him to 'a water . . . be a wood-side' to christen him. It is a witches' christening, of course, in which they appeal to the three-headed Hecate, and after their prayers are answered they proceed to name the 'urchin' Polwart, deliver it to Nicneven to nurse it and carry it off to a witch to rear it, fetching its food from the 'Pharie'.[43]

This poem is interesting evidence of the beliefs current in Scotland a generation or so after Dunbar's day. In spite of its burlesque manner it describes the different classes of spirits and their characteristics quite clearly. The fairies with their king and queen form one group. In their character of incubi and succubi they appropriately beget the child and leave it under a fairy thorn, probably the famous thorn tree of Polwarth itself round which newly married couples used to dance.[44] The Weird Sisters next arrive and preside, take charge of the new-born child, prescribe its physical constitution, and predict its 'weird' or fate in this world and the next. Triple divinities of this kind are familiar in the case of the Roman *Parcae*, whom the Renaissance equated with the Weird Sisters, and also in the case of the Scandinavian Norns. These last were apparently

47

originally goddesses who protected the newly born; they were once numerous, then reduced to nine in number, and finally to three.[45] This original function may also have been shared by the *Matres* who are sometimes referred to as *Matres Parcae*, notably in an inscription found at Carlisle.[46] The Weird Sisters may represent one form in which the *Matres* survived. Inscriptions show that one of their functions was protection of childbirth.[47] Most references to the Weird Sisters in the Middle Ages are from Scotland or the north of England and this is precisely the area where most of the inscriptions to the *Matres* in Roman times have been found.

The third group mentioned by Montgomerie looks very like the Maidens already described. Their number is not mentioned but is said to be 'anew' (enough), from which one would suppose that it is a definite number, not an indefinite rout like the fairies. They are all female and are under the command of a superior goddess Nicneven, a name sometimes given to the Fairy Queen and sometimes to the consort of the devil in the witch cult, but here suggesting rather the goddess of wells and groves with her nine attendants. The author calls them nymphs and says that their 'cunning consists in casting of a clew', which suggests the magic threads by which the fairies bind their victims or their lovers, and the threads and rags hung up at sacred wells. They take the child for its pagan baptism to what is apparently a sacred well in a grove. The spells by which he is bound to abjure the Christian faith and follow the triple-headed Hecate are a verbal charm, thirty knots tied in blue thread, and the members of a hundred men which they have taken from them. They are sarcastically referred to as nuns, but the line

> Thir venerable virgines whom the world calles witches

suggests that Montgomerie and his audience knew quite well that there was a difference and that the identification of the witch cult and that of the Maidens was a recent one. Moreover, they are said to come from Caithness and Ross. These parts of the country which in common with others had formed part of the old Pictish kingdom were also particularly noted for 'maiden' sites.

One could pursue this subject indefinitely, but my object has simply been to suggest reasons for thinking that, if Dunbar's audience took the three ladies in the arbour on midsummer evening for fairies, they may have been able to make a quite specific identification among various trios of supernatural females which undoubtedly were parts of popular beliefs at the time. These are identifications which we can perhaps no longer make. We can only keep in mind some of the possibilities and there were certainly others of which we no longer know. We can at least say that Dunbar and his courtly audience under James IV would not have been less informed about the various kinds of beings they might choose from than Montgomerie's audience at the court of James VI. But they would probably have seen the popular superstitions of the day through a colouring of literary tradition, particularly those provided by the Arthurian romances. They are also likely to have had their views of the world of faery less coloured by the obsession with witchcraft which marks Montgomerie's treatment as it did the mind of his royal master. It is to the literary tradition that we must now turn our attention.

4

Fays and Goddesses

ARTHURIAN romance was both read and written in Scotland in the fifteenth century. Dunbar in his 'Lament for the Makaris' mentions the death of Clerk of Tranent near Edinburgh—

That maid the Anteris of Gawane.

The courtly audience of his day would have been as well acquainted with the main figures of the Arthurian legend as anyone in Europe. According to R. S. Loomis the romance influence in southern Scotland goes back to the reign of David I in the early part of the twelfth century when there was 'a powerful influx of Anglo-Norman culture'.[1] The main tradition would have been, on the one hand, that of Geoffrey of Monmouth's *History of the Kings of Britain* and the various chronicles based on that work; these purported to be history and were still often treated as such. On the other hand were the numerous French romances and Breton *lais* and their English and Scottish counterparts. These, one might say, set the tone, but there seems also to have been an undertone, something peculiar to Scotland and suggesting an independent tradition. There is reason to think that wherever the historical King Arthur lived, the stories about him in their earliest form came into Welsh literature from the Gwyr y Gogledd, the Men of the North—that is the inhabitants of the British kingdoms which occupied Cumberland, Strathclyde, and the rest of Scotland south of the Firth of Forth after the departure of the Roman armies. One of the two main theories among scholars is that Arthur was indeed a North British prince. These kingdoms were absorbed by English-speaking Angles and Gaelic-speaking Scots between the sixth and the tenth centuries, but if, as K. H. Jackson argues, British continued to be spoken in some parts of Lothian as late as the eleventh century, then it is as likely that the speakers preserved oral traditions about Arthur and his exploits as they did about the nearly contemporary St Kentigern.[2] The *Annales Cambriae* puts their deaths only seventy years apart. These Men of the North had a heroic poetry, some of which has been preserved in Welsh, and they probably had written histories, perhaps composed at Whithorn as Nora Chadwick suggests.[3] A separate Scottish tradition about Arthur and his court is inherently likely and would help to explain why the medieval Scottish historians differ so sharply from Geoffrey of Monmouth in their account of Arthur, Mordred, and Guenevere. Mordred is represented as a Pictish prince, no villain, and the legitimate heir to the Pictish throne, Arthur as illegitimate, usurping, and treacherous. In Boece's version at least he is a man of immoral habits, who celebrates Christmas with disgraceful orgies.[4] An old Yorkshireman whom J. S. Stuart Glennie met about 1869 at Upper Heskett, south of Carlisle, recited to him a ballad which begins

> When as King Arthur ruled this land
> He ruled it like a swine

Other versions of the ballad have as their second line 'He was a thievish King' and 'He was a goodly King', but this last is ironic since it goes on:

> He stole three pecks of barley-meal
> To make a bag pudding.[5]

Even Andrew of Wyntoun, who is an exception in treating Arthur in Geoffrey's manner as the *flos regum*, seems embarrassed. He says he took his account from Huchon of the Aule Ryall's *Gest of Arthur*. Huchon must have taken his account from Geoffrey of Monmouth. Andrew of Wyntoun goes to what seem unnecessary lengths to explain how reliable Huchon is, even though, he says, some may think both himself and Huchon careless and ill-informed. A little later he complains that he could find no written account of Arthur's death. The manuscript of Huchon's tale must therefore have been defective or incomplete. Andrew tells all he knows, which is that after being wounded in battle Arthur was taken to an island and was never seen again.[6] One concludes that his information on this point came from an oral source and his embarrassment about Huchon's account suggests that the oral tradition in Scotland in the early fifteenth century was strongly against Geoffrey of Monmouth's picture of Arthur as the perfect king.

The Scottish view of Arthur's queen seems to have been even more at variance with that of the romances. It suggests that there had been some fusion of literary and folklore traditions or that a mythology had gathered round the historical king and his court independent of that which grew up in Wales and Brittany in the Middle Ages as accretions on the recorded facts. This was to be expected once the British population of the north had lost contact with Wales. Guenevere, or Guanora as she appears in Bellenden's free version of Boece in 1536, was captured by the Picts and died among them. She was accompanied by many ladies and their tombs at Meigle near Dundee are

> had in grete reuerence of the pepill, and specialie the sepulture of Gwanora as the titill writin therupoun schawis.[7]

Boece adds that if any woman stamped on the tomb she would be barren from that time on, as Guanora was. The 'tomb', which was constructed of sculptured Pictish stones, was described in the late eighteenth century by Dr James Playfair, the minister of Meigle. After giving much the same account as Bellenden, he adds:

> The character of that unfortunate personage has been drawn in the blackest colours. She has been represented as one who led a lascivious life and held an unlawful correspondence with Mordred, a Pictish King, which provoked the jealousy of her husband and excited him to take up arms in revenge of the injury. As a punishment of her enormous crimes, it is added, she was torn in pieces by wild beasts; her body was buried in Meigle and a monument erected to perpetuate her infamy.[8]

The two accounts bear witness to two aspects of the legend, one the lascivious nature and habits of the great queen and the other the superstitious awe with which her tomb was regarded in the sixteenth century. Remembering that the power to confer fertility on women or to make them barren was a property of sacred wells and stones and that Guenevere's name in Welsh—Gwenhwyfar—means white fairy, enchantress, or phantom, we may deduce that, in Scotland, legend had in time transformed Arthur's wife to one of the amorous and maleficent fays whom we meet in the romances. Various folk tales picture Arthur riding at night like the fairy king, and a local legend has him sleeping in a .cavern under the Eildon Hills and beneath the Eildon tree where Thomas the Rhymer met the Queen of Fairyland.[9] Perhaps Guenevere always had this character and it it is the romances which have euhemerised her. In the Welsh Triads, there are said to have been three Gwenhwyfars who were great queens at Arthur's court. This may be a jest or it may represent an older Welsh tradition.[10] In this case Guenevere would seem to have been a triple goddess who appears in later legend as a trio of sister fays or queens, like those who take Arthur to Avalon in the later romances. Scotland may well have preserved this tradition which later became overlaid by the romance view of her as Arthur's human but wanton wife. There is nothing in this, however, to connect her with Edinburgh and the fays of literature or, in particular, with our three ladies in a grove at midnight.

A more likely candidate is Arthur's sister Morgain la Fée, the enemy of his wife, Guenevere. This magnificent creature is one of the great imaginative triumphs of romance literature, a figure whose full beauty, energy, power, and mystery only emerge from the narratives of dozens of poets and the researches of hundreds of scholars. She is represented as one of two, four, but usually of three sisters, all powerful enchantresses, all resourceful and amorous and all royally imperious by nature, subtle, dangerous, fascinating and elusive, but Morgain is the principal. Her name with variations persists in all the tales, those of her sisters vary and sometimes they are nameless. Of her alone it was remembered that she was once a goddess, a title given her by at least four medieval authors. According to Loomis she is a composite character, inheriting characteristics of the Morrigan, chief of the trio of Irish war goddesses, Fand, daughter of the Irish god Dagda and wife of the god of the sea, Manannan, and Modron who in Welsh mythology is daughter of Avallach, wife of Urien, mother of Owain and ultimately the Celtic triple goddess Matrona, probably identical with the *Matres* or Mothers already discussed. In the romances she first appears as a powerful enchantress, living with her nine maidens on an island which has the character of a Celtic paradise. She is skilled in healing and illusion. She appears thus in the poem attributed to Geoffrey of Monmouth, the *Vita Merlini*. In a later romance she appears as an amorous fay and sorceress, mistress of a magic castle. But, as Loomis points out, her complex origins and the inconsistencies that these involve also lead to her appearing under other names or under no name at all and in particular as mistress of a Castle of Maidens. In the twelfth century the Anglo-Norman romance influence in Scotland combined with local legend to identify the local Maiden Castle, as Edinburgh was coming to be known, with the castles and islands and magic vales peopled with fays or besieged maidens in the romances. Chrétien de Troyes makes its mistress not Morgain but Morcades, wife of Lot, King of Lothian, but Loomis argues that this is really Morgain in disguise and that so is Malory's Dame Lyones, Lyones being a corruption of Loenois, i.e. Lothian.[11] Whatever one may think about the details of such arguments, it seems likely that in Dunbar's time Edinburgh Castle would be more closely connected with Arthurian legend than with the Maiden cult to which it probably owed its appellation of *Castellum Puellarum*. Arthurian legend was already firmly located in the city. The great hill to the east of the town was already known as Arthur's Seat, as Dunbar's flyting with Kennedie shows (l. 336). John Major in his *History of Greater Britain* (1521) clearly sets out the view of the times:

> At Edinburgh in Scotland was Arthur's Kingly seat and to this day that spot near Edinburgh bears his name.[12]

The legend that Merlin had paved a wynd or alley near the Tron Church and was buried at the head of it, mentioned by Robert Fergusson in the eighteenth century,[13] is possibly just as old. Arthur's Seat, the Castle, Calton Hill, and the Tron seem all to have had associations with the supernatural world. If Dunbar's audience was expected to take the three ladies, at first sight, for denizens of that world, they may have been just as likely to see them in terms of ladies of Arthurian romance, which had been associated with Edinburgh since the days of King David I, as in terms of the more popular fairies. Indeed literary and popular traditions were not likely to have been sharply distinct. Arthur's queen at Meigle was obviously no mere literary figure but a powerful local spirit who could strike any woman barren who trod on her 'tomb', just as the spirit in the Clach-na-Bhan, the Woman Stone near the boundary between Braemar and Kirkmichael, could bestow fertility on a barren woman who sat in its hollow.[14] If literary tradition had associated Morgain la Fée or any of her sisters with localities in and around Edinburgh, the tradition would almost certainly have been reinforced by beliefs in local spirits who would be assimilated to them and take their names. A tree or a standing stone associated with such names is sure to have been the residence of a powerful spirit before the romance ascription occurred, in the same way as with stones or wells which now bear the names of saints, and in the same way as the saint or the romance figure takes on the attributes or powers of the original tutelary spirit. A remarkable stone at Heriot in Midlothian was known in the eighteenth century as Lot's Wife, though the minister of the parish said no one knew why.[15] It is possible that the name refers to or was confused with the Biblical Lot, but in view of the number of Arthurian place names in the Lowlands, it seems more likely that Lot, the eponymous King of Lothian in Geoffrey of Monmouth and the romances, was meant. Lot's wife in Geoffrey's work is Anna, sister of King Arthur, though he seems confused in his traditions since a few pages later he gives Anna another husband and Lot another wife.[16] Layamon's *Brut* calls Arthur's sister Aene (ll. 19270-3). Lucy Paton and other scholars attempt to identify her with Anu, one of the trio of Irish goddesses of war, who is later replaced by Morrigan (Morgain) in Irish legend.[17] In some romances Arthur's sister and the wife of King Lot is called Morcades, who is probably only Morgain under another name. But in any case it is clear that Lot's wife to the audience of Dunbar's day would have been Arthur's sister and a powerful fay.

A similar instance of fusion of romance and local legend was noted by F. S. Child in the case of Thomas the Rhymer, who, in the ballad and the fourteenth-century verse romance, meets the Queen of Elfland under the Eildon Tree, becomes her lover, and is taken away to Fairyland with her, spending seven years there before being returned to this world. Child has pointed out that this is a version of a tale told of Ogier the Dane and Morgain la Fée and must be based on a French original.[18] The Eildon Tree is supposed to have stood on the spot now marked by the Eildon Tree Stone and both were obviously fairy haunts which must have housed local spirits before the romance tale was attached to them. But in the ballad and in the romance the Queen of Elfland appears as a typical fay. True Thomas as he lay on Huntley Bank, like Ogier the Dane in his encounter with Morgain, took the lady at first for the Virgin Mary, which is odd since she is dressed and equipped for hunting.

> Swylke one ne saghe j neuer none;
> Als dose the sonne on someres day
> That faire lady hir selfe scho schone.
> Hir selle it was of roelle bone,
> ffull semely was that syghte to se!
> Stefly sett with precyous stones,
> And compaste all with crapotee,
> Stones of Oryente, grete plente;
> Hir hare abowte hir hede it hange;
> Scho rade ouer that lange lee;
> A whylle scho blewe, a-nother scho sange
>
> .   .   .   .
>
> And als clere golde hir brydill it schone,
> One aythir syde hange bellys three.
> And seuene raches by hir thay rone.
> Scho bare an horne abowte hir halse,
> And vndir hir belte full many a flone.[19]

This is clearly a description of a fay of the type called by Lucy Paton *La Damoiselle Cacheresse*, and she corresponds to the description of Niniane in the *Huth Merlin* as she rides into Arthur's hall accompanied by a pack of hounds, dressed in a short green dress, with an ivory horn round her neck and carrying bow and arrows. In this romance she is identified as the Lady of the Lake. In addition, in the romance of Thomas of Erceldoune, she has the characteristic features of her kind, the fairy light that shines from her as bright as the sun itself, her hair hanging loose. Like Nimiane she is making a good deal of noise blowing her horn and singing.[20] Now Nimiane, the Lady of the Lake, and Morgain all interchange roles at times in the romances. If, as seems to be the case, the existing versions of the poem are based on a Scottish original which may even have been by Thomas of Erceldoune himself, then we have here an interesting example of fays from the literary romances not only assimilated to local spirits of stones and trees in Scotland, but attached to a historical person, the famous poet and prophet of Berwickshire in the thirteenth century. Morgain la Fée and her sisters could easily have appeared to the inhabitants of Edinburgh, or of Lothian in general, not merely as literary personages but as local tutelary spirits. Morgain may even by Dunbar's day have assumed the character of the Queen of Elfhame in local beliefs. There would be nothing surprising then in the view that Dunbar might have intended his audience to take his three ladies for Morgain and her two sister fays.

The three ladies in Dunbar's poem resemble the fays of romance in more than their appearance. The ambition of the two young wives is to escape from marriage altogether and to choose themselves lovers as often as they like, keep them for as long as they wish, and dispose of them at will, and this the widow has actually done. Moreover from time to time she assembles many lovers in her house and denies herself to none of them. The objects of their choice are young men of mettle, vigour and good birth:

> . . . baronis, knychtis,
> And othir bachilleris, blith blumying in youth, . . .
>
> (ll. 477-8)

To choose, lure, and detain young heroes as their lovers is, of course, one of the commonest habits of the fays. It is nearly always they who take the initiative and they often set a term to the period of the relationship. In the *Bataille Loquifer*, the hero Renoart is sleeping beside the sea when three fays, who turn out to be Morgain, her sister Marrion, and an attendant, fly towards him and carry him off to Avalon where he becomes Morgain's lover. In the prose *Lancelot* the hero is found sleeping beneath an apple tree by Morgain la Fée, Sebile l'Enchanteresse, and the Queen of Sorestan who come riding by. Pleased by his beauty each wishes to have him for her lover, and after some argument about this they take him to a castle belonging to the Queen of Sorestan. In the morning they ask him to choose one of them as a mistress but Lancelot refuses and manages to escape. A similar tale is told in four romances about Morgain's capture of Alisander l'Orphelin, famous for his beauty and his prowess in battle. In *Claris and Laris*, Morgain and her fays capture two brave knights to live with them in love and delight in a palace in an enchanted valley. In other versions of the theme the fays attend the christening or effect the capture of a baby destined to become a great hero with a view to providing themselves with future lovers. This procedure reminds us of the first wife's plan, when she has acquired a new lover, to provide for a replacement when she has exhausted the present incumbent:

> Fra I had preveit his pitht the first plesand moneth,
> Than suld I cast me to keik in kirk, and in markat,
> And all the cuntre about, kyngis court, and uther,
> Quhair I ane galland micht get aganis the nixt yeir,
> For to perfurneis furth the werk quhen failyeit the tother;
>
> (ll. 80-4)

In *Floriant et Florete*, Morgain and two other fays capture the hero as a baby for this end; similar tales are told of Lancelot and the Lady of the Lake and of Ogier the Dane.[21] In the latter case Morgain and five other fays attend and make gifts to Ogier at his birth and Morgain in terms of her prophecy later lures him to Avalon to become her lover. In the related story of Thomas the Rhymer and the Queen of Elfland, the fay does not wait, but binds her lover by an immediate union which tests his sexual prowess much in the spirit of the ladies in Dunbar's poem. In the ballad the compact is sealed and the hero bound by kissing the Elf-queen three times, but the fourteenth-century romance probably preserves the original and more earthy version of the lost Scottish romance:

> Downe thane lyghte that lady bryghte,
> Vndir-nethe that grenewode spraye;
> And, als the storye tellis full ryghte,
> Seuene sythis by hir he laye.
> Scho sayd, 'mane, the lykes thy playe:
> What byrde in boure maye delle with the?
> Thou merrys me all this longe daye,
> I praye the, Thomas, late me bee.'[22]

This is the kind of performance Dunbar's ladies are looking for. That the Elf-queen here is in fact Morgain la Fée is suggested by the fact that after making love she loses all her beauty and appears as a blue and naked hag. In *The Prophecies of Merlin* she appears similarly and when her sister fay, la Dame d'Avallon, points out that this is surprising in view of the fact that she has been naked in bed with many a handsome knight, she replies that in those cases she appears in the freshness and firmness of youth by magic baths and ointments.[23] If Morgain could appear not many miles from Edinburgh in this guise in a thirteenth-century poem, it would not be surprising to find her, in the neighbourhood of her Castle of Maidens, in a poem of the fifteenth or early sixteenth century.

The widow, it may be noticed, selects her lovers much as the first wife proposes to do, but she summons them to her lodging by means of a trustworthy servant. Again one is reminded of the various messengers and magic beasts used by the fays to bring young heroes to their palaces and enchanted isles or valleys. The widow's occasional festive orgies at which she describes herself as surrounded by a crowd of lovers all wooing her at once, all under her control and all enjoying her favours in turn, is hard to accept as a realistic scene in the Scottish capital, loose as the morals of the upper classes may have been. It is in any case hardly consistent with her claim:

> Yit am I haldin a haly wif our all the haill schyre,

(l. 472)

since such doings could hardly remain secret for long. But it does suggest in some ways the crowd of captive knights in some of the fairy castles and even more the endless feasting and love-making of some of the Irish isles of women and other Celtic paradises.

Another resemblance between Dunbar's ladies and the fays of romance is their common hostility to marriage. With the fays this is partly a natural result of their ambitions and habits in seeking the love of a succession of human heroes, many of whom are already married or betrothed. Renoart in the *Bataille Loquifer* has a wife Aalis whom he forgets in Morgain's arms; but, prompted by anxiety for his lost son, he leaves Morgain, to her fury, and then remembers his wife and repents of his infidelity. In the tale of Alisander l'Orphelin, Morgain to gain her ends has first to use her magic arts to aggravate Alisander's wounds, then to cure him and, as a price of his recovery, to forbid him to marry the maiden to whom he is engaged—she is, it must be admitted, a rival fay. Such incidents are not uncommon in the romances and arise easily enough from situations of rivalry and jealousy. But the series of stories in which Morgain sends a magic horn or a magic mantle to Arthur's court suggest a more definite antipathy. The drinking horn usually has the property that only a faithful wife can drink from it without spilling the wine; the mantle will fit only a constant wife. The main object is to discredit Arthur's wife, the mistress of Lancelot whom Morgain had tried unsuccessfully to win from her. The trick is used by other fays than Morgain and against other rivals. But the hostile attitude to marriage comes out in the fact that in most of such tests the horn or the mantle or whatever object is used is tried out on the whole court in question and that very few manage to pass the test. Whether as husbands or wives, they tend to discredit the institution of marriage itself.[24] Bercilak de Hautdesert, in *Sir Gawain and the Green Knight*, explains that the first purpose of Morgain la Fée in sending him on his errand to Arthur's court was

> For to assay the surquidré, gif hit soth were
> That rennes of the grete renoun of the Rounde Table
>
> (ll. 2457-8)

and only secondly to annoy and endanger Gaynor (Guenevere). The method of testing the pride of the members of the Round Table as displayed in the poem shows clearly that Morgain was primarily concerned to challenge their claims of chastity and fidelity in love which her own practice so signally ignored. As Loomis and Paton point out, the earliest form of the story of her relations with Arthur probably showed her, not as his sister, but as a fay thwarted in her attempts to win him as her lover in Avalon.[25]

Still another likeness of the widow and her two companions to the fays of the romances lies in their complaints about the husbands they have been saddled with—an old man, an impotent young man, and in the widow's case two husbands roughly similar to these. In all the comparisons already made the differences are as important as the similarities and suggest that, if Dunbar is following a literary tradition, it is either a degenerate tradition or he is deliberately making fun of it. As we have already seen, the theme of sexual impotence is raised by the poem in an ambiguous way. The ladies complain about this defect in their husbands but they treat the whole subject with superior amusement and derision. It is only what is to be expected of marriage which is a worthless institution in any case. The narrator on the other hand refers to the scene and the day as one which might well kindle a man's sexual powers again and ends with his sly question as to which of the ladies his auditors would choose for a *wife* if he had to marry one of them.

One of the commonest aspects of Morgain and many other fays as well as of their prototypes in Irish literature is their power of magically inducing disease or wounds. A favourite way of getting lovers into their power is to cast on them a great bodily weakness or general impotence and then to transport them to their palace or castle and cure them as the price of their becoming lovers. The earliest account of Morgain, the *Vita Merlini* composed about 1148, stresses this aspect of her nature:

> Morgen ei nomen, didicitque quid utilitatis
> Gramina cuncta ferant, ut languida corpora curet

Here is a possible answer to a question raised earlier—why, if Dunbar is satirising women, he should allow his first two ladies such excellent cases to plead by giving them repulsive and impotent husbands. If he is following a degenerate literary tradition it may be that in the original source the fays restored the heroes at midsummer in their magic garden as the fairy Fand heals Cuchulinn on the Plain of Delight, her island paradise. This tale of 'Cuchulinn's Sick Bed' suggests a possible prototype for the case of the second wife, though the original cause of the man's impotence has been forgotten and is now attributed to excessive amatory exercise. Similarly the case of the first wife suggests that in a possible original the old man was to be made young again. Ogier the Dane is brought to Morgain's island when he is already a hundred years old. She puts a ring on his finger which makes him young again; for two hundred years he then lives as her lover in restored vigour and among every imaginable pleasure.[26]

But there is another and perhaps a more likely prototype suggested by the well-known romance tradition of the association of the fay Nimiane or Viviane with the enchanter Merlin. We have already noticed her likeness to the Queen of Elfland in the romance of Thomas the Rhymer. Merlin and Thomas are constantly associated in the patriotic prophecy literature of Scotland. In the prose *Merlin*, a fifteenth-century English version of a thirteenth-century French romance, there are a number of points to suggest aspects of Dunbar's poem. Merlin in his later years meets a beautiful maiden by a well from which issues a charming stream. She is Nimiane, daughter of a nobleman called Dionas, himself the godson of the goddess Diana. She lives in a valley beneath a mountain bordering the forest of Briok. Merlin has disguised himself as a fair young squire. He falls deeply in love with the girl, and to win her love he brings a company of knights and ladies sporting from the forest, by his magic, and creates an orchard for them to dance and make merry in. The girl is won, or says she is, and, in return for his teaching her his magic arts, promises to be his love. Merlin promises to return on Midsummer Eve and fulfil his part of the bargain. He returns at the appointed time and his love is waiting for him at the well:

and whan she hym saugh she made hym grete chere, and ladde hym
in to the chambres so prively that he was not a-perceyved of no man;
and she asked and enquered hym of many thinges, and he her taught
all her askynge for the grete love that he hadde to hir; and when she
saugh he loved her so wele, she asked hym how she myght make a
frende for to slepe and not to a-wake till that she wolde . . . and it
fill on a day that thei were in a gardin by the fountayne hem to
disporte, and were sette vpon an ympe, and the mayden made hym to
slepe in hir lappe, and hilde her so with hym that Merlyn loved hir
merveillously wele. Than the maiden required hym that he taught hir
to make oon slepe, and he knewe hir menynge right wele; but neuer-
theles he it hir taught . . . and he taught hir iij names that she wrote
for to helpe hir-self at alle tymes whan she sholde with hym ly, and
that were full of grete force, ffor neuer as longe as thei were vpon
hir, ne myght neuer man touche her flessly; and fro thens-forth she
tysed euer Merlin to come speke with hir, for he ne hadde no power
to dele with hir agein her will, and ther-fore it is seide that woman
hath an art more than the deuell.

On two further visits Merlin continues to impart his magic to the
wily maiden, without her fulfilling her side of the bargain:

and she made hym the grettest ioye that she myght, and ete and dranke,
and lay in oon bedde; but so moche cowde she of his connynge that
whan he hadde will to ly with hire she hadde enchaunted and coniured
a pelow that she kepte in hir armes, and than fill Merlin a-slepe; and
the story maketh no mencioun that euer Merlin hadde flesshly to do
with no woman, and yet loved he nothinge in this worlde so wele
as woman.

On his fourth visit she induces him to teach her how to make a
tower of air from which there would be no escape, on the pretext
that now she wishes to have him in her arms night and day to
keep her promise at last and forever. Merlin is not deceived but
loves her so well that he consents:

till it fill on a day that thei wente thorgh the foreste hande in hande,
devisinge and disportinge, and this was in the foreste of brochelonde,
and fonde a bussh that was feire and high of white hawthorne full of
floures, and ther thei satte in the shadowe; and Merlin leide his heed
in the damesels lappe, and she began to taste softly till he fill on
slepe; and whan she felt that he was on slepe she a-roos softly, and
made a cerne with hir wymple all a-boute the bussh and al a-boute

Merlin, and be-gan hir enchauntementz soche as Merlin hadde hir taught.[27]

The result of these enchantments is that Merlin wakes up in a tower, the finest in the world and invisible to others, from which he cannot ever escape though Nimiane goes in and out at her pleasure. In other versions of the tale she hates Merlin and tricks him into a cave or tomb in which he lies, however, in a magic sleep. Nimiane is represented as a creature of this world, but in earlier versions she was undoubtedly a fay. The same story of acquiring magic arts from Merlin in return for an offer of love is told of Morgain la Fée in *Sir Gawain and the Green Knight*:

> The maystres of Merlyn mony ho hatz taken;
> For ho hatz dalt drwry ful dere sumtyme
> With that conable klerk. . . .

(ll. 2447-9)

Nimiane's well and her fairy thorn are clear enough indications of her nature, and the valley and the garden and the chamber are clearly euhemerised versions of an original Celtic paradise. The fact that Merlin chooses St John's Eve to win her love is also significant, but even more so is the fact that each of Dunbar's ladies has made her husband or husbands pay for their embraces, embraces which, like Nimiane, they are anxious to avoid. The second wife, like Nimiane, has invented a trick to keep out of them. The widow in particular has managed to strip both husbands of their goods and obtain the mastery by hypocritically pretending love to the first and daunting the second with her superior birth and standing, as Nimiane systematically robs Merlin of his knowledge, his power, and in some versions of the tale, of his life. Merlin is acquiescent in this process because of his love for her, just as the widow's second husband is. Merlin's impotence, induced by the spell he teaches Nimiane, and his attempts to make love to her in spite of this, are reminiscent of the second wife's husband, particularly as Merlin is said never to have had carnal relations with a woman though it was his chief desire: 'yet loved he nothing in this world so well as woman.' The second wife remarks

My husband wes a hur maister, the hugeast in erd.
Tharfor I hait him with my hert, sa help me our Lord!
He is a young man ryght yaip, but nought in youth flouris;

(ll. 168-70)

Of course the differences are as striking as the likenesses: Merlin's
impotence is due to magic (and perhaps some natural disability);
the impotence of the second wife's husband is due to over-indulgence,
and so on. But it is not suggested that one situation is in any way
the original or derived from the original of the other, merely that,
allowing for a good deal of euhemerisation, Dunbar's poem could
represent a late stage of a theme which was originally a romance
one, or possibly that it is a satire or a parody of similar themes in
romance. Perhaps, as I have already suggested, the poet, for some
reason obvious to his audience but lost to us, wished to do no more
than lend his human women a colouring or appearance of super-
natural beings, and if he seriously intended to present them as more
than this, then the original features of the legend or legends asso-
ciated with them must have been garbled or forgotten.

However, this is more or less what normally happens in the
romances. We have already seen it as a process of 'humanising' the
fays in the case of Nimiane just discussed, and the ambiguity of her
appearance, neither of the magic fairy world nor wholly of the
ordinary human world, is characteristic of the way the literature of
the romances gradually reduces and tones down their supernatural
aspects. They begin as Celtic high goddesses; with the process of
time they pass from real divinities to the status of half literary,
half folklore figures, though still supernatural beings. The next step
is to be viewed as human beings with exceptional magic gifts, while
in the final stage they appear simply as legendary or even contem-
porary human beings. The same thing happens to the settings: the
Celtic otherworld, the island in the fabled sea, becomes an enchanted
castle, valley, or wood located however vaguely in the real geography
of this world. Finally Avalon becomes an ordinary castle and its
mistress a human princess who has learned some magic tricks. The
next step is perhaps the one Dunbar presents us with, where the
ladies have become ordinary citizens of the contemporary world

and all the aspects of the original legends have been given a rational everyday explanation.

The euhemerisation of divine beings is apt to follow much the same paths in folklore and popular superstition as it does in literature. The history of the Irish fay Aine is a case in point. T. F. O'Rahilly argues that at an earlier stage of pagan belief she must have been one of a trio of sun goddesses, Aine, Grian, and Eriu. Possibly they were local aspects of a triple goddess or of one goddess, since they give their names to a number of specific localities, including, in the case of Eriu, a river in Scotland.[28] In ancient Irish literature, however, Aine appears as a member of the *síde* and she lives in her fairy hill at Knockainy in Limerick with her father Eogabul, son of Durgabul (Yew-fork son of Oak-fork). *The Battle of Mag Mucrama* from the *Book of Leinster*, a text not later than the tenth century and dealing with events said to have occurred in the second century, preserves a tale about her in which the son of the King of Munster encountered and outraged her on Knockainy itself.

> One Hallowe'en Oilill went to pasture his horses on Áne Cliach (Knockaney). A bed was made for him on the hill. That night the hill was stripped bare and none knew who stripped it. Twice it happened to him thus. He wondered at that. He sent messengers to Ferches son of Comman, a poet who dwelt on the boundary of Leinster. He was a prophet and a warrior. He came to speak with him. They both went on Hallowe'en to the hill. Oilill waits on the hill. Ferches was apart from him. Oilill falls asleep listening to the grazing of the cattle. They came out of the fairy-mound, and Eogabul son of Durgabul after them, and Áne daughter of Eogabul with a bronze lyre in her hand playing before him. Ferches went against him and dealt him a blow. Eogabul fled into the fairy-mound. Ferches strikes him with a great spear which broke his back as he came up to Oilill. Oilill lay with the girl while he was there. The woman bit his ear so that she left neither flesh nor skin on it, and none ever grew on it from that time. And Oilill Bare-Ear is his name ever since.[29]

In this charming illustration of the manners of a heroic age, Aine retains some of the characteristics of a goddess and a fairy queen. She later threatens Oilill with reprisals which she will undertake herself. One may suspect that the choice of Hallowe'en and the setting up of a bed on the fairy hill was originally the point of the story, the purpose being that Aine should come out at the propitious season and sleep with the king's son, and this in turn may rest on the ritual marriage of the king to the local goddess on her mound at the festival of Samain, the beginning of the old Celtic year. But apart from these traces, euhemerisation has gone to a point where she appears as 'human' enough to be caught and forced by a mortal against her will. In the late fourteenth or early fifteenth century the Earl of Desmond also caught her while she was combing her hair by her river after bathing—for Aine is a water spirit too, like her neighbouring fay Graney—and he was able to get her into his power by snatching her cloak. More gallant than the prince of Munster, he married her and she lived with him for several years and bore him a son before she returned to her own world. In this incident her 'human' characteristics predominate. A report dating from about 1834, quoted by Máire MacNeill, mentions various places, a fort, a well, and a mound among them, named after Aine in Derry in the parish of Lissan. The report continues:

> The Aine who gave names to all these places is said to have been taken away at night by the wee folk from her husband's side and never returned. She is living still and particularly attached to the family of O'Corra . . . who are believed to be her descendants because whenever one of them is about to die she is heard wailing . . . in the wild glen of Alt na Síon . . . adjacent to the fort of Lios Aine.[30]

MacNeill points out that Aine here is confused with Etain or Eithne, but either way the euhemerisation is complete. The confusion with the legend of Etain may be due to a half-remembered or garbled version of how Aine deserted her husband the Earl of Desmond and returned to her fairy haunts. But Aine is now a mortal woman captured by the fairies from whose world she continues to take an interest in her human descendants, a local family. Another report gathered from people living at or near Knockainy in 1876 illustrates a stage in this process which presents Aine in an ambiguous role, neither quite supernatural nor quite an ordinary human being, or rather a little of each, and this is particularly relevant to Dunbar's poem since he seems to present his ladies in just this way. The account is also worth quoting since it has points of resemblance with 'The Two Married Women and the Widow':

Áine is sometimes to be seen, half her body above the waters, on the bosom of Loch Guirr, combing her hair as the Earl of Desmond beheld her by the bank of the Camóg. The commoner account is that she dwells within the hill which bears her name [Cnoc-Áine] and on which she has often been seen. Every St John's Night the men used to gather on the hill from all quarters. They where [*sic*] formed in ranks by an old man called Quinlan whose family yet (1876) live on the hill; and clíars, bunches, that is, of straw and hay tied upon poles, and lit, were carried in procession round the hill and the little moat on the summit, *Mullach-Crocain-lámh-lé-leab'-an-Triúir* (the hillock-top near the grave of the three). Afterwards people ran through the cultivated fields, and among the cattle, waving these clíars, which brought luck to crops and beasts for the following year. . . One Saint John's Night it happened that one of the neighbours lay dead, and on this account the usual *clíars* were not lit. Not lit, I should say, by the hands of living men; for that night such a procession of *clíars* marched round Cnoc-Áine as never was seen before, and Áine was seen in the front, directing and ordering everything. On another St John's Night a number of girls had staid late on the hill, watching the *clíars* and joining in the games. Suddenly Áine appeared among them, 'thanked them for the honour they had done her,' but said that now she wished them to go home, as *They wanted the hill to themselves.* She let them understand whom she meant by 'they', for calling some of the girls she made them look through a ring, when behold, the hills appeared crowded with people before invisible. . . .

. . . Áine is spoken of as 'the best hearted woman that ever lived' and the oldest families about Knockainy are proud to claim descent from her. These Sliocht-Áine (descendants of Áine) include the O'Briens, Dillanes, Creeds, Laffins, O'Deas. We must add Fitzgeralds, what few remain thereabouts.[31]

What is particularly interesting about this account, in view of our present inquiry, is the persistence of a fully developed and consciously organised fairy cult as late as the second half of the nineteenth century in Christian Ireland. The possibility of a similar cult in fifteenth-century Scotland is immediately apparent. But what is even more interesting is the way the whole process has been euhemerised.

Aine is obviously a fairy and a powerful one. But she is not referred
to in these terms. 'She is the best hearted *woman* that ever lived' and
she is the ancestress of a number of local families who of course are
just as human as you and I. She is a Good Neighbour, in Scottish
terminology. The whole thing is as tactfully presented as possible
to avoid a clash with the Christian point of view. The pagan
ceremony is presented as a local, almost a family, custom connected
however vaguely with the celebration of the feast of St John. Behind
this the ancient sun and fertility goddess looks after her own as she
must have done a millennium before with the possible omission of
overt sexual rites suggested by the tale of Oilill Bare-Ear and other
legends in which she offers her favours to men. The strength of such
beliefs of course depends largely on the fact that those who retain
them are farmers. The Midsummer Eve fires taken round the fields
and among the cattle are as much an essential part of husbandry
as ploughing or shearing, and the church may as well try to
abolish one as the other. In Ireland there was a strong conviction
that the prosperity of the crops was directly due to the fairies, that
the fairies of one district fought an annual battle with those of
another and whichever was the victor obtained the luck of the crops
for the next season at the expense of their neighbours. Aine was
reputed to engage in such an annual battle with Donn of Knock-
feerina, a fairy king whose *sid* was a few miles from Knockainy.[32]

Aine's marriage to the Earl of Desmond and presumably, in local
legend, to the ancestors of several local families is another illustration
of the way in which, at a certain stage of euhemerisation, these
legends can present their otherworld figures as belonging also to
this. It could explain the main problem which arises in any attempt
to see Dunbar's three ladies as fairies or fays: that they are citizens
of the town and married to men of position and standing. Fairy-
marriages occurred in Scotland as elsewhere in medieval Europe.
There was not in those times the sharp distinction which we tend
to draw between spiritual and corporeal beings. The fays and fairies
were as much creatures of flesh and blood, when they appeared, as
the children of Adam. There is thus nothing really incongruous in
Dunbar's opening and closing sections of his poem, where his ladies

are presented in the guise of supernatural beings, and the middle section where they appear very much as beings of the ordinary human world.

However, it is precisely their marriages that form the real objection to our taking these ladies as fays. In folklore and in romance it is not the bond of marriage itself which is the compelling force in a union between a mortal and a member of the fairy race. It is rather a symbolic or ritual act which puts one in the power of the other, the possession of a formula or talisman, or the observance of a particular taboo. If such magic conditions are broken or circumvented in any way the mortal is free to return from fairyland and the fairy wife or husband vanishes and is seen no more in human society. There are no traces of such magic conditions in Dunbar's poem and the bond against which the ladies revolt is marriage itself, the ordinary legal and social constraints of husbands and kinsmen. Euhemerisation will not explain the retention of fairy elements in the beginning of the poem and their entire absence in the middle, supposing the poem to be based on some lost original. But there is another possibility which would reconcile the discrepancy: this is the view that our three ladies are not presented as fairies themselves but are just what they claim to be. Their appearance in fairy costume in a grove on Midsummer Eve is due to their being members of a fairy cult and their celebration of a cult festival. There is a good deal of evidence for the existence of such cults and to this we must now turn.

5

The Fairy Cult

SOME writers, dealing with the origins of witchcraft and other pagan survivals in Europe, speak of the Old Religion, as though there had been only one. This is of course absurd. There is little evidence that the cults of the very large number of divinities worshipped by Celtic peoples formed part of a single religious system and it is improbable, if the witch cult, as some suppose, is a survival of the ancient worship of the Horned God, that this was its sole source. Many cults survived and many of them became merged in others. On the other hand the case of Irish Aine mentioned in the last chapter is an illustration of a local cult surviving untouched by others and practically uncoloured by Christian beliefs. The religion of the Celts seems in fact to have been one of many independent, though related, cults, often confined to one locality. There is plenty of evidence that some of them survived and remained relatively intact until modern times. In sixteenth-century Scotland, as we have seen, it was still possible to distinguish beliefs in such groups as the Maidens, the Weird Sisters (the *Matres*), and the fairies.

To prove the existence of a specific cult, however, requires more than to demonstrate the survival of a belief. People may believe in witches or fairies without doing anything about them beyond taking the ordinary Christian precautions against evil spirits. This does not constitute a cult. There must be a practice in which the believers enter into relationships of a definite kind with the powers they believe in, invoking them by prayer, or combining to coerce or propitiate them. On the other hand the mere existence of super-stitious practices is not in itself evidence of an active cult. People may keep up the customary practices and rites of May Day or the New Year without the least idea of what they once meant, and in ignorance of the gods or spirits once involved. Or they may continue the rites transferring them to another cult. At a sacred well such as St Fillan's Well at Comrie in Perthshire (see p. 33) all the once pagan ceremonies were observed, but the curative effects, the restoration of fertility, and the granting of easy childbirth were attributed to the saint; whereas the same rites at Loch Siant Well in Skye, described by Martin Martin in 1695, were apparently attributed to a pagan spirit. A century later the minister of the parish of Kilmuir said of the crowds who once gathered there that they left small rags, pins, and coloured threads 'to the divinity of the place'.[1] This was apparently a genuine survival of a pagan cult and many instances from all over Scotland have been recorded right down to the present century. Others can be inferred merely from the awe or veneration in which some tree, well, stone, or Druid circle was held by the local inhabitants. At Halkirk in Caithness in the eighteenth century there was a monumental stone nine feet high:

> in John Sinclair's time, late of Ulbster, proprietor of that land, a set of ruffians broke it wantonly, who immediately were pursued by the neighbors; and on their being overtaken, a scuffle ensued, to which numbers resorted, and was the occasion of bloodshed.[2]

Sir John Sinclair, who was the local sheriff, restored the stone, fenced it, and fined the 'ruffians' a cow apiece. But soon the sacred sites began to be destroyed by the people themselves. At Kilmuir Easter in Ross, a number of small mounds, according to the minister, were regarded with peculiar terror and avoided by the people:

> So late as 1768, one of these tumuli, not so much larger than a cartload of earth, was left an impediment on the middle of the road, at the principal entry of the village of Milntown; and no argument could prevail with the inhabitants to remove it.

When a man was at last found reckless enough to do so and it was observed that he suffered no ill effects, the spell was broken and the villagers began to destroy all the mounds.[3] In parish after parish *The Statistical Account of Scotland* records similar events.

Other instances of survival of a pagan cult occur in accounts of customary practices at the great annual festivals of the old Celtic year. The minister of Callander in Perthshire in 1794 reported a Beltane custom which he said was then general all over the Highlands though fast dying out. The boys in this case, in other districts the herdsmen, met on a hill or on the moors, lit a fire, and prepared a feast which was eaten at a table made by cutting a trench in the turf. A cake was then broken and the pieces, one of them blackened, drawn out of a bonnet:

> Whoever draws the black bit is the devoted person, who is to be sacrificed to Baal, whose favour they mean to implore, in rendering the year productive of the sustenance of man and beast. There is little doubt of these inhuman sacrifices having once been offered in this country . . . although they now pass from the act of sacrificing, and only compel the devoted person to leap three times through the flames.[4]

Pennant in his *Tour of Scotland* describes another instance of the same custom and adds the details of a libation poured to the spirit or deity at the beginning of the feast, and the invocation which accompanied flinging knobs moulded on the sacrificial cake over the shoulder.

> Each person then turns his face to the fire, breaks off a knob, and flinging it over his shoulders, says, 'This I give thee, preserve thou my horses; this to thee, preserve thou my sheep; and so on.' After that, they use the same ceremony to the noxious animals: 'This I give to thee, O fox! spare thou my lambs; this to thee, O hooded crow! this to thee, O eagle.'[5]

The fact that the 'victim' in these feasts was known as the *cailleach beal-tine*[6] suggests that the deity addressed and the one to whom the sacrifice of the unlucky man was originally made was the Cailleach we meet in the same parts of Scotland in connection with the unlucky farmer in the harvest rites. But the nine knobs—or nipples, as another report calls them—on each of the cakes brought by each of the worshippers, and the fact that apparently a separate divinity was addressed at each throw, may also suggest that, as in the harvest festival, the Cailleach was associated with a Maiden, the one bringing ill-luck and the other prosperity. It would thus be the same cult but with different rites for husbandry and the herdsmen.

The survival of other cults is sometimes revealed by times of famine, plague, or public calamity, when recourse to Christian ceremonies has not proved effective. The bull was one of the sacred cult animals of prehistoric Europe and of the Celts in general. In the first century A.D. Pliny, who had been in Gaul, described a Druid ceremony involving a bull sacrifice on the occasion of the discovery of mistletoe growing on a sacred hard-oak, where it is rarely found:

> and when found, it is gathered with a solemn religious ceremony, especially if it should be on the sixth day of the moon (since by the moon they reckon their months and years and also their generations (or ages) of thirty years). And this is because the moon is then waxing and has not reached mid-crescent. They call the mistletoe by a name in their language which means All healing. They prepare for a sacrifice and a banquet beneath the tree and bring up two white bulls whose horns are then bound for the first time. A priest dressed in a white robe then climbs the tree, cuts the mistletoe with a golden sickle and it is caught in a white cloak; whereupon they kill the victims praying the while that the god will make his gift beneficial to those on whom he has bestowed it. They believe that mistletoe given to animals in drink will impart fertility to any of them and that it is an antidote to every poison.[7]

Bull sacrifices appear to have been common to the Celtic world. The famous Gundestrup Bowl from Denmark, believed to be Celtic work, has a panel showing what seems to be the sacrifice or ritual slaying of three bulls. In Ireland there is reference to a bull sacrifice followed by a bull feast (*tarbfeis*) when a new king was to be chosen.[8] The bull appears on a number of Pictish monuments, and on a stone cross slab at St Vigeans, Angus, there appears what looks like another bull sacrifice: a naked man holding a sword at a bull's throat as he kneels before it. The scene occurs on a Christian cross, just below another showing the legend of the meeting of St Anthony and St Paul. Isabel Henderson says of this and another pagan rite depicted on the same cross that these scenes 'probably had no significance for the sculptor beyond its artistic form'.[9] In view of the fact that bull sacrifices continued to be made in Scotland until quite recently, this seems unlikely. It suggests perhaps that Pictish Christianity made concessions to local cults or was unable to suppress them. Bull sacrifices, with nominally Christian associations, continued to be made until modern times. In 1656 an inquiry conducted at Applecross, then a remote village which had been without a minister since the Reformation, was held by the Presbytery of Dingwall in Ross. They found,

> amongst wthyr abominable and heathenishe practizes that the people in that place were accustomed to sacrifice bulls at a certaine tyme wppon the 25th August, which day is dedicated as they conceave to St Mourie, as they call him.[10]

The Presbytery had never heard of St Maolrubha, the missionary to Applecross in the eighth century, and confessed that they could not discover from the people whether he was a pagan god or a former papist saint—not that they regarded one as more heathenish than the other. It is probable, in view of the fact that the sacrifices were performed on the shore of Loch Maree at about the period of Samain, that it was a pagan god discreetly covered by a saint's name whom the people had continued to worship from time immemorial. What could happen at Applecross in the seventeenth century could easily have happened at St Vigeans a thousand years earlier.

Some thirty years later the same Presbytery of Dingwall had trouble with the clan Mackenzie. Hector Mackenzie of Mellan, with three of his sons and a grandson, was summoned to answer for

> sacrificing a bull in ane heathnish manner in the iland of St. Ruffus, comonlie called Ellan Moury in Lochew (Loch Ewe) for the recovering of the health of Cirstane Mackenzie, spouse to the said Hector Mackenzie, who was formerlie sick and valetudinarie.[11]

The Mackenzies failed to answer the summons, which is not perhaps surprising since Kirstan Mackenzie had apparently recovered her health and the Presbytery seemed to have been unable to enforce their decisions in many cases, even in comparatively minor events such as the worship of sacred wells and the ceremonies on St John's Eve at midsummer which they had decreed must be extirpated.

That these bull sacrifices were not merely traditional procedures but a fully preserved pagan rite is suggested by the description of another sacrifice at the island of Mull in 1767. As a result of an epidemic disease among the black cattle the islanders agreed to the ceremony, although they considered it wicked. They took a wheel and nine oak spindles to the top of a hill, put out every fire in the houses in sight of the hill, and then by turning the wheel *deasil* over the spindles kindled need-fire by friction. One householder refused to put out his fires and they had at last to bribe his servants to do so before the fire could be kindled. They then sacrificed a heifer suffering from the disease, cut out the diseased parts and burned them in the newly kindled fire, re-lit their own hearths from the fire, and feasted on the remains of the beast: An old man from Morven on the mainland recited incantations during the whole fire ceremony. He too believed it sinful and that repeating the incantations on former occasions had reduced him to beggary, but he did it just the same.[12] There could be no clearer evidence of the way such cults survived in spite of Christianity.

What is even more interesting is the integrity of the cult ceremony, which suggests that it had had a continuous practice from the earliest times and was not merely a revival of moribund superstition. At first sight there may not seem to be much likeness between this ritual and the ceremony described by Pliny. In both cases there is a cattle sacrifice accompanied by special prayers or incantations uttered by a priest or initiate. Both ceremonies are concerned with health and fertility of cattle and the prosperity of their owners. But in fact the cutting of the mistletoe and the kindling of the need-fire have much in common. Mistletoe makes barren animals fertile, is an antidote to all poisons, and is considered all-healing. 'All-healer' was reported to have been a Celtic name for the mistletoe in modern Brittany, Wales, Ireland, and Scotland.[13] But the same properties were ascribed to the need-fire kindled at the Beltane feasts just described. John Ramsay of Crieff in Perthshire, a friend of Sir Walter Scott, gave a long account of these ceremonies and says of the need-fires, in words which seem to echo Pliny:

This fire had the appearance of being immediately derived from heaven, and manifold were the virtues ascribed to it. They esteemed it a preservative against witchcraft, and a sovereign remedy against malignant diseases, both in the human species and in cattle; and by it the strongest poisons were supposed to have their nature changed.[14]

Mistletoe too was held to be heaven-born when found on an oak tree. Pliny says:

The Druids . . . held nothing more sacred than the mistletoe and the tree on which it grows, provided that tree is an oak. . . In fact, they think that anything growing on an oak tree has been derived from heaven.[15]

In some parts of Europe mistletoe is cut on Midsummer Eve and is considered a specific against witchcraft, and there are traces of the same belief in Wales and the north of England. Frazer suggests that these virtues may have arisen from an earlier belief that mistletoe was due to a lightning flash, and cites its name of 'thunder-besom' in one district of Switzerland.[16] More significant is the fact that need-fire was kindled with oak wood spindles in the case in question and that in Scotland and on the Continent oak wood was most often used for this purpose. This suggests that originally it was the sacred oak, which was the source of the magic properties of both fire and mistletoe. Finally we may notice that the mistletoe was cut if possible on the day that began a new month, year, or cycle of years: the need-fire is similarly kindled at the great festival periods, especially Beltane, and the wheel, with which it is kindled in many instances, is probably the emblem of the sun's disc, used at these festivals and consulted in divination. Pliny's account of the white oxen and the white robes of the officiants also suggests that the deity invoked may have been one of the Celtic divine personifications of the sun or the moon. In this case it was probably the moon, since the plant had to be cut before the moon had reached its half crescent. In the sacrifice on Mull it was noted that the ceremony of raising need-fire would be ineffective unless completed before the sun had reached its midday point in the sky. There is thus good reason to suppose that the two ceremonies, if not identical, spring from the same tradition and this tradition must have been preserved over many centuries in a living religious cult of which there are many traces not only in Scotland but all over Europe, so that it probably is older than the Celts themselves. And not only the cults but the deities concerned sometimes survived without the usual euhemerisation into saints, devils, or fairies. *The Chronicle of Lanercost* records a curious instance of what may have been the open practice of the phallic cult of a fertility god in Fife in the year 1282, led by the village priest himself.[17] Martin Martin writing at the end of the seventeenth century recounts that a certain John Morison of Bragair in Lewis told him that when he was a boy, that is in the mid or early seventeenth century,

> The inhabitants of this island had an ancient custom to sacrifice to a sea-god called Shony: The inhabitants round the island came to the Church of St. Malvay, having each man his provision along with him; every family furnished with a peck of malt, and this was brewed into ale; one of their number was picked to wade into the sea up to the middle, and carrying a cup of ale in his hand, standing still in that posture, cried out with a loud voice saying: 'Shony, I give you this cup of ale, hoping that you'll be so kind as to send us plenty of sea-ware for enriching our ground for the ensuing year;' and so threw the cup of ale into the sea. This was performed in the night time. At his return to land they all went to church, where there was a candle burning upon the altar; and then standing silent for a little time, one of them gave a signal at which the candle was put out, and immediately all of them went to the fields where they fell a-drinking their ale, and spent the remainder of the night in dancing and singing, & c. Next morning they all returned home being well satisfied that they had punctually observed this solemn anniversary, which they believed to be a powerful means to procure a plentiful crop. Mr Daniel and Mr Kenneth Morison, minister in Lewis, told me they spent several years before they could persuade the vulgar natives to abandon this ridiculous piece of superstition; which is quite abolished these 32 years past. [*c.* 1662][18]

Alas for Mr Daniel and Mr Kenneth Morison and their like! But at least they seem to have shown no sense of Christian outrage and the simple way in which the pagan cult and Christian observance had been combined by their parishioners, perhaps for centuries before, is eloquent testimony to the way such rites and beliefs managed to survive. It is worth remembering in connection with the fairy cult which we have next to consider, because its unhappy association with the cult of witchcraft and the resulting persecutions leave one with an impression that it must always have been a stark alternative to Christian belief. The first thing the newly recruited witch had to do was to renounce the Christian faith and swear fealty to the Devil. But the fairy cult, where it was uncontaminated by witchcraft, seems to have made no such demands, and in fact seems to have aimed at the sort of compromise adopted by the natives of Lewis before the Morison brothers interfered.

This compromise was partly a practical accommodation which grew out of the social importance of the fairy people to their human neighbours. But it also acquired its rationale, a theory that fairies were neutral spirits, either 'of a middle Nature betwixt Man and Angel', a view recorded by the Reverend Robert Kirk as held by his neighbours in Perthshire in the seventeenth century,[19] or, more usually, spirits who were expelled from heaven with the rebellious angels, but not condemned to hell, since they had neither consented to the revolt nor opposed it. They formed what was sometimes called the Middle Kingdom of spirits between the angels and the demons. It is not known just when this idea finally crystallised but we can trace some of the steps that may have contributed to it. The sixth chapter of Genesis begins:

> And it came to pass, when men began to multiply on the face of the earth, and daughters were born unto them, that the sons of God saw the daughters of men that they were fair; and they took them wives of all which they chose . . . and also after that, when the sons of God came in unto the daughters of men, and they bare children to them; the same became mighty men, which were of old, men of renown.

In the Vulgate they are called 'the sons of God', but Saint Augustine following the Septuagint calls them 'angels of God'. This latter view was conflated with the apocryphal Book of Enoch in which the first account of the fall of angels occurs (late second century B.C.). The giants who were the offspring of these unions—Genesis is not specific on this point—were so wicked that God sent the Deluge to destroy them and sentenced the amorous angels to be buried under mountains until the Day of Judgement. Later legend introduced the view that it was the women who seduced the angels sent by God to keep watch over men. These views were taken up and discussed by nearly all the church fathers, some of whom opposed and some of whom extended and elaborated the notion. Clement of Alexandria and Ambrose, for example, introduced the idea that these fallen angels revealed their secrets to women and became the originals of the pagan gods. Tertullian attributes astrology to them and approves the idea of the Book of Enoch that they introduced magic and divination. Eusebius, without approving the idea, quotes from Porphyry the classical view that there were both good and bad demons, and puts forward the idea that on the fall of the angels some were allowed to remain on earth instead of being cast into Tartarus. St Augustine, while hesitating over the whole theory, brings in the classical notion of Fauns, Sylvans, and Dusii, nature spirits whose intercourse with women 'it would seem arrogant to doubt'. Isidore of Seville introduces yet another idea: that there was a terrestrial order of angels created to inhabit the space between air and the firmament. It was they and not the celestial angels who fell, and this space is now occupied by the souls of those just men who await the Day of Judgement, a view still current in Perthshire in the seventeenth century according to Robert Kirk:

> There may be many Places called Fairie-hills, which the Mountain People think impious and dangerous to peel [rob] or discover by taking Earth or Wood from them; superstitiously believing the Souls of their Predicessors to dwell there. And for that End (say they) a Mote or Mount was dedicate beside every Church-yard, to receive the Souls till their Adjacent Bodies arise, and so become as a Fairie-hill.[20]

It was from such elements as these, in what seems to have been a widespread and popular discussion in the early centuries of Christianity, that an unorthodox but even more widespread view seems to have been created in the later Middle Ages: that there were certain angels, neither good nor particularly bad, who had been condemned to live underground rather than inhabit hell. They were held to be creatures of intermediate state between human beings and angels, able and willing to have commerce with men or women according to their sex and to beget and bear children by this inter-course. They were corporeal but could render themselves visible or invisible as they pleased, were great dealers in magic, could fly through the air, and divine secrets and predict the future. They were possessed of supernatural wisdom which they could transmit to favoured mortals, especially their lovers. The spirits of the dead sometimes lived among them till the Last Judgement. They were the entities behind the gods and spirits of woods, fields, wells, trees, hills, and rivers to be found in the local legends of any part of Europe. In short they were the explanation of the popular belief in fairies. Fairies were not demons and a Christian could associate with them, as he could with Jews or Mohammedans, as long as he observed due discretion. The church of course never gave assent to this view and continued to regard them as evil spirits. But in practice it must have partly come to terms with the belief as it did with that in astrology which it continued to denounce, without effect, until at least the seventeenth century.

It is uncertain just where and when this theory of the fairies as the Middle Kingdom first took shape, but early expression of it in the British Isles occurs in Walter Mapes's *De Nugis Curialium* in the twelfth century. One of the anecdotes in this amusing and charming work tells a then fairly conventional story of a rich young nobleman who foolishly wastes his great inheritance and is finally reduced to beggary. When he is at his lowest a spirit appears before him and promises to restore all and more than he has squandered if he will accept the spirit's control and advice. Not without reason, the young man suspects and fears that he is being tempted by the Devil. He shows both stupefaction and hesitation and the spirit, guessing the reason, explains that he need not fear that he is being trapped to his damnation because he is destined to live to a ripe old age and will have plenty of time to make his peace with heaven. Part of the bargain is that well before his death he will be given three clear signs of its advent. As the young man still shows doubt he explains the nature of the demons whom he fears and the difference between them and the class of beings of which he himself is a member:

81

For they flatter in order that they may lead into perdition, they raise up in order to dash down; and the world rightly holds them in detestation. But we, alas, though innocent, are painted with their infamous reputation. Yet indeed we have absolutely no interest in robbing men of their goods, or in the destruction of cities; we do not thirst for their blood nor hunger for their souls, nor do we long to work even more evil than we are able to bring about. It is enough for us to exercise our freedom fully in things short of death. I confess that we are by nature prone to amusing and sportive tricks; we contrive illusions, devise phantoms and make spectres appear, so that an empty and entertaining contest may appear once the facts have been covered up. We are able to do anything that makes for laughter, nothing that provokes fears. For I am one of those exiles from heaven, who, without assisting or consenting in the sin of Lucifer, acted foolishly like vacillating partisans after the crime was committed. And if the Lord in his wrath cast us out as unworthy of heaven, yet in his mercy, he allowed us, because of the slighter nature of our offence, to be, some in the empty wilderness, some among the dwellings of men. The ancients, in their delusion, called us demi-gods or demi-goddesses, names serving to distinguish the sexes according to the bodies in which we appeared. From the uninhabited places or from our different functions we were known as Trolls, Silvans, Dryads, Oreads, Fauns, Satyrs and Naiads, over whom, according to their designations, Ceres, Bacchus, Pan, Priapus and Pales hold sway.[21]

Walter Mapes, as a good churchman, of course, represents these arguments as fallacious. The spirit really is a demon. But the view he promotes was apparently a common one and seems to have been accepted by many of Walter's contemporaries.[22] It was clearly a very convenient way of assimilating local spirits and minor deities of the countryside, and the practices associated with them, to the body of Christian doctrine on the subject of spirits and their powers. This was a subject in which, as the history of witchcraft shows, the greatest confusion and the widest variety of opinion obtained in the church itself till modern times. Until commerce with fairies came to be treated as witchcraft by the lay and the ecclesiastical courts, there was at least a chance that a Christian could claim in good conscience that his recourse to the Good Neighbours for aid in securing bountiful crops or for medicine for man and beast had nothing to do with diabolic practice. In fact, as we shall see, the fairies were often propitiated and courted as an aid against the witches and sorcerers who held the Devil's commission to plague mankind and drew their power from him.

Nevertheless the connection with hell and its powers was there. The inhabitants of the Middle Kingdom had been expelled from heaven for the sin of the church at Laodicea. If they were not actively evil, neither were they actively good, and one aspect of the theory about them was that they were bound to pay a tithe of souls to hell. This was a reason given for their luring mortals to Fairyland and for their kidnapping babies, though it is an accretion on earlier pagan views that these were recruited as lovers or that the souls of the dead lived in fairy mounds. In the Scots ballad of 'Tam Lin', which seems to be in origin at least as old as the early sixteenth century, the hero has been taken by the Queen of the Fairies to live in a fairy mound:

> And pleasant is the fairy land
> But, an eerie tale to tell,
> Ay at the end of seven years
> We pay a tiend to hell;
> I am sae fair and fu o flesh,
> I'm feard it be mysel

The hero is rescued by his human mistress at midnight on Hallowe'en when the fairies ride abroad and the Fairy Queen, whose lover he had obviously been and whose victim he was no doubt destined to be, expresses her chagrin in forcible terms.[23] But in the fourteenth century romance of Thomas of Erceldoune it is the Fairy Queen herself who returns her lover to the world of men in order to save him from becoming the Devil's tithe after he has been in Fairyland 'three yere & more'. Previously she had stopped him eating the fruit of the fairy trees in her kingdom on the grounds that this would have put his soul in the Devil's power. In this poem Fairyland is definitely represented as a Middle Kingdom. It lies three days' journey underground and, with his head on the lady's knee, which apparently gives him second sight by contact with her, Thomas is able to see the roads that lead from there to Heaven, to the Earthly Paradise, to Purgatory, and to Hell. The latter is the enemy of the fairy people as it is of the human race. The Fairy Queen shows herself benevolent to Thomas and teaches him the powers of prophecy and of minstrelsy.[24] We need not doubt that all this was in the Scottish original on which the five surviving English versions are based, since the point of Thomas's voyage to the fairy kingdom and his continued meetings with its queen after his return was clearly to give the authority of the fairies' foreknowledge of events to the prophecies of Thomas of Erceldoune, which form the second fytte of the poem. Since these prophecies were pro-Scottish and enjoyed an immense reputation in fifteenth- and sixteenth-century Scotland, it seems likely that the idea of the Middle Kingdom was well known in Dunbar's day.

This attempt to give respectable standing to the fairy people was no doubt due to their real importance in the daily lives of most of the inhabitants of Scotland in the Middle Ages. This importance extended into almost every part of social life; the fairies had to be considered in birth, marriage, and death, in the production of crops, the catching of fish, and the raising of cattle on which survival depended from day to day; they were concerned in justice, in contracts and oaths, in treaties and the law of nations in war and in defence against war; people had recourse to them for medicines against natural ills of man and beast and for spells and counter-charms against the practices of witches and sorcerers, for success in love, for knowledge of the future and for the discovery of hidden treasure or the recovery of lost or stolen belongings. In Scotland as elsewhere fairies were apt to take a hand either for aid or for mischief in the humblest domestic matters of the dairy and the kitchen, and various charms and magic plants had to be placed at doors and windows to keep them out of houses and away from byres and barns. Women in childbirth and babies in cradles had to be protected and watched to prevent their abduction by fairies. In many places they were propitiated at weddings and they were consulted as to the hour and manner of death and the prospects of return from perilous journeys and enterprises. All this is so much a commonplace of folklore that examples are needless. The beliefs and customs persisted to the present day in many parts of the country.

Others appear to have died out fairly early, though traces remained in occasional ceremonies or in tales and legends. *The Statistical Account of Scotland* makes mention of natural or artificial mounds, usually two in number and often near the church or some other public place in almost every parish and in many towns and villages. They were known as laws, law hills, *tom-a-mhoid* (hill of the court of justice), moats, moot-hills, gallows-hills, gibbet hills. The local legends about them were that there in former times the people met to administer justice, make laws, and undertake solemn contracts such as the signing or witnessing of treaties of peace. The people round Dunsinane in the late eighteenth century were still able to point out the Lawton, a hill nearby where King Macbeth once used to sit and dispense justice to his subjects, while at Little Dunkeld not far away another report says:

> A round mount at the bottom of Birnum hill on the south east side is worthy of remark. It is faced with steep oaks, except for a few yards where it was fortified by art. This eminence has been known for time immemorial by the names of *Courthill* and Duncan's-Hill, and is believed to have been on some occasion occupied by the unfortunate Scottish King of that name.[25]

Another name for these mounds was Hills of Peace. As nearly all green hills and artificial mounds were regarded as fairy dwellings and the fairies themselves were often known as the People of Peace, it is natural to suppose that they were chosen for their purpose in order that the fairy people should share in the pacts and acts of judgment and their execution, and that these acts should have the solemn authority of the sacred place on which they were performed. In the course of time as the hills were no longer actually used for these purposes, the association was often forgotten. In the parish of Dunipace, Stirling, there were two hills of peace from which the parish was supposed to have taken its name, but the reason given for the name was a vague tradition that they marked the place where 'peace had been concluded between the Romans and the Scots'.[26] Either the memory of the folk was better in the parish of Blair Atholl and Strowan, Perth, or they were more willing to confide in their minister who reports:

Strath-dhrnaidh, in Strath-groy, is one of those roundish green hills that they [the Highlanders] call Sioth-dhun, i.e. the Hill of Peace; because on these they made peace, and other contracts of old. They probably reckoned the matters here transacted, the more solemn, too, that they believed the Sighichin, or Fairies supposed to dwell in those hills, to be witnesses of their transactions. The hills were generally natural, but some times artificial.[27]

The origin of the practice may have been a pact with spirits believed to live in the mounds or the witness of the souls of the dead, also believed to live there—or perhaps both, since often these two beliefs coexist. There is an interesting but improbable story about Malcolm Canmore which crops up in several of the early chronicles. Shortly after his accession to the throne he learned that a certain great nobleman was conspiring with his enemies to murder him. The king imposed silence on his informant and waited for the nobleman to return to court, which he did with a very large retinue. The king received him affably and, early next morning, ordered the huntsmen to be ready and called on all the nobles and knights to accompany him to the hunt. Once at the hunting grounds he sent everyone to their stations and contrived to be left alone in the forest and unobserved with the traitor. He then dismounted, reproached the man with his intended crime, and challenged him to single combat there and then. The traitor, overcome with remorse and shame, fell on his knees, confessed, and put himself at the king's mercy; the king then, on certain sureties, pardoned him.[28] John Major, telling the story five centuries later, remarks severely that the story makes no sense and that Malcolm showed none, to put his enemy in the position to carry out his crime and to make him desperate by revealing that he knew of his purpose.[29] But Ailred of Rievaulx's account, followed by John of Fordun,[30] suggests a possible solution of the problem. The story, unless it is an interpolated folk tale, is likely to be based on fact since Ailred had been brought up at the Scottish court with the sons of David I, one of Malcolm's sons. Now in his version and that of Fordun there is a significant detail omitted in other accounts. The king with his hunt comes to a certain plain, which was surrounded in fashion of a crown by the closest forest; and in the middle of it was seen a knoll swelling up, as it were, which embroidered with flowers in a beautiful variety of different colours offered daily a pleasant resting place to knights wearied in the chase.

Upon this the King took his stand, higher than the rest; and according to the hunting law which the common people called the 'Tryst', assigned a separate place to each of the nobles with his dogs, so that wherever the quarry chose to emerge, besieged on all sides, it should find its fate.[31]

The only way to make sense of the tale is to suppose that in the original version the king led his treacherous subject to a fairy hill which, in Ailred's description, the knoll so closely resembles, and that there he either held a court as his position when assigning the hunting stations suggests, or that having disposed his courtiers around the edges of the forest, watching the plain, he remained alone on the hill with the traitor and there made his accusation before the witness of the supernatural beings within it. This would account for the nobleman's immediate and awed confession and for his failure to take advantage of the situation. Ailred's version of the story is likely to have been censored for the sons of the saintly King David, to remove the imputation of pagan practices from his father and the husband of St Margaret—even if the result was a reflection on his common sense. If the source of the story, as Fordun asserts, was Turgot, St Margaret's biographer and confessor and her chief helper in purifying Scottish Christianity, this may well have been the case.

However this may be, the people long continued to associate justice, the execution of criminals, the burning of witches, the taking of oaths and making of agreements, with fairy hills and mounds. In other cases they were associated with sacred groves or fairy trees, as at Heskett in Cumberland, where the court for the Forest of Englewood was held annually under a thorn tree on St Barnabas' day.[32] The same close association of the fairy race and the human may account for the holding of fairs at fairy sites or the annual processions to such sites from towns and official bodies. An example of the former was the holding of an annual Fair at Carnock (Fife) on 28 May round a fairy mound surmounted by a thorn tree, half-way between the church and the Law Knowe, the second fairy mound usually to be found in such sites.[33] The thorn tree was blown down in 1832 but the fair was only discontinued in 1867. Another fair at Longforgan, Perth, was held round the Market Knowe on the Muir of Forgan, described as a beautiful green mound though the ground around was covered with heath and broom—a typical feature of a fairy hill.[34] At Dunfermline, Fife, there stood in the churchyard a venerable thorn reputed in the eighteenth century to be four hundred years old;

> at the foot of this tree in Popish times, the people are said to have held a market on Sabbath, before assembling for public worship.[35]

At Brechin in Forfar at the Trinity and Lammas fairs, the youngest of the bailies with a posse rode to the North-water bridge, about five miles from the fair which was held on Trinity Muir. This was to prevent forestalling, selling of cattle or horses without paying the fair dues or customs:

> At the same time, the whole citizens proceed on foot with great pomp and solemnity . . . to the Law of Keithoc alias Hare-Cairn which is about midway between Brechin and the North-water Bridge.

The purpose was said to be to give help to the bailie, should he meet with violence or opposition, but this can only have been a secondary purpose, the principal being a ceremonial visit to the fairy mound with which the ruins of a temple had once been associated.[36] At Culross, Fife, until recently on St Servan's Day the people of the town marched in procession carrying green boughs and, after decorating the town cross, made their way to the Borestane near Kincardine where they made an offering of leeks on the altar of the sacred stone.[37] Many other instances could be given to suggest that in former times the public life and institutions of the people must have been closely connected with the fairy race. One of the most curious was the custom of the members of the Masonic Lodge at Arbroath, Angus: they used to walk in annual procession on Midsummer Day to the Maiden Castle cave on the coast. They had walled in the entrance and given it a gate and a door. Here they admitted new members to the lodge. It suggests that Masonic initiation had been deliberately associated here with older initiation ceremonies connected with a maiden or fairy cult.[38]

Co-operation between the human and the fairy races in warfare must once have been just as common. The fairy battles for the 'luck of the crops' in Ireland, accompanied by fights between the inhabitants of the neighbouring districts in the same interest, have already been mentioned. There are some traces of similar ideas in the harvest customs in parts of Scotland. At Mousewald a group of stones were believed to be reapers so punished for 'Kemping' (fighting) during the harvest, while at Monquhitter, Aberdeen, 'the corn growing on the bloody butts of Lendrum has never been reaped without blood or strife among the reapers'.[39] The minister's explanation that this was due to the influence of a ferocious three-day battle once fought on the site is less plausible than that it was a reapers' fight in sympathy with a possible fairy fight in aid of the crops. There were three tumuli in the area.

But there is evidence that on a number of occasions the fairies took sides in actual warfare or were partisans of particular clans. The best known instance is that of the Macleods of Skye who possessed, and still do, the famous fairy flag, which has been carried into numerous battles but is only displayed in desperate situations. After the massacre of a large number of Macleods in the church at Trumpan in 1578, the chief sent a force from Dunvegan Castle to catch the MacDonalds, the perpetrators, as they were scattered for plunder. He had ordered the fairy flag to be taken out of the iron chest in which it was kept.

> As soon as the Macleods encountered the forces of the enemy, the latter fled in panic towards the shore, for, as the story-teller puts it, 'the very grass blades were changed to armed men as soon as the folds of the magic banner were unfurled in the breeze.'[40]

According to various versions of the story about the origin of the fairy flag, the head of the clan Macleod must have been either the descendant of a fairy marriage or of a fairy changeling, so that the fairy host was perhaps supporting its own side. Robert Kirk says that his neighbours believed the fairies to be divided into tribes and clans like their human counterparts and had feuds and battles as they did.[41]

But the two races did not simply live side by side. Members of both were believed to live among and share the lives of the other race, either involuntarily or of their own free will, for periods which might vary from a lifetime to an occasional visit or resort for feasting and revel at regular intervals of time. Children were interchanged in their cradles and some humans grew up in Fairyland, while there were always liable to be a few fairy children playing in any group in the street, such as the fairy boy of Leith casually pointed out by the landlady of an inn at Leith to Captain Burton about 1670.[42] A 'shargie', that is a child that did not thrive, was liable to be taken for an elf-child, and some of them grew up and lived normal lives among their neighbours with this reputation, though others were sometimes burnt or exposed or otherwise disposed of in an effort to force the fairies to return the human child.[43] The fairy folk moved freely among humans and, except that they were sometimes rather smaller, were not distinguishable from them in appearance or clothing unless they gave themselves away by word or action. Bessy Dunlop, an Ayrshire woman, tried for witchcraft in 1576, told the court that once when she was in childbed

> ane stout woman com in to hir, and sat doun on the forme besyde hir, and askit ane drink at hir, and sche gaif hir; quha alsua tauld hir, that that barne wold de.

Bessy did not recognise the woman and asked Thom Reid, the *revenant*, who first introduced her to the fairies, who she was, to be told: 'that was the Quene of Elfhame his maistres'.[44]

While later legend tended to dwell on the dangers of being captured by the fairies and the practical impossibility of escape, earlier views seemed to suppose a fair amount of coming and going between the two worlds though various cautions might have to be observed: silence, abstaining from fairy food and drink, the use of talismans or protective charms such as iron, fernseed, or a twig of hazel. The Scottish witch trials cannot be taken as evidence of what the accused really saw and did, since the confessions were usually extracted under terror and torture, and the methods of interrogation frequently suggested to the victims what they were expected to confess. As far as the details of the witch cult are concerned, with its devil worship and sabbat ceremonies, they are probably quite unreliable. But as far as commerce with fairies is concerned what the victims confessed fits in with independent evidence and gives at least an idea of what ordinary people at the time believed to be the case. The details of the witch cult appear to be only evidence of what the judges believed and to have been largely imported from elsewhere in any case.[45] But the homely details of dealings with the fairies carry a conviction of day-to-day customs as the horrific and revolting details of the sabbat do not. And it is clear from these accounts that certain people at any rate were able to pay frequent visits to fairy mounds to make love, feast, and obtain medicines and healing charms. Bessy Dunlop, in one of the earliest circumstantial accounts, refused to go to Elfhame, and all her commerce with the fairies was through Thom Reid who had died some years before at the battle of Pinkie, but she seems to have met him at frequent intervals. Alesoun Peirsoun, tried in 1588, seems to have visited the fairy world a number of times over many years, guided and protected by William Sympsoun, her paternal uncle, who told her he had been carried away by them. At times she lived with them for considerable periods and he warned her, when they heard the noise of a whirlwind in the sea, to keep out of the way and cross herself to avoid being taken away as part of the 'teynd of hell'; William, who wore fairy dress, was apparently not confined and could come and go as he pleased. Christian Lewingstoun of Edinburgh, tried in 1597, declared that her daughter had been taken away by the fairies but she apparently met her frequently and it was through her that she gained her occult knowledge. Issobell Haldane of Perth, tried in 1623, spent three days in a fairy hill from Thursday till Sunday noon when she was returned by a man with a grey beard who appears to have become her intermediary with the fairies. Issobell Gowdie from Nairn, tried in 1662, seems to have

91

gone several times into the Dounie Hills to the Queen of Elfhame's court and returned without difficulty; but she was a witch and under the direction of the Devil.[46] Andro Man of Aberdeen confessed to his prosecutors in 1597 that for the past thirty-two years he had been visiting 'the Queen of Elphen' and that she had visited him and had a number of children by him.[47] A woman called Janet Drever a few years after this stood trial for fostering a baby to the fairy folk: a not uncommon belief was that the fairies preferred human milk. She nursed the child in a fairy hill, referred to her hosts as 'our good neighbours', and said that she had been having 'carnal conversation' with them for more than twenty years.[48] It seems to have been perfectly friendly intercourse. John Stewart, tried for sorcery in 1613, declared that after two meetings with the King of the Fairies, each at Hallowe'en, he had been accustomed to join these people every Saturday night at seven o'clock and spend the night with them in fairy hills.[49] These and other accounts may not suggest that such things actually happened or even that the narrators believed they happened, though it is often difficult to think otherwise, but it is certain that they told such things as would be accepted as probable happenings. In other words, there was a common belief in the later sixteenth and the seventeenth centuries that certain initiates in human society were accustomed to visit the fairy kingdom, that there was in fact an active fairy cult as there was a witch cult. An earl of Menteith is said to have made a grant of

> The Cui-n'an-Uriskin, or Cave of the Fairies in Ben Venue, at which says Dr Graham in his *Sketches of the Picturesque Scenery of Perthshire*, 'the solemn stated meetings of the order were regularly held'. . . The Earl in question was spoken of as 'overlord of the faery folk'.[50]

The cave at Arbroath where Masonic initiations were held on Midsummer Day has already been mentioned. At Closeburn, Dumfries, in a rocky defile supposed to be inhabited by fairies, there was at the entrance:

> a curious cell or cave, called the Elf's Kirk, where, according to the superstition of the times, the imaginary inhabitants of the linn were supposed to hold their meetings . . . many fabulous stories were told and perhaps were once believed concerning this curious linn.

One of several caves at Wemyss, Fife, was

> visited by the young people of Easter Wemyss, with lights, upon the
> first Monday of January, but from what this custom took its rise the
> writer could never learn.[51]

It was possibly a ceremony like the annual procession of young
men and women to the Dragon's Hole cave on May Day in Perth-
shire,[52] and this and a number of other references to meetings
held in caves with supernatural associations suggest cult meetings
and initiation ceremonies. A number of caves, which were apparently
used as places of Christian worship in the Middle Ages, particularly
in the west of Scotland,[53] would suggest that, as with sacred wells,
the church took over former cult sites. That this was not always
a quite successful take-over is shown by the legend attached to a
miracle-working cave said to have been occupied by St Columba
on an island off the coast of Argyll. In spite of its sacred associations
the cave was the object of superstitious veneration till the end of
the eighteenth century on account of its reputation for preventing
the pregnancy of women who made love there.

> The cave preserved its reputation till of late; and but for the following
> untoward accident would have remained an object of terror till this
> day [1797]. A pair more solicitous about gratifying their passions
> than promoting the political interest of their country went into it,
> with a view to bring its influence to the test of experiment. They were
> disappointed. The female became pregnant, and the whole neighbour-
> hood sceptics . . . the miraculous excellencies of the island have now
> ceased.[54]

This amusing but slightly irrelevant anecdote seems to be a good
point at which to end the chapter. Its object has been to assemble
some specimens of the evidence surviving for the persistence of
various pagan cults, including that of the fairies, in Scotland at
periods mostly after the fifteenth century. The assumption is that,
as in most European countries, such cults declined progressively with
the efforts of Christianity to extirpate them and with the growth of
civilisation and the spread of education. It is fair to argue that in
Dunbar's day they were more vigorous and specific than in the

sixteenth, seventeenth, and eighteenth centuries, when the progressive decline of the superstitions in which they were rooted is well attested.

Most of this later evidence, however, comes from the witchcraft trials, which are not only suspect in themselves, but represent a mixture of beliefs and cults and probably a corruption and degeneration of the fairy cult by that of the witches. Apart from the witch trials the evidence that there was a specific 'cult' of fairies, in which initiates with a common set of observances met to celebrate their relations with them, is rather slight. It is, of course, incredible that men and women of flesh and blood actually entered hills and mounds as they said they did. Caves are more likely meeting places but there is not enough evidence—though what there is is suggestive.

The next point therefore must be to see what the earlier form of the fairy cult is likely to have been, before its contamination with the witch cult.

6

Love and Ceremony

ANY study of the Scottish witchcraft trials, particularly the early ones, shows that there were at least four kinds of practice which the courts treated indifferently as witchcraft: healing by herbs and charms, commerce with fairies, sorcery and, lastly, commerce with the Devil or witchcraft proper. The first two were usually combined but are quite distinguishable and the same is true of the last two. Sorcery procures the death, maiming, disease or blasting of men, animals or crops, the destruction or loss of goods, and the frustration, perversion, or impotence of natural processes and human designs and activities. It may be brought about by natural magic or demonic aid, and in Scotland, as in most parts of the world, it is as old as man and older than history. There are occasional references to sorcery for political ends throughout Scottish history and there is no doubt that it was common in everyday life. The Synodal Statutes of the Diocese of Aberdeen in the thirteenth century prescribe excommunication four times a year against sorcerers and notorious fire-raisers. On the other hand there is little evidence for the existence of a witch cult in Scotland before the Reformation. What distinguishes this cult from sorcery in general is the proceedings of the Sabbat, the periodical association of witches and warlocks at meetings with the Demon or his representative, usually at night in lonely parts of the countryside, the initiations involving a foreswearing of baptism and swearing allegiance to Satan, the ritual murder, ritual cannibalism, and ritual fornication with the Devil reported on such occasions, with other more ludicrous ceremonies such as kissing the Devil's buttocks as a sort of homage or penance, riding on broomsticks, and dancing naked back to back. Whether any of this went on in Scotland before the Reformation is not certain. There was no Inquisition in Scotland and the Scottish church seems to have made little real effort to suppress sorcery, beyond burning an occasional flagrant offender.[1] After the Reformation the Protestants instituted prosecutions based on what were by then classical witch cult beliefs current in England and the Continent. It is questionable whether the 'cult' in the sense described above was not at least in part created by the prosecutions themselves and by the literature of the subject eagerly read and discussed at the time.

It is at any rate interesting to notice that the earlier witchcraft trials in Scotland are concerned mainly with sorcery, the practice of healing and protective magic, and the cult of the fairy people. The trial of Janet Douglas, Lady Glamis, in 1537 for attempts on the life of James V by sorcery, was a patent piece of political manipulation and the evidence on which she was convicted and burned was contemptible. But it was in terms of sorcery, not of a witch cult; in fact the indictment simply charges her with a conspiracy to poison the king.[2] Bessy Dunlop, though she refused to visit the fairy dwellings, met a group of 'the gude wychtis that wynnit [lived] in the Court of Elfhame'. The men were dressed like Scots gentlemen and the women wore plaids. On another occasion returning home with her husband, Andrew Jack, she saw the fairy hunt ride by and disappear into the neighbouring loch. The inducements offered her by Thom Reid were purely material, better clothes and gear, horses and cattle and entertainment if she would visit the fairy court. Bessy and her husband were probably poor cotter farmers in Ayrshire and there is hardly anything but the ordinary country superstitions about fairies in her confessions. The 'fairies' she met were indistinguishable from ordinary country people and could indeed have been just that: members of a cult group. There is hardly a hint of a Sabbat ceremony, or of witchcraft and sorcery.[3] Alesoun Peirsoun had 'good acquaintance' with the Queen of Elfhame, she said, and many friends in the fairy court, which she visited for music and entertainment. The clothing of the man who came to her when she lay down sick and alone at Grangemure was green; what she

96

saw the good neighbours do, making salves and gathering herbs before sunrise, was common fairy and indeed country practice. She herself was a healer and among her patients was Patrick Adamson, Archbishop of St Andrews. There is no evidence of witch cult or of malicious sorcery in her depositions. Like Bessy she saw a number of people believed to be dead among the fairy folk.[4] Thomas Greave appears to have been simply a healer. He did not confess to meeting either fairies or witches but his methods suggest fairies rather than witchcraft. There is no malice, no blasting or destructive magic, and the healing charms—putting a thread in the chimney and making the patient pass nine times through it, heating a coulter and dipping it in water from the Holy Well of Hillside, washing the shirt of a patient in a southward running water at night and replacing it on the sick man—are all suggestive of fairy magic. On one occasion he had warned his companions, at one of these nocturnal sark washings, to expect terrifying supernatural noises but could not produce anything more horrific for the court than to remark:

> thair was ane grit noyse maid be ffoullis or the lyll beistis that arraise and flichteret in the water.[5]

Not much evidence of witchcraft or demonology here one would say. Poor Thomas Greave, they strangled and burned him just the same!

Cases such as these form a sharp contrast to those in which the victims confess to procuring murder by sorcery, by devilish poisons, by images and pictures burned or pierced with pins and knives, to cattle destroyed, shipwrecks procured, to raising the Devil and grotesque intercourse with him, to Sabbat meetings and witches' rides. One cannot help believing that there were distinct and separate cults, though as time goes on the two tend to be confused. Even where they are, there seems in some cases to have been a clumsy combination of the two elements. Andro Man adds to his almost purely fairy scene at the court of Elphen and the praise of his fairy mistress the details of the ceremony of kissing her buttocks and those of the Devil in the form of a stag. These appear so out of

97

place that they are almost certainly imported from the witch cult.[6] The curious and detailed confessions of Issobell Gowdie in 1662, apparently made voluntarily, without torture or threat of torture, mention visits to the court of the Queen of the Fairies inside the Dounie hills and also meetings of witches presided over by the Devil. It is true that there is some mingling of the two cults in this rambling and absurd account. Witches visit the fairy court, the Devil is dressed in fairy clothing, one of the familiar spirits of the witches is called Thomas a Fearie, and so on. But another of these Auldearne witches, Janet Breadheid, while confirming a good deal of Issobell's account of the witch meetings and activities, makes no mention of fairies or fairy hills.[7] The two cults may only have had some members in common, if indeed the whole thing was not the invention of a crazy woman. But in any case it confirms the view that the witch cult and the fairy cult were thought of as separate and having different organisations and places of meeting even at this late date. That they were actually distinct is very probable. This was the opinion of Sir Walter Scott[8] and of King James the first of England and sixth of Scotland, both of whom had studied the evidence and talked to people who held these beliefs. James in his *Daemonologie* distinguishes four kinds of evil spirits, those that haunt houses and solitary places, those that cause demoniac possession, the amatory spirits called incubi and succubi, and the fairies. The first three are actively associated with witchcraft and sorcery, the last he thinks most likely are illusions caused by the Devil to mislead 'sundry simple creatures, in making them beleeue that they saw and harde such thinges as were nothing so indeed'.[9] The only confusion of witches and fairies occurs in the records of the trials, between 1563 when the law against witchcraft and sorcery was passed and the end of the trials in the early eighteenth century. In the records of Scottish folklore since then the witches and the fairies may occasionally do similar things but there is no confusion of the two in the popular mind. A good deal of fairy magic, such as resort to wells and stones, was to obtain charms and remedies against sorcery, so that fairies were clearly regarded as allies against the malice of witches. Around Kirkmichael in Banff, where belief in both fairies and witches was still strong into the last century and many people claimed to see both, the country folk used to resort to a professional witch-opposer.[10] A trial in Bute in 1662 brought out evidence of opposition between the witch cult and the fairy cult in the area. It appears that the Devil had actually warned his witches of the evil deeds of the fairies, and a witch is represented as repairing the damage caused by a whirlwind which the fairies had raised. This, of course, is a reversal of the usual roles.[11]

Since the evidence of the witch trials is both suspect in itself and certainly shows a fairy cult confused or contaminated by the witch cult, it is necessary to try to see what the former was like in its 'pure' state, before the courts began treating it as a mere variant of the latter and the wretched victims perhaps complied by confessing anything required of them. King James, in fact, gives an admirably concise summary in the passage in the *Daemonologie* in which he treats the fairy beliefs as mere illusion:

> To speake of the many vaine trattles founded vpon that illusion: How there was a King and Queene of *Phairie*, of such a iolly court & train as they had, how they had a teynd, & dutie, as it were, of all goods: how they naturallie rode and went, eate and drank, and did all other actiones like naturall men and women.

He adds the following beliefs: that people carried by the fairies visited fairy hills which opened, and that they met the Fairy Queen there; that she would give them a magic-working stone; that they saw various people there whose deaths they were able to foretell. He adds the shrewd observation that people accused of witchcraft confessed to dealing with fairies since, to their way of looking at it, fairies seemed better and more innocent than unclean spirits. People hoped in this way, he said, to be more leniently treated by ignorant magistrates.[12] The contrast between the two cults as it appeared to such people is well brought out by one of the illustrations to a little book, *Newes from Scotland*, published in 1591 and describing the trial of Dr Fian, Agnes Sampson, and a number of other witches on various charges including an attempt to kill the king by sorcery. James himself was present at their examination on more than one occasion and took a great interest in the case. The main part of this picture shows the witches at their devilish work. A horrific demon preaches to them from the pulpit of 'North Barrick Kerke', while Dr Fian acts as their scribe. In the top left-hand corner they are shown flying over the sea with their sieves in their hands, procuring the wreck of the king's ship; in the top right-hand corner they are shown standing by a cauldron on a fire brewing poisons for the destruction of the king and other victims. All this is relevant to the text of the book. But in the right centre and the lower right corner are two fairy scenes which have nothing to do with the trial at all. In the upper one a traveller with his staff and wallet lies sleeping on fairy ground, probably on top of the mound itself, which was the best way to ensure being carried into a fairy dwelling. In the lower scene the same man is shown, still sleeping, inside the mound while three fairy ladies banquet at a table behind him and a row of casks down one side of the chamber ensures unlimited supplies of wine. It looks as though the author in compliment to James I, whose *Daemonologie* had appeared four years earlier, was representing the king's view of the two cults in his illustration. On the one hand are the witches and demons malevolently active and real, on the other is the illusion of the fairy world, no less the work of the demon, but represented as a mere dream of the traveller incautious enough to lay himself open to the power of witches. What is even more interesting is that while the witches in the picture form a crowd of varying numbers, the fairies at the feast in the mound are three in number, like the ladies in Dunbar's poem. The side of the mound is represented as cut away so that the inside can be seen, but this is more than a pictorial device since many tales tell of seeing into the mound once a charm or talisman gives the power or if the person concerned happened to be there at the right time, such as the stroke of midnight. In fact the effect in this crude woodcut is of seeing three ladies at a feast in an 'arbour'. The fairy light is represented by a large candle on a side table. As far as one can tell the ladies are represented as well-dressed and young and one of them appears to be talking, laughing, or singing in a lively way.[13] The resemblance to Dunbar's scene is striking enough to make one wonder whether three fairies at a feast were not familiar enough to be recognised in the fifteenth and sixteenth centuries. Was there a well-known fairy trio which Dunbar's opening description could be counted on to suggest to his audience without his having to do more than set the scene in an appropriate way? If so, this is perhaps the trio represented in the picture, since most earlier and contemporary accounts speaks of the fairy mounds as thronged with revellers of both sexes.

If there was really an actual cult, involving meetings attended by initiated persons and sometimes by the uninitiated who chanced on the meetings by accident, the feast with music and dancing, drinking and love-making, either in a fairy cave, mound, or grove must have been the essence of it. This is what all the earlier and later accounts have in common and what they have in common with prototype accounts in Irish and Welsh myths and legends and the romances of chivalry based on these.

Two anecdotes of the twelfth century are particularly interesting, among the mass of vague legend and folk tale, because they are circumstantial, datable, and refer to well-known historical characters. One is William of Newburgh's account of the famous fairy cup.

In the province of Deiri [Yorkshire] also not far from the place of my nativity, an extraordinary event occurred, which I have known from my childhood. There is a village, some miles distant from the Eastern Ocean [the North Sea], near which those famous waters commonly called Gipse, spring from the ground at various sources . . . A certain rustic belonging to the village, going to see his friend, who resided in a neighbouring hamlet, was returning, a little intoxicated, late at night; when, behold, he heard, as it were, the voice of singing and revelling on an adjacent hillock, which I have often seen, and which is distant from the village only a few furlongs. Wondering who could be thus disturbing the silence of midnight, with noisy mirth, he was anxious to investigate the matter more closely; and perceiving in the side of the hill an open door, he approached, and looking in, he beheld a house, spacious and lighted up, filled with men and women, who were seated, as it were, at a solemn banquet. One of the attendants, perceiving him standing at the door, offered him a cup: accepting it, he wisely forebore to drink; but, pouring out the contents, and retaining the vessel, he quickly departed. A tumult arose among the company, on account of the stolen cup, and the guests pursued him; but he escaped by the fleetness of his steed, and reached the village with his extraordinary prize. It was a vessel of unknown material, unusual in colour, and strange in form: it was offered as a great present to Henry the elder, King of England, and then handed over to the queen's brother, David, King of Scotland, and deposited for many years among the treasures of his Kingdom; and a few years since, as we have learned from authentic relation it was given up by William, King of the Scots, to Henry the Second, on his desiring to see it.

These and similar matters would appear beyond belief, were they not proved to have taken place by credible witnesses.

He adds the speculation that God may indeed permit evil angels to make such exhibitions partly by illusion and magic as in the case of the nocturnal revel on the hill and partly in reality as in the case of the cup, adding in reference to another story:

Indeed, the nature of those green children, who sprang from the earth, is too abstruse for the weakness of our abilities to fathom.[14]

What is interesting about this tale of a twelfth-century Tam o' Shanter is that the facts related by the historian have a reasonable chance of being true. William of Newburgh is remarkable for his accuracy and his reliability among the historians of his age. He suspends judgment on other marvellous events which he feels are well enough attested to relate, but he tells of this one as something established by reliable witnesses. He was probably born at Bridlington a few miles from where the fairy hillock stood and says that he had often seen it and had no doubt examined it with his usual care. He had heard the story when he was a boy and the events could hardly have happened more than a generation before his birth in 1136, since Henry I to whom the cup was presented came to the throne in 1100. As William entered the monastery at Newburgh, some thirty miles away, when he was between nine and eleven years of age, that is, shortly after 1145, he would have heard the story when there were probably a number of people in the village who had been alive at the time. The story has the air of having been heard on the spot and William is unlikely to have told it unless he had confirmed the account he heard as a boy. In fact he vouches for this. There is no reason to doubt the existence or the description of the cup itself. It was obviously famous and other stories of alleged fairy cups show how greatly their medieval owners prized them. Henry I married Edith of Scotland in 1100 but is unlikely to have presented her brother David with the cup before 1124 when the latter came to the throne. William of Newburgh implies that it was presented to David as king and placed in the royal treasury. Before 1124 it would have been natural to make such a gift to the reigning king, either Edgar or Alexander, the brothers of David, especially as Alexander had married Henry's natural daughter Sibylla. The latest date of the presentation would have been before 1135 when Henry died. William the Lion, who returned it to Henry II, may have done so early in his reign but is more likely to have handed it over after the Treaty of Falaise in 1174 when he had fallen into Henry's power after an unsuccessful invasion of England. William of Newburgh implies that it was not a gift and that it was handed over at Henry's demand. This would fit in with his statement that the return of the cup had happened a few years before the time of writing and this was probably during the year 1199. Moreover, for description of the cup and of the esteem in which the Scottish kings held it, William probably did not have to depend on hearsay. He either spent his whole life at the little priory of Newburgh, or, after being educated there, re-entered the priory as a canon in 1182. But within a short distance were the great monastic houses of Byland and Rievaulx which William visited and where he was well known. It was Ernald, abbot of Rievaulx, who asked him to write his history. Now from 1134 till 1143 the famous Ailred of Rievaulx was there as Master of Novices, and again from 1147 to 1167 as abbot. Ailred was himself a historian and as a boy he had lived at the court of David I as the companion of David's eldest son Henry. The king was fond of him, made him steward of the royal household, and later offered him a bishopric. If the fairy cup went to Scotland between 1124 and 1135, as seems probable, Ailred had almost certainly seen it and may even have had it in his custody. He would know its story and with William's thoroughness and scrupulousness about evidence there is not much doubt that he and Ailred would have exchanged views. William may not have been the only person Ailred talked to. He was influential also with Henry II and spent some time with him in 1162. As the Plantagenets were rumoured to have fairy ancestry, Henry, if he paid any attention to the fable, may well have been more than usually interested in the fairy cup his grandfather had once owned along with a fairy horn similarly seized which had been presented to him by a Lord of Colchester.

I have gone to some length to argue the bona fides of William of Newburgh's story, in the first place because this can so rarely be done with such stories from earlier centuries. One example is the story of the fairy cup supposed to have been seized at a banquet of the elves by one of the Musgraves and still preserved at Edenhall in Cumberland in Sir Walter Scott's day.[15] In the second place many of these stories are so like William's—the setting, the fairy feast, the seizing of a cup, a jewel, or a fairy bride, or the capture of the intruder by the fairies—that one cannot ignore them. Yet most of them can be dismissed as mere superstition as far as any real evidence goes. It is more difficult, I think, to do this with William of Newburgh. One should at least look for another possible explanation. If one dismisses the idea that William was simply fooled by the locals, which seems less likely as he was one of them himself, only two probable alternatives suggest themselves. One is that the cup was a genuine enough treasure recovered from a burial mound but that local superstition or duplicity had explained its presence and possession by the story of the farmer seizing it from a fairy banquet. The other is the supposition that all occurred as reported. William and all his contemporaries including the farmer himself obviously believed that the revellers were fairy folk, the 'green children who sprang from the earth'. This is a phrase which he uses of another story about two green children who appeared in East Anglia in the reign of Stephen.[16] But he tells the two stories together and plainly regarded the green children and the revellers alike as fairy people. His admirably objective narrative gives a different impression. The farmer was slightly drunk, though not too drunk to take precautions or to be able to outstrip his pursuers. No doubt as it was midnight and he had always regarded the mound and probably the nearby magic springs as fairy ground, he later told the story in terms of his superstitions. But what he actually heard was simply singing and the noise of a revel; what he saw was a hillock with lights and a number of men and women in or on the hillock engaged in a gay but apparently ceremonial banquet. He was obviously taken for a late arrival and offered a draught accordingly, but his behaviour immediately showed the company their mistake and they chased him to recover their stolen property. The fact that they failed to catch him suggests that they were not supernatural beings since the fairies were credited with the power to travel through the air with incredible swiftness. In short, what William of Newburgh seems to be reporting is a fairy cult meeting composed of human beings, some of whom would be neighbours, though they probably believed that some of those they were associating with were genuine fairies.

The evidence of the fairy banquets and visits in the Scottish witch trials is in entire agreement with this view; the fairies are indistinguishable from their human neighbours, the 'queen' at these gatherings appears to order the proceedings, and there is music, dancing, and love-making as well as feasting. The fairy boy of Leith in the seventeenth century was solid enough for George Burton to drag him back into the room when he 'vanished' and showed no signs of supernatural power, though he wanted to escape badly enough. He describes the company who met at the banquet each Thursday inside Calton Hill not as fairies but as 'men and women' (see Chapter 7). Modern Scottish folklore is often romanticised and its fairies often have a suspiciously literary flavour, but where the belief is recent or still persists, the incidents are often quite matter of fact. For example:

> Two young men in Deeside [Aberdeenshire] were returning home on Hallowe'en night, each with a jar of whisky on his back, and, seeing an opening, entered a fairy dwelling [in an elf-hill]. There was music and dancing. One, without laying down his burden joined the dancers. The other suspecting the place and company stuck a needle into the door as he entered and thus got away when he liked. The former was left behind. His companion returning a year later found him

still dancing with the whisky on his back. When brought to the open air he was only skin and bone.[17]

Incredible details naturally occur in such stories, but in essentials they boil down to meetings of men and women for what they believe to be fairy rites and merriment on fairy ground. The sort of thing that could grow into the kinds of tale we have been referring to occurs in the diary of a Scots country gentleman, Andrew Hay of Craignethan, Lanarkshire, in the middle of the seventeenth century.

> 10 [October] Munday, 7 a'cloak—This morning, after I was ready and had breakfasted, I went to Skirling [*where he dined and chatted with the minister*] . . . we were also informed that Jon Cleghorn, Kirklawhill, did one dark nyt see a good many men and women dancing, and with a great lyt wt them, which imeditlie disappeared, and which he sayes were witches.[18]

They might equally well have been 'fairies', yet men and women just the same.

Another aspect of the fairy tradition that is best explained by the existence of an actual cult with human initiates is the occurrence of fairy marriages. Once again there are plenty of instances of families who claimed to have a fairy ancestress. An Earl of Desmond has already been mentioned and possibly the Macleods of Dunvegan and the Plantagenets, who were credited with a descent from a demon on the mother's side, were in the same class. So probably were the McDuffs, earls of Fife, who were reputed to have a castle or fortress on the fairy hill or Maiden Castle at Markinch, with a subterranean passage into the hill below, and the Lord Forbes of Putachie whose family was associated in local legend with the Nine Maidens of Auchindoir and whose arms bore the boar's head in memory of the ancestor who killed the boar which had killed the Maidens.[19] Sir David Lindsay of the Mount who came from Fife and was Lord Lyon, as the chief Scottish herald in the early fifteenth century, thought fairy descent important or common enough to lay down the proper armorial bearings for a family claiming fairy blood.[20] There are numbers of instances of humbler folk who made the same claim. Andro Man of Aberdeen in 1597, as we have seen, confessed to a regular union lasting thirty-two years with the Queen of Elphen by whom he had several children whom he continued to meet. Unfortunately there is a great cloud of witnesses but a great paucity of anything like real evidence. But a story related by a contemporary of William of Newburgh is nearly as circumstantial as his and again suggests that the so-called fairies seen at night in lonely places were often in fact human enough members of a cult group.

Edric the Wild (that is, in Latin, *silvestris*), so called because of his quickness of limb and his gay and ready tongue and behaviour, was a man of great honesty and lord of North Ledbury. Returning late from hunting through the Forest of Dean* and wandering about uncertain of his way until midnight, attended only by a lad, he arrived at a house set in the opening of a large grove. It was of a sort of which the English used to have one to each district, taverns which they called *ghilhus*.† Drawing near, he saw a light in the building and, looking inside saw a number of distinguished looking women taking part in a lively ring-dance. They were extremely beautiful and as elegant in dress as adorned by native grace, but of larger build and taller than women among us. Our warrior noticed one among them who outshone the rest for beauty of face and figure and was attractive beyond all the pleasures of kings. The ladies were encircling her with light and cheerful movements and with subdued voices were singing in solemn harmony. A delicate melody was audible but the words were in an unknown tongue. The moment he saw her, the knight's heart was pierced and, scarcely able to sustain the fire shot from Cupid's bow, all aglow, all in flames, he was made reckless by passionate desire for this loveliest of plagues, this golden peril. He had listened to popular tales of superstitions about nocturnal bands of evil spirits, [the night-riders with] Diana, the assemblies and hostings of forest fairies; he knew perfectly well how these supernatural beings hit back if disturbed, how, if surprised, they instantly punish the offender, how they keep themselves inviolate and dwell apart hidden and unknown. He knew too how they detest those who try to steal into their counsels in order to pry and publish, and what care they take to keep themselves from view, lest being seen they should be held of no account . . . but forgetting all, as blind desire prompted him . . . he rushed round the

* Or 'through forest glades'.
† *giest-hus* (?).

building, found the entrance and, dashing in, seized on her who had already seized him by her charms. The rest of the company at once threw themselves on him and a furious struggle took place for some time, until by his own efforts and those of his boy, they broke free. But their feet and shins showed what damage the teeth and nails of the female sex can effect. He succeeded in carrying the lady with him and for the space of three days treated her as his bride. But in this time has was unable to wring one word out of her, though she bore his ardent love-making placidly enough. On the fourth day, however, she spoke to him as follows: 'Good health, my darling, and indeed you shall prosper and enjoy good fortune both of person and of goods. But this shall be on condition that you speak no ill of me or of my sisters from whose company I was torn, nor of the place nor of the grove from which I was taken nor of anything in their neighbourhood. Be assured that from the very day you fall from grace, I shall be taken away and you will find yourself exposed to continual misfortune, and indeed you will have advanced your last hour by your insolent behaviour.' He promised to be a steady and faithful lover on any terms he could fulfil. So he invited his neighbours and even noble families living at a distance and when a great number of them had assembled, joined her to himself in the solemn bonds of matrimony.

At that time, William the Bastard, then newly King of England, was on the throne. He had heard of this remarkable event and wanted to investigate and to know for sure whether it was a fact. So he summoned both husband and wife to come to London. They came and many witnesses with them and many testimonials from those who were not able to be there in person. There was a tremendous amount of discussion about the conditions under which a woman of this sort, never before seen or heard of, could have appeared and while everyone was still lost in amazement they were sent back to their estates.

It happened, when a few years had gone by that Edric, having returned from the chase about the third hour of the night and looking for his wife, failed to find her. So he called her and told others to call her too. When at last he saw her coming slowly towards him, he got angry and said: 'Haven't those sisters of yours kept you rather a long time?' He uttered other reproaches too, but to the empty air, for she had heard the voices of her sisters and vanished. The young man, of course, repented his disastrous outburst and sought out the place from which he had captured her, but neither by tears nor by laments could he induce her to return. He continued to mourn for her day and night, but this was foolish of him, for his unremitting grief put an end to his life.[21]

Walter Mapes, who tells this story, is not as reliable or as convincing a witness as William of Newburgh. William in fact would probably have denounced him as he denounced Geoffrey of Monmouth for passing off ridiculous fictions as history. His *Court Trifles* devotes itself to the fables and gossip which William eschewed. Nevertheless it is reliable enough when it treats of historical events, especially events dealing with the English court between the conquest and his own day. Unlike many of the fabulous tales he tells, the one just related appears perfectly credible and the events if they really happened would have been only a little over a generation before the narrator was born and would have been a matter of local gossip. Ledbury is in Herefordshire and it is very probable that Walter was himself a Herefordshire man. At any rate he was, as he tells us, from the Welsh Marches, he owned land not far from Hereford and had constant associations with the city during most of his life. His work is full of local legends and anecdotes and the present one seems to have been gathered on the spot, since the local details are precise and those relating to London fairly general. However, he could also have collected some details from London where he had been a court official. The work was written at court in fragments which were later assembled not in any particular chronological order and rather hastily, for Walter did not notice that he had told the story of Edric the Wild twice. It obviously impressed him. The second version is shorter, the details are mainly about the London end of the story and suggest some notes taken from documents or traditions preserved at the court. In both versions, however, the story leads up to the donation of the Ledbury estates to the see of Hereford by Edric's son, Alnod, in gratitude for being cured of a palsy to which he had been subject. Walter's connections with the cathedral seem to have been close ones. He held a living in Gloucestershire, among his other benefices, which was in the gift of the vicars choral of Hereford, and in 1199 he was strongly backed by the chapter of the cathedral in his unsuccessful attempt to become their bishop. It is more than likely that he had access to cathedral records and traditions. He must have talked to people who had known Alnod, and if, as is supposed, he was born near

Hereford about 1140 he could have talked to people who had known Edric and his fairy wife. Edric had been one of the great landowners of the Welsh Marches at the time of the Norman Conquest, distinguished by his wealth, courage, and ability. The Norman castle at Hereford used to harry his lands in Shropshire and Herefordshire on the grounds that Edric had never made formal submission to William the Conqueror. In 1067 Edric joined with two Welsh kings in a full-scale revolt and continued to harass the Normans until 1070 when he made his peace with the Conqueror, and must have been confirmed in some of his estates since North Ledbury is mentioned as his in Domesday Book.[22] Two years later Edric went with the king to conquer Scotland.[23] The marriage could not have taken place until after the reconciliation and, in fact, Walter's second version of the story says William summoned the wife to London at the time of a council there so that she could tell her story in public. This places the marriage shortly before one of the two councils he held in London, one in 1075 and the other in 1078. Unlike many marvels and portents related in the *De Nugis Curialium*, this story seems to have a solid backing of historical facts and to refer to persons so well known and an event so notorious that it would be unlikely to be pure fiction.

It is also unlike most of the similar stories in Walter's repertory in that there is nothing particularly supernatural about the events narrated. This aspect is purely in the interpretation placed on them by the actors in the story and the author himself. Edric losing his way in the woods at night comes not to a fairy mound, an enchanted castle, or magic lake or well but to a common enough type of Anglo-Saxon house. Because it is on the stroke of midnight and the place is filled with women dancing and singing, he naturally takes them for supernatural beings. But, in fact, their behaviour when surprised is very different from the behaviour reported of such beings in legend and folk tale. They cast no spells, do not vanish mysteriously, change shape, or create illusions to baffle the intruder and when he escapes they do not pursue him by aerial flight like the night riders with Diana, Herodias, or Dame Habundia with whom Walter obviously associates them. In fact they behave very much as ordinary women of flesh and blood would. They surround the ravishers and lay hold of them hoping to prevail by force of numbers. Even so it cannot have been very formidable opposition since most of them seem to have quickly ended up on the floor where they continued the scuffle by holding, scratching, and biting the legs of Edric and his boy attendant. They managed to escape in a struggle with a large number of women, though encumbered by having to carry with them an unwilling girl of more than usual height and weight. There is not much evidence of supernatural powers in any of this, nor in the subsequent history of the ravished bride. She obviously managed to persuade her husband and many other people that she possessed such powers but her vague threats, promises, and prophecies are almost the only attempt to exercise them. Her sudden disappearance at the end is a characteristic fairy trick, but need not be taken for anything more than what any skilful conjuror can do. It is easy to fool an audience who are persuaded that they have never moved their eyes from an object which appears to vanish as they watch, whereas they have simply had their attention diverted for a moment. The fairy boy of Leith practised this trick quite successfully though he was being watched by a number of people whose object was to prevent his going to the Thursday night meeting of the cult.

> The boy came again, at the place and time appointed, and I had prevailed with some friends to continue with me (if possible) to prevent his moving that night. He was placed between us, and answered many questions, until, about eleven of the clock he was got away unperceived of the company; but I, suddenly missing him hasted to the door, and took hold of him, and so returned into the same room; we all watched him and, of a sudden, he was again got out of doors.

This time he escaped but there was obviously no magic in the trick and he was as much a creature of flesh and blood as Captain Burton who reported the incident.[24]

What this story of Walter Mapes does suggest, of course, is that Edric saw through the window members of a women's cult group whom he took for fairies or spirits, and that they encouraged him and others to believe that they were. In the second version of the tale he is said to have snatched his wife from among the dead.[25] There is some reason to believe that such communities of women existed in Britain from very early times. This is a subject to which we shall return in a later chapter, but it is interesting to notice some likeness between the scene Walter Mapes describes and the one in Dunbar's poem. In the one the women meet at midnight in a house in a grove; Walter uses the words *nemus* and *lucus* to describe the latter so that he clearly has a sacred grove in mind. In the other the ladies meet in a bower in what appears to be a sacred or fairy grove. In both accounts the hour is midnight and the women have the appearance of fairies and are therefore probably dressed on purpose to look like them. In both cases the entertainment or ritual consists of singing and dancing. The hostility to the male sex is something else they have in common and the 'fairy' bride dominates, hoodwinks, and leaves her husband when she pleases, a theme which is the subject of the discussion of Dunbar's ladies.

With Walter Mapes and William of Newburgh we are lucky perhaps to get stories of cult meetings reported before popular imagination had begun to add impossible details and to change real events into fabulous. *The Romance of Partenay* or *Lusignan*, sometimes called *The Tale of Melusine*, illustrates how such stories of actual events misconstrued could turn into real fairy stories which no one now could possibly credit. This early sixteenth-century romance is translated from a fifteenth-century French version and is thus roughly contemporary with Dunbar's poem. It begins with the story of Raymond, adopted son of a rich earl of Poitou, who had the bad luck to kill his adoptive father during a boar hunt. Sunk in gloom he is returning, or rather, riding aimlessly through the forest, and passes a fairy well or healing spring:

> Uppon thys fontayn ther had verilie
> which was right holsome, ful clere as crestal
> Thre fair laydes of gret seignorie.
> In hys forth-passyng saw non of them all,
> Such dolorous thoughtes to hym gan call.
> Then spak the moste gentillest of thaim thre,
> The most goodlokest And iolyest to se;[26]

This charming creature is Melusine, one of three fairy sisters who greets Raymond, predicts his future fortune and offers to marry him provided he promises to observe a certain condition, which, of course, he later breaks, like Edric the Wild. Like Edric, Raymond falls deeply in love with her and does everything she tells him, including arranging a great wedding before as many and as noble witnesses as possible. They enter a fairy chapel—Melusine it appears is a good Catholic—and are married in the presence of fairy knights and ladies as well as of the earl's human neighbours. Melusine's fairy host builds them a castle to her designs. In its elements the story is very similar to and has apparently grown out of a story like that related by Walter Mapes. But this is now pure fairyland. Melusine is not only a genuine fairy but the daughter of a fairy and of a Scottish king who similarly broke the condition imposed by his bride. For this he has not only lost his wife but his three daughters have imprisoned him in a fairy mountain where he is guarded by a giant. The interesting thing about this fantastic non-sense is that the various French versions of the tale treat it as based on fact. The original of the English version was undertaken at the request of William Lord of Parthenay at the end of the fourteenth century and claims to be based on family tradition and documents, as no doubt it was. These nobles of Poitou claimed descent from the fairy ancestress, were proud of it and believed the castle they lived in to be of fairy construction.[27] It is probable that a more matter-of-fact tale like that of Edric lies at the back of it all and that the original Melusine was a real woman but a member of a women's cult group.

Much the same sort of explanation naturally fits best the numerous tales of fairy lovers and fairy mistresses enjoyed without the benefit of matrimony. Many of these of course belong merely to myth and folklore; but there is a considerable remainder of stories that suggest that the 'fairy' was a human member of a fairy cult and that the children of such unions were regarded as human enough. At Aberdeen, in 1597, Isobel Strathaquin's daughter was tried for witchcraft. She alleged in her defence that 'what skill so ever she has, she had it of her mother; and her mother learnt it of an elfman

113

who lay with her'.[28] Andro Man in the same series of trials testified that the fairies 'have playing and dansing quhen thay pleas; and als that the quene is verray plesand and wilbe auld and young quhen scho pleissis, and lyis with any scho lykis'.[29] The Reverend Robert Kirk in the seventeenth century reports the beliefs of his neighbours around Balquhidder and Aberfoyle in Perthshire—beliefs which he seems to have shared—

> For in the Highlands there be many fair Ladies of this aereal Order, which do often tryst with lascivious young Men, in the quality of Succubi, or lightsome Paramours and Strumpets, called *Leannain Sith,* or familiar Spirits.[30]

Evans Wentz notes that the 'black chanter of Clan Chattan' was said to have been given to a famous Macpherson piper by a fairy woman who was in love with him and that the Mackays like the Macleods had a fairy flag which was the gift of a fairy mistress.[31] The belief in Leannan Shi has persisted in parts of Scotland to the present day. J. M. McPherson mentions an old shoemaker in Tomintoul, Banffshire, who as a young man had had a 'lanan shi' as a mistress,[32] and there is record of a young man in Barra, Inverness-shire, who was so worn out by his fairy mistress, who insisted on meeting him every night, that he migrated to Nova Scotia. But she followed him there.[33] Such tales may be all nonsense but they are told by people who believe them to be fact and they fit in with beliefs and practices which are consonant with a fairy cult. The existence of such a cult would help to explain some of the anomalies that dismissing them as mere superstition sometimes leaves unresolved. It is naturally impossible to prove the existence of an active and actual fairy cult beyond all doubt, but enough has perhaps been said to suggest that there are reasonable grounds for supposing that a number of pagan cults did survive here and there in Scotland until recent times, that they were therefore likely to have existed in Dunbar's age in greater force, and that among them were at least two sorts of cult practice connected with belief in fairies and human membership of a fairy group. One of these had the character of a general meeting of initiates for a feast and revel at regular intervals, the other that of a women's secret society or 'mystery' from which men were excluded. The tale of Edric the Wild suggests that they had a secret language or a ritual including songs or hymns in an archaic speech, like those of the Arval Brethren in Rome. Edric would have recognised Welsh but found the words of the song to which the ladies danced unintelligible, though after her three days' silence his stolen bride appeared to address him in his own language which was probably hers as well.

One remark of Walter Mapes illuminates what is perhaps the main reason why we know so little about such cults. The obvious one, of course, is that people who practised them kept quiet about things that would certainly have brought down on them the censure and perhaps the punishment of church and lay authority. His first account of the rape of the fairy bride is, as I said, apparently gathered from report and tradition around Ledbury and Hereford. It gives a detailed account of what happened there and suggests that William I sent for Edric and his wife mainly out of curiosity. The second account which appears to know little of local details and suggests an extract from a court record says that

> The King, having heard of this extraordinary occurrence, both on account of her beauty and of the rape, wondered and had the woman brought to him while he was holding a council in London and produced her before everyone, and when she had confessed he sent her home [*confessamque remisit*].[34]

This looks more like a judicial inquiry. The report of the event in Wales makes no mention of fairies and puts the emphasis on the fact that one of William's important thanes had married a woman caught in an illicit rite (*coetu nocturno foeminarum choreantium*). *Remisit* may simply mean that when he had heard her tale the King sent her home, but may equally well mean that when she had confessed he let her off without penalty. No doubt he would not be ill-pleased at the opportunity to have an additional hold over his troublesome and powerful marcher lord, Edric the Wild, by the threat of a suspended sentence for sorcery against his wife. The judges who examined Joan of Arc regarded her confession that with the other girls of the village she used to sing and dance under the Fairies' Tree near Domrémy as a very serious and damaging admission on her part. As time went on and the campaign against witchcraft increased in ferocity it became even more dangerous to be known to have anything to do with superstitious practices of any sort.

But Walter's comment on Edric's knowledge of the popular beliefs of the time reveals an older and in the end a more compelling reason for keeping the cult, its rites, and its membership concealed from everyone but the initiates. He says that Edric was well informed (*edoctus*) about the way certain nocturnal assemblies of women demons, of whom he mentions three types, revenge and punish attempts to take them by surprise and

> how they keep themselves inviolate and dwell apart hidden and unknown. He knew too how they detest those who try to steal into their counsels [or councils] in order to pry and publish, and what care they take to keep themselves from view lest being seen they should be held of no account [*ne visa vilescant*].

The last phrase means literally 'lest things seen, should grow worthless' and therefore includes the rites and the performers. This in turn could mean that the sacred mysteries would be profaned and rendered ineffective, but could equally well mean that every effort was made to create an air of terror and supernatural horror and a condition of sudden and terrible magical powers of retribution, because if anyone saw that these were not divinities but human women, no one would think anything of them or their rites. This is not what the author means, of course. Like all but the most enlightened of his contemporaries he was convinced that these assemblies were manifestations of demons. But it is undoubtedly the primary reason why such cults are always surrounded with secrecy in all parts of the world, even when there is no fear of punishment from the state.

The other reason why we have so little to go on is that, along with the church's tendency to regard such superstitious practices as damnable, went the serious historian's tendency to regard them as trifling and unworthy of the dignity of being recorded in their pages. It is only by chance that some instance of the sort recorded by Walter Mapes or William of Newburgh finds a place in the chronicles because they happen to be connected with persons or events of historical interest to the chronicler. It is even rarer to find writers like Walter Mapes, Gervase of Tilbury, or one of the anonymous compilers of *The Chronicle of Lanercost*, simply recording these trifles for their own sake. Secrecy in order to preserve the power of the cult, secrecy to protect its members from punishment, and the indifference or contempt of those who have left us records of past times, are all reasons why we have so little to go on, but perhaps the most important of all is the mere loss of documents and records. The evidence that remains should be treated with the greatest caution, but it should not be dismissed simply because sometimes only a single instance may survive of what may once have been a widespread practice. We must now consider a case in point.

7

The Fairy Cult in Edinburgh

WE would have not much evidence on this subject but for the narrative of Captain George Burton quoted in a book published at the end of the seventeenth century, *Pandemonium, or the Devil's Cloister*, by Richard Bovet. As Burton says the events occurred about fifteen years before the time of writing, and that was apparently while Bovet was composing his book, published in 1684, we may place the date as probably between 1660 and 1670. Burton was a visitor to Leith; from his narrative he appears to have been sceptical and his account is as circumstantial and objective as one could wish.

> About fifteen years since, having business that detained me for some time at Leith, which is near Edinburgh, in the Kingdom of Scotland, I often met some of my acquaintance at a certain house there, where we used to drink a glass of wine for our refection; the woman which kept the house was of honest reputation among the neighbours, which made me give the more attention to what she told me one day about a fairy boy (as they called him), who lived about that town. She had given me so strange an account of him, that I desired her I might see him the first opportunity, which she promised; and not long after, passing that way, she told me there was the fairy boy, but a little before I came by; and, casting her eye into the street, said, Look you, sir, yonder he is at play with those other boys; and designing him to me, I went, and, by smooth words, and a piece of money, got him to come into the house with me; where, in the presence of divers people, I demanded of him several astrological questions, which he answered with great subtilty; and, through all his discourse, carried it with a cunning much above his years, which seemed not to exceed ten or eleven.
>
> He seemed to make a motion like drumming upon the table with his

fingers, upon which I asked him, Whether he could beat a drum? To which he replied, Yes, sir, as well as any man in Scotland; for every Thursday night I beat all points to a sort of people that used to meet under yonder hill (pointing to the great hill between Edenborough and Leith). How, boy? quoth I, what company have you there? There are, sir (said he), a great company both of men and women, and they are entertained with many sorts of musick, besides my drum; they have, besides, plenty of variety of meats and wine, and many times we are carried into France or Holland in a night, and return again, and whilst we are there, we enjoy all the pleasures the country doth afford. I demanded of him how they got under that hill? to which he replied that there was a great pair of gates that opened to them, though they were invisible to others; and that within there were brave large rooms, as well accommodated as most in Scotland.—I then asked him, how I should know what he said to be true? Upon which he told me he would read my fortune, saying, I should have two wives, and that he saw the forms of them sitting on my shoulders; that both would be very handsome women. As he was thus speaking, a woman of the neighbourhood coming into the room, demanded of him, What her fortune should be? He told her that she had two bastards before she was married, which put her in such a rage, that she desired not to hear the rest.

The woman of the house told me that all the people in Scotland could not keep him from the rendezvous on Thursday night; upon which, by promising him some more money, I got a promise of him to meet me at the same place, in the afternoon, the Thursday following, and so dismist him at that time.[1]

The 'fairy' boy may, of course, have been fooling Captain Burton to the top of his bent, but it seems unlikely since the story was apparently accepted by the neighbours and by Burton's own local acquaintances who met him at the inn, some of whom bore witness to the boy's own belief in his tale. It is a story which suggests that meetings of a fairy cult group in Calton Hill were taken very much as a matter of fact and certainly treated as an unexceptional occurrence by the ordinary citizens of the capital at a time when anyone professing or confessing or even suspected of such meetings was still liable to be arrested on a charge of witchcraft. Yet both the boy and the neighbours seem to have talked to Burton without any signs of apprehension. It confirms the impression one gets from the witch trials themselves and from the researches of folklore experts in later times: that beliefs and practices of this sort were very widespread, if not universal, among the general run of people, but that they were able to keep it from the authorities and quite successfully for the most part. It was the unlucky ones who got caught. When they were caught, as the trials again show, it was often due to a quarrel which caused the parties to forget or ignore the ordinary precautions, and make accusations that could lead themselves as well as their enemies to the stake or the gallows. Even so, the authorities were often unwilling to have this sort of trouble on their hands unless pushed on by the zeal of ministers and courts of session. There are many instances in burgh records where they simply contented themselves with fines or cautions or exile from the town limits. If, as it appears, a regular fairy cult meeting could be held in Edinburgh in the seventeenth century, it is even more likely that such meetings could take place there in the fifteenth or the early sixteenth century and be winked at or ignored by authority. Dunbar in that case need not have made his reference explicit: everybody would have known what his poem represented without his giving more than the bare hints that occur at the beginning and end of the poem.

The story told by Captain Burton is interesting because it throws light on the main problem that arises if we try to take most of the accounts of fairy feasts and meetings seriously, that is as accounts of actual meetings of a cult group. It seems to require us to believe two impossible occurrences which crop up again and again in these accounts and form part of them as far back as we can go in myth and folk tale. One is the transport of human bodies for considerable (often very great) distances through the air and their return in an impossibly short time; the other is, of course, that the feasts and meetings are constantly said to have taken place in underground houses within mounds and hills and even, in some cases, beneath the waters of a lake, a river, or an arm of the sea. This seems to prove that the meetings were as much delusions as the underground houses and aerial flights must have been. This does not affect my argument in the case of Dunbar's poem, since we are dealing with a work of literature. What matters is not what actually took place, but what people believed could and did take place. But in fact there is a possible and quite credible explanation to be found in the widespread phenomenon of the Second Sight, especially common in the Celtic or former Celtic areas. When Captain Burton naturally enough asked the fairy boy how the men and women who attended the Thursday night revels managed to get inside the hill, he answered that 'there was a great pair of gates that opened to them though they were invisible to others'. The illustration to *Newes from Scotland* showing the traveller sleeping in a fairy mound with three ladies feasting behind him also shows in the side of the mound an elaborate arched gateway with pillars and a closed door or doors, so that the idea was apparently familiar enough. Other reports speak of a doorway into fairy hills or mounds, others again simply tell of the hill itself opening and closing behind them. Can we make any sense of such reports? About the same time that, according to the fairy boy, this was going on in Edinburgh, the Reverend Robert Kirk in Perthshire was questioning his neighbours about their fairy beliefs and practices. He was a Gaelic scholar and so could make direct contact with those of his parishioners who spoke no English. He reports that the persons usually able to see the fairies in their migrations were those gifted with this double vision:

> They [the Fairies] remove to other Lodgings at the Beginning of each Quarter of the Year . . . and at such revolution of Time, SEERS, or Men of the SECOND SIGHT (Faemales being seldome so qualified) have very terrifying Encounters with them.[2]

In fact it is clear from his careful and soberly recorded account that he himself had never seen any fairies and that all his direct information, apart from tradition or hearsay, came from 'Seers or Men of the Second Sight', who in particular saw them 'eat at Funeralls [and] Banquets'.[3] It is clear that, whether Captain Burton recognised it or not, the fairy boy was also gifted with this Second Sight. When he predicted the Captain's two wives, in order to satisfy Burton's doubts, he said that he saw the 'forms' of those ladies sitting on his shoulders. In Martin Martin's discussion of Second

Sight, again almost contemporary with Kirk's and Bovet's books, he gives a list of typical 'visions' together with the interpretations put on them by the seers. A woman's form seen at a man's left hand was a sure sign that she would be his wife at a later date.[4]

Martin Martin was a native of the Western Isles, a careful but sceptical observer who did not subscribe to the superstitions he noted down as the Reverend Robert Kirk seems to have done. The chapter in which he deals with the phenomenon of Second Sight in the Highlands and Islands is particularly detailed and interesting:

> The Second Sight is a singular faculty of seeing an otherwise invisible object, without any previous means used by the persons that see it for that end; the vision makes such a lively impression upon the seers, that they neither see nor think of anything else, except the vision as long as it continues: and then they appear pensive or jovial according to the object which was represented to them.
>
> At the sight of a vision, the eyelids of the person are erected, and the eyes continue staring until the object vanishes. This . . . occurred more than once to my own observation, and to others that were with me.

Discussing how this faculty is acquired he says that it did not seem to be hereditary, nor could he learn from anyone, by the strictest inquiry, that there were any known means of acquiring it or communicating it to others. Some were born with it but others apparently acquired it suddenly and without any known reason. Most of the visions were of a sort that predicted future events or events occurring some distance away. It was a common thing for the seers to see 'houses, gardens and trees, in places devoid of these'. Often the same things were seen simultaneously by seers several miles apart. Most important of all, however, one seer could transmit his vision to another by touch.

> All those who have the second sight do not always see these visions at once, though they be together at the time. But if one who has this faculty designedly touch his fellow-seer at the instant of the vision's appearing then the second sees it as well as the first; and this is sometimes discerned by those that are near them on such occasions.[5]

Cases of mass hallucination on a much larger scale are well known and it is obvious that this would form a perfectly good explanation of how a number of human initiates in a fairy cult, most of whom would possess Second Sight, could persuade themselves at their meetings that they travelled to distant places through the air, or that they entered the mounds and hills on which they met, and enjoyed feasting and revelling within. Whatever the psychological explanation of such 'visions' may be, we need go no further than the case of William Blake to be assured that such things happen to people who are not in other ways deranged. Blake did not go into a trance and was aware of what was going on around him while he saw things and persons, including on one occasion a fairy, which those around him could not see. There are other examples of this curious faculty recorded and it was certainly common in Scotland at one time. Martin remarks:

> It is observable that it was much more common twenty years ago than at present; for one in ten does not see it now, that saw it then.[6]

As for the uninitiated who happened on such things as revels in hillsides and the fairy cavalcades on earth or in the air, these seem mostly to have done so at times such as midnight or during periods like Beltane, Midsummer, or All Hallows when it was supposed that the invisible world was open to anyone's view. In other cases it was the result of sleeping or lying on fairy ground or using or wearing certain charmed objects. People prepared by superstition readily see what they expect to see. Sometimes such chance visits seem to have ended in recruitments to the cult as a modern instance would suggest in the case of a Nithsdale young man who, passing through a lonely place at night, heard delicious music and, approaching, saw a fairy company, as he supposed, at a feast:

> A green table with feet of gold was laid across a small rivulet, and supplied with the finest of bread and the richest of wines. The music proceeded from instruments formed of reeds and stalks of corn. He was invited to partake in the dance and presented with a cup of wine. He was allowed to depart in safety and ever after possessed the gift of second sight. He said there were several of his former acquaintances who were become members of the fairy society.[7]

When we recall that our problem is not to prove that there were cult meetings of fairy societies in Dunbar's day, but merely that it would be enough that Dunbar's audience should believe that their fellow citizens took part in such meetings, it should be clear that he should have had no difficulty in presenting three Edinburgh housewives in the guise of fairies, depending on his hearers to make this assumption.

If they did they would probably have, like the citizens of Leith two hundred years later, a good idea of the place in which the meetings were supposed to be held and one can, I think, make a reasonable guess at this. As we have already seen the ladies meet in a hawthorn grove of great age and therefore probably a sacred grove. It is outside the city and in a deserted place since the participants are sure that there is no spy near them. This in itself would suggest a spot likely to be avoided by the superstitious, since on a night of universal celebration like the Midsummer Eve festival, the revellers could be expected to range widely. The description of morning at the end of the poem gives several more precise details:

> Thus draif thai our that deir night with danceis full noble,
> Qhill that the day did up daw, and dew donkit flouris;
> The morow myld wes and meik, the mavis did sing,
> And all remuffit the myst, and the meid smellit;
> Silver schouris doune schuke as the schene cristall,
> And berdis schoutit in schaw with thair schill notis;
> The goldin glitterand gleme so gladit ther hertis,
> Thai maid a glorius gle amang the grene bewis.
> The soft sowch of the swyr and soune of the stremys,
> The sueit savour of the sward and singing of foulis,
> Myght confort ony creatur of the kyn of Adam,
> And kindill agane his curage, thocht it wer cald sloknyt.
> Than raise thir ryall roisis, in ther riche wedis,
> And rakit hame to ther rest through the rise blumys.
>
> (ll. 511-24)

The place, if it is an actual spot round Edinburgh, must be one that is surrounded by flowery meadow and with copses and stretches of brushwood; it is set in a 'swyre', that is a pass or declivity near the top of a hill or mountain or between two hills and there is a stream or streams nearby flowing actively enough to be heard. It is also suggested that it is one of those spots where a spring and a sacred grove were the resort of those wishing to be healed of various ills including impotence. It is a place which would be likely to have associations with fairies.

There are various places outside and close to the city as it was in Dunbar's day which might have answered to some of these requirements. There is the Castle Rock itself, which, as we have seen, probably had associations with the cult of the Maidens and was known as Maiden Castle, but it would be both inhabited and guarded at the time and we need a deserted spot. There was the ridge north of the city on which the New Town was built in the eighteenth century, which Fergusson in his poem 'Auld Reikie' refers to as fairy ground.

> While our new city spreads around
> Her bonny wings on fairy ground.[8]

If this is not a merely literary flight of fancy there may have been a belief surviving in 1773, when the poem in its first form was published, that it was 'given ground', that is property belonging to the fairies. A similar belief is recorded at Monquhitter, Aberdeenshire, in the same century:

> Fairies held from time immemorial certain fields which could not be taken away without gratifying these merry spirits by a piece of money.[9]

Similar pieces of fairy property are known all over the country. 'Given ground' was also a frequent place for nocturnal meetings. But in Dunbar's day this area was separated from the city by the Nor' Loch. Then there is Calton Hill itself which we have seen was believed as late as the seventeenth century to be a fairy hill. Its name apparently indicates that it was once the site of a sacred grove: *Calltuin* in Gaelic is said to mean hazel grove and the hazel, like the rowan and hawthorn, has special magical associations with fairies. There were Caltons in various parts of Scotland[10] and the hazel grove that inspired such awe at Loch Siant Well in Skye has already been mentioned. An account of Edinburgh written between 1500 and 1532, and therefore nearly contemporary with Dunbar's poem, refers to it as *Collis Apri* or Boar's Hill and the boar, as we have seen, is occasionally associated with the cult of the Maidens. The author of the account, Alexander Alasius or Alesse, also mentions that the Cowgate a few hundred yards away was then inhabited by the rank and aristocracy of the city, to which Dunbar's ladies who 'weddit war with lordis' would have belonged;[11] Calton Hill would have been a convenient resort for their midnight party and it has or had a declivity that could perhaps be described as a 'swyre', but as far as I know no spring or stream of running water answering to the description in the poem. Before the Reformation, moreover, it was the site of a Carmelite monastery which after this became a leper hospital.

Perhaps the most likely spot would have been the region round St Anton's or St Anthony's Well in the hollow between Arthur's Seat and Salisbury Crags. It is exactly what can be described as a swyre. A spring issuing from under a boulder flows down the precipitous rock face. A chapel dedicated to St Anthony was built near it in the later fifteenth century and the Lord High Treasurer's accounts have several references to offerings made there so that it was apparently a healing well. Perhaps the dedication to St Anthony indicates that it was regarded as particularly helpful to sufferers from erysipelas or St Anthony's Fire.[12] We have already seen that the execution of criminals in Scotland was anciently associated with fairy mounds or law hills. Witches and sorcerers were burnt there. Both Castle Hill and Calton Hill in Edinburgh were used for these executions, but apparently in Dunbar's day Arthur's Seat shared this function. In the flyting between Dunbar and Kennedy, Kennedy is made to say to our poet:

> Renounce thy rymis, bath ban and birn thy bill;
> Heve to hevyn thy handis, ande hald the still:
> Do thou not thus, bogane, thou salbe brynt
> With pik, fire, ter, gun puldre, or lint,
> On Arthuris Sete, or on ane hyar hyll.
> (ll. 332-6)

At Beltane on May Day this meadow-like area was visited by the maidens of the town searching for patches of dew to wash their faces in, a custom referred to by Robert Fergusson as accompanied by ring dances in his day:

> On May-day in a fairy ring
> We've seen them round St Anthon's Spring
> Frae grass the caller dew draps wring
>   To weet their ein,
> And water clear as chrystal spring
>   To synd them clean.[13]

The custom was still being kept up in 1842[14] and the fairy associations of the spot seem clear. But readers of *The Heart of Midlothian* will recall the superstitious terror which caused all to avoid the place at night in Scott's description of Jeannie Deans's meeting with Robertson, and even in the daytime it struck Dorothy Wordsworth as Scott described it: 'a desert even in the immediate vicinity of a rich and populous and tumultuous capital'. Dorothy's journal for 16 September notes:

> We set out upon our walk, and went through many streets to Holyrood House, and thence to the hill called Arthur's Seat, a high hill, very rocky at the top and below covered with smooth turf, on which sheep were feeding. We climbed up till we came to St Anthony's Well and Chapel . . . we sate down on a stone not far from the chapel, overlooking a pastoral hollow as wild and solitary as any in the heart of the Highland mountains.[15]

I like to think of her sitting there beside William, gazing perhaps at the spot where Dunbar imagined his three ladies expressing sentiments of which she would certainly have disapproved, but would perhaps have understood—William perhaps not.

As Dorothy's remarks show, the 'swyre' could be reached by a comparatively easy walk from the Cowgate, and no place can be imagined more suitable for the meetings of a women's fairy cult whose members wished to be alone and protected by superstitious dread from intrusion or inquisition.

We have reached the end of the first part of this ramble through suggestions and possibilities, not perhaps without profit by the way, but they have led to no conclusion such as scholars could approve. For this is a Wild Goose Chase. The goose is never caught, the purpose and pleasure is in the chase. But the object of these earlier chapters has been to suggest that there are at least reasons for thinking that Dunbar may have planned his poem to amuse and puzzle his audience by basing it at first on their own background of fairy belief, fairy romance, and fairy cult practice. The chapters that follow will consider in more detail what the wanton wives discuss and try to show that the theme and tone of the central part of the poem is not as out of keeping with the romantic and fairy setting as has sometimes been supposed.

8

The Blest Bond

As the women begin their conversation we move from a nebulous fairy world into a real and coarsely definite one. The contrast is perhaps greater for modern readers than for the original auditors, since fairies in their day were by no means the ethereal creatures they have become since then and there would be little incongruity in three fairy women talking as these do. If they were meant to be real women at a cult celebration there would be no incongruity at all. But fairy women or real women, they are discussing matters of real life and it is worth while looking at what the discussion is about.

The descriptions of the miserable husbands and what happens to them is so vivid and entertaining that it is easy to see this as the main point: the two young wives ridicule and complain of their unsatisfactory bed-mates, the widow describes hers as a lesson in how to deal with such situations. The whole thing is satire on the female sex of a common enough type in medieval literature. But to take this view of the poem as no more than satire is to miss the fact that, in essence, the women are not simply complaining about their husbands or even about husbands in general. They are in revolt against the institution of marriage itself considered as a permanent and unbreakable bond, requiring strict monogamy on the part of the wife and giving the wife no say in the choice of her husband before marriage and no power to decide anything afterwards without his consent. The descriptions of their husbands are, in a sense, merely illustrations of this initial complaint, which in itself is a prelude to the real discussion: how to abolish or circumvent marriage. This explains why Dunbar appears to give the two young wives such good cases against their husbands. The first is old, repulsive, and enfeebled, the other is impotent from self-indulgence. These are simply extreme cases of what may happen to a woman who has no say in the choice of a husband. The complaint is not against the particular men, but against the institution itself that makes such things possible. The illustration in one sense could equally well have been husbands chosen by families for family reasons who were sadists or idiots. Sexual deficiency is no doubt chosen because it brings out more sharply the fact that such marriages defeat the very purpose of the institution. The first words of the widow make the main subject of the discussion perfectly clear:

> Bewrie, said the Wedo, ye woddit wemen ying,
> Quhat mirth ye fand in maryage sen ye wer menis wyffis;
> Reveille gif ye rewit that rakles conditioun?
> Or gif that ever ye luffit leyd upon lyf mair
> Nor thame that ye your faith hes festinit for ever?
> Or gif ye think, had ye chois, that ye wald cheis better?
> Think ye it nocht ane blist band that bindis so fast,
> That none undo it a deill may bot the deith ane?
>
> (ll. 41-8)

From here the discussion develops along the lines of considering some alternatives to marriage as it is, and then considering how marriage itself may be used to attain the same general ends: the sexual freedom of women and freedom to choose and reject, to govern and dispose in domestic matters. These questions are treated with an air of hilarious amusement and of confident derision of the male sex, in marked contrast to the tone of complaint adopted by the two young wives in describing their husbands.

The first wife answers each of the widow's questions in turn. Marriage is not a blest bond; it is harmful, joyless, and a cause of strife. It is not a question of choosing better, but of choosing not to be made a prisoner of marriage. It is power to change her partner that she would prefer if the choice rested with her. She then proposes the first alternative: marriage contracted for a year only, with women having the sole right to say whether it should be continued for a further term, the right to change partners when it pleases them, and, of course, the freedom to choose or reject their partners. The second wife replies that if, like the birds on St Valentine's Day, she had the privilege of choosing a new mate, then chastity adieu! What she seems to be saying is that if annual marriage were the rule why stop at that? Why should she not choose and change when she feels like it? Why keep a man for a whole year or until his vigour fails him? Her option, it would seem, is for promiscuity. The widow in her reply to these arguments changes the whole emphasis. Women, she says, should accept marriage, presumably because there is no practical alternative but principally because the right to make their own sexual choices is less important than the actual power to do so. Unrestricted enjoyment of the pleasures of love is inferior to enjoyment of complete power over the other sex. It is not really such a bad thing to be married to an old man because a young wife can flatter and cajole him easily, get his goods and be sure to outlive him and then be free while still young and attractive to follow her own desires. This is what happened in the case of her first husband. Her second marriage illustrates an even more successful road to power for a woman. She marries a rich merchant and, using the initial advantage of her aristocratic birth and higher social position, dominates him to such a point that she not only gets all his wealth and the control of his affairs into her hands, but then proceeds to break his spirit completely. When he, too, dies, she is rich and free to choose and change lovers as often (and as many times) as she likes. The two other women had obviously thought in terms of one husband or one lover at a time, but the widow's picture of her own apotheosis dispenses with marriage altogether. It has no point, once it has made her independent. Her final triumph consists in her holding a kind of Court of Love, in which crowds of lovers compete for her favours together, and none in the end is disappointed. But even in this account the emphasis is firmly on the woman's dominance and enjoyment of power rather than on the unlimited gratification of desire. The two young wives agree that the widow's theory of things is preferable to theirs, applaud her highly and resolve to follow her example and her 'sovereign teaching'. In the end the theme of the poem is not the problem of marriage but the problem of power; sensuality is not the driving force of these women but the gratification of the will.

A good many critics have pointed out that the widow seems to be modelled on Chaucer's Wife of Bath. In their unlimited sexual appetites and their passion for having the mastery over the other sex they are, of course, similar. But these are commonplaces of medieval satire against women. In temperament and character the two have little in common and their views of marriage are completely different. What the Wife of Bath demands of life is well summed up at the end of her tale:

and Jhesu Crist us sende
Housbondes meeke, yonge, and fressh abedde,
And grace t'overbide hem that we wedde;
And eek I praye Jhesu shorte hir lives
That wol nat be governed by hir wives.

(ll. 1258-62)

She is not, of course, averse to love adventures outside marriage, but marriage itself is an institution that she accepts and the five husbands she has had at the church door and the sixth she is prepared to welcome when he appears are thought of primarily as husbands. To the widow marriage is an institution to be manipulated for the wealth, power, and independence it can provide and then to be abandoned for free love. She no more accepts marriage in itself than the two young wives accept it. Her motives are purely those of expediency and the whole tenor of Dunbar's poem is that of an attack on and rejection of Christian marriage and the church's view of the proper relation of the sexes.

One interesting thing in all this is that Dunbar, writing for a court audience, is clearly putting a view that mainly concerned women of the upper classes. The medieval church took a view of marriage in which, at least in theory, the woman was entirely subordinate to the man, but in practice, in Scotland at any rate, it seems to have been little concerned with duties and obligations. Before the thirteenth century its main interest seems to have been to prevent marriages within the forbidden degrees and, after that, to see that banns were properly published in accord with the decrees of the Fourth Lateran Council of 1215. This was to prevent clandestine marriages. In the lower classes of society women seem to have enjoyed considerable freedom of choice but in the upper classes where property or political alliances were concerned they found themselves increasingly restricted. The second wife in Dunbar's poem, for example, has been married off by her kinsmen, not against her will, for at first she thought she was getting a jewel of a husband. But had she known the truth before marriage it would have made no difference and once married there was no redress:

> Apone sic materis I mus, at mydnyght, full oft,
> And murnys so in my mynd I murdris my selfin
> Than ly I walkand for wo and walteris about,
> Wariand oft my wekit kyn, that me away cast.
>
> (ll. 211-14)

In Scotland as in England at the time, the transfer, sale, or abduction of heiresses or widows with property was common enough. But in the poem the most important objection of these women of position and property is not to the economic and legal enslavement that marriage involves, nor to its being arranged without their consent, it is simply to its *permanence*, to the fact that it was in effect a life sentence.

The medieval church did not concern itself much with the custom and procedure of marriage. It encouraged people to seek the blessing of the church on their union but a mass or even the intervention of a priest were not necessary to a valid marriage. In Scotland the ceremony was ordinarily in two stages. The first was the betrothal at which the parties agreed to take each other and the arrangements as to dowry and so on were concluded between the two families. The second was the ceremony of handing over the bride by her father or her nearest male relative. These were private transactions and took place outside the church, usually at the door, where it became customary for the priest to give a blessing, and the parties would then hear mass inside the church. But neither the mass nor the blessing were part of the ceremony and neither were essential to it. The essence of marriage was in fact that the couple should declare their present intention of taking each other as man and wife and this declaration if followed by intercourse was all that was necessary to a valid marriage. The Fourth Lateran Council forbade clandestine marriages but it did not and could not make them invalid. It could only punish the offenders. This was the case until the Council of Trent in 1563 decreed that a valid marriage must be celebrated before a priest and in the presence of witnesses. But by that time Scotland was in the throes of the Reformation and informal marriages by declaration only continued to be legal until 1939. Nevertheless the Scottish church from the beginning of the thirteenth century made increasing efforts to condemn marriages not performed with a previous publication of banns and with religious sanction and blessing. A decree of the Diocese of Aberdeen in that century forbids clandestine marriages and forbids its priests to have anything to do with them on pain of canonical punishment.[1] The continual repetition of such decrees right up to the Reformation and the increasing penalties prescribed suggests that they were not effective, and in fact several loose and illegal kinds of union, some of which were of a temporary nature, continued to be practised side by side with regular marriage. Some of these were no doubt corruptions or misunderstandings of the form of marriage just described, but others were certainly due to the survival of customs and views of the relations approved between the sexes. Such customs went back to the pagan past of the various Celtic peoples, British, Pictish, and Irish, whose descendants made up the Scottish nation in the Middle Ages. Before we consider these alternative and looser forms of marriage, it is interesting to see what ancient writers tell us about their customs. It is interesting for one thing, because almost all of them describe a state of affairs that would have delighted Dunbar's ladies or would at least have seemed to them an arrangement preferable to that of their own society.

In the first century B.C. Julius Caesar, speaking apparently about tribes he had not seen in the interior of Britain, says:

> They have their wives, ten or a dozen together, in common and for the most part this holds between groups of brothers or of fathers

and sons; but the children born from them they consider to be his who takes a woman's virginity.[2]

The peoples he is referring to do not sow corn but live on milk and flesh and are clothed in skins. He seems to have been mis-informed in thinking that these were the customs of all the Britons of the interior of the island, but the description of a pastoral people, clothed in skins, would fit the tribes of the far north. Caesar is for the most part very reliable in his accounts of native peoples and seems to have taken a good deal of pains to inform himself about their way of life.

Strabo, writing about half a century later, but whose information is possibly a good deal older, in some cases based on Pytheas, c. 300 B.C., gives an account of the Irish which he admits is unsupported by actual reports from people who had been there:

> Concerning this island I have nothing to tell, except that its inhabitants are more savage than the Britons, since they are man-eaters as well as heavy eaters, and since further, they count it an honourable thing when their fathers die, to devour them, and openly have intercourse, not only with other women, but also with their mothers and sisters; but I am saying this only with the understanding that I have no trust-worthy witnesses.[3]

Not much in that perhaps, though there might be if Strabo is really depending on information dating from the fourth century B.C., since there is some evidence for cannibalism among the Celts in prehistoric times.

Dio Cassius, writing at the end of the third century or the begin-ning of the fourth, is our next witness, and probably a good one since he was intimate with the emperor Septimius Severus who had campaigned in Scotland and forced the Caledonians to come to terms. He appears to have seen the memoirs of Severus. Among the northern tribes subdued by Severus were the Meatae and the Caledonians, the two principal nations. Dio Cassius places the former near 'the crosswall which cuts the island in half', probably the Antonine wall, and he places the Caledonians beyond them. As Ptolemy places the Caledonians in the area which corresponds to modern Perthshire, they are probably the nation which came later to be known as the

Picts.[4] Of both these principal nations Dio says, or rather, the eleventh-century monk Joannes Xiphilinus whose recension of this part of the work survives, says:

> There are two principal races of the Britons, the Kaledonioi and the Maiatai, and the names of the others have been merged in these two. . . Both tribes inhabit wild and waterless mountains and desolate and swampy plains and possess neither walls, cities, nor tilled fields, but live on their flocks, wild game and certain fruits. . . They live in tents, naked and unshod, possess their women in common and in common rear all offspring.[5]

In the prayer which Dio Cassius puts into the mouth of Buduica (Boadicea) these characteristics are attributed to the Iceni of the first century A.D., probably without any justification. But since he almost certainly took the details from what he had heard of the tribes of Scotland, the passage can be regarded as a further statement of the case. Buduica is made to say to her tribal goddess Andraste:

> Those over whom I rule are Britons, men that know not how to till the soil or ply a trade, but are thoroughly versed in the art of war and hold all things in common, even children and wives, so that the latter possess the same valour as the men.[6]

In the next century we find St Jerome saying much the same thing about the *natio Scotorum*, that is the Irish, in his polemic work *Adversus Jovinianum* written about 395: speaking of the curious foods and food taboos of the barbarian tribes he observes:

> What could I mention about other races, since even when I was a young man in Gaul, [I heard tell of] the Atticoti, a British People feeding on human flesh; and that when, ranging the forests they come on herds of swine and cattle and flocks, they cut off the buttocks of the herdsmen and their wives and the breasts of the women, and consider these the daintiest of foods? The Irish race do not have individual wives and almost as though they had read Plato's Republic and followed Cato's example, none among them has a spouse exclusively his own, but they sport and wanton after the manner of cattle, each as it seems good to him. The Persians, Medes, Indians and Aethiopians, no mean countries and comparable with Rome itself, form unions with their mothers and grandmothers, their daughters and their granddaughters.[7]

St Jerome had been in Gaul as a young man and he kept up a correspondence with various friends there all his life. Among them was Hedibia, the last of the line of the Druids of Armorica and an educated woman.[8] He was in a position to know the current gossip about the wilder Celtic tribes beyond the Roman frontiers. His tone is amused and contemptuous, as the references to Plato and Cato show, but he regards the behaviour of these people as fairly normal for barbarians and adduces similar customs in Africa and the East.

None of these accounts is perhaps very trustworthy, not in the sense that the reports may not have been accurate enough, but in the sense that the authors who recorded them may have been unable to grasp the sort of marriage and kinship system involved. A wide variety of endogamic kinship organisations, which might fit Caesar's summary account, is known among primitive peoples. 'Possessing their women in common' may be a misunderstanding of an intricately regulated and by no means promiscuous system by which a brother marrying a wife is regarded as married to all her sisters and she as married to all his brothers. But in known examples of this sort of marriage, the whole thing is governed by specific custom as to occasion and priority of rights. On the other hand all the writers cited may be taking festivals and ritual occasions of promiscuous sexual intercourse as evidence that these Celtic tribes had no specific system of marriage, a conclusion that is certainly not justifiable. This sort of orgy seems to be implied by Jerome's phrase *ut cuique libitum fuerit, pecudum more lasciviunt.* But the possibilities are endless and the discussions of scholars inconclusive.

On one point, however, all these writers are agreed and are definite: incest was general among the Celts who lived in the wilder parts of the British Isles and had a pastoral and hunting economy. It is interesting to notice that a system of marriage which permitted relationships which the church regarded as incestuous apparently continued in Scotland, Ireland, Wales, and the Celtic south-west of England well into the Middle Ages and that the church was unable to eradicate it. The Irish heroic sagas, though written down in Christian times, reflect a pre-Christian age, and they contain a number of stories of incest, as in the case of Conchobor and his sister (in some versions his daughter) Dechtire, who was his charioteer, or of Créidne who had three sons by her father, the King of Ireland.[9] The stories of these relationships are recounted as a matter of course. *The Tripartite Life of St Patrick* records that even the holy St Mel, whom Patrick installed as bishop in Ardagh, was assumed by the newly converted population to be living in incest with his sister Eiche, because she shared his house. St Patrick had to separate them, though they were proved innocent by a couple of miracles. But the scandal was still recounted locally in the nineteenth century.[10] St Patrick's efforts appear to have been vain, for incestuous unions seem to have been widespread at the end of the twelfth century. The Synod of Cashel called together in 1171 to settle affairs after the Norman conquest of Ireland laid it down as one of the most important reforms that

> Firstly it is decreed that all the faithful throughout Ireland are ordered to put away those with whom they have formed unions, who are related to them either by blood or by marriage; and that when they have done so they shall contract lawful marriages and stick to them.[11]

Fifteen years later Giraldus Cambrensis was shocked, not so much at the incest, which he admits was common in his native Wales, as at the degenerate state of Irish religion which permitted such practices. The Irish he says are

> A people, of all peoples, the most uninstructed in the elements of the faith; they do not even now pay tithes and first-fruits; nor even now do they contract lawful marriages, but they fail to avoid incest and, what is truly detestable not only to the Christian faith but against common decency, in many parts of Ireland, brothers marry, indeed I say traduce the wives of their dead brothers; it would be truer to say that they seduce them, so evilly and incestuously do they mate with them.[12]

Things appear to have been no better among the Britons than among the Irish. According to Nennius, Vortigern, the powerful British tyrant who was credited with having invited the Germanic invaders under Hengest and Horsa into Britain, 'married his own daughter, by whom he had a son. When this was made known to St. Germanus, he came, with all the British clergy to reprove him.' Vortigern, according to the story, summoned his daughter and ordered her to present her son to St Germanus and declare that Vortigern was indeed the father. She did so and St Germanus and the synod cursed Vortigern who fled, and St Germanus adopted and fostered the child.[13] He was called Faustus. Now Vortigern and his daughter may be rather shadowy historical figures but St Germanus, the great bishop of Auxerre, whom Pope Celestinus I sent to Britain to combat the Pelagian heresy, was certainly not. Nor was his foster child Faustus, bishop of Riez and friend of Sidonius Apollinaris. At any rate it was possible for Nennius in the ninth century to impute an incestuous origin to Faustus, though this may reflect no more than the common custom of imputing illegitimate birth to heroic early saints in imitation of the doubtful paternity or illegitimate birth attributed to the heroes of pagan Celtic legend.[14] Nora Chadwick, who discusses the question in detail, thinks the incest story may have arisen from spite but that St Germanus was probably Faustus's maternal uncle and therefore his natural foster parent.[15] On the other hand the story may be further evidence of a well-known practice of royal incest in pagan and semi-pagan British kingdoms. Nennius was writing well after the event, but Gildas was a contemporary of the south British princes whom he denounces in his *Liber Querulus de Excidio Britanniae*. It is usually supposed that the book was written about the middle of the sixth century. It is not strictly speaking a history: Gildas is not concerned to recite facts but to awaken the consciences of the Welsh princes of his own day. The *Liber Querulus* is a work similar in purpose and method to the famous *Sermon of Wulfstan to the English*. Compared with Archbishop Wulfstan he is an inept Jeremiah and he does not resort nearly enough to the most telling ammunition for polemic, facts. According to Stenton the work is unbalanced because Gildas mentions only five of the very large number of contemporary British kings: 'A King who sinned in moderation had no interest for Gildas.'[16] It is clear, however, that he chooses the worst examples as symptoms of the way the whole country is going. Moreover he knew what he was talking about and he is not likely to have used these examples unless he also knew that what he said was notorious. Now what he tells us about these five princes is that, while nominally Christians, they are renegades to the faith, irresponsible tyrants, and sunk in sexual debauchery. Constantine of Dammonia (Devon), son of an unclean mother, has stained himself with many adulteries, put away his wife and perhaps, for Gildas's passionate rhetoric is hardly clear, has become a sodomite. Aurelius Conanus, prince of Powis, is swallowed up in horrible murders, fornications, and adulteries. Next comes Vortipore or Vortiporix, king of the Demetae in south-west Wales, an elderly man who, in addition to many adulteries, has repudiated his wife and now lives in incest with his daughter. Cuneglassus, another south Welsh prince, has relapsed into heathenism, thrown his wife out of doors, and now commits adultery, incest, and sacrilege with her sister, a former nun. Maglocunus, Maelgwn of Gwynedd, the greatest of the contemporary Welsh princes, fittingly receives the finest flowers of Gildas's eloquence: 'as if soaked in the wine of the Sodomitical grape, foolishly rolling in that black pool of thine offences'. Maelgwn, it appears, was once a monk, but has relapsed into heathen ways and is now surrounded by drunken court poets singing his praises. He abandoned his wife to become a monk, took her back after his relapse, and then, despising her, took as his mistress his nephew's wife and lived in incest with her. Warming to his work he then had his wife and his nephew murdered and publicly married his niece.[17]

Christianity had been introduced in late Roman times to this part of England but Devon and Cornwall had only been converted as a whole in the sixth century so that we may see in these rulers and in the south Welsh princes a relapse into or survival of pagan marriage customs in which incest was accepted. In an early life of St Samson, who took part in the missionary effort just mentioned, it is recorded that travelling through a district called Triconium he saw pagan people dancing and worshipping a stone idol, a young man racing on a horse, and the local chieftain watching the ceremony.[18] As St Samson was born about A.D. 480 and died about 560, this evidence of active heathenism in the area must have happened only a short time before Gildas wrote his attack.

Romance as well as history supports the notion of royal incest.

A sixth-century funerary inscription in Cornwall appears to read: 'Here lies Drustaus (or Circusius) son of Cunomorus'. There was a Breton king called Conomorus, who may be identical with the Cornish one since they were contemporaries, and there was a Dumnonia on both sides of the Channel. The founder of the Breton Dumnonia a generation before was said to have ruled on both sides of the Channel. A life of the Breton saint St Pol de Leon states that King Mark was known also by the name Quonomorius; so that Drustaus or Drustanus, son of Cunomorus, may possibly be equated with Tristan, nephew of King Mark, of the famous legend.[19] It would be an interesting case of royal incest of a son or nephew with the king's wife. King Arthur himself, shadowy figure as he is in history, carries several legendary traits in the romances hardly in keeping with the picture of the perfect Christian prince which these works present. Geoffrey of Monmouth drawing on Gildas, Bede, Nennius, and probably on Welsh oral and written sources, the 'idle tales of the Britons' rejected by William of Malmesbury, makes Arthur's birth the result of an adulterous union, does not impute incest to Arthur himself, but does impute it to his queen Guan-humara and his nephew Modred.[20] In one of the manuscripts of Wace's *Brut*, Modred appears as brother to Ginievre, Arthur's wife, so that the incest is between brother and sister. A Welsh chronicle, based on Geoffrey's *History*, makes Modred Arthur's *nepos* (grandson or nephew), and a Magdalen College manuscript makes him Arthur's son by a concubine, all ideas which complicate the incest relationship.[21] But a later and more persistent legend is that Modred was Arthur's son by an incestuous union with his sister Anna, wife of King Lot of Lothian. This is the view most familiar to modern readers from the pages of Malory, who tries to save Arthur's reputation by suggesting that he did not know that the lady who visited him at Carlyon was in fact his sister. Now Arthur as a historical character would have lived a generation before the Welsh princes whose incestuous ways were condemned by Gildas, and the simplest explanation of the incest story is that it was either an independent tradition due to the fact that Welsh princes did practise incest, or that legend gave Arthur the expected relationships as his fame grew through the romances. At any rate we may suspect that it was not a custom confined to princes and royal houses. Giraldus Cambrensis, himself a Welshman on his mother's side, and extremely proud of his Welsh blood, nevertheless confesses this as a weakness of his countrymen. Book II, Chapter 6 of his *Description of Wales* is devoted to the bad qualities of the Welsh as Book I had been devoted to their virtues as a nation. He begins with the point that incest is peculiarly an aristocratic failing in Wales but has spread among all classes.

> The crime of incest has so much prevailed not only among the higher, but among the lower orders of this people, that having the fear of God before their eyes, they are not ashamed of intermarrying with their relations, even in the third degree of consanguinity. They generally abuse these dispensations with a view of appeasing those enmities which so often subsist between them, because their 'feet are swift to shed blood'; and from their love of high descent, they unite themselves to their own people, refusing to intermarry with strangers, and arrogantly presuming on their own superiority of blood and family.

In the same section of the book he reports that incest also 'took root in Armorica [Brittany] and [is] not yet eradicated', and this was, he says, in spite of a church council summoned to put an end to it.[22] This was at the end of the twelfth century or the beginning of the thirteenth.

As one might expect, Scotland shared this peculiarity with the other Celtic areas of the British Isles and with Brittany. The Irish in Dalriada and the Highlands must have brought their customs with them, which would have reinforced or fitted in with those of the British peoples and the Picts already mentioned. Dio Cassius's remark that the Picts (Caledonians) possess their women in common, and in common rear all offspring, is about the last we hear on this subject until the sixth century, when St Kentigern conducted his mission in Glasgow and Cumbria. The anonymous *Life of St. Kentigern*, composed in the middle of the twelfth century on the basis of a written account of his miracles and of oral tradition, describes the saint's labours in his new bishopric at Glasgow:

The renowned warrior began to make war upon the shrines of demons, to throw down images, to build churches, to dedicate those he had built; to mark out parishes with fixed boundaries . . . to ordain clergy; to dissolve incestuous and unlawful marriages; to change concubinage into lawful wedlock.[23]

As Kentigern's diocese was among British people of Cumbria and, according to the *Life*, he spent some time in Wales, the practices referred to would be, if the tradition on which the life is based is an old one, those we have already seen as attributed to the Welsh and the British kingdoms of the south-west of England. That the efforts of the Darling Saint were ineffectual may be supposed from the fact that the Celtic church in Scotland had apparently still failed to combat these customs when St Margaret became the queen of Malcolm Canmore. Her biographer Turgot, writing between 1100 and 1107, mentions among the reforms which she pressed forward:

Illegal wedlock with step-mothers, as also a surviving brother's marriage with the wife of a brother who had died (unions that used to take place there previously) she showed to be exceedingly execrable, and to be avoided by the faithful like death itself.[24]

The narrative remarks that the Scottish clergy could think of no reply and agreed to do what the queen suggested. But they seem to have had an uphill task. A century later they were still legislating anxiously against incestuous marriages within the fourth degree of consanguinity or affinity and especially between sons and daughters of godparents or a godchild and the child of his godfather or godmother. The latter cases were not only technically and theologically incest in the eyes of the church and canon law, but were likely to be incest in a more modern sense since godparents were often closely related by blood or marriage to their godchildren. During this period there are frequent records of appeals to the Pope for dispensation to allow bastards to hold ecclesiastical office and a typical condition of granting this—*dummodo non fit de adulterio, vel incestuoso coitu procreatus*—suggests that Rome was well aware of the state of morals in Scotland.[25] The general attitude towards the Scots is depicted by Richard of Hexham in his account of events after the battle of Clitheroe, events of which he had first-hand knowledge: after describing the slaughter of the inhabitants by the Scots who spared neither sex nor age he continues:

> then alas! promiscuously with the other women and their spoil, they carried off as well the noble widowed matrons and the chaste maidens. Stripped also, and bound and fastened together in troops by cords and thongs, they drove them away before them, goading them with their spears and arrows. This same thing they did in other wars but to a greater extent in this. Thereafter when these were apportioned with the spoil, certain of [the enemy] were moved to pity, and set some of them free, giving them up to the church of St Mary in Carlisle. But the Picts and many others took with them to their country those who fell to their lot. And then these bestial men, who regard as nothing adultery and incest and other crimes, after they were weary of abusing these most hapless creatures after the manner of brute beasts, either made them their slaves or sold them to other barbarians for cows.[26]

Such events must have been barbarous indeed to stand out and win special comment during the anarchy of Stephen's reign so vividly described by the *Anglo-Saxon Chronicle*. And it is well to remember that this raid on the north of England was conducted by the saintly King David I, who took peculiar pains to see that his followers respected church property. Richard of Hexham distinguishes between the degrees of barbarity of the Lowland or southern Scots and the wild Scots of the north and west whom he calls Picts. But it is clear that the latter were regarded as indifferent to all sexual irregularities, and indeed the attitude seems to have persisted among them until well after the Reformation. The minutes of the Synod of Argyll in the first half of the seventeenth century provide a good example. The unfortunate Synod seems to have laboured despairingly against the indifference among the local population of every rank to the heinous sins of fornication, adultery, and incest. Sometimes one suspects deliberate provocation and contemptuous amusement at the condemnations and the penalties imposed by the ministers and their exhortations to reform. In 1643 the Synod excommunicated a man who 'married his uncle's wife and wilfully retaines her' and a few extracts from the records over the next few years will show that such things were not accidents or chance occurrences:

144

1654. 'One Nicomas in the Isle of Bute hes comited incest with her own unkle', shue knowing the relation and he not. . .

1654. 'Allan McNeill who committed incest with his step-daughter. . .'

1654. [Name missing] mc Illmichall of Inercholane suspect and accused of incest with his god-mother and while the trial is pending the Synod 'inhibit him to cohabite with his goodmother'. . .

1654. The Synod ordains summary excommunication 'considering the great and grievous guiltiness of Duncan mc Callum in Kilmartine laying under the sins of incest and severall adultrees. . .'

1655. The Synod excommunicates 'Donald mc Phersane and [Dirval] mc Vurich for 'relapse into incest'. As Donald's wife was Elizabeth mc Vurich, Dirval was apparently his sister-in-law. . .

1657. Alexander Rosse and Isobell Campbell 'one mother's bairnes have committed incest together in Ila, and the childe procreated be them left in fostering in Lochaber, and they themselves fled away to Ireland. . .'

1656. 'Rorie Dou mc Innus Tuaich, being guiltie of foule incest and horrible murther as is aleadged, for the which he is fled out of Mull where the same was committed into some bounds within the presbyterie of Sky.'[27]

The cases of Rorie Dou McInnes and Alexander Rosse show why the Synod's measures were ineffective in the Western Islands. The culprits could easily move elsewhere and other presbyteries had enough problems of their own. The frequent appeals of the Synod of Argyll to have the offenders apprehended and sent back appear to have met with practically no success. Public opinion was often against them though it did not take quite so drastic a form as a century earlier when the priest of Kirkmichael in Banffshire, on refusing to marry an uncle to his niece, was seized by the uncle and his supporters, laid upon a faggot bound to a stone and, the faggot being set on fire, burnt to death. This stone in the eighteenth century was still known as the Priest's Stone, but whether this was a memorial on the principle of *pour encourager les autres* is not recorded.[28]

Similar evidence could be produced from the records of Scottish trials to show that incest persisted in many parts of Scotland until the end of the seventeenth century, practised by people who regarded themselves as married and as having a right to marry within the forbidden degrees, a right established by custom no matter what church or state might say.

It is clear from the cases already mentioned that there were two elements involved in this. One was an older family or dynastic practice connected with succession and right to property which was probably also connected, as the remarks of Giraldus Cambrensis show, with the organisation of the clan or 'great-family'. Under early Welsh law, the oldest texts of which belong to the period of Giraldus, the wife was regarded as belonging, in matters concerning tribal or family feuds, to her original family group (*cenedl*) and not to her husband's. Moreover, a girl came into the possession of her property at the age of twelve and was then marriageable. It was the duty of kinsmen to arrange her marriage and for obvious reasons it was more convenient in many cases to marry her within the clan, and this seems to have been the usual practice. 'Marry in the kin and fight the feud with the stranger' was reported to have been an old tribal saying. Sir John Lloyd who quotes this saying concludes his discussion of the organisation of the *cenedl* by remarking:

> The study of the cenedl reveals to us the oldest elements in Welsh society which had resisted the influence of Roman law and government, of Christian ethical teaching and of royal authority.[29]

What the church called incest both in Wales and in Scotland was in fact often essential to the cohesion of the clan or the safeguarding of property, and in these areas the clan was paramount. In the Highlands it successfully resisted the feudalism which was imposed on the Lowlands in the eleventh and twelfth centuries. Moreover there seem to have been customs in both countries by which what the church called an incestuous marriage was, by ancient custom, the established method of the succession to the throne or the chieftain-ship, though the claimants might be the brothers, nephews, or sons of the late ruler. Church and state were still not successful in eradicating these practices in seventeenth-century Scotland. A local tradition in Sutherland preserved the memory of a certain judge Morison:

> This judge had King James VI's commission for maintaining justice and good order in that country [the Isles]; and though he was murdered

by this M'Leod himself, but in revenge of his being instrumental in putting to death one of that family who acted as laird of Lewis. The preceding laird of that place dying without lawful issue, but leaving a number of natural sons (some say sixty) a contention arose among them about the succession to the estate.

The clan elected not the eldest, who was unpopular, but another, the son of a gentlewoman whose parents were of considerable influence among the Macleods. Judge Morison recognised him as chief of the clan. Later the judge and the newly elected chief fell into the hands of the eldest claimant, who hanged his brother and let the judge go. The clan Macleod suspected that the judge had had some complicity in the death of their chief, and their next leader, John Macleod, caught him unawares and killed him. The surprising thing in this otherwise normal tale of manners and customs in the Highlands and Islands, is that immediately he had killed the king's representative, John Macleod went to Lewis and married the judge's widow. He was apparently following an ancient customary procedure which must have been the reason for many cases of incestuous marriages.[30]

The second obvious reason why the church and the state failed to eradicate incestuous marriages in Ireland, Wales, and Scotland was indifference to sexual irregularities, acceptance of a good deal of promiscuous behaviour, and the view that marriage was not necessarily a permanent union at all. In the following chapters we shall see that the changes proposed by the two young wives and the widow in Dunbar's poem were by no means flights of their own fancy. They were demanding for themselves freedoms which many of their countrywomen in lower walks of life or in areas remote from the capital actually enjoyed.

Among forms of marriage more favourable to women we may notice here the system which seems to have been in force among the Picts, at least in royal families, before the collapse of the Pictish Kingdom in the ninth century. This matrilineal and probably matrilocal system seems to have died out in the early Middle Ages and was apparently not even remembered in Dunbar's day, so that it is not relevant to the present discussion. It will be considered in another context and in a later chapter.

9

St Valentine's Day

It is the first young wife who fully sets out the program of annual marriage and explains in detail how she would proceed to keep up a constant supply of annual husbands.

> God gif matrimony were made to mell for ane yeir!
> It war bot merrens to be mair, bot gif our myndis pleisit:
> It is agane the law of luf, of kynd, and of nature,
> Togiddir hairtis to strene, that stryveis with uther:
> Birdis hes ane better law na bernis be meikill,
> That ilk yeir, with new joy, joyis ane maik,
> And fangis thame ane fresche feyr, unfulyeit, and constant,
> And lattis thair fulyeit feiris flie quhair thai pleis.
> Cryst gif sic ane consuetude war in this kith haldin!
> Than weill war us wemen that evir we war fre;
> We suld have feiris as fresche to fang quhen us likit,
> And gif all larbaris thair leveis, quhen thai lak curage.
> My self suld be full semlie in silkis arrayit,
> Gymp, jolie, and gent, richt joyus, and gent[ryce].
> I suld at fairis be found new faceis to se;
> At playis, and at preichingis, and pilgrimages greit,
> To schaw my renone, royaly, quhair preis was of folk,
> To manifest my makdome to multitude of pepill,
> And blaw my bewtie on breid, quhair bernis war mony;
> That I micht cheis, and be chosin, and change quhen me lykit.
> Than suld I waill ane full weill, our all the wyd realme,
> That suld my womanheid weild the lang winter nicht;
> And when I gottin had ane grome, ganest of uther,
> Yaip, and ying, in the yok ane yeir for to draw;
> Fra I had preveit his pitht the first plesand moneth,
> Than suld I cast me to keik in kirk, and in markat,

And all the cuntre about, kyngis court, and uther,
Quhair I ane galland micht get aganis the nixt yeir,
For to perfurneis furth the werk quhen failyeit the tother;
A forky fure, ay furthwart, and forsy in draucht,
Nother febill, nor fant, nor fulyeit in labour,
But als fresche of his forme as flouris in May;
For all the fruit suld I fang, thocht he the flour burgeoun.

(ll. 56-88)

The second wife after her complaint returns to this theme:

Ye speik of berdis one bewch: of blise may thai sing,
That, one Sanct Valentynis day, ar vacandis ilk yer;
Hed I that plesand prevelege to part quhen me liikit,
To change, and ay to cheise agane, than, chastite, adew!
Than suld I haif a fresch feir to fang in myn armes:
To hald a freke, quhill he faynt, may foly be calit.

(ll. 205-10)

The first thing that strikes one about this enterprising proposal is that it is worked out in such precise and practical detail that it seems to be more than a pipe-dream or a flight of fancy. These young women give the impression of describing a familiar procedure rather than inventing a hypothetical one. It is true that the first of them says:

Cryst gif sic ane consuetude war in this kith haldin!

But this may be taken to mean either: may Christ grant that such a custom was observed in this country, or alternatively, that such a custom was recognised in this company or in these social circles. In the first case it would probably be ironical, since it seems likely that a very similar custom was in fact in force in Scotland at the time. It was probably limited to lower ranks of society for the most part, though in the Highlands it may have been general. If this second sense is intended, then the phrase 'in this kith' would be equivalent to 'among women of our class'. The second wife refers to the right to change and choose again as a 'privilege', a word at that time denoting a law granting special and usually exclusive advantages to a particular person or class of persons, for example

149

the clergy, the nobility, the merchant guilds and so on. Women of her condition, she implies, have not this privilege.

The reference to St Valentine, of course, is in the first instance to the common medieval belief that on St Valentine's Day, 14 February, the birds choose new mates for the ensuing year. To follow the example of the birds, as the first young wife points out, is to follow the law of love, of our human constitution (kind) and of Nature in general, while to join incompatible persons together in a permanent yoke is perverse and unnatural. In Chaucer's *Parlement of Foules* these three laws are associated in his description of the meeting of the birds on St Valentine's Day; the poet first visits the temple of Venus representing the law of love, then attends the 'parliament' presided over by the goddess Nature whose law extends to all creatures. But each of the groups of birds has its individual way of choosing its mates (the law of kind) and these groups correspond roughly to different classes in human society. The comparison of humans with the birds in Dunbar's poem is meant to emphasise the unnaturalness of a marriage system which compels those who strive against each other to live together, thereby perverting the law of love; the unnaturalness of compelling a woman to live with an impotent husband and thereby thwarting the purpose of marriage itself and so perverting the law of Nature; and, thirdly, the unnaturalness of denying her rational choice in marriage, and thereby perverting or thwarting the law of kind, since the specifically human attribute among animal natures is that of rational choice. In the images that follow in the first wife's account of the lovers she would choose, we feel the force of freshness, renewal, natural growth, and fruition, and she herself might appear almost as the continuing force of Nature herself, ruling the seasons and providing for a fresh crop of vigorous life every spring, except that it is all done in her own interest alone. It is in this that the comparison of her proposals with the customs of the birds is seen to be a superficial one. The birds do, according to legend, choose fresh mates for the year on St Valentine's Day. But they do it as birds obeying the laws of love, kind, and Nature. The first wife actually proposes no such thing; the choosing is to be all on one side in her case; the love is to be at first a matter of baiting a trap and, in the result, a ferocious duel ending always in the defeat and destruction of the male partner; the Nature appealed to is no kindly goddess but a savage embodiment of the principle of *vae victis*!

St Valentine's Day had, however, other associations. It was not only the birds who chose their mates on that day, but, at an earlier period, perhaps human beings as well. The pretty customs associated in modern times with this festival are like the pretty legends of the fairies as they appear in modern literature. Both mask or replace older, more human, and less romantic customs. There are in the main three sets of practices associated with 'Valentines'. The first is the modern custom of choosing someone of the opposite sex to be one's Valentine, sending them a card or a present together with a formal declaration of love which need not be more than a compliment. It is a practice which goes back at least as far as the fifteenth century. The second is the belief that the first man a young woman meets on the morning of St Valentine's Day will be her future husband. This takes its place among the divinatory practices, marriage omens, charms and prognostications associated with many other festivals, including Midsummer's Eve. A number of others are associated with St Valentine's Eve. Probably nothing but the fact that St Valentine's Day was associated with lovers and the choice of partners attached such predictions to the festival. In the third and apparently the oldest Valentine customs the choice of lovers is arranged by lot. Description of the ceremony as it was practised in Morayshire in the nineteenth century brings out the essentials of the primitive custom:

A number of the young people of the town or village assembled in some particular house for the purpose of drawing their Valentines. Fate had to settle the matter. A sheet of paper was cut up into slips sufficient in number for the boys and young men who were to put their fortunes to the test. Upon these slips the names of the girls were written. When ready the slips were placed in a hat and well shaken together. Then the drawing took place. Slips for the girls were prepared in the same way. . . Every one had in like manner [to proceed to the Valentine's home to announce the event] to establish his claim to his Valentine. . . On the presentation of the slip of paper, every

one drawn as a Valentine had to make some small present to the
wooer, such as an apple, etc. As it was with the boy drawers, so it
was with the girls. This was the original way of observing Valentine
day and was undoubtedly a survival from pagan times.[1]

The couples so chosen remained Valentines for a year and there is
little doubt that in more primitive times the custom was not the
innocent game it appears in the account given above, but one in
which a lover or a mistress or a temporary spouse was selected for a
year with the option of changing at the end of it. The ballad that
Shakespeare's Ophelia sings in her madness apparently refers to the
same custom, by which the young man or woman, selected by lot,
was expected to go to the house of his or her Valentine and announce
the fact. The result is probably what was originally a method of
establishing the relationship and showing acceptance after the
exchange of presents or pledges. But in Shakespeare's day the fact
that it was an actual marriage custom had been forgotten and the
young man regards it simply as an opportunity to be made the most of:

> To-morrow is Saint Valentine's day,
>   All in the morning betime,
> And I a maid at your window,
>   To be your Valentine.
> Then up he rose and donned his clothes,
>   And dupped the chamber door,
> Let in the maid, that out a maid
>   Never departed more.
> By Gis and by Saint-Charity,
>   Alack, and fie for shame:
> Young men will do't, if they come to't,
>   By Cock they are to blame.
> Quoth she, before you tumbled me,
>   You promised me to wed.
> So would I ha' done by yonder sun,
>   And thou hadst not come to my bed.[2]

Marriage was not the only matter arranged on St Valentine's Day:
it was an occasion on which the Scottish Parliament in former times
ordained that the commissioners of shires should draw lots 'and
valentines yeirlie at ilk parliament for thair places', and Charles I

when at Edinburgh in 1641 had some difficulty in preventing the Scottish Parliament from choosing their Lord Chancellor by the same method of putting names on slips of paper into the hat of the Clerk of the Parliament, 'as they do Valentines'. Charles apparently won his point by deferring the matter till 14 February was well past.[3] It is clear that this date, which is just after the beginning of the old Celtic year at Imbolc or St Bride's Day, 1 February, was a ceremonial occasion of very wide significance. It was, in England at any rate, the occasion of a number of the great hiring fairs at which house and farm servants were hired for the year. There must have been many more of these but those where the custom survived into modern times include the St Valentine's Fair at Faversham in Kent referred to in *Arden of Faversham* at the end of the sixteenth century and continued to the end of the eighteenth, and fairs continuing to the present day at Bath, Devizes, Biggleswade, Dorchester, King's Lynn, Bromley, and Wymondham.[4] The association of fairs with St Valentine's Day is important because of the association of other fairs with customs of annual marriage which seem to be presupposed in the ordinary ceremonies of the days as recorded in the last few centuries.

The most famous of these fairs was that at Teltown in County Meath in Ireland. Oenach Tailten, held there from the most ancient times, was one of the great national assemblies, and for a number of centuries was presided over by kings who claimed the kingship of Ireland. The legends about it connect it with the mythological sovereignty of Ireland. The assembly was the occasion of games and feasting and the celebration of the festival of Lughnasa, the beginning of the harvest. Although as a royal assembly it seems to have ended with the Norman conquest of Ireland, it survived as an assembly of country people and a fair until 1770. In the nineteenth century several people gathered from the local peasantry a curious tradition of a marriage custom there, said to have been practised in pagan times. The most circumstantial and careful account was that of John O'Donovan in 1836:

> a hollow called Lag an Aonaigh i.e. *the hollow of the Fair*. Here according to tradition marriages were celebrated in pagan times. A

well springs in the centre of this hollow, a short distance . . . to the south of which a wall . . . [now a ditch] was erected, and in this wall there was a gateway closed by a wooden gate in which there was a hole large enough to admit a human hand. This is the spot at which marriages were celebrated according to the odd manner following. A number of young men went into the hollow to the north side of the wall, and an equal number of marriageable young women to the south side of the wall which was so high as to prevent them from seeing the men; one of the women put her hand thro' the hole in the gate, and a man took hold of it from the other side, being guided in his choice only by the appearance of the hand. The two who thus joined hands by blind chance were obliged to live together for a year and a day, at the expiration of which time they appeared at the Rath of Telton and if they were not satisfied with each other they obtained a deed of separation, and were entitled to go to Laganeeny again to try their good fortune for the ensuing year. This tradition has given rise to a phrase in the country 'they got a Tailteann marriage' by which is meant that they took each other's word for nine months. The natives of Telton think that there was a great deal of fair play in this marriage. . . .[5]

Although this account belongs to the nineteenth century, Máire MacNeill from whom I have quoted O'Donovan's words brings together evidence to show that the custom was ancient and concludes: 'It may be accepted that both early and later tradition agree in testifying to a peculiar marriage custom at Tailtiu.'[6] One may add that the precise details that O'Donovan was able to get from the local inhabitants and their approval of this form of marriage do not support their assertion that the custom belonged only to pagan times. Indeed it would be surprising in view of the state of marriage and morals in Ireland at the time of the Norman invasion if the custom had not continued well into the Middle Ages and perhaps even later. The mere persistence of the fair would have been a strong argument for the persistence of its customs. Some of the evidence adduced by MacNeill suggests that this form of temporary marriage was in the tenth century identified or confused with a hiring or buying of concubines, an ancient practice at these fairs.

In the tenth century Cormac, writing in Cashel, when explaining the word 'coibhche' was reminded of Oenach Tailten [he had mentioned a mound there called Tulach na Coibhche]. He glossed the word as 'cendach' (buying), but the word, according to Gwynn, had the special meaning of 'bride-price' or 'marriage contract', and turns up in an anglicised rendering 'caif' or 'cayf' (meaning temporary marriage or concubinage) in such Anglo-Irish documents as the Statute of Kilkenny.[7]

In the twelfth century Giraldus Cambrensis noted similar practices among his countrymen in Wales:

> They do not engage in marriage, until they have tried, by previous cohabitation, the disposition and particularly the fecundity of the person with whom they are engaged. An ancient custom also prevails of hiring girls from their parents at a certain price and a stipulated penalty in case of relinquishing their connection.[8]

The resemblance between the customs of St Valentine's Day and the Welsh and Irish practices is evident. St Valentine is associated with choice of sweethearts for a year, to be decided by lot rather than by personal selection and to be followed by exchange of presents or pledges. His day is also the occasion of hiring fairs when servants were engaged for the year. These fairs were often occasions of great festivity and licence. At Teltown marriages were arranged for a year and could then be dissolved, according to some accounts, by the parties climbing one or both of two adjacent mounds and turning their backs on each other. They could then marry again by the same method as before. The name of one of the mounds preserves the tradition of a present (bride-price) and pledges. The Teltown Fair took place at Lughnasa, the first day of August by the Julian calendar, and was therefore not a suitable time for marriage and not one of the regular marrying times in Irish custom: the beginning of spring, St Brigid's (or St Bride's) Day, 1 February, would seem a more suitable time. St Brigid is mentioned in an eleventh-century poem as one of the patron saints of the fair and she had a site of her own just across the river to which in the nineteenth century the games associated with the fair were transferred. It is possible that originally the marriage custom of Teltown occurred at another time of the year. St Valentine's Day of course falls shortly after St Brigid's Day and is a more suitable date for marriage and fertility rites than the time of harvest. At any rate there seems to be good reason to believe that annual marriage, probably connected with spring fairs and festivals, was once a practice in Ireland and possibly in Wales. The account of Giraldus Cambrensis suggests that in Wales as probably at Teltown as well there were two associated practices, trial marriage by mutual agreement and hiring of concubines for a definite period accompanied by pledges of indemnification if the hirer returned the girl. In spite of the efforts of the church, the Welsh in the Middle Ages continued to practise divorce and to regard marriage as terminable at will:

> the ancient rule that a man might put away his wife, if so minded, was still valid . . . But the law took care that it should not be frivolously put into operation by providing for a substantial payment known as the *agweddi*, to the divorced woman, and allowed even this only during the first seven years of marriage. After the lapse of this period the husband . . . had to resign to the first wife half of all his possessions, exactly as if the separation had been brought about by his death.[9]

The ancient Welsh laws would not have been likely to make these provisions unless the period of cohabitation mentioned as a regular practice by Giraldus had been regarded as in fact marriage of a temporary sort. Indeed the laws seem to treat the first seven years as a more or less probationary period.

It would be surprising if similar customs were not found in Scotland, and in fact there is evidence that they were. Máire MacNeill mentions traditions of the presence of St Ciaran at the Teltown Fair. In the long poem by Cúan O Lothchain composed for a revival of the fair in 1007, after it had lapsed for eighty years, St Ciaran is mentioned as one of the three guarantors of the Oenach, the others being St Patrick and St MacEirc. St Ciaran died in the first half of the sixth century and was founder of the great monastery of Clonmacnoise. Máire MacNeill suggests that the story of a miracle he performed in favour of one of the two wives of the king presiding at the fair was probably originally told not of the assembly at Teltown but of that at Uisneach,[10] but his name may have been associated with the annual marriage customs in popular legend as the following story from Scotland suggests. It was told by the learned Dr John Smith, minister of Campbeltown in Kintyre, Argyllshire, who wrote a long historical account of the district in 1793 and had obviously consulted both the Irish and the Scots Chronicles and was well versed in local tradition. Campbeltown, which was formerly known as Kilkerran, and Kintyre in general have many associations with St Ciaran or Kieran. The doctor, having reached the sixth century in his account, continues:

It was towards the middle of this century, when St. Ciaran, Querin or Quirinus, the father and founder of the monastery of Clen upon Shenan [Clonmacnoise] became the apostle of Kintyre. . . St. Ciaran was one of the masters of St. Columba, the apostle to the Picts and Western Isles, who addressed a Latin hymn to him, which is said to be still extant . . . Campbeltown consisted until lately of four distinct parishes. One of these . . . was dedicated to St. Ciaran. The three others were dedicated to the Saints Couslan, Michael and Caomhghin (pronounced Coivin, and translated Clement). . . These two saints, however, Couslan and Coivin, though both of unquestionable piety, seem to have had ideas on some subjects totally different. Couslan, for instance, inculcated in the strongest manner the indissolubility of the marriage tie (a point probably as necessary to be inculcated in his time, as in *our own*); and if lovers did not yet find it convenient to marry, their joining hands through a hole in a rude pillar near his church, was held, as it continued to be till almost the present day, an interim tie of mutual fidelity, so strong and sacred that it was generally believed, in the country, none ever broke it, who did not soon after break his neck, or meet with some other fatal accident.

Coivin, in his district, took quite a different course. He proposed that all who did not find themselves happy and contented in the married state should be indulged with the opportunity of parting, and making a second choice. For that purpose he initiated an annual solemnity, at which all the unhappy couples in his parish were to assemble at his church; and, at midnight, all present were sufficiently blindfolded, and ordered to surround the church three times at full speed [no doubt *deasil*] with a view *of mixing the lots in the urn.* The moment the ceremony was over, without allowing an instant to recover from the confusion, the word *cabhag* (seize quickly) was pronounced; upon which every man laid hold of the first female he met with, whether old or young, handsome or ugly, good or bad, she was his wife till the next anniversary return of the solemnity . . . The saint soon brought his parishioners to understand, that they had reason to be satisfied with a condition, which, with all his Christian licence, there was little prospect of mending by a change, and, for many ages, the custom has been only handed down by tradition.[11]

The similarity of these customs with those at Teltown is obvious and each report supports the other since neither narrator is likely to have known the other legend and would probably have mentioned it if he had. St Ciaran was a popular saint in Scotland and many sites were dedicated to him in the west and north of Scotland and in Perthshire and other central shires. St Kiernan's Cave, about five miles from Campbeltown, has been identified as perhaps the earliest Christian chapel in Scotland. His association with two centres of an annual marriage custom is interesting. At Carnock in Fifeshire an ancient fair was held round the thorn tree cross, a fairy thorn surmounting a fairy mound, placed between the church and the Law Knowe. The fair was held in May on the festival of St Ciaran,[12] though whether anything suggestive of annual marriage customs was associated with it I have not been able to learn; but hiring fairs were common all over Scotland. One at the Thirlstane between Auchtermuchty and Abernethy was locally reputed to go back to Roman times.[13] The Thirlstane is a huge flat stone with a hole in the centre such as were common all over Scotland and were commonly used for handfast ceremonies of marriage or betrothal as in the case at St Couslan's parish in Kintyre. The same ceremony could have been used in annual marriage as at Teltown, and at least one annual fair in Scotland had a tradition similar to the Teltown one. This was in the parish of Eskdalemuir in Dumfriesshire. The account of the minister of the parish is very close to one given in Pennant's *A Tour in Scotland* about twenty years earlier (1772):

> In mentioning the remarkable things in this parish, it would be wrong to pass over in silence, that piece of ground at the meeting of the Black and White Esks, which was remarkable in former times for an annual fair that had been held there time out of mind, but which is now entirely laid aside. At that fair, it was the custom for the unmarried persons of both sexes to choose a companion, according to their liking, with whom they were to live till that time next year.

This was called *hand-fasting*, or hand in fist. If they were pleased with each other at that time then they continued together for life; if not, they separated, and were free to make another choice as at the first. The fruit of their connexion (if there were any) was always attached to the disaffected person. In later times when this part of the country belonged to the Abbey of Melrose, a priest to whom they gave the name of Book i' Bosom (either because he carried in his bosom a bible, or perhaps a register of the marriages), came from time to time to confirm the marriages.[14]

If this tradition is reliable it would be evidence that in Dunbar's time annual marriage was in fact practised in Scotland, since Melrose Abbey was finally destroyed in the Earl of Hertford's invasion of Scotland in 1545 and was probably never restored. Book i' Bosom could hardly have been operating later than 1568 when Bothwell, whom Queen Mary had made commendator of the Abbey, was proscribed. He was probably doing his best to mend the devil's handiwork in the fifteenth or early sixteenth centuries.

Perhaps the best known account of annual marriage in Scotland comes from Martin Martin's account of Skye written about 1695:

It was an ancient custom in the islands that a man should take a maid to his wife, and keep her the space of a year without marrying her; and if she pleased him all the while, he married her at the end of the year, and legitimised these children; but if he did not love her, he returned her to her parents, and her portion also; and if there happened to be any children, they were kept by the father: but this unreasonable custom was long ago brought into disuse.[15]

The last remark may have been made in good faith but some of Martin's fellow islanders had apparently not heard the news. A few pages earlier in his narrative he records:

When Mr. Morison, the minister was in Rona two of the natives courted a maid with intention to marry her; and [she] being married to one of them, afterwards the other was not a little disappointed, because there was no other match for him in this island. The wind blowing fair, Mr. Morison, sailed directly for Lewis, but after three hours sailing, was forced back to Rona by a contrary wind; and at his landing, the poor man that had lost his sweetheart was overjoyed, and expressed himself in these words: 'I bless God and Ronan that you are returned again for I hope that you will now make me happy and give me the right to enjoy the woman every other year by turns so that we may both have issue by her.'[16]

In fact 'long ago' is a misleading phrase since Martin must have been aware of the war between the two great clans of Skye at the beginning of the century in which he was writing. This was known as *Cogadh na Cailliche Cairne* or War of the One-Eyed Woman and is said to have been caused by the fact that Donald Gorm Mor, chief of the MacDonalds, had contracted a trial marriage with Margaret, the sister of Rory Mor, chief of the Macleods of Dunvegan Castle. In the course of the contractual year and a day she lost the sight of one eye and Donald Mor is said to have sent her home to her kin mounted on a one-eyed horse, escorted by a one-eyed groom and followed by a one-eyed dog. It was of course the insult of the method of returning the lady, not the return itself, which caused the war.[17] William Skene, commenting on this custom of trial marriage for a year and a day among the Highland chieftains, refers to a case in the sixteenth century.[18]

An article in *The Scottish Historical Review*, by A. E. Anton, a lecturer in law at the University of Aberdeen, argues strongly that there is no real evidence for the existence of this form of marriage in Scotland at all. Not one of the cases cited in evidence, he says, suggests that temporary unions were recognised in medieval Scotland.[19] He makes out a good case for this view, but fails, I think, to demonstrate that temporary marriages did not in fact take place nor that a large part of the nation accepted them as genuine marriages, whatever the secular or the canon lawyers might say. Anton argues that cases cited by Vinagradoff and others, which may be regarded as direct sources for the claim, may be reduced to three. The first is a history of the clan Maclean compiled by Seanachie, a member of the clan, who described a union contracted by John, fourth laird of Ardgour, who died in 1547. The marriage is described as arranged for a definite term of years and it appears that at the end of the time he sent the lady away. A history of the clan Maclean, also written by a reverend gentleman, a member of the clan, in 1899, denies that the lady's children by the marriage were regarded as legitimate, as Seanachie declares they were. Who is the more reliable witness? One can only suspend judgment on this case. His second case is the one, already quoted, of the annual handfast marriages in the upper part of Eskdale. He argues that Pennant, whose account he quotes, was not a very reliable observer, which may be true. But he practically ignores the fuller and more circumstantial account of the minister of the parish published in *The Statistical Account of Scotland*. He appears to know nothing of the Irish and Welsh parallels or of the account of similar events in Kintyre, and he argues, not very convincingly, as he admits himself, that if such a custom did exist in Eskdale and perhaps in other remote parts of Scotland around 1600, its origin may have been a Germanic one, introduced into the country by the Anglican invaders and settlers. The example he quotes comes from Jutland and it has nothing to say about annual marriage or concubinage. Anton's other example is the passage about trial marriage for a year in Martin Martin's book:

> What Martin's informants were describing was probably the 'mariages contracted for certane yeiris,' forbidden by the Privy Council in the so-called 'Statutes of Iona' in 1609.[20]

The Statutes of Iona is really the report of a commission of inquiry and reform. It gives an account of the beliefs and customs of the Western Islands. The inquiry may have been partly set up on account of the War of the One-Eyed Woman. Anton suggests that the reforms were directed against concubinage, which undoubtedly existed in the area as it did in Ireland and Norway from which the Western Isles drew many of their customs. But it is interesting to see what the *Statutes* actually said; they refer (and he quotes them) to:

> the grite grouth of all kynd of vice, proceiding pairtlie of the laik of pasturis [pastors] plantit, and pairtlie of the contempt of those quha are alreddy plantit, ffor remeid quhairoff they hauf all aggreit in ane voice [the reference is to the members of the court, their witnesses, friends and tenants, in short, the whole population acting through their chiefs] lyk as it is presentlie concludit and inactit, that the ministeris alswelle plantit as to be plantit within the parochynis of

the saidis Illandis salbe reverentlie obeyit, thair stipendis dewtifullie payit thame, the ruynous kirkis with reasonable diligence repairit, the sabothis solemplie keipit, adultereis, fornicationis, incest and sic uther vyle sklanderis seveirlie punisht, mariageis contractit for certane yeiris simpliciter dischairgit, and the committaris thairof haldin, repute and punist as fornicatouris.[21]

Anton may be putting the point of view of the time among the Edinburgh lawyers and the bishop in charge, but it is plain that this was a new doctrine to the Isles. The local members of the commission, which included a number of the chieftains or their representatives, candidly confessed that they, as well as the 'haill commonalitie inhabitants of the Illandis . . . were in grite ignorance of this',[22] that indeed they took these for valid marriages and distinguished them from fornication, adultery, and incest, which they admit to have been very common among them. Anton's point appears to be sound but rather academic. Temporary and annual marriages were never recognised by Scottish law or the Scottish church, but they appear to have been accepted by the Scottish people. Once again, as far as the Highlands and Islands were concerned, it seems likely that in Dunbar's day temporary or annual marriage was known, practised, and accepted in those areas.

The value of Anton's article is that it clears up a great deal of misunderstanding about the so-called handfast marriages of Scotland. The handfast marriage was not in essence anything irregular since ordinary marriages approved by the church usually involved the declaration and handclasp normal to a contract. Its origin in fact was the conclusion of the agreement over the bride-price or the 'tocher' or dowry. Associated with this was a ceremony in Scotland and Ireland of making the handshake through a sacred holed stone —the Bore-stanes, Maiden Bower Stones, Thirlstanes, Swearing Stones, Plighting Stones, Betrothal Stones, and Bridal Stones as they were variously known. This was, in general, merely a means of giving added solemnity to the undertaking and need not have implied any pagan superstition or confusion with the forms and procedures of temporary marriage. As long as the parties to the marriage declared their present intention to take each for husband

and wife and followed this by 'carnal copulation expremit be the wordis of the present tyme', as Archbishop Hamilton's catechism of the mid-fifteenth century put it, the marriage was valid, no matter whether the church might consider it illegal and insufficient. What both the medieval Catholic Church and the Reformed Church were more concerned about was marriage *per verba de futuro*, in which the parties or their parents or guardians made a promise of future marriage or announced their future intention of taking each other as husband and wife, and proceeded then to carnal copulation. This was not a valid marriage at all and there was nothing to prevent the parties concerned later denying the engagement and choosing other partners. This practice became increasingly common and achieved the same end as annual or temporary marriage with which it was no doubt confused. But no doubt too, many simple people believed that a marriage *per verba de futuro* was valid enough, and the constant reference both to such marriages and to marriage where present intention had been declared as 'handfast marriage' shows that many people did not understand the technical difference. The taking of hands accompanied by a declaration was supposed to be the essence of the ceremony. The effect of this confusion was two-fold: valid but clandestine marriages came to be regarded as not binding, and invalid promises of marriage as constituting actual marriage. It was for this reason that the church insisted on publication of banns and a public religious ceremony *in facie ecclesiae*. Handfast marriage by the sixteenth century had often come to mean a loose union which the parties could complete or abandon as they wished. In 1562 the Aberdeen Kirk Session showed the state of affairs by which many used the forms of betrothal to constitute what was in effect a system of temporary or indefinite marriage:

> Becaus syndrie and many within this toun ar handfast, as thai call it, and maid promeis of mariage a lang space bygane, sum sevin yeir, sum sex yeir, sum langer, sum schorter, and as yit vill noch mary and compleit that honorable band, nother for fear of God nor luff of thair party, bot lyis and continewis in manifest fornicatioun and huirdom: heirfor, it is statut an ordanit, that all sic personis as hes promeist mariage faythfully to compleit the samen betwix this and Festeranis Evin nixt cummis.[23]

In this decree the Reformers were only continuing the struggle of the Catholic Church in Scotland before them, a struggle which appears to have been in the main as ineffective before as after the Reformation.

Other customs not recognised by the church or the law probably contributed to the confusion in the minds of ordinary people about the permanence of marriage. One of these was the custom of selling or hiring wives to other men. In 1073 Pope Gregory VII complained to Lanfranc that he had heard the Scoti both deserted and sold their wives, and this probably refers to inhabitants of Scotland rather than of Ireland because usually at this date Scoti means Scots and not Irish, and the *Register of the Bishopric of Moray* records abuses of this sort in 1225 and 1251.[24] Typical of the kinds of incident that keep occurring too often to be a matter of chance are two entries in the *Register of the Kirk Session of Humbie*: in 1639 William Williamson, a stranger to the district, bought Agnes Crawfurd, spouse to Robert Baird, giving her six Scots pounds and her husband eight for the sale. In 1646, James Steill, a farmer of Humbie, sold his wife temporarily to Patrick Fowler, a shearer he had hired, in return for twenty days' shearing. The deal was arranged 'in ane idle mirriment at drinking'.[25] In Dundee in 1556 Jonet Gilchrist sold to her husband Robert Thomson the right

> to use his body and dispone thereupon as himself pleases, to marry or live chaste as he shall think expedient.

The price for this release was 'forty pounds with ane stand of clething'. This was part of a documentary agreement to a divorce which the parties expected to be ratified by the church.[26] But above all we should consider these looser sorts of marriage custom not in isolation but, as any of Dunbar's three women would have viewed them, in the setting of widespread promiscuity and indifference to sexual irregularities of any kind which seems to have been a characteristic of the Scottish people at all stages of their history. This will be the subject of the next chapter. But it should be clear that when the two young wives discussed annual marriage and temporary marriage they were probably talking about actual practices which only their place in society and the control exercised by their husbands and their kinsmen prevented them enjoying.

10

Wae Worth Maryage!

THE widow concludes her 'sermon' on how to manage men and defeat marriage by a vivid and amusing account of a riotous feast and saturnalia at her house, and this is followed by an avowal of her complete promiscuity with men of all classes:

> Bot yit me think the best bourd, quhen baronis and knychtis,
> And othir bachilleris, blith blumyng in youth,
> And all my luffaris lele, my lugeing persewis,
> And fyllis me wyne wantonly with weilfair and joy:
> Sum rownis; and sum ralyeis; and sum redis ballatis;
> Sum raiffis furght rudly with riatus speche;
> Sum plenis, and sum prayis; sum prasis mi bewte,
> Sum kissis me; sum clappis me; sum kyndnes me proferis;
> Sum kerffis to me curtasli; sum me the cop giffis;
> Sum stalwardly steppis ben, with a stout curage,
> And a stif standand thing staiffis in my neiff;
> And mony blenkis ben our, that but full fer sittis,
> That mai, for the thik thrang, nought thrif as thai wald.
> Bot, with my fair calling, I comfort thaim all:
> For he that sittis me nixt, I nip on his finger;
> I serf him on the tothir syde on the samin fasson;
> And he that behind me sittis, I hard on him lene;
> And him befor, with my fut fast on his I stramp;
> And to the bernis far but sueit blenkis I cast:
> To every man in speciall speke I sum wordis
> So wisly and so womanly, quhill warmys ther hertis.
> Thar is no liffand leid so law of degre
> That sall me luf unluffit, I am so loik hertit;
> And gif his lust so be lent into my lyre quhit,
> That he be lost or with me lig, his lif sall nocht danger.
>
> (ll. 476-500)

How seriously can we take this Rabelaisian scene? It can hardly be taken quite literally, as I have already remarked, since the widow could not have kept up her reputation for virtue and holiness for long if she had held many parties of this kind. But there is nothing improbable in the entertainment itself which recalls the picnics of Theodora before she became empress as described by Procopius:

> Never was anyone so completely given up to unlimited self-indulgence. Often she would go to a bring-your-own-food dinner party with ten young men or more, all at the peak of their physical powers and with fornication as their chief object in life, and would lie with all her fellow diners in turn the whole night long: when she had reduced them to a state of exhaustion she would go to their menials, as many as thirty on occasions, and copulate with every one of them; but not even so could she satisfy her craving.[1]

Procopius, who detested his empress, may have been repeating and inflating malicious gossip, but whether the story is true of Theodora or not it is certainly taken from contemporary Byzantine life. The question is whether Dunbar was doing the same sort of thing and whether his audience would have taken such scenes of sexual promiscuity, with perhaps a more equal mingling of the sexes, as a fantasy or as an ordinary occurrence? On the whole it seems probable that promiscuous sexual intercourse was very common in Scotland at all times and that the end of the fifteenth century was no exception.

The ancient authors already cited, in addition to imputing incest to the Celtic tribes outside the Roman frontiers, all say or imply that they were promiscuous in their sexual relations. Such reports at second or third hand by civilised foreigners talking about people they regard as ignorant savages must be treated with caution. But comparative anthropology affords many examples of ritual or festive occasions of sexual promiscuity and there is some evidence that formal occasions for a sexual free-for-all did exist from the earliest times and survived in some cases to the present in Scotland.

The first of these occasions were the fixed and recurring festivals of the Celtic and the Christian year: New Year's Eve or Hogmanay, New Year's Day, Imbolc or St Bridget's Eve and Day, Beltane or May Day, Easter, Midsummer or St John's Eve and Day, Lammas or the festival known as Iuchar in the Highlands and Lughnasa in Ireland occurring at the time of the corn harvest, Samain or Hallowe'en and the following All Hallows' Day, and Yule or Christmas Eve and Day. Of these the spring and summer festivals seem particularly to have been associated with sexual licence.

Beltane or May Day had this reputation in England as well as in Scotland. Philip Stubbes's sour puritan description of the festivities is probably not the less accurate for being a jaundiced view.

> Against May, Whitsonday or other time, all the yung men and maides, olde men and wiues, run gadding ouer night to the woods, groues, hils & mountains where they spend all the night in plesant pastimes; & in the morning they return, bringing with them birch & branches of trees to deck assemblies withall.

After a description of bringing home the maypole and the dancing that followed he continues:

> I have heard it credibly reported (and that *viva voce*) by men of great grauitie and reputation, that of fortie, threescore, or a hundred maides going to the wood over night, there haue scaresly the third part of them returned home again undefiled. These be the frutes which these cursed pastimes bring forth.[2]

The Beltane festivals in Scotland included fires as at Midsummer, rolling cakes and fiery wheels down hills and, originally perhaps, human sacrifices, but the bringing home of branches, trees, and the maypole after a night spent in the woods or on the hills was part of the entertainment as was the election of a May Queen. An Act of the three Estates of the Realm in 1555 tried to suppress these and other festivities:

> Statut and ordainit that in all tymes cumming na maner of person be chosin Robert Hude nor Lytill John, Abbottis of Unresson, Quenis of the Maii,

while women who impeded the traffic in the streets of burghs or landward towns 'about simmer treis (maypoles) singand' were to be sentenced to ducking.[3]

An entry in the fourteenth-century *Chronicle of Lanercost* records what is probably the earliest account of a Beltane festival in Scotland

and one that strongly suggests that the occasion had originally been marked by great sexual licence. The entry is for the year 1282 and the account is apparently more or less contemporary with the events recorded:

> About this time the parish priest at Inverkeithing organised the profane rites of Priapus in Easter week. When the young girls had assembled from the town and had arranged their ring dances, he made them dance around Liber Pater. And having these females enlisted, he himself, from mere wantonness led the dance, carrying in front of them simulacra of the human sexual organs mounted on a pole. As he capered around, he kept inciting all the onlookers to lustful practices by means of songs, mimic gestures and shameless speeches. Those who held respectable matrimony in honour were affronted by so scandalous a performance, though they showed respect to him as a parson because of the dignity of his position. If anyone, from kindly motives took him to task, he became worse and assailed them with insults.[4]

John the priest was obviously a crank or an eccentric and this story is merely a prelude to one that tells how later in the year he met his death, which the writer of the chronicle regards as divine retribution. During Penance Week, when his parishioners were assembled in the church at dawn for the usual penitential service, he insisted that some of them should strip while others pricked them with goads on the bare flesh. Inverkeithing was a royal burgh of some importance and a favourite resort in the previous century of King David I who had a house there. The burgesses resented their priest's methods of penance and he was knifed that same night. Inverkeithing seems to have been the site of one of the last struggles of the Culdees or Keledei, those mysterious relics of the old Celtic church whose communities at Lochleven and St Andrews had been put down by David I. Another community at Inverkeithing was said to have been suppressed by a decree of Alexander III in 1250.[5] The Keledei were reputed to have become degenerate at the end of their existence but this may be a rumour due to the bitter hostility of the Roman clergy. At any rate it is possible that the chronicler's story of the eccentric parish priest has some malice behind it and is intended to illustrate the unorthodox practices which the influence of these hermit communities could be expected to produce.

Various interpretations have been placed on the festivities at Inverkeithing, including the idea that they represent an early instance of celebration of the witch cult or the revival or reappearance of the primitive worship of a phallic god. The first is unlikely, the second possible since the ancient Celts certainly had such deities as well as their female counterparts. But had it been an actual image of a pagan god that the girls danced around at the command of a Christian priest, we would have expected the church to take some action. The event seems to have been widely known, but there is no hint that the priest was reproved or punished. The scandal seems to have been less at the festivities themselves than at the priest's organising, leading, and directing them. Easter week in 1282 would have been from 29 March to 5 April, old style, which is too early for Beltane in a general way. But the week after Easter, as the end of the Lenten fast, was a period of general festivity which appears to have taken much the same form on high days right through the summer season. Easter, of course, often fell much closer to May Day. As late as 1625, for instance, five men and a piper, according to the records of the presbytery of Lanark, were condemned as profaners of the Sabbath for fetching home a maypole and dancing about it on Pasche [Easter] Sunday which in that year fell on 19 April. William Kennedy in his *Annals of Aberdeen* (1818) notes that the first Sunday in May and the first Tuesday after Pasche were the ordinary days set aside for the ancient games, farces, and plays of the season which included, in Dunbar's day, the plays of Robin Hood and his men, the Maypole, the revels of the lords of Misrule and so on,[6] afterwards banned by the Reformers. But the main reason for thinking that *The Chronicle of Lanercost* is describing Beltane rites is that they are so similar. Clearly Pater Liber, an ancient Italian fertility god whose name was sometimes applied to Bacchus, and Priapus the ancient Italian garden god with his well-known phallic attributes, were not worshipped by the inhabitants of Fife in the thirteenth century! Both names are probably used by the monkish chronicler to express the nature of the emblem displayed and his abhorrence of the maypole, crowned as it originally was with the representation of a phallus. The songs, the obscene mimicry, and the coarse language were probably just as traditional as the dance round the maypole effigy. In May 1591, the Kirk Session of Perth took action against 'filthy and ungodly singing about the Mayis',[7] and such songs continued to be the despair of the godly not only at fairs and bridals but at wakes and funerals for the next two centuries. There is no doubt either that the incitement to general sexual licence did not stop at that. We have already noted that the May Day processions to the Dragon Hole at Perth in 1580 were 'not without suspicion of filthiness after to follow', and 'superstitious games', that is to say the usual May Day sports and revels were celebrated there by the young men and women of the city. The Records of Elgin contain more than one attempt in the sixteenth century to stop nocturnal misbehaviour in the Spynnie Wood on the Eve of May Day,[8] and the results of such jollifications are probably represented by an extract from the *Records of the Parish of Auchterhouse*, Angus,

> On Sunday, the 25th of May, 1645, Andrew Smith confeste that he had carnal copulation with Jein Mores. Sicklich Jo. Williamsonne confessed, that he had adoe with Elspit Low; therefore thay are ordained to mak their repentance the Sabbath following.[9]

The characters of Robin Hood and Little John adopted by two of the citizens on these occasions were not merely disguises for plays and sports, but, in many cases, were appointments by the municipal authorities to try to restrain the excesses of the festivals. There are several records of prominent citizens begging to be excused owing to the expense and the impossibility of keeping control of the holiday crowd. When the 'disguisings' were abolished by the Reformers they found themselves equally unable to restrain drinking, sexual licence, and fighting. A magnificent picture of what such an occasion was like in the fifteenth century is presented by 'Peblis to the Play', a poem attributed to James I but probably nearer in time to Dunbar's day.

> At beltane quhen ilk bodie bownis
> To peblis to the play
> To heir the singin and the soundis

> The solace suth to say
> Be firth and forrest furth thay found
> Thay graythhit thame full gay.

This was the time of the great Beltane Fair at Peebles, twenty-three miles from Edinburgh, to which crowds of people came from the neighbouring countryside.

May Day in Scotland seems to have been primarily a women's festival. The account of *The Chronicle of Lanercost* mentions the young women assembling outside the town and in 'Peblis to the Play' it is the women who begin the festivities: they are pictured in the most homely way getting up early in the morning and ironing their head-dresses amid a great hubbub of chatter and jokes:

> All the wenchis of the west
> war vp or the cok crew
> ffor reilling thair micht na man rest
> ffor garray and for glew
> An[e] said my curches ar nocht prest
> Than ansuerit Meg full blew
> To get ane hude I hald it best
> be goddis saull that is trew (quod scho)
> of peblis to the play.[10]

It would seem that the men are still trying to get some sleep in all this uproar. But some husbands are up. In the next stanza the excited young wife choosing the hood suggested by her friend hears her husband exclaim:

> Quod he thy bak sall beir ane bend

to which she replies

> In fayth quod scho we meit nocht

which seems to sum up the proceedings. He expects her to be laid on the grass by a lover and she replies that it is none of his business. On this day it is everyone for himself or herself. In the next couple of stanzas she is unable to eat for excitement and then bursts into tears because, she says, she is too sunburnt to approach the men:

171

> I dar nocht cum among na ging
> I am so ewill sone brint
> amang yon merchandis my erandis do
> Marie I sall anis mynt
> Stand of far and keik thaim to
> as I at hame wes wont.

Now the young men set out, leave the town, and start across the moor to the wood. They are dressed in their best and armed and one of them livelier than the rest

> Said mirrie maidinis think nocht lang
> The wedder is fair and smolt
> He cleikit vp ane hie ruf sang
> 'Thair fure ane man to the holt.'

Before they have gone half the way the maidens come upon them and each man gives his idea as to how to split up into couples. After some discussion they do so. There seems little doubt from the young men's comments as to how the coupling will end. The rest of the poem recounts in an equally spirited way how they all trooped back to the tavern, got drunk, quarrelled, and the whole affair ended, as it usually did, in a riotous fight in which some who resorted to their weapons were thereupon put in the stocks. Dancing followed outside the town and the girls began to go into action. Thisbe took Will Young by the hand and walked off with a broad invitation which brought guffaws from the men:

> Than tisbe tuik him by the hand
> wes new cuming fra the hekill
> Allace quod scho quhat sall I do
> And our doure hes na stekill
> And scho to ga as hir taill brynt
> And all the cairlis to kekill

It is easy to see why the Reformed church felt it had to suppress these festivals but depressing to read the account of Peebles given some two centuries later by its minister, the Reverend Dr William Dalgliesh:

The people are regular in their attendance on the institutions of religion, sober, peaceable and virtuous . . . In the way in which holidays of human institution are now observed in Europe, it is of advantage to industry, to virtue and to religion itself that we have so few of them in Scotland. . . . Our holidays are mostly observed with the same religious sanctity as the Sabbath.[11]

Fortunately for Scotland the church militant was not everywhere so triumphant. The maypoles continued to be set up even in Edinburgh itself. Alexander Scott in the mid-sixteenth century in his poem on May speaks of the women's games:

> In May gois dammosalis and dammis
> In gardyngis grene to play lyk lammis
> Sum at the bairis they brace lyk billeis
> Sum rynnis at barlabreikis lyk rammis
> Sum round abowt the standand pilleis.[12]

Prisoners' Bars and Barley-break are two running and capture games still played by children, the third game may be a sort of tig played round a post or pillar but is more likely to be a dance round a may-pole under an ambiguous name referring to its original phallic emblem. In Dunbar's poem 'Of a Dance in the Quenis Chalmer', he describes his own part in the dancing:

> And thair he dancet the dirrye dantoun;
> He hoppet lyk a pillie wanton,
> For luff of Musgraeffe, men tellis me;

The editor professes not to know what a 'pillie wanton' may be, but the sense is perfectly clear from Robert Burns's poem, 'Here's his Health in Water':

> He follow'd me baith out an' in,
> Thro' a' the nooks o' Killie;
> He follow'd me baith out an' in,
> Wi' a stiff stanin' pillie.
> But when he gat atween my legs,
> We made an unco' splatter;
> An' haith, I trow, I soupled it,
> Tho' bauldly he did blatter;[13]

Wright's *Dialect Dictionary* gives the word as current in the northern counties of England and in Scotland with the forms *pill*, *pillick*, *pilluck*, *pillie*, and *pilly* and the meaning: 'the male organ, the penis'. Maypoles were banned in 1561 on pain of death, but appeared again in Edinburgh in 1621 when

> Manie of the profainer sort of the town were drawn out upon the sixt of May [the old May Day] to May games in Gilmerton and Rosseline; so profanitie began to accompany superstition and idolatrie, as it hath in former times. Upon the first of May the weevers of St. Paul's Worke, Englische and Dutche, set up a highe May pole, with their garlants and bells hanging at them, whereat was a great concurse of people.[14]

The 'profainer sort' were still at it in the nineteenth century when Arthur's Seat was their favourite resort for May Day revels. A letter dated in April 1826 describes the beginning of the concourse of people about four o'clock in the morning moving through King's Park to Arthur's Seat till the whole hill was a moving mass of people. The maypole was set up at the summit and the craftsmen were dancing around it while vendors of whisky moved about among the crowd and the ground was littered with the bodies of the dead drunk. An accompanying illustration shows as wild and drunken a scene as any in fifteenth-century Peebles.[15]

Another poem that strengthens this impression of the Scottish Beltane ceremonies occurs in the same manuscript collection as Dunbar's poem and is probably roughly contemporary with it. It is ascribed to a poet called Clapperton about whom nothing else is known, and its setting is at Bowden in Roxburghshire, about twenty miles from Peebles. The occasion is Black Monday, that is Monday in Easter week when festivities like those of Beltane were celebrated.

> In bowdoun, on blak monunday
> Quhen all was gadderit to the play
> Baith men and women semblit thair
> I hard ane sweit ane sicht and say
> Way worth maryage for evirmair

The 'sweet one' complaining is a young woman whose plight is comparable to that of Dunbar's first wife. She is married to an elderly husband who is incapable of 'Venus' works':

> Thus am I thirlit on to ane schrew
> quhilk dow nothing of chalmer glew
> Off bowre bourding bayth bask and bair

and who stops her going to the festivals. If she could be rid of him, she says, she would never marry again and would give herself up to entertaining lovers promiscuously:

> Luffairis bayth suld heir and se
> I suld luif thame that wald luif me
> Thair hartis for me suld never be sair
> Bot ay vnweddit suld I be
> Way wourth maryage for evirmair[16]

The point of the poem is that she had formerly expected to enjoy these freedoms at the Easter week festivals from which her niggardly husband has excluded her.

Both the first wife and the widow mention pilgrimages as likely occasions for picking up new lovers and this was a common cause of complaint in the Middle Ages, as the proverbial rhyme quoted by the Wife of Bath suggests:

> Whoso that buildeth his hous al of salwes,
> And priketh his blinde hors ouer the falwes
> Aud suffreth his wyf to go seken halwes
> Is worthy to been hanged on the galwes.
> (ll. 655-8)

One of the most famous pilgrimages in Scotland was that to the Chapel and Hermitage of Lareit, Our Lady of Loretto, in Mussel-burgh, five miles from Edinburgh. Alexander Scott in the poem already quoted refers to it in terms which suggest that the pilgrimage was anything but religious:

> In May gois madynis till Lareit,
> And hes thair mynyonis on the streit,
> To horss thame quhair the gait is ruch:
> Sum at Inche-bukling bray they meit,
> Sum in the middis of Mussilburch

In fact it had a bad reputation and Sir David Lindsay of the Mount in his 'Dialog Betuix Experience and ane Courteour', attacking the laxity of the Catholic Church in moral matters, records what he had observed before the shrine was destroyed by the Earl of Hertford in 1543. The pilgrimage was finally suppressed by the Reformers in 1590: Lindsay wrote the work about the middle of the sixteenth century:

> I have sene pass one mervellous multytude,
>> Yong men and wemen, flyngand on thare feit,
> Under the forme of feynit sanctytude,
>> For till adore one image in Loreit,
>> Mony came with thare marrowis for to meit
> Committand thare fowll fornicatioun:
>> Sum kyst the claggit taill of the Armeit
> Quhy thole ye this abominatioun?

After some attack on idolatry, especially the supposed miracles worked by the hermit, he goes on:

> Ye maryit men, that hes trym wantoun wyffis,
>> And lustie dochteris of young tender aige,
> Quhose honestie ye suld lufe as your lyffis,
>> Permyt thame nocht to passe on pylgramage,
>> To seik support at ony stok Image:
> For I have wyttin gud wemen passe fra hame,
>> Quhilk hes bene trappit with sic lustis rage,
> Hes done returne boith with gret syn and schame[17]

Lindsay is obviously piling it on. There were other aspects of the Chapel of our Lady and there were genuine pilgrimages, but there is no reason to doubt that the pilgrimage in May was marked by riot and sexual promiscuity and that as he says

> Sic pylgramage heth maid mony one hure,
> Quhilk, gyf I plesit, planelye I mycht preve.

Nor is there any reason to think that things were any different in Dunbar's time half a century earlier.

It would not be surprising to find that the Midsummer festival had the same character as that of Beltane, since they were really two parts of the same summer celebrations. As early as the twelfth century Belethus, a monk who died in 1162, explains the fires on St John's Eve by the fact that bones then are burnt to drive away dragons which at this season are abroad in earth, air, and water and spread incitement to lust. While another monk at Winchelscombe, after quoting Belethus in a sermon, observes of St John's Eve:

> This vigil ought to be held with cheerfulness and piety, but not with such merriment as is shown by the profane lovers of this world, who make great fires in the streets, and indulge themselves with filthy and unlawful games, to which they add gluttony and drunkenness, and the commission of many other shameful indecencies.[18]

It is clear that in the Middle Ages at any rate the 'mirriest of nichtis' tended to follow the pattern of Beltane. In 1601 the Kirk Session Records of Perth, on a certain Janet Syme confessing 'her sin of fornication committed with John Barrie, a cripple, at Midsummer last', made strict inquiry as to whether 'any other had carnal dealing with her'. Obviously they expected this to be the case on such an occasion.[19]

It was not a character of the Midsummer festival confined to Scotland. The wakes held at holy wells by young men and women in England as well as in Scotland at this time of the year were apt to end in the same manner. There are numerous accounts of debauchery, drunkenness, fighting, and fornication at midsummer gatherings round sacred wells in Ireland such as St Ronogue's Well near Cork and St Patrick's Wells at Struell, County Down.[20] At the latter, the wells were supposed to overflow miraculously at midnight on Midsummer Eve and an observer in 1836 noted that the sexes bathed naked and promiscuously in the wells and that after the ceremonies the pilgrims went to their tents in the nearby fields for a revel; it was generally understood that as long as they remained on the sacred site they could not contract new guilt after their purification.[21] A charming anonymous English ballad of the fifteenth century gives an impression of the way things were expected to go on Midsummer Eve. The young girl is recounting her frolic:

> Ladd Y the daunce a Myssomer Day;
> Y made smale trippus, soth for to say.

Jak, oure haly-water clerk com be the way
And he lokede me upon; he thout hit was gay
    Thout yc on no gyle.

Jak, our haly-water clerk, the yong strippelyng,
For the chesone of me he com to the ryng
And he trippede on my to and made a twynkelyng;
Euer he cam ner; he sparet for no thynge.
    Thout Y on no gyle.

Jack after flattering her and promising her a pair of gloves, arranges to meet her after evensong and invites her to go to his chamber to get the gloves. Still thinking no guile she goes and all follows as one might expect:

Schetus and chalonis, ic wot, were yspredde;
Foresothe tho Jak and y wenten to bedde;
He prikede, and he pransede; nolde he neuer lynne;
Yt was the murgust nyt that euer Y came ynne.
    Thout Y on no gyle.

Wan Jak had don, tho he rong the bell;
Al nyght ther he made me to dwelle.
Of y trewe we haddun yserved the reaggeth deuel of helle;
Of othur smale burdus, kep Y nout to telle
    Thout Y on no gyle

That Monday at prime Y com home, as ic wene;
Meth Y my dame, coppud and kene:
'Sey, thou stronge strumpeth, ware hastu bene?
Thy trippyng and thy dauncyng, wel it wel be sene.

As indeed it was.[22] It is a pity this little piece is not better known.

Beltane, Midsummer, and Lammas, because of the warmer weather, naturally gave more opportunities to the licentious and the cheerful who thought no guile, but Kirk Session and Burgh Records in Scotland show much the same concern over riotous and immoral behaviour at all the great fixed festivals. In between these were numerous occasions of revel and celebration to which we must now turn.

11

The Ball o' Kirriemuir

THE markets and the great annual fairs of Scotland were equally occasions of licence of the sort associated with the fixed festivals just discussed. Many of these fairs were of great antiquity. Some of their charters and grants go back as far as the twelfth and thirteenth centuries, but the assemblies themselves were probably often very much older and possibly as old as the fixed festivals of Beltane, Midsummer, and Samain at which some were held. Ancient Midsummer fairs were held at Ayr, Cullen in Banffshire, Clatt in Aberdeenshire, and Dumbarton, among others. The numbers of persons attending them were often enormous. As many as five to ten thousand visitors are reported in the eighteenth century or earlier, and the festivities and sports as well as the sale of cattle and merchandise sometimes went on day and night for a week or a fortnight. They were often held outside the town or city with which they were associated, on open ground which, as we have seen, was in many cases associated with a fairy mound or some other sacred site of pagan times. Some, like the great June fair at Largs in Ayrshire, known as Comb's or Cosme's Fair (St Columba's Fair), were occasions of general mixing of the people of the Highlands and the Lowlands. Largs, on the coast facing the island of Bute, is well placed for such meetings of populations which at other times were usually actively hostile to one another. A report of the fair in 1794 calls it a Midsummer Fair. As it appears to have begun on the second Tuesday in June it probably continued to and took in the Midsummer festivities. The account continues:

It might be called a congress between the Highlands and the Lowlands; and occasioned a vast concourse of people, for some days. The spectacle of boats from all quarters, the crowds of people, the sound of music; ashore, dancing and hilarity day and night on the green; and further up, a new street, or town, formed of the stands of the merchants formed an amusing spectacle. Of late this congress has decreased much; because there are many shops now through the Highlands and travelling chapmen frequent almost every part of that country. However there is still a respectable concourse of rustic beaux and belles, from east and west, by land and sea.[1]

Another account two years later adds the information that Largs had two moats or mounds of earth called the Law Hills one at each end of the village and it was here that the fair was presumably held. After speaking of the crowds the Friend to Statistical Enquiries, who considered the minister's account just quoted as defective, remarks:

Such a vast multitude cannot be accommodated with beds; and the Highlanders in particular, do not seem to think such accommodation necessary. They spend the whole night in rustic sports, carousing and dancing on the green to the sounds of the bagpipe . . . The candidates for the dance are generally so numerous that it is kept up without intermission during the whole of the fair.[2]

The state of sexual morals in the Highlands at that time leaves little doubt of the other activities pursued under the stars at Comb's Fair. At Inverkeithing, where the priest led the Maypole dances three and a half centuries earlier, the Lammas Fair was described in 1652 as a day for 'fun, frolic, fit races, ale and drunken foks, gentle and simple and folks came frae near and far to it'.[3] At Ecclesgreig, Kincardine, the Reverend William Walker remarked of the annual hiring fairs:

One of these markets for hiring servants is held on the Hill of Garvock, and the other at Laurencekirk. The congress of masters and servants, at these places is very numerous, and, almost in every point of description resembles the SATURNALIA of the ancient Romans.[4]

Robert Burns writing a verse epistle to John Lapraik of Dalquhram in 1773 refers to his own part in these revels at the fairs:

> There's ae wee faut they whiles lay to me,
> I like the lasses—Gude forgie me!
> For monie a plack they wheedle frae me
>   At dance or fair;
> Maybe some ither thing they gie me
> They weel can spare.
>
> But Muchline Race or Mauchline Fair,
> I should be proud to meet you there; . . .[5]

Burns's history at Mossgiel is evidence enough that the Lowland lasses were no less generous with their favours than their Highland counterparts at the time.

It was while he was farming near Mossgiel that Burns wrote his famous description of another type of fair by which the kirk had in past times hoped to draw the godly away from the unseemly revels of the profaner fair assemblies. The 'Holy Fair' at Mauchline was held on the second Sunday in August and great crowds came from the neighbouring farms and villages. Like most of these assemblies the Mauchline 'Holy Fair', as Burns describes it, had degenerated into a mixture of religious observance and disreputable revel. In the church the communion was being administered while a succession of ministers preached from a 'tent' or movable pulpit in the churchyard which was full of people of both sexes eating, sleeping, listening, talking, cursing, falling into religious ecstasy, making love, making assignations, and drinking themselves senseless.[6] The proceedings, like those of the secular fairs, often went on for as much as a week and they were no less an occasion of fornication and promiscuity among the young who often came precisely with this purpose in mind.[7]

> Some swagger hame, the best they dow,
>   Some wait the afternoon.
> At slaps the billies halt a blink,
>   Till lasses strip their shoon:
> Wi' faith an' hope, an' love an' drink,
>   They're a' in famous tune
>   For crack that day.

How monie hearts this day converts,
    O' sinners and o' lasses!
Their hearts o' stane, gin night are gane
    As saft as ony flesh is.
There's some are fou o' love divine,
    There's some are fou o' brandy;
An' monie jobs that day begin,
    May end in Houghmagandie
                Some ither day.

What went on at fairs and festivals was only a public aspect of what went on at more private and occasional celebrations such as wakes and weddings and christenings, harvest and haymaking. As Henry Grey Graham remarks of eighteenth-century Scotland:

All the great domestic events were accompanied by roystering and drinking—at a christening there was much, at a funeral there was more, at a wedding there was most . . . However the Kirk might threaten and punish the people danced defiantly; for to dance 'promisky' [i.e. men and women together] as they called it, was their great delight and lairds and farmers sent money and food and drink to supply the festival. That these scenes were often wild and indecorous was certainly the case.[8]

These entertainments, which were the object of the reforming zeal of the Presbyterians after the Reformation, were clearly customs carried over from the Middle Ages. The 'penny bridal' in particular seems to have drawn the condemnation of the kirk—and with good reason. In 1647 an Act of the Presbyteries of Haddington and Dunbar, following an Act of the General Assembly at Edinburgh two years before, declares:

The brethren and ruling elders of the two presbiteries of Hadingtone and Dunbar . . . finds the number of persones above twentie convened to pennie bridles and the prices exceeding 12s the man and 8s the woman occasiones great lasciviousness and hurt to the poorer sort; as likewise finds that piping and dancing befor and after dinner or supper, and the staying of persones conveened for drinking, the dinner and supper being ended, occasiones great lasciviousness; and moreover that lowse speaches and filthie communication and singing badie songs and prophane minstrelling in time of dinner or supper tends to great deboshrie.[9]

Such efforts seem to have been quite unavailing. The penny bridals continued to be immensely popular down to the end of the eighteenth century when the minister at Monquhitter, Aberdeenshire, described the custom which, he said, was then falling into disuse:

When a pair were contracted, they, for a stipulated consideration, bespoke their wedding dinner at a certain tavern, and then ranged the country in every direction to solicit guests. One, two, and even three hundred would have convened on these occasions, to make merry at their own expense for two or more days. This scene of feasting, drinking, dancing, wooing, fighting &c. was always enjoyed with the highest relish, and, until obliterated by a similar scene furnished ample material for rural mirth and rural scandal.[10]

Another account from Avach, Ross, gives much the same details and mentions that

A barn is allotted for the dancing and the house for drinking. And thus they make merry for two or three days, till Saturday night. On Sabbath, after returning from church the married couple gives a sort of dinner or entertainment to the present friends on both sides.[11]

Hume Brown in his *Early Travellers in Scotland* quotes from Thomas Kirke, *A Modern Account of Scotland by an English Gentleman* (1679). Kirke, though thoroughly biased and hostile to the Scots, seems to have known Scotland well and to have reported facts even if he used them maliciously, as he obviously did. His account of a handfast wedding which was obviously a penny bridal concludes:

however, 'tis this performed, the young couple, being attended with tagrag and bobtail, gang to Kirk. [A parody of the ceremony follows.] Home they go with loud ravishing bag-pipes, and dance about the green, till they part by couples to repetition [rehearsal], and so put the rules into practice . . .[12]

Among the poems collected by Burns, and recently printed in their original form from the only surviving copy of *The Merry Muses of Caledonia* in Lord Rosebery's library, is a description of such a wedding, certainly not hostile to Scotland and confirming Kirke's observations a century and a quarter earlier. This is the song 'Blyth Will an' Bessie's Wedding'. After the two opening stanzas describing the circumstances of the wedding, the song proceeds to the behaviour of the guests at what was again obviously a penny bridal:

> [Tam]mie Tamson too was there,
>   Maggie Birnie was his dearie,
> He pat it in amang the hair,
>   An' puddled there till he was weary.
>
> When e'enin' cam the town was thrang,
>   An' beds were no to get for siller;
> When e'er they fand a want o' room,
>   They lay in pairs like bread an' butter.
>
> Twa an' twa they made the bed,
>   An' twa an' twa they lay the gither;
> When they had na room enough,
>   Ilk ane lap on aboon the tither.[13]

A poem in Allan Ramsay's *Tea Table Miscellany* (1724) records a similar instance of customary—and no doubt at one time ritual—fornication among the guests at such weddings. This is the well-known 'Polwart on the Green'. We have already met the village of Polwarth in Berwickshire, in connection with Alexander Montgomerie's flyting with Sir Patrick Hume of Polwarth in the sixteenth century. As this poem apparently mentions the famous thorn tree of Polwarth, the poem cited by Ramsay may be older than it appears or at least may rest on an old tradition. The local tradition about the thorn trees in the middle of the village green at Polwarth at the end of the eighteenth century was as follows:

> In the middle of the village there are two *thorn trees* at about six yards distance from each other, around which, it was formerly the customs, for every new married pair, with their company, to dance in a ring; from hence the song of *Polwarth on the Green*. But this custom has fallen much into disuse, there not having been above 2 instances of it these 20 years.[14]

Robert Chalmers in 1800 noted that there were by then three thorns replacing an aged thorn tree, blown down several years before after surviving for centuries, so that it was probably the same fairy thorn mentioned by Montgomerie.

The poem itself appears to refer to one of these popular wedding celebrations lasting two or three days and involving such a crowd of visitors that there were not beds enough to be found for them in the village. The time is the hay-making, that is June, the popular month for weddings, many of which were no doubt necessary after the celebrations in May which was deemed an unlucky month for marriage. The speaker in the poem is a young woman inviting her lover to share her bed after the day's revels:

> At Polwart on the Green
>   If you'll meet me the morn,
> Where lasses do convene
>   To dance about the thorn,
> A kindly welcome you shall meet
>   Frae her wha likes to view
> A lover and a lad complete,
>   The lad and lover you.
>
> Let dorty dames say *Na*,
>   As lang as e'er they please,
> Seem caulder than the sna'
>   While inwardly they bleeze;
> But I will frankly shaw my mind,
>   And yield my heart to thee;
> Be ever to the captive kind,
>   That langs na to be free.
>
> At Polwart on the green
>   Amang the new-mawn hay
> With sangs and dancing keen
>   We'll pass the heartsome day.
> At night, if beds be o'er thrang laid,
>   And thou be twined of thine,
> Thou shalt be welcome, my dear lad,
>   To take a part of mine.[15]

As the minister of Monquhitter noted, the tendency to regard certain months as propitious for marriage meant that during two or three months of the year the penny bridals and their licentious accompaniments must have been an almost continuous orgy.

Funerals were almost as riotous occasions as weddings. In 1675 the Synod of Moray, the Lord Bishop, and the brethren were deeply disturbed by 'the heathenish customs practised at lyke wakes'; they mention the dancing in which the family of the deceased were supposed to take part, the excessive drunkenness, the 'bawdrie songs' and the 'lascivious exercises', the 'guising' and 'gaming' customary on such occasions. Another account in the eighteenth century describes the dancing and revels in which even the widow was expected to join and says that the custom had once been universal in Scotland. The Kirk Session at Elgin in 1621 tried to forbid 'singing bawdrie songs nor na lewd fassones' at wakes. Other references to the same customs are frequent from the sixteenth to the eighteenth centuries.[16]

The end of the harvest was another occasion for revels. The celebration, as we have seen, must originally have had a religious purpose connected with the corn spirits known in various places as the Maiden, the Cailleach or Old Wife, the Bride, the Corn-Baby and so on. Their purpose was to ensure the fertility of crops and stock for the following year, and ritual sexual promiscuity is a feature of such celebrations in various parts of the world. Some of the Scottish harvest customs suggest that they too must at one time have been occasions of this sort of licence and that, as an actual person was chosen each year to be the personified May Queen, so someone became the Maiden or the Cailleach at each harvest and was actually 'married' to the farmer or the reaper who cut the last sheaf. It has been pointed out that, as women were the original cultivators, these are predominantly women's ceremonies and are designed to propitiate and placate the female spirits or deities who preside over the growth and yield of the crops. On such occasions women naturally took the initiative in sexual advances. In a number of places in Fifeshire and elsewhere there are variants of a practice by which a stranger passing or entering a harvest field would be set on and tumbled by the women. The same custom in other parts of Europe show that originally he would have been bound up in a sheaf and so become the harvest bridegroom who would be mated with the Harvest Queen or the Maiden.[17] In one description if a man entered the field during the harvesting

> before he knew where he was, he was seized by two or three females and laid on his back. Then one of them held him down and laid herself flat on the person, and another female tumbled over the two as they lay. This was called Kipping and the man after he was allowed to get up, was expected to give a small sum of money by way of providing some refreshment.[18]

In other places newly engaged harvest hands were treated in a similar way. The last handful of grain reaped in Berwickshire was as elsewhere known as the Maiden and the favoured girl who cut it became the queen of the harvest; no doubt in earlier times she would have been the Maiden personified. In another instance the Maiden was carried on the back of the mistress of the house at the harvest dance held in the barn or granary, and in yet another the man who led off the dance had the Maiden attached to his breast. When such examples are compared with the vast number of recorded variant customs all over Europe, it becomes clear that one feature of the ancient custom was sacred fertility nuptials between the corn goddess and her human devotees. It would not be surprising to find that the worshippers followed suit in unions which were originally designed to promote and support the fertility of the next season's produce.

The natural time for this would be the feast and dance that followed the getting in of the harvest at which the maiden ceased to be a maiden and became the fruitful wife, whether in effigy or in person. Such dances were usually held in the barn or granary of the farm. The farmer and his friends would attend part of the entertainment and would then retire and the shearers (reapers) would keep up the festivities till the following morning.[19]

What these festivities often involved is illustrated by the well-known and very popular obscene ballad, 'The Ball o' Kirriemuir'. According to James Barke, this had its origin in an actual incident near Kirriemuir, a small town in Angus:

This ballad-song developed from a twenty-verse work celebrating an actual event . . . Some thirty ears ago [*c.* 1930] a local historian, in the Kirriemuir district, gave me this story of its origin. Around the 1880s a barn dance (harvest home or Kirn dance) was held in the barn of a neighbouring farm. On this occasion the young fellows gathered rose hips and removed the tiny yellow hirsute seeds. These were scattered on the earthen floor of the barn. The girls danced barefooted. Female drawers were not in general use but, where worn, were of the open crotch or 'free trade' pattern. In the stour of the dance the small hip seeds lodged around the pudendal hair and set up a pubic and vaginal itch. In other words they constituted a powerful external aphrodisiac. In addition to this, some wag had added a modicum of Spanish fly to the punch bowl. A final touch was the placing of a divot, or sod of grass, in the well of the hanging kerosene lamp. This shortened the life of the illumination to coincide roughly with the time the internal and external aphrodisiacs became effective.

The upshot was an orgy of major proportions and it was this orgy that was celebrated in the original Ball o' Kirriemuir.[20]

I have not been able to discover which were the original twenty stanzas. They have now been overlaid by an enormous number of added stanzas; but by comparing a number of versions and rejecting all items which in language or reference are obviously later than the last century, a fair idea of the original can be formed. And at once there appears a discrepancy between the song and the account just quoted. I do not question that events at Kirriemuir in the 1880s were much as described. Indeed I heard of a similar prank by two young men of another Scottish village, from one of the perpetrators. It happened in the 1920s and one consequence was that the two lads in question left Scotland and emigrated to Australia. What happened at Kirriemuir seems to have been a harvest ball that got a little more out of hand than usual rather than an exceptional orgy. But the song appears to celebrate an older and more traditional set of events. It is a satirical poem describing a ball attended by all the locals including, rather improbably, the parson and his family. There is no contrivance, the company meets in *expectation* of a Saturnalia. The lights do not go out, and the dancing and the fornication go on continuously and simultaneously both in the 'ball-room' and in the neighbouring fields, interspersed with festive obscenities, songs and games, such as we know occurred at fairs and wakes and penny bridals. Nearly all versions now begin with the entrance of four and twenty prostitutes who are out of place in this rural scene. It seems to me likely that in the original poem, which has plainly been merely roughly adapted to the events at Kirriemuir, the entrance of the 'maidens' of the harvest began the poem. In the ball described by James Barke the débâcle was arranged by the young men, and when the lights went out we are to understand that the men seized the women and indiscriminate copulation took place in the dark. But in the song it is the women who organise, dominate and take the initiative, and the refrain, probably the oldest part of the song, shows them, like Dunbar's ladies, exhausting one man after another and issuing new invitations to those who are fresh or have recovered their vigour for another bout:

> Wi' a fa'll dae it this time,
> Fa'll dae it noo?
> The mon that did it last time
> Canna dae it noo.

It is the women, too, who lead the dancing and who improvise most of the indelicate feats which appear to serve the purpose of interim entertainments to allow the males to recover. Allowing for a great deal of comic exaggeration it probably gives a good enough picture of what a harvest ball was like in former times, after the more respectable had retired to rest.

James Barke's enthusiastic praise of 'The Ball o' Kirremuir' is hardly justified. As verse it is the most incompetent doggerel; its humour is of the clownish variety; its powers of imagination will in no way compare with most of the splendid Scots bawdy in *The Merry Muses of Caledonia*; but it goes to an enchantingly vigorous tune and it has in it what seem to be, in the older portions, a vigour of movement to match the tune, a vigour that recalls that of the widow and her two companions in Dunbar's poem.

But apart from these customary occasions of promiscuity, it is clear that in earlier times the Scots, of the lower classes at any rate, were in fact accustomed to promiscuous intercourse as the flesh or the spirit moved them. Surviving from the Middle Ages there are occasional bits of evidence that the reports of Dio Cassius, Jerome, and others had some foundation. An entry in *The Chronicle of Lanercost* for the year 1277 has a precious piece of local gossip preserved because it tickled the fancy of the monk who kept the record:

I include here, because it is amusing, a certain document to which Robert of Roberstone, a Scots Knight, drew my attention, and in the presence of many witnesses, at my insistence, he claimed that it was quite reliable. There was a nobleman living in Annandale, in the diocese of Glasgow, who had leased a village and its fields to the people who occupied it. And these folk, becoming wanton from good living and lit up after leaving the tavern, used to fornicate promiscuously with one another's wives and daughters. By this practice they used to keep the coffers of the local archdeacon full, since in consequence they were almost constantly on his books. But when the lord of the manor asked for his land-rents, they used to say that they could not pay or to ask for a deferment. As he was a just and kindly man he said to them 'Why should I, seeing that my other tenants pay me their dues without remission? But if the lease is set too high, I could adjust it and if you are not able to meet it, then give it back to me.' Whereupon one of them guffawed and said in bantering tone: 'None of the things you mention, sir, is really the cause, so much as our own incontinence which consumes the goods in which both we and you our overlord abound'. He answered at once: 'This is the rule I now lay down for you: if any of you has connections outside marriage, let him immediately give me back my land.' They were thoroughly alarmed and to prevent the penalty gave up their illicit pleasures, applied themselves to work and husbandry and from penury returned to easy circumstances again, while their names on the Archdeacon's books decreased from day to day. And one day, enquiring why he found no men from this particular hamlet on his list, he was told of the rule the lord of the manor had imposed on them. He was incensed at this, and happening to meet the Knight on the road, he said in a high and mighty way: 'Who, Sir Robert, has made you an Archdeacon or appointed you to clerical office?' When the Knight denied it, he went on 'Well you are behaving as if it were so, insofar as you are forcing your tenants to obey these penal rules of yours.' 'The rule I made,' said the other, 'was in respect of my lands not in respect of the sins involved; but you, in making them redeem themselves for their sins, have consumed the returns from my farms. I see well that as long as you can keep your purse always full, you couldn't care less who gets their souls.' At this the exploiter of crime and lover of transgressions was silent.[21]

This gem of local history appears to have been questioned at first by the chronicler not because there was anything surprising in the behaviour of the villagers but because the archdeacon's blackmail needed verification. It is unlikely that the custom of promiscuous sexual intercourse after leaving the tavern grew up by chance simply as a result of the easy circumstances of the villagers. It fits in too well with earlier and later reports of promiscuity among the lower orders in Scotland. Also in the thirteenth century we find the Diocese of Aberdeen legislating against 'low and indecent pastimes such as provoke to lasciviousness' in churches and churchyards.[22] Aeneas Silvius Piccolomini, later Pope Pius II, who visited Scotland in the early fifteenth century, noted the licence among the common people:

> The men are small of stature and brave, the women white and beautiful and very prone to love. To kiss a woman means less there than to touch her hand in Italy.[23]

Aeneas Silvius complied with the custom of the country and left an illegitimate child in Scotland, where bastardy was lightly regarded. On his return from Scotland he disguised himself as a merchant and travelled by a roundabout route in order to deceive the enemies in England who wished to intercept him.[24] His first night in England is one of the most entertaining passages in his autobiography. The people of Cumberland just across the border were of much the same stock as the Lowland Scots and similar to them in customs, morals, and manners. Somewhere across the Solway Firth, probably not far from Bowness, he was offered hospitality in the house of a farmer. The whole neighbourhood gathered to see the stranger and after supper the men and the children all left saying that they were taking refuge for the night in a tower some way off for fear of the Scots who often raided across the river when it was low at ebb tide. They refused to take Aeneas with them

> although he earnestly besought them, nor yet any of the women, although there were a number of beautiful girls and matrons. For they think

the enemy will do them no wrong—not counting outrage a wrong. So Aeneas remained behind with two servants and his one guide among a hundred women, who made a circle round the fire and sat up all night cleaning hemp and carrying on a lively conversation with the interpreter. But after a good part of the night had passed, two young women showed Aeneas, who by this time was very sleepy, to a chamber strewn with straw, planning to sleep with him, as was the custom of the country, if they were asked. But Aeneas, thinking less about women than about robbers, who he feared might appear any minute, repulsed the protesting girls, afraid that if he committed a sin, he would have to pay the penalty as soon as the robbers arrived.[25]

Aeneas was rewarded for his continence and continued his journey next day after a rather uncomfortable night with the goats and heifers stealing the straw from his bed and a wild alarm in the middle of the night which turned out to be a party of friends, not the wild Scots, though the result as far as the women were concerned was probably much the same. When Aeneas talks about 'the custom of the country' he is probably referring to Scotland where he spent some time rather than England of which he had little experience. When he speaks of the Scottish women being 'easily won' or 'very prone to love', he is most likely speaking of them in much the same terms as those in which he describes the women of Cumberland.

There is evidence that things remained much the same after the Reformation. A 'Lewd Ballet' (1571) preserved in the State Papers Office comments on the fact that the Reformation made little difference to the sexual morals of the ordinary population:

> Bot, seing quhow all erdly thingis wor subject to mutatioun,
> Than fand I it no grett mervall, albeit the congregatioun
> Wor no les than the puir Papistes Inclynit to fornicatioun.[26]

Gardiner in his *History of the Commonwealth and Protectorate* quotes a letter from a soldier in Cromwell's army during the campaign of 1650 in Scotland. It gives an English Puritan's impression of what the Protestant Reformation amounted to with the mass of the people:

I believe the people have as much of proffession, as any people that call themselves Christians . . . It is usual with them to talk religiously and with a great show of piety and devotion for a time, and the very next moment to lie, curse and swear without any manner of bounds or limits . . . for the sins of adultery and fornication, they are as common amongst them as if there were no commandments against either. They call those only broken women that have but six bastards. For the committing of adultery, the Kirk Books of some of the ministers which we have found will show the names of their parishioners who have stood on the stool from time to time, and many have fallen into relapses after they have undergone that punishment.[27]

This impression of a foreigner, who, like his general, Cromwell, was disappointed in the Scottish reform of religion, is amply borne out by the local Scottish records. In spite of an Act of Parliament in 1528 pronouncing the severest penalties for the crime of rape it continued to be treated as trivial offence by the courts. In 1556 harlots were ordered to wear a distinctive dress in Edinburgh and the reason was apparently to distinguish the professionals from the amateurs and to give some protection to honest women, as appears from a minute of the Town Council of Dundee in 1559:

It had been reported to the great defame, slander, and shame of honest men's wives, their daughters, and women servants, that they had been seduced by panders and procurers to use themselves unlawfully in fornication.[28]

Three years later the Town Council of Edinburgh passed a regulation against 'idolators, whore-masters and harlots' which included the penalty of death for the third offence.[29] In 1561 the bailies of Edinburgh tried to banish adulterers. Had they succeeded they would have depopulated their city. In the following year they prepared a hole in the North Loch for dipping or ducking fornicators, but by November of that year the number of fornicators apprehended had risen to such a degree that it was necessary to order the preparation of a special prison for their reception.[30] Yet the records of the seventeenth century show that things were, if anything, worse.

In the Highlands the same practices continued in all ranks of society well into the eighteenth century. The records of the Synod of Argyll in the seventeenth century are even fuller and more despairing in their attempts to stamp out widespread fornication and adultery than in their battle against incest already mentioned. In 1651 they gallantly attempted to bring to book Sir Hector Maclean of Dowart and censured the Presbytery of Kilmore for not acting with vigour against persons of quality. Nothing happened, so the next year they proceeded to excommunicate Sir Hector:

> considering that Hector mcLeane hath falline verie many tymes in fornicatione and adultrie and that he hath made only a mocke of the publick professione of his repentance. . . .[31]

It seems that he also harboured others excommunicated for the same sins. Edward Burt, who appears to have been with General Wade in Scotland in the first half of the eighteenth century and who was an amused, detached, and by no means a hostile observer, noted that in the Highlands girls of the lower class

> if they have no Pretensions to Family (as many of them have, though in Rags), they are vain of being with Child by a Gentleman; and when he makes Love to one of them, she will plead her excuse, in saying he undervalues himself, and that she is a poor Girl not worth his Trouble, or something to that Purpose.
>
> This easy Compliance proceeds chiefly from a kind of Ambition established by Opinion and Custom; for as Gentility is of all things esteemed the most valuable in the Notion of these People, so this kind of Commerce renders the poor plebeian Girl, in some Measure, superior to her former Equals.
>
> From thence forward she becomes proud and they grow envious of her being singled out from among them to receive the Honour of a Gentleman's particular Notice: but otherwise they are generally far from being immodest.[32]

In Dunbar's age neither the nobility nor the church gave much lead by their example to discourage the excesses of the commons. Dunbar's own descriptions of the morals of the court make this perfectly clear, as does Sir David Lindsay's *Ane Satyre of the Thrie Estatis* in the next century. John Major, Dunbar's contemporary, discussing the feast given by Henry II which led to the murder of Becket, turns aside to speak of the Christmas orgies at court among the Britons, and his model is contemporary Scotland as well as England:

the days that follow this sumptuous banqueting they spend in develish dances and lewd songs;—so far do they carry it, that the Kings send for their nobles of the kingdom and their wives. These men show themselves most unwise in thus taking their wives with them to these orgies of the court, for it would better become a chaste matron to stay at home.[33]

Hector Boece describes a parliament held at Perth in 1431 to find measures to check riotous banquets and subsequent orgies among all classes, but specially the noblemen and courtiers. He blames the custom on friends of James I who had been brought up at the English court, but his own history shows that he knew well enough that it was a native custom of the Scottish courts. A speech, attributed to Bishop Wardlaw of St Andrews at this parliament, describes the customs of the upper classes at banquets:

> First rysing be intemperance sik inordinatte lust that may na wayis be dissoluitt fra the samyn, eftir quhilk follis revising [ravishing] and defloracioun of madynnis, matronis and violacion of spousage.[34]

This party sounds just the widow's cup of tea and makes her description of her own entertainment almost a modest and ladylike affair by comparison. Certainly Dunbar's young wives need have had no fear of lack of opportunity when they decided to follow the widow's advice.

As for the church, there seems to be general agreement that in the fifteenth and early sixteenth centuries the morals of many of the clergy were not calculated to deter the laity from promiscuous behaviour. In the thirteenth century the church wrestled unsuccessfully with the problem of parish priests who kept mistresses and concubines. The Aberdeen Synod issued a general ban on these ladies and forbade them to enter churches or enjoy the use of holy water or the kiss of peace 'or any share in the communion of the faithful'. Another statute of the time declares:

> Although the rulers of the church have always sought to drive far away from the homes of churchmen that filthy contagion of lustful naughtiness whereby the good fame of the church is shamefully discredited, yet the vice exists in such wantonness that it always shamelessly introduces itself.[35]

This was indeed the case. The situation was unchanged two centuries later when we find Archbishop Forman of St Andrews ordering priests to put away their wenches or household companions (*focariae*) and concubines (*concubinae*). Alexander Scott, in his New Year gift to Mary, Queen of Scots, in 1561, advises her to take action against the wicked pastors whom their own bishops and public condemnation are powerless to amend or shame

> For wantonness thay wald nocht wed na wyvis,
> Nor yit leif chaste, bot chop and change thair cheir:
> Now, to reforme thair fylthy licherous lyvis
> God gife the grace aganis this guid new yeir.[36]

Scott and Lindsay might be suspected of exaggeration since they were in sympathy with the Reformation, but the records support them; among the higher clergy in the early sixteenth century who legitimised their bastard children (and in many cases married them into the Scottish nobility) were the abbot of Aberbrothock, afterwards an Archbishop of St Andrews, William Stewart, Bishop of Aberdeen, William Chisholme, Bishop of Dumblane, Alexander Stewart, Bishop of Moray, and Patrick Hepburn, Bishop of the same diocese. This last had five bastard sons and two bastard daughters legitimated. As late as the eighteenth century the people at Criech in Fifeshire used to point out a castle that had belonged to Cardinal Beaton, Archbishop of St Andrews, papal legate and Chancellor of Scotland in the sixteenth century. The local legend was that he used to keep 'a little country seraglio' there, where he could relax from the cares of state.[37] Little wonder if the efforts of honest churchmen to reform the parish priests went unregarded! Dunbar's widow gives an instance of the curate of her church who has enjoyed her favours, if he did not actually seduce her in the first place, as she hints:

> I wes apperand to be pert within perfit eild;
> Sa sais the curat of our kirk, that knew me full ying:
> He is our famous to be fals, that fair worthy prelot;
> I sal be laith to let him le, quhill I may luke furth.

> (ll. 305-8)

In illustrating the topic of this chapter I have limited myself to the more entertaining examples, but a great deal more evidence could be brought forward to show that the complete promiscuity desired by the two young wives and practised by the widow was not a fantasy of sex starvation, but was, and continued to be, very much the way a large part of the population of Scotland customarily behaved. It was part of the old Celtic way of life which they had never abandoned. Even Dr Johnson seems to have come under the influence of the prevailing manners during his famous tour of the Hebrides. During their stay at Dunvegan Castle Boswell records one of the most surprising and delightful of Johnson's observations:

> After the ladies were gone from the table, we talked of the Highlanders not having sheets; and this led us to consider the advantage of wearing linen—JOHNSON, 'All animal substances are less cleanly than vegetables. . . I have often thought, that, if I kept a seraglio; the ladies should all wear linen gowns,—or cotton;—I mean stuff made of vegetable substances'. . . To hear the grave Dr Samuel Johnson, 'that majestick teacher of moral and religious wisdom', while sitting solemn in an arm-chair in the Isle of Sky, talk *ex cathedra*, of his keeping a seraglio, and acknowledge that the supposition had *often* been in his thoughts struck me so forcibly, with ludicrous contrast, that I could not but laugh immoderately.[38]

Which was unfortunate for Boswell. Johnson withdrew himself from dreams of promiscuous bliss, resumed the majestick mantle of moral and religious wisdom and savaged his disciple in the accustomed manner.

12

The Thing That Women Most Desire

In the delightful tale told by Chaucer's Wife of Bath, a young knight at Arthur's court is sent out by the queen, on peril of his life, to find the answer to the question:

> What thyng is it that wommen moost desiren?

He learns the answer from a woman who, in spite of the Christian curtain lecture she reads him in the end, is really one of the fays of romance. He first encounters her in the form of a hideous old crone in a forest glade where he has surprised a company of fairy ladies at their customary ring dance. Later, after she has saved his life and demanded him in marriage, she obtains his entire submission to her will and changes into a ravishing young woman and a charming wife. The answer she teaches him is precisely the one Dunbar's ladies would have given to the same question, and the narrator says that there was no woman in Arthur's court who dissented from it:

> 'My lige lady, generally,' quod he,
> Wommen desyren to have sovereynetee
> As wel over hir housbond as hir love,
> And for to been in maistrie him above.
>
> (ll. 1037-40)

This was a sentiment which medieval satirists and moralists alike readily attributed to the female sex. In the later Middle Ages the elaborate *Frauendienst* involved in the game of Courtly Love may have given some colour to the view; but in fact this was little more than a courtly and literary game. In the real world no one was in any doubt: women were to be kept in their place and that place was an inferior one as custom, church, and law all agreed. St Paul had laid it down that 'the husband is the head of the wife even as Christ is the head of the church'. Eve, as Chaucer's parson points out (l. 330) typifies the flesh as Adam typifies the spirit and therefore Adam's was a double sin in disobeying God and in subverting the order of nature by allowing the inferior nature to overmaster the higher, desire to supplant and direct rational judgment. Dunbar and his contemporaries would have agreed with the reformer John Knox a generation later when he declared, in *The First Blast of the Trumpet against the Monstrous Regiment of Women* (1558), that:

> To promote a Woman to bear rule, superiority, dominion, or empire above any realm, nation, or city is repugnant to nature, contumely to God, a thing most contrarious to his revealed will and ordinance, and finally, the subversion of good order, and of all equity and justice.[1]

God, of course, the only ruler of princes, might himself approve a female ruler who came to the throne by divine right, even though it was impious for men to take it on themselves to 'promote' a woman to such an office. But below the throne the rule held of women generally. God's will and Nature's order demanded their subjection. Knox later got into difficulties with the Protestant queen of England and with his own Mary, Queen of Scots, and tried to argue that the words just quoted applied only to 'that wicked Jezebel of England', Mary Tudor.

> 'But,' said the Queen of Scots, with her sharp intelligence 'ye speak of women in general.'

Knox, who tells the story, was forced to admit it:

> 'Most true it is, Madam, (said the other), and yet it appeareth to me that wisdom should persuade your Grace never to raise trouble for that which to this day hath not troubled your majesty.'[2]

This advice from the great reformer is oddly similar to that which the widow gives to her rebellious companions: accept things as they are and make the best use of them, rather than try to change the established order. Mary would have done well to follow Knox's advice, for her problem was essentially one of preserving her authority, and the problem of Dunbar's ladies is similar: how to preserve a power already in their possession but threatened by church and state, rather than that of establishing a new order of things and claiming rights and privileges previously unknown. In the Celtic regions and in Ireland, Wales, and Scotland in particular, in this as in other respects, customs, beliefs, and manners had survived down to Dunbar's day which were at variance with the established attitudes of the church, the secular and the canon law, and the habits of feudal society. Nevertheless, if they existed, they did so on sufferance, and all the forces of society were organised to diminish them. In one respect at least the proposals of Dunbar's three ladies are typical of most revolts of oppressed or underprivileged populations: they want not reform but reversal of the *status quo.* Their schemes show no belief in the equality of the sexes; there is no concept of freedom of the person, no thirst for natural justice behind their revolt. They wish to have the mastery in the fullest sense, to rule the male sex, to use them for their own ends, discard them when they are no longer of any use, and if possible to humiliate them as well in order to demonstrate the omnipotence of female power. The widow's treatment of her second husband after she had got control of his business and his wealth is the clearest possible expression of this intransigence:

> Quhen I the cure had all clene and him ourcummyn haill,
> I crew abone that craudone, as cok that wer victour;
> Quhen I him saw subject and sett at myn bydding,
> Than I him lichtlyit as a lowne and lathit his maneris.
> Than wox I sa unmerciable to martir him I thought,
> For a best I broddit him to all boyis laubour:
> I wald have ridden him to Rome with raip in his heid,
> Wer not ruffill of my renoune and rumour of pepill.
>
> .   .   .   .   .
>
> I maid that wif carll to werk all womenis werkis,
> And laid all manly materis and mensk in this eird.
> Than said I to my cumaris in counsall about,
> 'Se how I cabeld yone cout with a kene brydill!

The cappill, that the crelis kest in the caf mydding,
Sa curtasly the cart drawis, and kennis na plungeing
He is nought skeich, na yit sker, na scippis nought one syd:'
And thus the scorne and the scaith scapit he nothir.

(ll. 325-32, 351-8)

But if their dream is one of absolute domination and of retribution on their oppressors, it is one which only increases a power and independence that women seem already to have enjoyed at the time. The Spanish envoy to the court of James IV, Don Pedro de Ayala, in 1498 thought it worth while to comment on this, no doubt comparing them with his countrywomen in Spain, who themselves enjoyed a considerable amount of independence:

> I mention this because they are really very honest, though very bold. They are absolute mistresses of their houses, and even of their husbands, in all things concerning the administration of their property, income as well as expenditure. They are very graceful and handsome women. They dress much better than here [England], and especially as regards the head-dress, which is, I think, the handsomest in the world.[3]

Except for their honesty, about which Dunbar had other and, as we have seen, possibly better informed views than Ayala's, this is a company to which the widow belongs and her two young companions will belong to it as soon as they have learned the lesson she teaches. Dunbar is not describing an exceptional case of female enterprise and depravity, but satirising what he regards as a general characteristic of the Scottish women of the day—a characteristic which as a churchman he must have regarded as a subversion of the natural order and the will of God. Yet it is a state of affairs which he treats with amusement rather than with the denunciation of a stern moralist. When he asks his 'auditors most honourable' at the end of the poem which of the three they would choose as a wife if they had to pick one, the point of the question does not seem to be: could you imagine yourself choosing any of these monsters at all, or any one in preference to the others? This would seem, in fact, a pointless question to ask. The sting seems to lie in the assumption that if they choose any wives at all, the chances are that this will be their nature and that their views will be those expressed at this Midsummer frolic.

Dunbar's poem 'Of the Ladyis Solistaris at Court' supports Ayala's observation of the power and independence of Scottish women in the management of their husbands, their estates and their affairs, though it gives a different view of their 'honesty' and implies that they were free with their favours:

Thir ladeis fair, That maks repair
And in the courte ar kend
Thre dayis thair, Thai will do mair
Ane mater for to end
Than thair gudmen, will do in ten
ffor ony craift thai can
ffor weill thai ken, Quhat tyme and quhen
Thair meynis thai sould mak than

Withe litill noy, thai can convoy
A mater finalie
yit myld and moy, Thai keip it coy
On ewynnis quyetlie
Thai do no mys, Bot gif thai kyss
And kepis collatioun
Quhat rak of this, The mater is
Brocht to conclusioun

Ye may wit weill, thai haue grit feill
A mater to solist
Traist as the steill, Syne never a deill
Quhone thai cum hame is myst
Thir lairdis ar, me think rycht far
Sic ladeis behaldin to
That sa weill dar, Go to the bar
quhone thair is ocht ado

Thairfoir I rid, gif ye haue pleid
Or mater in to pley
To mak remeid, send in your steid
your ladeis grathit vp gay
Thai can defend, ewin to the end
Ane mater furthe expres
Suppois thai spend, it is onkend
Thair geir is not the les

In quyet place, And thai haue Space
within les nor twa houris
Thai can percace, purches sic grace
At the compositouris
Thair compositioun, without suspitioun
thair finalie is endit
with expeditioun, and full Remissioun
And selis thairto appendit

All haill almoist, Thai mak the coist
with sobir Recompence
Rycht litle loist, thai get indoist
all haill thair evudens
Sic ladyis wyis, ar all to pryis
To say the verite
Sic can devyis, and none Supprys
Thame throw thair honeste

Another poem on the same theme is more outspoken:

The vse of court so weill I knaw
The ladeis ar solistaris aw
At hame remanis the sarie lairdis
That giffis no giftis nor yit rewardis
Bot sendis thair wyffis behind the yardis
To further erandis fra ewin faw
The vse of court so weill I knaw

In cloikis thai come so quentlie cled
And rowndis to get thair erandis sped
Thai gif no buddis bot on the hiddis
And gettis grit scuddis in naikit bed
Thair buclair is bowit and bakwart borne
And all the caus is quhyt forlorne
vp gettis thair wame thay thin[k] na schame
And syn bringis hame the laird the horne
Thair buclar is borit and bakwart borne[4]

The state of affairs described by Ayala and hinted at in these poems
is not likely to be a sudden development of the fifteenth century.
In fact there is a good deal to suggest that control of affairs was
something inherited, though in a diminished way, from even greater
power and position held by women in ancient Celtic society. Because

the poem seems to reflect this tradition and to regard the institution of marriage in Christian and feudal society as the cause of its decline, it is of interest to see what the status of women had been in former times and what memory of it was likely to have survived. Once again there is little direct or connected evidence and perhaps we cannot get beyond some plausible conjectures. But to speculate on 'what song the sirens sang' may not be without its rewards, even though no definite answer is, in the nature of things, to be expected.

The status and prestige of persons and animals in primitive societies is apt to depend either directly on their strength, ferocity, or magic power or indirectly on the taboos or sanctions attached to their persons or their functions. One would on the whole expect that women, being physically weaker than men, would have a dominating or an independent status in a society only by virtue of their magic or sacred powers or of traditional methods of counting descent and inheritance of rule or property through the female line. There is no doubt that the high standing of women in ancient Celtic societies was in part due to such things, but it is surprising to find that it was at least partly due to their strength, ferocity, and skill in war. The traditional distinguishing characters of the two sexes are, as anthropology has shown in recent years, largely as a matter of social convention and conditioning. Societies in which women are the aggressive, combative, and dominant sex and men the gentle, domestic, and artistic sex are not unknown. There was nothing particularly gentle or domestic about the average male in any Celtic society of the Heroic Age, but many of their women seemed to have matched them in aggressive personality, warlike enthusiasms, and independence of spirit and action. 'Roman history', says Nora Chadwick, 'recorded no male enemies in Celtic Britain of the stature of Boudicca and Cartimandua.'[5] As these two are historical characters and well attested ones, we may begin our survey with them. When the Romans occupied Britain in the first century they found the great tribe, or federation of tribes, the Brigantes, under the rule of a queen Cartimandua, who appears not only to have been capable of waging a military campaign on her own account, but of changing a husband without losing her position as queen. She was clearly not merely the wife of a reigning monarch, but queen in her own right. Boudicca (usually known as Boadicea) is an even more interesting person. She organised the revolt of the Iceni and led the army in person and almost succeeded in destroying the Roman power in Britain. One can imagine a tribe following its queen to battle when the king was dead, as was then the case; but it was not only the Iceni who did so: the neighbouring tribes such as the Trinovantes followed her command and we hear nothing of the leadership of their kings and chiefs. Indeed Tacitus, writing about a generation after the event, and in a good position to have accurate knowledge through his father-in-law Agricola, expressly says that the Iceni did not distinguish between the sexes as military commanders and that the Britons were accustomed to make war under the leadership of women.[6] Dio Cassius described Buduica's appearance as the queen addressed her army:

> In stature she was very tall, in appearance most terrifying, in the glance of her eye most fierce, and her voice was harsh; a great mass of the tawniest hair fell to her hips; around her neck was a large golden torque; and she wore a tunic of various colours over which a thick mantle was fastened with a brooch. This was her invariable attire. She now grasped a spear to aid her in terrifying all beholders and spoke as follows:[7]

These are probably Dio's own words since Xiphilinus' epitome more often than not preserves Dio's text in passages of dramatic narrative or anecdote, but it was written about a century and a half after the revolt. Dio obviously had access to information not used by Tacitus, but the speech he puts into Buduica's mouth contains references to the Britons as having their wives in common and not practising agriculture which are known not to be true of the southern British tribes. It seems likely that he filled out his sources with details based on court gossip about Severus's campaign in Scotland or even from Julia Domna herself, the wife of Severus, who had seen and talked with some of the Caledonian women. But he may quite well have drawn on current beliefs about the size, warlike character and vigour of these redheaded Celtic women. Ammianus Marcellinus gives much the same impression of the women of Gaul, whom he would have seen when he was there between A.D. 354 and 357:

> The Gauls are almost all rather tall in stature and red-headed, fierce and threatening in the glance of their eyes, passionately fond of quarrelling and haughtily arrogant. Nor could even a crowd of foreigners withstand one of them in a brawl, if he should call in his wife, by far more powerful than he and with flashing eyes, especially when swelling out her neck and gnashing her teeth, she brandishes her enormous snow-white arms and proceeds to let fly punches and kicks, just like catapults delivering volleys from their twisted cords.[8]

This reads very like a description of some fracas which Ammianus had actually seen and it bears out Buduica's statement that the British women were just as valiant as the men[9]—a statement that may be really based on what Dio had heard of the Caledonian women. It is probable from what Tacitus says that Boudicca was not alone but that the other women were resolved to fight and probably did take part in the battle in which her army was defeated.[10]

What the classical historians have to say about the women of Gaul and Britain is well borne out by the epic tales of the Irish Heroic Age. Women warriors abound and are the nursery of arms:

> In Irish and Welsh stories of Celtic Britain the great heroes are taught not only wisdom but also feats of arms by women. In the Irish saga known as the Wooing of Emer, Cú Chulainn is trained in all warrior feats by two warlike queens—Scáthach, who is also a *fáith*, i.e. a 'prophetess', an expert in supernatural wisdom—and Aífe. In the Welsh story of 'Peredur' (later Percival) the hero is trained by the nine *gwiddonad* of Gloucester, who seem to be women of a similar profession. They wear helmets and armour, and they instruct Peredur in chivalry and feats of arms and supply him with horse and armour. These women also train other young men, and they live with their parents in a 'llys' or court. The establishment seems to have been in the nature of a military school.[11]

It is interesting to note that Scathach and Aife had their training schools not in Ireland but in Scotland. Cuchulainn first attended the training school for boys maintained by Conchobor, King of Ulster, and then went to what was obviously a finishing course with Scathach in Scotland. In the *Tain Bo Cualnge*, Cuchulainn meets Fer Diad who studied under Scathach with him and it appears from this passage that the third part of the course, the apprenticeship being over, was a sort of journeyman's course, in which the young heroes were sent overseas to get experience in various parts of Europe where Scathach maintained establishments under the direction of stewards. One battle against the Germans on the border of the Tyrrhenian Sea is mentioned. Another of Cuchulainn's fellow students at Scathach's academy, before meeting him in battle, is unwilling to fight him because Cuchulainn is his foster brother and bound to him by a perpetual covenant. Cuchulainn feels the same way about the duel and appeals to Ferbaeth 'by his foster brotherhood and by Scathach, the foster mother of them both'.[12] It would seem that the formal relationship of teacher and pupil in such academies was that of the common Irish institution of fosterage. At the beginning of the saga, Queen Medb, just before a battle, while getting her charioteer to turn her chariot *deasil* in order to avoid bad luck from curses laid on her by those parted from lovers and friends, encounters another woman warrior fully armed in her chariot who turns out to be Fedelm, the prophetess of Connaught. She is quite a young woman and has just come back from Scotland after taking a course in the art of prophecy.[13] The fact that prophecy, and no doubt magic, were also taught at such establishments may be a clue to the original role of the woman war leader, since magic and divination were as essential parts of the art of war as skill in arms. Women may first have come to exercise these skills in virtue of their supernatural powers. In Britain, as the first line of defence when the Romans attacked the Druid stronghold at Mona (Anglesey), the shore was lined with packed troops of armed warriors, while running among them were women dressed like Furies, with dishevelled hair, brandishing torches.[14] They were probably prophetesses or priestesses but were apparently part of the fighting force and were cut down by the legionaries among the fighting men and the Druids. According to Dio Cassius Buduica was not only the military commander of the revolt, but the priestess of the tribal goddess who was a goddess of war. Dio interprets the goddess's name as meaning Victory. As

Boudicca or Buduica also appears to mean Victory the reigning queen and the tribal goddess may originally have been identified. In his account of her address to her army, which is unlikely in the circumstances to have been reported at first hand to the Romans, but which is probably based on similar events, he says:

> When she had finished speaking, she employed a species of divination, letting a hare escape from the fold of her dress; and since it ran on what they considered the auspicious side, the whole multitude shouted with pleasure, and Buduica raising her hand towards heaven, said: 'I thank thee, Andraste, and call upon thee as a woman speaking to a woman.'[15]

When the campaign had got off to a successful start the woman commander sacrificed women captives to the woman war goddess.

> They hung up naked the noblest and most distinguished women and then cut off their breasts and sewed them to their mouths, in order to make the victims appear to be eating them; afterwards they impaled the women on sharp skewers run lengthwise through the body. All this they did to the accompaniment of sacrifices, banquets and wanton behaviour, not only in all their other sacred places, but particularly in the grove of Andate [Andraste]. This was their name for Victory, and they regarded her with the most exceptional reverence.[16]

Cartimandua, Queen of the Brigantes, also ruled over a tribe whose tribal goddess was a warrior divinity, Brigantia, whom some scholars equate with the Irish goddess Brigid. Although in the attributes of an orientalised Minerva, the well-known relief from Birrens in Dumfriesshire shows her on a platform, under an arch, holding a spear and wearing the wings of victory very much as Boadicea must have appeared to her countrymen and very much as they must have imagined their own tribal goddess Andraste: a powerful female warrior with a thick mass of hair curling down behind over her shoulders, standing as if about to address her troops before battle. But as Nora Chadwick observes:

> Our fullest and most authentic picture of Ireland in the earliest historical period [perhaps, more or less contemporary with Boudicca and Cartimandua] is the great prose saga of *Táin Bó Cualnge*, The Cattle Raid of Cooley, which has preserved us an intimate record of European Society in the late Iron Age.[17]

The hero of this saga is Cuchulainn, the greatest of all the Irish heroes and rightly compared with Achilles in classical legendary history. His antagonist is Medb, wife of Aillil, King of Connaught. Medb is the dominating figure of the saga. It is she who starts the war when her possessions become less than those of her husband because the supernatural bull Findbennach left her herd to join Aillil's. She proposes to capture an even more famous bull from the Ulstermen. It is Medb who controls the army, plans the strategy, gives the orders, and negotiates with the allies of Connaught. She takes part in the fighting at the climax of the campaign and she openly uses her sexual favours to secure political advantages and her husband has to accept this. He remains in fact a comparatively minor figure. Like Cartimandua and Buduica, she has female aid in the divine world, war goddesses who intervene on her behalf. The queen in her own right acting as war leader and allied with if not actually representing the tribal goddess seems to have been a feature of earlier Celtic society.

At the same time the examples mentioned seem to show it as a system on the way out. Tacitus says that the Britons were accustomed to women commanders in war, but Cartimandua and Boudicca are our only known examples, so that it cannot have been a common practice. Cartimandua, who, like Medb, appears to have decided policy and strategy, even if she did not engage in battle herself, was in a precarious position. Tacitus expressly says that at least part of the cause of the revolt of the northern Brigantes against her was a feeling of ignominy at having to submit to a woman commander.[18] Prasutagus, King of the Iceni, appears to have been at least able to dispose of his kingdom by willing it to Caesar and his two daughters, and Boudicca his wife became war leader in what may be regarded as exceptional circumstances. This does not, as we shall see, mean that she did not actually control policy before her husband's death. Aillil, in the *Tain Bo Cualnge*, makes policy and gives orders but only with the consent of his formidable wife. But in fact the Irish saga also suggests that the system was decaying there. Both sides in the conflict criticise women's methods in war and policy as contrary to the code of honour and fair play. When Medb wants to massacre the Leinstermen so that they will not get all the credit for the expected victory, Aillil and Fergus protest and together they override her plan:

> 'We will not hide that this is a woman's plan,' said Aillil, 'what you say is not good.'

Cuchulainn, when Medb offers to meet him to make peace, is warned by his charioteer that she is without chivalry:

> 'Great are Medb's deeds,' said the charioteer; 'I fear a hand behind the back with her.'

Perhaps the most significant thing is the fact that Cuchulainn defeats Medb's war goddess, the terrible Morrigan, and then Medb herself in the last battle of the campaign.

> Cuchulainn overtook Medb then when he went into the battle. 'Protect me,' said Medb. 'Though I should slay thee with slaying, it were lawful for me,' said Cuchulainn. Then he protected her because he used not to slay women.

In the end Morrigan has to come to Cuchulainn to be healed of the damage he has done her, and heal her he does, though she tricks him into it.[19] The *Tain Bo Cualnge* is of course not historical and most scholars regard Medb as a euhemerised goddess, though the saga probably reflects manners and customs of the Heroic Age. But that the Irish did have women warriors is well attested historically. The continuation of the practice well into Christian times was perhaps due to conditions applying to the inheritance and holding of land. For example, under ancient Irish law a daughter, when there were no sons in the family, was liable to military service if she inherited all her father's land but could evade this by taking only half the inheritance.[20] Women fought one another in some circumstances. In the *Tain Bo Cualnge*, Medb conducts a raid against what seems to be a force of women led by Findmor, wife of Celtchar Mac Uthidir.[21] Scathach and Aife were rivals and made war against each other. The Irish laws make provision for what appears to have been a grudge fight or duel between a *cetmuinter* or principal wife and a secondary wife when the latter was taken into the household. The period was strictly limited to three nights and fines were settled if either party continued reprisals beyond that period. The chief wife was permitted to inflict any injury short of death. The secondary wife was allowed to defend herself but not to wound her rival, though she had the right to inflict damage with her finger nails, utter insults, punch and bruise and tear her antagonist's hair.[22] This jolly ceremony no doubt had the effect of making anyone who contemplated a secondary marriage think twice about it.

Custom seems to have condoned the practice of warfare by women as well as men until the end of the seventh century when it was abolished by the Law of Adamnan. According to a thirteenth-century commentator, St Adamnan, the biographer of St Columba, was induced to propose the law by his mother:

> On a certain day Adamnan chanced to be passing through Mag Breg, with his mother on his back; and they saw two battalions attacking each other. Now Ronait, Adamnan's mother, happened to see a woman with an iron hook in her hand dragging another woman from the opposite side, with the hook fastened in her breast. For men and women used to fight in battle alike at that time. Thereupon Ronait sat down, and said: 'Thou shalt not take me from this place until women are freed forever from this condition, and from battles and campaigns.' So Adamnan promised this thing. Then there happened to be a great council in Ireland, and Adamnan went to that council with men chosen from the priests of Ireland, and he freed women there.[23]

The Cain Adomnain, passed in 697, in its original form apparently protected clerics, women, nuns, monks, and tenants of church lands but in the surviving form it is most specifically directed against the killing of women. It forbids the employment of women in military operations of any kind, assaults, raids, hostings and fights and imposes very heavy penalties both on the leaders who permit or order a breach of this law and on every man taking part in the operation.[24]

Scotland seems to have been, no less than Ireland, the home of fighting women. Adamnan came from Scotland to attend the council at which were also Eochaid, King of the Dalriatic Scots and Brude son of Derile, King of the Picts.[25] The latter was one of the sureties named for seeing that Adamnan's Law was observed in his part of

Scotland. The sureties for the Scottish Kingdom were clerics.[26] Irish legend, as we have seen, placed the academies for heroes and prophets in Scotland and there are local legends of famous women warriors preserved there down to modern times. A fourteenth-century manuscript preserving a chronicle of the Picts says that the ancestors of the Picts and Scots were neighbours of the Amazons.[27] The facts alleged are nonsense but the remark about the Amazons may be an attempt to account for the fact that the women of these nations took part in warfare. Martin Martin records the preservation of the legend of a famous 'Amazon' in the island of St Kilda, noted for her skill in hunting as well as for her prowess in war.[28] Hector Boece in the sixteenth century remarks that before the great change in manners and institutions which occurred in the time of Malcolm Canmore:

> The wemen war of litil les vassalage and strenth than was the men; for al rank madinnis and wiffis, gif thay war nocht with child, yeid als weill to battall as the men.

He also records that among the people of Annandale, before their conquest by the Romans, the people were cannibals and ate their prisoners and that

> The wyvis usit to slay thair housbandis, quhen thay were found cowartis or discomfist be thair ennemis; to gif occasioun to otheris to be more bald and hardy quhen danger occurrit:[29]

These may be tales—Boece is not reliable on the early history of Scotland—but they show at least that in Dunbar's time the tradition of the fighting past of Scottish women had been preserved.

In fact it was still being practised, especially in the Highlands which had not undergone the change of customs introduced by feudalism to which Boece refers. In the reign of James IV Knock Castle in Sleat, Skye, was taken by the Macdonalds from the Macleods. The Macleods laid siege to the castle which was successfully defended by Mari Chaistail, Mary of the Castle. Her defence gave the clan time to rally and she forced the attackers to raise the siege,[30] a feat comparable to that of the famous Black Agnes, Countess of March who, in the fourteenth century, defended the Castle of Dunbar for five months against an English army led by the Earls of Salisbury and Arundel. She took part in the fighting according to Andrew of Wyntoun and even her foes praised her:

> off this ilk sege in hething
> The Inglismen maid oft carping:
> 'I wow to God, scho beris hir weill,
> The Scottis wenche with hir ploddeill
> For cum I airly, cum I lait
> I fynd ay Annes at the yait.'[31]

She also used to appear daily on the walls and taunt the Englishmen. In the end she forced them to raise the siege. Pitscottie, speaking of her father, Earl Thomas Randolph, records with the same pride as Andrew of Wyntoun:

> He . . . had daughteris of quhame the eldest was callit Blak Annas be ressone scho was blak skynnit. This Annas was ane woman of greit spreit mair nor became ane woman to be, quho was mareit wpoun Patrick earle of Marche.[32]

In the troubled times between the death of James V and the accession of James VI, women took their part in the deeds of violence then so common in Scotland as to be almost the rule. In 1549 Margaret Hume, Prioress of North Berwick, conducted a private war with Alexander Oliphant of Kellé or Kelly, each of the parties on various occasions having waylaid, attacked, or besieged the others and their servants. In the same year Issobella McFarlane was banished from the Stewartry of Strathearn in Perthshire for attacking Jonet Glass under cover of night, burning her house to the ground and destroying all her provisions, goods, and cattle. A few years earlier another virago was executed for a similar attack on the laird of Rosyth in Fife.[33] Other instances show them directing the operations rather than taking part in the actual assaults. In 1556 Mariota Montgomery, Lady Symple, set her servants on to attack and murder Gilbert Rankyne and others 'in the castle of Laven' and abducted and imprisoned others.[34] In 1594 the Marquis of Huntley, raising troops before the battle of Glenlivet, applied not to the head of the clan Gordon but to Bessie Gordon, his wife, who arranged for her husband and eight sons with followers to join Huntley without even consulting them, though her husband was present at the interview—or so the local legend ran in the eighteenth century.[35] In 1612 as a result of hostility between the clans Neish and McNab, some of the Neish clan raided some McNabs as they were sitting down to Christmas dinner and escaped with the roast. It seems to have been no more than a rough practical joke, but the wife of McNab urged her sons to vengeance; they caught the Neish's unprepared and killed the whole family, except two small children, beheaded the bodies and took the heads back to their mother—to the old lady's immense satisfaction. A seventeenth-century manuscript by Alexander Campbell tells a story of the wife of the chief commander of the Isle of Islay, Janet of Dunstaffnage, his maternal grandmother (though the narrator was not aware of this relationship):

> —this wicked woman was in practice of seizing in the night all the followers of the Family of McDonald who was and still is the chief of the inhabitants upon that Island. By this womans orders the people would be bound hand and foot and carried away in boats and Birlines in the night time and before day left on Desart Rocks and Islands in the sea there to perish . . . There was another wicked woman at Dunstaffnage that had the same practice of persecuting the remains of the Coll McDonalds.[36]

It was obviously Janet of Dunstaffnage and not her husband George Campbell of Airds who was really in chief command in Islay.

These are a few examples of the independence and masterly behaviour of women of the upper classes and they could be multiplied many times over. Their sisters of the common people were no less noted for intransigence and valour, not to mention a complete disregard for St Paul's view of their proper station. One of their most popular sports was rioting. Pitscottie's chronicle for the year 1460 notes a strange and terrible example of the cannibalism which St Jerome had heard of and which seemed to have persisted in parts of Scotland until this date. A 'brigand' who lived in a remote part of Angus was captured and with all his family burnt alive for this crime, all except a child of one year old who was put with foster parents in Dundee. This was apparently only because she had not reached the age of reason (seven years). When she came to the age of womanhood, she was tried, convicted, and burnt to death for the same crime. As an early example of women's riots and also of the temper of the Scottish female of the period, Pitscottie's account is worth quoting:

> It is said that quhen this young womane was command fourtht to the place of executioun, that thair gaderit wnnumerabill mulltitud of pepill about hir and spetiall of wemen curssand and warieand that scho was sa wnhappie to commit sa dampnabill deidis, to quhome scho turnit about witht ane wode and furieous contienance, sayand, 'quhairfoir cheide ye witht me as I had committit ane unworthie act. Gif me credit and trow me, gif ye had experience of eittin of women and mens flesche ye wald think the same sa delicious that ye wald never forbeir it againe,' and sa witht ane obstinat mynd this wnhappie creature but signe or outward taikin of repentance dieit in the sight of the haill pepill for misdeidis that scho was adiudgit to.[37]

This tragedy is one of the first instances on record of the mob of women who figure so often in Scottish communal life from this time onwards. Oddly enough most of the earlier instances are of religious riots, but the behaviour of the mobs suggests that they enjoyed riot for its own sake. They were certainly adept at it. An early victim was the turn-coat bishop of Galloway:

> The first of November 1615, he wes transportet fra Perth to the chappel royal efter he had been 30 yeiris minister at perth, and upon the 25th of februar 1618, he departit this Lyffe, and it was thocht for greiff that the wyffes of edinburgh com in to him, and schewe to him his awin bukis aganes freiris buikis.[38]

This might appear a harmless exercise until we see how the ladies really emphasised their point of view. On the occasion of the introduction of Laud's Prayer Book in 1637 there were further riots led by women. Robert Baillie, a well-known Presbyterian divine, described the tumult they caused during the day, especially as directed at Reverend William Annan, Minister of Ayr. In the evening he decided to venture on the streets to visit his bishop:

> he was no sooner on the causey, at nine o'clock in a mirk night, with three or four ministers with him, but some hundreths of inraged women

of all qualities, are about him with neaves [fists], and staves, and peats [but] no stones. They beat him sore; his cloake, ruffe, hatt, were rent. However, upon his cryes, and candles set out from many windows, he escaped all bloody wounds; yet he was in great danger even of killing. This tumult was so great, that it was not thought meet to search, either in plotters or actors of it, for numbers of the best qualitie would have been found guiltie.[39]

The riot in St Giles's Church at Edinburgh on 23 July that year is well known. When the Bishop of Edinburgh appealed to the enraged women not to profane the house of God he had a 'creepie stool' thrown at him and the wildest uproar broke out which completely broke up the service till the women were finally ejected by the provost and the bailies. They continued to riot outside the church and planned their revenge on the bishop.

The Bishop . . . conducted the afternoon service which passed without incident, but no sooner was he come out of the kirk to go to his lodgings than he was set upon by a mob of women. The Earl of Roxburgh hustled him into his coach, which was pelted with stones by the rabble, which ran beside it. It was with great difficulty that the Bishop attained the safety of his lodging, the mob following him and trying to drag him down the stairs by his gown, one woman demanding that he should suffer the fate of Cardinal Beaton.

The women rioted at other churches in Edinburgh that day in what was clearly a planned insurrection. The bishop was lucky; a volume recording events between the accession of Charles I and the Restoration, published in 1682, describes the discomfiture of the Church Synod of Perth in 1652, at the hands of mobs of women:

Letters of the Synod's meeting at Perth, and citing the Ministers and people who had expressed a dislike of their *heavenly government* that, the men being got out of the way, their wives resolved to answere for them. And on the day of appearance, 120 women, with good clubs in their hands, came and besieged the church where the Rev. Ministers sat. They sent one of their number to treat with the females, and he threatening excommunication, they basted him for his labour, and sent a party of sixty who routed the rest of the clergy, bruised their bodies sorely, took all their baggage and twelve horses . . . these conquerors having laid hold on the Synod Clerk, beat him till he foreswore his office . . . thirteen of the ministers rallied about four miles from the place, and voted that the village should never more have a Synod kept in it but be accursed; and that although in the years 1638 and 39 the Godly Women were called up for stoneing the Bishops, yet now the whole sex should be esteemed unlucky.[40]

The curses of the unfortunate clergy may have given them comfort for their bruises: they only emphasised the triumph of the women. They raised another successful riot in Kirkcudbright in 1663 against the installation of a curate.[41] At Edinburgh in 1672 they showed their indomitable spirit by a riot in Parliament Close, presenting a petition to the Council 'because the men durst not'. They filled the close, threatened Archbishop Sharp, and only three were apprehended.[42] In 1682 a mob largely composed of women set on the military escort of a number of young men serving prison sentences who were being marched off to join the troops in Holland. The troops fired on the mob and two of the women were killed, one of them in an advanced stage of pregnancy. This was in Edinburgh. Seven years later the ladies of Glasgow showed their mettle:

It was customary every Thursday to have prayers and a sermon in all the churches. On Thursday January 17th 1689, a mob, chiefly of women, surrounded the cathedral, intending to drag down from the pulpit the curate, Mr. Milne . . . The viragoes caught him, tore first his gown off, then his other clothes, including his shirt. They were proceeding to strip him completely naked, when he begged, for the sake of decency, to be allowed to retain his small clothes. For answer they beat him severely and, says the 'Case of the Afflicted Clergy', 'used him in such an indecent manner as not fit to be named: but it cost him his life'.[43]

The spirit is rather that of Boudicca than of the followers of Christ and there is no doubt that the tradition of female intransigence had an unbroken tradition from the days of the British Warrior Queen. Riots led by women continued throughout the eighteenth century and in various parts of Scotland and during the notorious and barbarous Highland clearances, determined women, having got the men out of the way on several occasions, routed large parties of soldiers or police in pitched and sometimes bloody battles.

There is no reason to doubt that the female sex in Scotland in Dunbar's day, both in the upper and the lower classes of society, was any less formidable than their sisters of earlier and later times, or that they were any less determined 'to have the maistrie' of the opposite sex. As Alexander Scott remarked in the next generation:

> Thay wald haif all men bund and thrall
> To thame, and thay for to be fre;
> They covet ilk man at thair call,
> And thay to leif at libertie:
> So find I thair affectioun
> Contrar thair awin complexioun.[44]

It is clear that the second wife's program in Dunbar's poem was a *fait accompli* among many of her countrywomen, though another view, that of woman as the gentle and submissive sex by nature (complexioun), was being imposed on them by church and state, as by public and private opinion. But the older tradition was an 'unconscionable time a-dying' and indeed is, even now, not quite extinct in Scotland. It was not for nothing that Eric Linklater placed the scene of his modern version of the *Lysistrata* in the Scottish capital. *The Impregnable Women* gives a good picture of the traditional women's fighting mob and the equally traditional lack of respect or submission to the male sex, which preserved the ancestral memory of a day when women ruled the roost in a very real sense.

13

Mother to Daughter

THE power and prestige enjoyed by women in some human societies depends not on their prowess, or even on any special magical gifts, neither on their charms nor their aggressive personalities, but on the fact that the inheritance of land and property runs in the female line. This is sometimes associated with matrilocal forms of marriage in which the husband comes from another clan and the children of the marriage belong not to his but to his wife's clan or kinship group. In other cases the husband may not be a resident or even a permanent partner and the duty of supporting and protecting the woman and her children may then fall upon her brothers.

Most Celtic peoples as they appear in historical times are patriarchal and patrilineal in their organisation, in spite of the considerable power, prestige, and independence of the women, which we have already considered. But there are signs that at least some of them had once been matrilineal in their reckoning of inheritance, descent, and kinship, that the choice and change of husbands had been a woman's right or privilege, and that among royal or chiefly families the husband was often a stranger or a visitor, while the closest male relationship was that of a man to his maternal uncle. Once again the evidence is scrappy, often ambiguous, and allows us to do little more than build up a possible case, but it is at least fairly certain that the Picts, who at one time occupied almost all of Scotland, were accustomed to choose their kings and to count the descent in royal families according to a matrilineal system. Bede says clearly that it was their custom in his lifetime and the ancient lists of Pictish kings bear out what he says. Around this landmark of historically respectable fact we may arrange the less certain pieces of evidence and suggestion.

One of the earliest stories about a Celtic tribe as told by Livy is that in the time of Tarquinius Priscus, that is to say about 600 B.C., a high king of the Gallic Celts, Ambigatus by name, because the nation had grown too populous, decided to send his two nephews Segovesus and Bellovesus to find new areas of settlement. This relation of a king to his sister's sons, as H. M. Chadwick points out, suggests a matrilineal system of counting descent, and there are traces of the same relationship among the Teutonic, Latin, and Greek peoples.[1] Mythology, which often preserves traces of archaic custom and social organisation, suggests that at least some of the tribes of Wales and of Ireland counted descent in the female line. Heroes like Fergus Mac Roich or Conchobor Mac Nesa are named after their mothers and not after their fathers. Others like Cuchulainn are either known as the son of their mother, e.g. Cuchulainn son of Dechtire, or are considered illegitimate.[2] In Welsh legend, Math, lord of Gwynedd in North Wales, is called son of Mathonwy, who was his mother, but his father is not mentioned. When Math was unable or unwilling to make a progress through his territories or to lead the war-band, this duty devolved on his nephews Gilfaethwy and Gwydion, sons of his sister Don. In the next generation the responsibility seemed to rest on the son of their sister Aranrhod, Llew Llaw Gyffes. Don's husband, like Mathonwy's, is never mentioned, nor are the wives of Math and Gwydion. It is Gwydion who arranges his sister's marriage and defends her when she is in peril.[3] It looks like a matrilineal type of succession, though the south Welsh kingdom mentioned in the same tale appears to be patrilineal. The situation suggested by these legends of matrilineal and patrilineal systems existing side by side may have been one that persisted in Wales as late as the ninth century. The north Welsh dynasty of Merfyn and Rhodri Mawr, which did so much to unite the Welsh kingdoms at that time, did so largely by a series of judicious marriages. Merfyn's father married Ethyllt, daughter of the last king of the old dynasty of Gwynedd. Merfyn inherited Gwynedd through his mother and he married Nest, sister of the last king of the old line of Powys; their son Rhodri Mawr inherited Powys from his mother and by marrying the sister of the King of Ceredigion inherited another kingdom through his wife. Rhodri's grandson kept up the family tradition by marrying the granddaughter of Rhodri's neighbour, the King of Dyfed, and inherited Dyfed through his wife. In the end he inherited Powys through his uncles, the sons of Rhodri Mawr.[4] The new dynasty of course inherited in the male line but seems to have acquired its kingdoms by marrying into the old dynasties where inheritance may have run in the female line as it did among the contemporary Picts. Such a system would go a long way to explain the royal incest which seems to have been such a problem to the early churches in Wales and Scotland and provoked the horror of Gildas and St Kentigern in the sixth century and of St Margaret of Scotland in the eleventh. Under a matrilineal system succession goes through the female line, as long as the husbands chosen by the women or the clan also observe the matrilineal rules. But as soon as patrilineal systems are in competition with matrilineal, husbands chosen from outside the family or clan are likely to behave as the dynasty of Merfyn and Rhodri Mawr did. The best way to counter this, as Giraldus Cambrensis noticed, is to marry within the family or clan. With a royal family this is likely to lead to incestuous unions, as the choice is limited.

A similar period of competition between the two systems, with the patrilineal in the ascendant, may be reflected in the *Tain Bo Cualnge*. Medb uses the offer of her own love and of marriage with her daughter Findabair as the chief inducements to military and political alliances and as the means of persuading one hero after another to engage the invincible Cuchulainn in the battle of the Ford. One of the reasons why most Celtic scholars, with the notable exception of Nora Chadwick, believe Medb to have been a goddess and not a historical character is that she seems, on account of her numerous marriages, to have been a personification of sovereignty. The legends record that she was wife to nine kings of Ireland and that only one who became her consort could be king.[5] The problem could be solved by supposing that Medb and other such queens—for other kings in Ireland were wedded to their kingdoms—were real women closely allied with and perhaps representing the tribal goddess and the repository of the sovereignty and, through their daughters, of the succession. This rather than Findabair's beauty or even the alliance with the royal house of Connaught would be a more compelling reason, in a heroic age, for so many heroes to take on so desperate a venture—and even to set sacred obligations aside—as was involved in a duel with Cuchulainn. Queens like Medb may have been able to make and unmake kings as Cartimandua seems to have done in the first century in Britain. And like Cartimandua her position may have been precarious, faced with the competition of a patrilineal system among her neighbours.

Cartimandua may have been more or less contemporary with Medb, if the latter was in fact the legendary representative of an actual great queen. At any rate she seems to have been the repository of the sovereignty of the Brigantes. Her consort Venutius was apparently a brilliant war-leader, but according to Tacitus Cartimandua divorced him and took his armour bearer (*armiger*) as her consort instead.[6] This caused a revolt, since, among other things, her people did not wish to be subjected to the rule of a woman. This statement is somewhat suspect since all the evidence shows that this was no new thing. It was with Cartimandua that the Romans had made their original treaty, not with her husband Venutius. It was to Cartimandua not to Venutius that Caratacus appealed for refuge after his defeat by the Romans and it was Cartimandua who handed him over to her allies. It was Cartimandua whom the revolt tried to overthrow: there is no mention of the part, if any, played by the new consort Vellocatus. The Brigantes had already been ruled by a woman.

Now it is interesting to note that on the northern border of Cartimandua's domains were the peoples later to be known as the Picts who practised succession in the female line, and that on the borders of the Brigantes in the north-east English midlands were the Coritani, another Pictish tribe with their chief towns at Leicester and Lincoln.[7] We know nothing of their system of succession. But on the other side of the Coritani were the Iceni, whose queen Boudicca led the great revolt against the Romans.[8] Prasutagus, her husband, was recognised as the reigning monarch by the Romans. But he was a client king and if he had no male heir, as has been generally assumed, his kingdom would have lapsed to Rome. For this reason he made a will in which his two daughters and the Emperor Nero were named as co-heirs, in the vain hope of preventing annexation. In fact the senior officers of the military governor at once moved in and publicly flogged the queen, while the slaves of the procurator, the civil administrator, no doubt just as publicly, raped her daughters.[9] There seems to be little point in these operations which appear to have been part of an official plan of annexation, unless we assume that the Iceni, like their neighbours, counted descent in the female line. The flogging of the sacred person of the queen in whom the sovereignty resided and the servile outrage on the daughters in whose gift the sacred marriage of the next succession lay, would then have real political meaning. It would spell the end of the dynasty and the system of royalty. It would explain better why, when the revolt had begun, the noblest women among the captives were sacrificed to the tribal goddess. If Prasutagus was a consort like Venutius or Medb's husband Aillil, it would explain better how the Iceni and their allies unhesitatingly entrusted the campaign to the reigning queen rather than to any of their local war chiefs. Dio Cassius says explicitly that she rode at the head of her troops in her chariot and that she assigned the others to their several stations.[10] Taken together there are some striking resemblances between the three queens Medb, Cartimandua, and Boudicca. Such persons would help to explain the splendid funerary chambers of the Bronze Age with the most sumptuous ornaments and treasures accorded to women buried singly and not as consorts both on the continent and in south-western England.[11] The queens we have mentioned would appear to be survivors of a system which only some of the more conservative tribes preserved into the Iron Age.

Among these were the most northerly tribes of the British Isles and they seem to have preserved the system of matrilineal descent till the middle of the ninth century A.D. and possibly later. Two remarks by Dio Cassius who, as we have seen, was in a position to have first-hand information about the campaigns of Septimius

Severus against these northern peoples, throw some further light on their customs in the third century. He says that the Maiatai and the Caledonians had what he calls a democratic system of rule, by which he appears to mean that they elected their war-leaders who were clearly not hereditary kings.[12] A few pages later he recounts an anecdote about the treaty which Severus made with the northern tribes at the end of a campaign in which he claimed to have reached the northmost point of the country. The historian has just been mentioning the Emperor's measures against adultery in Rome and adds:

> In this connexion, a very witty remark is reported to have been made by the wife of Argentocoxus, a Caledonian, to Julia Augusta. When the empress was jesting with her, after the treaty, about the free intercourse of her sex with men in Britain, she replied: 'We fulfil the demands of Nature in a much better way than do you Roman women; for we consort openly with the best men, whereas you let yourselves be debauched in secret by the vilest.' Such was the retort of the British woman.[13]

Taken with the fact that the Picts, who are believed to be the descendants of these Caledonians, practised a matrilineal form of succession, this appears to be further evidence that it was the women who chose their partners and through whom the succession ran, while the war-leaders were elected and could be replaced. The Caledonian lady's remark that they chose the noblest suggests that the most distinguished war-leader became the consort of the queen and could be replaced if he failed to please her or the tribe. Cartimandua's mistake in fact may well have been that she chose to replace Venutius, whose prowess and skill in war were recognised, by an inferior warrior. An inscription from Colchester also of the third century dedicates a gift

> To the god Mars Medocius of the Campestres and to the victory of our Alexander Pius Felix Augustus Lossio Veda, nephew [*nepos*] of Vepogenus a Caledonian has dedicated [this] gift at his own expense.[14]

The authenticity of the inscription has been questioned but a number of scholars appear to accept it as genuine. If *nepos* means nephew rather than grandson here, it would be interesting to find a Caledonian, perhaps a hostage in southern Britain, worshipping a Celtic god, associate of the *Matres*, and naming his uncle, probably a maternal uncle, perhaps as his chief family connection. There are too many 'ifs' in all this but it could fit in with a matrilineal system of succession, by which the nephew was held as surety for his uncle, who in his turn was the chief male representative of a reigning queen or chieftainess, while the nephew would be next heir.

Both the contemporary account given by Bede in the eighth century and the lists of Pictish kings which have survived bear out the view that the husbands of the women of the royal families were never by custom kings themselves. To them it might have been said as the witches said to Banquo:

> Thou shalt get Kings though thou be none.

Bede, after giving a legendary account of the origin of the practice, says that it was the custom of the Picts to choose their kings from the female royal stock rather than from the male.[15] This would confine the succession to the brother, son, or daughter's son of a reigning queen. In fact the lists of Pictish kings down to the second half of the eighth century, that is about the time Bede was born, show brothers succeeding brothers, but not sons succeeding their fathers. Quite a number of the fathers seem to have been foreigners, such as the father of Brude I in the sixth century whose father Maelchon is equated by many scholars with Maelgwyn, King of Gwynedd, whom Gildas abused for his evil courses. Such a 'marriage' can hardly have been a permanent union. A number of other fathers were from the neighbouring Scots royal family of Dalriada and at least one was from the Anglo-Saxon kingdom of Bernicia.[16] H. M. Chadwick remarks:

> It is clear that a record of the Kings' fathers was kept, at least from the fifth century onwards. Some of the fathers, possibly all, were foreigners. It is not known whether any permanent form of marriage was contracted, or whether the fathers were merely casual visitors. All we know is that in actual fact some of them returned to their own countries, and reigned there later. The organisation of the royal

family would seem to have been matrilocal as well as matrilinear. The Kings themselves, however, had wives, families and permanent homes of their own; and their wives and children were apparently treated with special honour, and possessed some power.[17]

Some more or less legendary tales appear to have preserved memories of the same system and to suggest that the marriages were both temporary and at the will of the queens or princesses concerned. One is the fabulous tale of Cano in the *Yellow Book of Lecan*[18] which may be based on tradition going back to the seventh century. Another is in the *Liber Hymnorum*, an eleventh-century compilation, with prefaces to the Irish hymns. It is probably quite unhistorical but may preserve genuine customs and traditions. The preface to the hymn 'Parce, Domine' tells the story of a Pictish princess Drusticc, daughter of Drust 'King of the Britons at that time'. The time would be in the early sixth century. An Irish monk called Finnian of Moville had come over to Whithorn in Scotland, the original foundation attributed to St Ninian, missionary to the Picts in the fifth century.[19] The princess had been sent by her father to Mugint, the author of the hymn in question, for instruction in reading. Mugint who was in charge of the establishment had apparently brought Finnian over from Ireland to be her tutor. While at the monastery she fell in love with Rioc, one of the monks or novices, and she said to Finnian:

> 'I will give thee all the books that Mugint has to write [possibly books lent her by Mugint for copying] if thou wilt give me Rioc in marriage.' And Finnian sent Talmach to her that night in Rioc's shape, and he knew her and thereby Lonan of Treoit was conceived and born. But Drusticc imagined that Rioc had known her, and she said that Rioc was the father of her son. And this was false because Rioc was a virgin.[20]

The story, even if legend, is old enough to give a precious picture of a royal Pictish princess, exercising her sovereign right to choose her bed-mates as Dio Cassius had pictured the type two or three centuries before. The 'marriage' is evidently meant to be temporary and the monks, in spite of Christianity, are unable to thwart a custom which their religion naturally condemns. All they can do is to prevent sacrilege of the young man's vow of chastity by providing a substitute. The imperious nature of this young woman is recorded in the twelfth-century *Book of Leinster* which, in giving a list of mothers of the saints, says of her:

> Dustric daughter of Drust King of the Britons of the north, and mother of Lonan Talmach's son. Of her it is said: 'Drust, King of the free estuary from the shore had one perfect daughter, Dustricc, very haughty to others; the mother of Lonan, Talmach's son.[21]

The other interesting thing about her is that she was mother not to a king but to a saint. Legend, as we have seen, attributed illegitimate birth to a number of saints such as St Bridget of Ireland, St Dubricius of Wales, St Kentigern of Scotland and Faustus, bishop of Riez, son as well as grandson of Vortigern. The earliest stories were no doubt concerned to prove not the illegitimate, but the royal, or at least illustrious birth, of such Celtic saints. A good example is the famous St Mungo or St Kentigern, the patron saint of Glasgow.

The earliest life of St Kentigern was probably composed about the middle of the twelfth century from a little volume (or volumes) of the saint's miracles, which the author says he found, and 'from what was told me orally by trustworthy people'. His account of Kentigern's birth is that King Leudonus, a semi-pagan, who ruled the province of Lothian, had a daughter called Thaney. She refused a suitor, 'a most elegant youth', Ewen son of Erwegende of royal British stock. Rather than marry him she became the slave of a swineherd who was a secret Christian. Thaney was an avowed Christian and had decided to remain a virgin. Ewen dressed himself as a woman, followed the princess, and ravished her. Her father, learning that she was pregnant, tried to have her executed but was miraculously prevented. She was set adrift in a boat, and was washed up near Culross where she gave birth to her son. They were taken to St Serf who brought up St Kentigern, who in turn became an apostle to the Picts and to the Britons of Cumbria.[22] The office of St Theneuu in the Aberdeen Breviary calls Kentigern's father Euuen son of the King of Cumbria, born of the noblest British stock. The later accounts of the saint either attribute virgin birth to him or suppress the story altogether as scandalous or unseemly. The whole story has been exhaustively discussed by K. H. Jackson, who believes it to be fabulous but based on ancient and partly oral tradition.[23] In its present form it makes no sense and was rightly omitted by Jocelyn, who wrote another life of Kentigern some thirty years later, as an evil story and contrary to Christian belief. He picked up from 'silly and credulous people' in the diocese of Glasgow another legend that St Kentigern had been conceived and born of a virgin mother. But the whole thing looks like a garbled version of an ancient Pictish royal marriage. An eighteenth-century version of the story from Culross says that Kentigern was the son of Eugenius III, King of the Scots, and of a daughter of Lothus, King of the Picts. His mother Thanetis, finding herself with child, out of shame stole away from her father's court and entered a boat which was washed up at Culross where she left her child to nurse and returned home. He was brought up by St Serf.[24]

It seems likely that in the various versions which do not simply suppress the account of St Kentigern's birth we have attempts by Scots, British, or southern Pictish tradition to make an edifying story out of a legend in which the saint was the offspring of a royal Pictish marriage under the old system. The circumstances of a foreign prince who resides temporarily at the court, leaves the princess with child, and returns to his own kingdom and family, would have been a perfectly regular proceeding, but would seem scandalous to Christians of a later age who knew nothing of this form of marriage. They therefore tried to explain it as a rape or a virgin birth. On the other hand there may be other possibilities. The anonymous *Life* says that Thaney was 'ruled by a step-mother'. If Leudonus had lost his wife and married another member of the royal female line, say her sister—an event that must sometimes have occurred under the matrilineal system—in order to preserve his position, Thaney may well have been forced to flee if her rival's daughter was favoured in the succession. If on the other hand Thaney had been forced into a convent for the same reason, and had herself made the conventional Pictish choice of a visiting prince, her punishment and expulsion would be understandable. In any case this interpretation of the legends would mean that they go back at least to the ninth century when the Pictish system of royal marriage began to give way to a patrilineal system. But it was still recognised and remembered for a time. Constantine, the Pictish king who restored the Pictish power at the end of the eighth century, came to the throne by right of conquest rather than of succession. He was succeeded, perhaps in a normal Pictish way, by his brother Oengus. Oengus's son succeeded him, the first Pictish king whose succession was certainly patrilineal.[25] But when in 839 the two sons of Oengus and the King of Dalriada fell fighting the Norsemen, Alpin son of Eochaid, a Scottish prince of Dalriada, according to Boece, claimed the Pictish succession:

> Alpyne, herand the slauchter of twa emez but ony successioun of thair bodies on live, send his ambassatouris to the Princes of Pichtis, clamand the croun therof be reassoun of heretage because he was nerrest aire to his eme [uncle], King Hungus [Oengus], gottin on his sister Fergusiane, sen all uther children of Hungus war decessit.[26]

Boece, writing in the sixteenth century, had no idea of the real nature of the Pictish succession but he seems to be following a genuine tradition. Alpin, as sister's son of the reigning king, would have been the rightful heir, though he appears to recognise the new patrilineal succession introduced by his uncle.

But if the system of matrilineal succession was soon forgotten in the south of Scotland, among the northern Picts it may have lingered for several centuries more. H. M. Chadwick concludes from a study of the genealogies of the Scottish clans that it may have gone on to the twelfth century,[27] and the fourteenth-century chronicler Andrew of Wyntoun records a legend pointing to the custom in the case of Macbeth in the eleventh century.

It is well known, though perhaps not as well known as it should be, owing to the influence of Shakespeare's play, that the historical Macbeth was not quite the villain he is pictured by most of the Scottish chroniclers. His claim to the throne was as good as, if not better than, Duncan's and through his wife it was better still. He did not, in the earliest accounts, treacherously assassinate his cousin the king but defeated him in battle. Duncan was not a paragon of kingly virtue but a weak and unsatisfactory king and Macbeth when he succeeded him proved an able and fortunate monarch; his reign of seventeen years was one of great prosperity and only towards the end of it did he show the injustice and cruelty which led to his overthrow. But Macbeth was the representative of the reactionary Celtic north; he favoured the old Celtic church and possibly the old social organisation. It was in the interests of the descendants of Malcolm Canmore, after Macbeth's death, to discredit him, to represent him as a regicide, a traitor and monster, and this is precisely how history was written. Nevertheless the struggle of the native religion, customs, and social system continued for a long time in the north against the feudal and Norman revolution of the eleventh and twelfth centuries. The Highlands were never effectively feudalised and in Dunbar's day were a byword in the south for primitive manners and barbarous language and institutions. Andrew of Wyntoun tells the 'official' story of Macbeth's treacherous murder of his uncle and the incitement of the witches, though he honestly admits Macbeth's virtues as a king and his services to the church. In order, it would seem, to weigh the balance against Macbeth, the chronicler tells two other quite unhistorical tales which seem to show that the old Pictish customs were still alive and perhaps that these legends, which had gathered round Macbeth's name in the north, were witness to the fact that they were still remembered there. In the first place he says that as soon as Macbeth had killed his uncle he lay with his uncle's wife and made her both his wife and his queen,

> And thus gatis quhen his eme was dede
> He succedit in his steid.

To Andrew this shows only the depth of Macbeth's depravity in disregarding the degrees of affinity. But it is clearly an instance of the old custom which we have already noticed as persisting in the Highlands to the sixteenth century, by which marriage to the widow of the ruling chief secured the succession since that ran in the female line. It was such incestuous marriages which shocked St

Margaret in the next generation after Macbeth. By the Pictish method of succession, indeed, Macbeth was perhaps the truer heir since he was daughter's son of Kenneth II whereas Duncan was only granddaughter's son of the same monarch. It is about this princess, daughter of Kenneth II, that Andrew tells an even more curious story which I translate since Andrew's verse is as tedious and flat as his medieval Scots spelling is hard to read, and the tale is a longish one:

As we find in the legends about him, Macbeth was begotten in an unusual way. His mother was accustomed to repair frequently to the woods to enjoy the refreshing air. And one day, as she went alone to disport herself in the forest, she happened to meet a handsome man. It seemed to her at the time that she had never before seen anyone so well-built, so strong or good-looking, so well-proportioned in limbs and features. They soon got to know each other so well that in the course of sport and merriment the man lay with the woman and begot a son on her on that occasion, this same Macbeth who afterwards grew to such state, position, and power, as I have just related.

And when this person had sported and spent the day with her and made her pregnant with a son, he said he was of the race of demons but bade her not be afraid on that account. For he said that his son should be a man of standing and chieftainship and no man born of woman should be able to kill him. And in token of this he gave his mistress a ring, bade her keep it well and have it for love of him. Thereafter he often used to visit her and had to do with her in secret and told her many things that would come to pass. When her time came she was unburdened and bore the son that he had begotten and called him Finlach Makbeth. He became very famous as you have heard. This was the origin of Macbeth who later made himself King of Scotland according to one of the stories about him, though whether it happened in this way or whether he was born in the ordinary manner and like most other men I do not know. But he was cruel in his behaviour as you may hear and have heard tell.[28]

As related, the story is intended to discredit Macbeth and suggest his hellish nature, but when translated out of monkish language it means that Macbeth's father was a fairy prince and it is likely that this was a flattering legend that continued to be told in the north about the great Mormaer of Moray who so nearly saved his country from the domination of the Saxon and the Norman. And this legend in turn is quite possibly a folk-tale version of the hero of illegitimate birth which, traced back, is the story of the normal 'marriage' of a Pictish princess to a foreign prince who begets an heir to the throne and goes back to his own clan or nation. The original institution has been forgotten and turned into a fairy marriage in the case of Macbeth's mother, as it was turned into a tale of virgin birth in later versions in the case of St Kentigern's mother. Much the same thing might have happened to another Scottish hero, Robert Bruce, had his story come down through legendary history and folk tale instead of in the sober accounts of historians. Even so, the mother of the hero seems to have behaved very much as a Pictish princess of an earlier time might have behaved in the choice of a husband. One is tempted to believe that the tradition had been handed down from mother to daughter, even though all public memory of the institution that once gave them power and authority had vanished. In the annals which continue John of Fordun's *The Chronicle of the Scottish Nation*, and are probably also by Fordun (who wrote in the second half of the fourteenth century), the story is told as follows:

> In the year 1271 . . . Adam Earl of Carrick left an only daughter named Martha as his heiress and she succeeded him in his domain and earldom. After she had, therefore, become mistress of her father's domain, as she was, one day, going out hunting at random, with her esquires and handmaidens, she met a gallant knight riding across the same country— a most seemly youth named Robert Bruce, son of Robert, surnamed the Bruce, the noble earl of Annandale in Scotland, and of Cleveland in England. When greetings and kisses had been given on each side, as is the wont of courtiers, she besought him to stay and hunt and walk about; and seeing that he was rather unwilling to do so, she by force, so to speak, with her own hand made him pull up, and brought the knight, though very loath, to her castle of Turnberry with her. After dallying there, with his followers, for the space of fifteen days or more, he clandestinely took the countess to wife; while friends and well-wishers of both knew nothing about it, nor had the King's consent been got at all in the matter. Therefore the common belief of the whole country was that she had seized—by force as it were—this youth for her husband.[29]

Alexander III was irritated by this behaviour of a feudal tenant, promptly took Turnberry Castle and confiscated the countess's estates, but friends of both parties arranged an amicable settlement and the countess, who was a widow, made her second husband, as she had made her first, Earl of Carrick. This was not without precedent in medieval Scotland. For example, when Fergus, Earl of Buchan, died with a male heir, in the thirteenth century, his daughter Marjory married William Cummine of the family of Badenoch and in her right he became Earl of Buchan.[30] Such cases have a tone curiously reminiscent of the days when kings became kings and chiefs chiefs in the right of their mothers or their wives. In fact, though patrilineal inheritance and feudal custom had long obliterated the old system, the greater independence and often the dominance in matters of property and inheritance enjoyed by women in Scotland may well be due to the fact that women never forgot the power they once enjoyed and that they contrived, in spite of everything, to keep the substance of it, though the forms had vanished and the reason for it had passed into oblivion. Travellers to Scotland, from Ayala onwards, frequently commented on their status. Thomas Morer, who was chaplain to a Scottish regiment about 1689 and wrote *A Short Account of Scotland* noted that:

> The women of Scotland are capable of estates and honours, and inherit both as well as the males; and therefore after marriage may retain their maiden name;[31]

The way in which women retained their own names and often their own property in Scotland impressed many travellers. It was perhaps the last afterglow of an age in which the real power had been theirs to exercise and enjoy.

We can form only a shadowy idea of what succession and inheritance in the female line may have meant in ancient Scotland. But there are modern examples of peoples with similar customs from which we can perhaps fill out the picture.

In the fourteenth century the celebrated Arab traveller Ibn Battuta made a journey from Spain across North Africa and the Sahara to the Niger and back. He found the entire central Sahara occupied by a people who have been identified with the modern Tuareg. Of one section of this people, the Massufa, he says:

> Their women are of surpassing beauty, and are shown more respect than the men. The state of affairs amongst these people is indeed extraordinary. Their men show no sign of jealousy whatever; no one claims descent from his father, but on the contrary from his mother's brother. A person's heirs are his sister's sons, not his own sons. This is a thing which I have seen nowhere in the world except among the Indians of Malabar. But those are heathens; *these* people are Muslims, punctilious in observing the hours of prayer, studying books of law and memorising the Koran. Yet their women show no bashfulness before men and do not veil themselves, though they are assiduous in attending the prayers. Any man who wishes to marry one of them may do so, but they do not travel with their husbands, and even if one desired to do so her family would not allow her go.
>
> The women there have 'friends' and 'companions' amongst the men outside their own families, and the men in the same way have 'companions' amongst the women of other families. A man may go into his house and find his wife entertaining her 'companion' but he takes no objection to it. One day at Iwálátan I went into the qádí's house, after asking his permission to enter, and found him with a young woman of remarkable beauty. When I saw her I was shocked, and turned to go out, but she laughed at me, instead of being overcome by shame, and the qádí said to me 'Why are going out? She is my companion.' I was amazed at their conduct, for he was a theologian and a pilgrim to boot.[32]

This state of affairs applied to all ranks. When Ibn Battuta visited the 'Sultan' at a place called Tagadda, the chieftain met him wearing a blue cloak, trousers, and turban like the Tuareg of today, and accompanied by his sister's sons who were the heirs to his kingdom. In another part of the country he learned that no caravan could cross the region without a guarantee of protection from the Tuareg who, then as now, were formidable raiders and warriors. To his surprise, he found that a woman's guarantee had more authority than a man's.[33]

The modern Tuareg have had their warlike occupations reduced by European occupation of their territories but their social organisation is much the same as it was when Ibn Battuta visited them, though there are variations in the different groups of tribes into which they are now distributed, those of Tassili-n-Ajjer, the Ahaggar, Adrar-n-Ifoghas, and Air being the most important. They are a white race and speak dialects of the same language as the Berbers of North Africa but their original language and racial affinities may have been quite different as is their system of inheritance and descent. They are nominally Muslims but they treat a number of important Muslim laws and practices with scant respect and their women do not wear the veil, whereas the men do cover their faces in public. In this they resemble the Picts, on whom Christianity seems to have sat rather lightly and been unable to combat deeply-rooted pagan practices and sexual customs. Inheritance among the Tuareg is in the female line as it was among the Picts. Of the Tuareg of Air Lord Rennell, who lived among them, observes:

> A man's status, in Air, as elsewhere among the Tuareg, is determined by the caste and allegiance of his mother. . . If a woman marries a man of her own tribes the children, of course, belong to that tribe, but if she marries away from her people they belong to her own, and not to her husband's clan. In this case, were the husband to predecease his wife, the children and their mother would return to live with her tribe. . . The laws of inheritance and succession also show the strength of the matriarchal tradition. Although hereditary office is rare among the Tuareg nowadays, it seems to have been more frequent in the past [he then quotes Ibn Battuta]. . . The Tuareg of Ghat not only treat their women-folk in much the same way as their brethren further south [at Air], but Richardson specifically states that the succession of the chiefs and Sultans of those parts is similar to the practice of the Tekadda house and at Agades. It is the son of the sister of the Sultan who succeeds.[34]

The similarity of the system of descent to that prevailing among the Picts is matched by his account of the social prestige of their women and liberty of action and initiative of which Lord Rennell remarks:

> This ease of garb among the women and their unveiled countenances are in keeping with the perfect freedom which they enjoy. Irrespective of caste or circumstance, whether they be noble or slave, rich or poor, the women of the People of the Veil are respected by their men in a

manner which has no parallel in my experience. . . . The Tuareg women are strong-minded, gifted and intelligent. They have their share in public life; their advice is proffered and sought in tribal councils. Contrary to Moslem practice . . . a Tuareg woman may own property in her own name, and, more than that, may continue to own and administer it after her marriage without interference by her husband, who has no rights over it whatsoever. . . .

. . . Their bravery is famous in Africa. Instances are not lacking where they have played great parts in war. In one engagement in Air the Kel Fadé women led their men into battle, covering them with their own bodies and those of their children to prevent the French firing. When Musa ag Mastan, the Amenokal [chief] of Ahaggar, went to France in 1910 his sister ruled the people in his stead. Though no instances are recorded in Air itself of women becoming chiefs of tribes they rule several villages among the Kel Geres. By usage and by right their functions are more consultative than executive. They do not seek election to tribal councils. They enter them as of right and not in competition, but not even then do they order men about. Their function is to counsel and to charm. They make poetry and have their own way.[35]

Nevertheless on occasions, he notes, they have led their tribes even in battle and tradition records a Tuareg queen, Kahena of the Aures Hills, who led her people against the invading and conquering Arabs in the eighth century as Boudicca led the Iceni against the Romans in the first century.[36]

The Tuareg of the great Ahaggar massif in the central Sahara are essentially similar in their customs, according to a later observer who lived among them for a time, though he notes that in this group it is the men who govern at all levels of Ahaggar society and that women, though treated with the greatest respect, cannot hold any office and cannot appear in tribal councils or appoint speakers to represent them there. Occasionally, however, a noble-woman of high rank and renowned for her intelligence, strong character, and skill in diplomacy may intervene in a quarrel to prevent a blood feud.[37] Chieftainship is hereditary in the female line and passes in theory from a chief to his eldest sister's eldest son, though other sorts of succession occur, including brother to younger brother—another feature of the Pictish succession, and as there, probably only a variation of inheritance through the mother. In the Ahaggar:

> A child of Tuareg parents inherits rank and privileges through the mother, regardless of whether she is a member of the father's clan or not; but the child is known as 'such-and-such, child of so-and-so', the parent thus referred to being the father. Property is inherited from both parents, following the principle of Moslem law which provides that a male heir shall receive twice as much as a female heir who is related to the deceased in the same degree. Today a Targui [Tuareg], asked to give his ancestry, will recite the list of male forbears in his father's line, although in the fourteenth century Ibn Battuta wrote that descent was counted through the mother's brother, and that a man's heirs were his sister's children rather than his own.[38]

It is particularly interesting to notice that even where Tuareg customs appear to be passing over a patrilineal system, as in the Ahaggar, the commanding and dominating position of the women remains a living tradition and a reality in spite of the gradual lapse of customs on which it depended. Such a situation would go far to explain the independence and status of women in Celtic countries for many centuries after an original matrilineal society had disappeared. Tuareg women in the Ahaggar appear to preserve all their prestige and independence. They can for instance marry beneath them without losing social or economic status, and on the contrary, men, though they exercise the power, can only rise in social status, which in Tuareg society is finely graded, by means of marriage and they lose caste if they marry beneath them.[39]

It is in respect of marriage, sexual customs, and freedom of choice of partners that Tuareg women perhaps give us a lively picture of what may have been the situation of Pictish women hinted at by ancient writers. Ibn Battuta gives what looks like a view of a society in which Tuareg women in the fourteenth century, though married according to Muslim law, enjoyed before and after complete freedom in the choice of lovers. Modern accounts confirm that the choice of partners is still a female prerogative. Marriage is late by Muslim standards, normally about twenty-five for a woman and thirty for a man. Marriages are monogamous in spite of Muslim law which permits plurality of wives. Among the Tuareg of Ahaggar Briggs describes the afternoon and evening meetings at which the women sing and entertain. A girl will then indicate to a favoured suitor that he may return after the meeting breaks up.

> When a young couple are by themselves at last, they may begin by kissing mouth-to-mouth, but more often they breathe up each other's noses, nostril-to-nostril. From here on things proceed naturally, some-times going very far indeed, but rarely as far as many imaginative writers would have us believe. . . The fact that these ladies can allow a very considerable degree of sexual intimacy and still avoid actual intercourse without resorting to violence seems to be due essentially to the simple fact that they are held in great respect by their menfolk.[40]

This is an area where, as we have seen, the influence of Islamic law and custom seems to have modified the older society. But among the Tuareg of Air, according to Lord Rennell, the freedom noted by Ibn Battuta still prevails:

> Before marriage, which for Oriental women occurs comparatively late in life, Tuareg girls enjoy a measure of freedom which would shock even the modern respectable folk of Southern Europe. They do no work, but dance and sing and make poetry, and in the olden days they learned to read and write. The art of literature is unfortunately dying out, but the women still are, as they always were in the past, the repositories of tradition and learning. . . Half the poetry of the Tuareg deals with the loves and adventures of young men and women. Marriages are not arranged as among the Arabs. It often happens that a girl has two or more suitors, when her free choice alone is the deciding factor. It is common for a girl who is in love with a man to take a camel and ride all night to see him and then return to her own place. . . Fights between rivals are not uncommon. Illicit love affairs inevitably occur: if they have unfortunate consequences, the man is called upon to marry the woman, but infanticide is not unknown. Once married the woman is expected to behave with decorum and modesty.[41]

In another Tuareg group, that of the Tassili-n-Ajjer, very little visited by white men until recently, the women are reputed to be freely amorous and to get and hold the love of men they choose by enchantments and powerful love philtres called *borbors*, which diminish a man's resistance and leave him at the mercy of the woman who uses them.[42]

Enough has been said to suggest that the freedom, enterprise, and dominating position of Scottish women in the Middle Ages, even in a predominantly patrilineal and Christian society, may have been the result of a consciously preserved tradition handed down from mother to daughter from an originally pagan and matrilineal society in which they ruled the roost and disposed of their favours as they wished. But there is also the possibility already mentioned that such traditions were also preserved and fostered by women's societies or cult groups descending from remote antiquity till at least the sixteenth or seventeenth centuries. It is this possibility, speculative as it may be, that we shall next consider.

14

Islands of Women

SAILING across the calm Pacific and expecting a landfall, one often sees, especially at dawn or dusk, what appears to be a mountainous coast on the horizon. As the ship draws nearer these realistic hills often resolve into cloud formations, but once in a while turn out to be what they seem, the islands the ship was bound for. At other times the ship passes at such a distance that one cannot tell whether it was reality or illusion. In the world of prehistory, of legend and folklore, we continually come upon ideas which, if pursued with the aid of critical inquiry, archaeology or comparative anthropology, can sometimes be established as facts or demolished as myths. But there are others which tantalise us with uncertainty no matter how far we pursue them. One such idea which has haunted the European imagination is that of islands, communities, or nations of women. The Argonauts on their way to Colchis found the island of Lemnos inhabited by women alone, under their queen Hypsipyle, and stayed there a year to marry and beget children before they sailed on to win the Golden Fleece. Bran son of Febal and Maelduin in Irish legend visit islands of women, are entertained there and make love to their hostesses. Much the same thing happens to Odysseus returning from Troy, though the islands in both cases are inhabited only by a single nymph by whom he has children. There was also the island inhabited by the Sirens who lured sailors to their doom and the island of the Hesperides who guarded the sacred apple tree of Hera. Another magic apple island is Avalon, described by Geoffrey of Monmouth, though he ascribes the tale to Telgesinus. There Arthur visits Morgain who lives in eternal youth and summer with her eight sister-fays. These and similar stories, like those told by Herodotus and Diodorus Siculus about the Amazons, are the insubstantial clouds of myth and legend. Scholarship resolves them into romanticised forms of ancient nature-myths or of legends about the world of the dead.

But under the clouds there is sometimes evidence of real islands, records of cult centres sacred to women worshippers from which men were either excluded or admitted only on special conditions. An island of course has an obvious advantage for a cult community or for cult meetings of this sort, but it is not essential; a sacred grove or a sacred mountain will do as well, or even a sacred occasion, provided the terror inspired by the divinity or the force of custom is enough to keep intruders away. In the Mediterranean countries it is sometimes difficult to disentangle the native cult from a later oriental cult imposed on it. Thus the legend that the worship of Dionysus or Bacchus was introduced from Asia Minor was generally accepted in both ancient Greece and ancient Rome. Yet it would seem from the myth of Orpheus to have been a native Thracian cult sacred to women alone. In the *Bacchae* of Euripides, Dionysus is represented as bringing a new religion to Thebes from Lydia. The majority of the worshippers are women, but men also take part in the orgiastic rites and King Pentheus, the spokesman for native religion and custom, speaks of the rites as a mere excuse for sexual promiscuity:

> Our women, I discover, have abandoned their homes on some pretence of Bacchic worship, and go gadding about in the woods on the mountains, dancing in honour of this upstart Dionysus, whoever he may be. They tell me, in the midst of each group of revellers stands a bowl full of wine; and the women go creeping off this way and that to lonely places and there give themselves to lecherous men, under the excuse that they are Maenad priestesses.[1]

The herdsman who reports to Pentheus later in the play denies this rumour of lascivious behaviour. The women as he saw their rites were alone, possessed by divine frenzy and in fact liable to tear to pieces any man who intruded on their rites—a fate which shortly befell Pentheus himself. Nevertheless Pentheus was probably voicing

241

popular opinion about a cult in which men and women feasted and revelled at night in the woods or in sacred groves in honour of a fertility god whose rites were realistically carried out. And this cult seems to have taken over another cult peculiar to women and native to Thebes. Teiresias, the local prophet, assures Pentheus that no chaste-minded woman will come to harm in the rites of Bacchus and we learn in the course of the play that, in spite of the fact that the cult is supposed to be newly introduced from the East, the tomb of Semele, mother of Dionysus, is in Thebes with a perpetually burning fire at her shrine, and that Dionysus was in fact born in Thebes itself. A women's cult of Semele involving the tending of a sacred fire would seem to have been native to Thebes.

One gets the same impression from Livy's account of the famous Bacchanalian scandal at Rome two centuries after the *Bacchae* was written. In 186 B.C. the consuls Spurius Postumius Albinus and Quintus Marcius Philippus, taking much the same view as King Pentheus, were engaged in eradicating the Bacchanalian cult which had become, they believed, a cloak for political insurrection, debauchery of the young, and even commerce in organised murder. The tradition that had come down to Livy was that the orgiastic cult of Bacchus had been introduced by a Greek into Etruria and had spread to Rome and to every part of Italy. The celebrations at Rome took place on the Aventine at night:

> There were initiatory rites which at first were imparted to a few, then began to be generally known amongst men and women. To the religious element in them were added the delight of wine and feasts, that the minds of a larger number might be attracted. When wine had inflamed their minds, and night and the mingling of males and females, youth with age, had destroyed every sentiment of modesty, all varieties of corruption first began to be practised, since each one had at hand the pleasure answering to that to which his nature was most inclined. There was not one form of vice alone, the promiscuous matings of free men and women, but perjured witnesses, forged seals and evidence, all issued from this same workshop: likewise poisonings and secret murders so that at times not even the bodies were found for burial. Much was ventured by craft, more by violence. This violence was concealed because amid the howlings and the crash of drums and

cymbals no cry of the sufferers could be heard as the debauchery and murders proceeded.[2]

The rites were found to be in the charge of four men who acted as priests and controlled the festivals for criminal ends, but the greater part of the worshippers were women. However, the freedwoman Hispala Faecenia, who was the consul's first informant and who had previously been an initiate, declared that originally it had been a purely women's mystery and quite respectable:

> At first she said it was a ritual for women, and it was the custom that no man should be admitted to it. There had been three days appointed in each year on which they held initiations into the Bacchic rites by day; it was the rule to choose the matrons in turn as priestesses. Paculla Annia, a Campanian, she said, when priestess, had changed all this as if by the advice of the gods; for she had been the first to initiate men, her sons Minius and Herennius Cerrinius.[3]

Moreover, the rites were held in a grove on the Aventine Hill near the Tiber, sacred to Stimula, a goddess identified with Semele, the mother of Bacchus. So that here as at Thebes we appear to have a foreign orgiastic cult of Bacchus taking over a native women's cult of a goddess identified with the mother of Bacchus. Semele was destroyed by fire from heaven. Her name, however, suggests that she was originally a moon-goddess and the sacred fire tended by her worshippers need have had nothing originally to do with the lightning of Zeus.

What is interesting in Livy's account is the resemblance between the two cults and certain medieval fairy cults which we have already noted. The latter appear to have been divided into one cult in which women alone danced and celebrated in woods and forests and others in which mixed companies of men and women, supernatural and mortal, held feast and revel accompanied by promiscuous sexual intercourse. The latter appear, as at Rome and Thebes, to have largely displaced the former in the course of time. One feature of the orgies on the Aventine Hill—which apparently had caves, galleries, or catacombs within it—was that victims whom the murder racket wished to dispose of were tied to a machine which whisked them into the interior of the hill. The worshippers were told that they had been carried off by the gods. It looks as though the gang were turning to their advantage a feature of the cult which reminds one of the mortals held captive in fairy hills and mounds. It was the moon-goddess Selene, for example, who kept the shepherd Endymion as her lover in a cave on Mount Latmos, in much the same way as Morgain la Fée kept Ogier the Dane on her apple island of women, Avalon. The magic sleep of Endymion is matched by the magic oblivion of Ogier caused by the ring that his mistress gave him; both Ogier and Endymion are endowed with perpetual youth by their divine captors. We may have here relics of older women's religions preserved in many parts of Europe and only partly assimilated to the new masculine-dominated pantheons of later ages. Tacitus mentions a goddess whose shrine was on an island in the North Sea, who was worshipped with great reverence by six Germanic tribes, including the Anglii who later settled northern Britain and gave their name to England. This goddess he calls Nerthus (or Erthus) and identifies as an earth goddess. Her image stood in a cart in a sacred grove on her holy island, covered with a cloth which no one but the priest could touch. She made occasional journeys in her car drawn by cattle through her territories and was then restored to her island after a ritual purification in a sacred lake on her island. The slaves who performed this lavation were immediately drowned in the lake. Tacitus speaks of a priest—not priestesses—but the original officiants may have been women as in the case of the Naharvali, another Germanic tribe who worshipped twin gods in a sacred grove served by a priest dressed as a woman.[4]

The Celtic lands preserve a number of traces of cult centres conducted by women and excluding men. Strabo, apparently quoting Poseidonius from the early first century B.C., tells of an island off the mouth of the river Loire inhabited by women priestesses:

> In the ocean he [Poseidonius] says there is a small island, not very far out to sea, situated off the outlet of the Liger river; and the island is inhabited by women of the Samnitae, and they are possessed by Dionysus and make this god propitious by appeasing him with mystic initiations as well as other sacred performances; and no man

244

sets foot on the island, although the women themselves, sailing from it have intercourse with the men and then return again. And he says it is a custom of theirs once a year to unroof the temple and roof it again on the same day before sunset, each woman bringing her load to add to the roof; but the woman whose load falls out of her arms is rent to pieces by the rest and they carry the pieces round the temple with the cry of Ev-ah and do not cease until their frenzy ceases; and it is always the case, he says, that someone jostles the woman who is to suffer this fate.[5]

These rites are perhaps no more likely to have been originally in honour of Dionysus than those on the Aventine, but they are obviously similar to those and to the rites at Thebes and in Thrace. But the mention of Dionysus suggests that, as at Rome and at Thebes, the original rites may well have been in honour of a Celtic goddess, perhaps a moon-goddess, and that in later practice they were transferred to the son or consort of the goddess. Similar rites and worship by communities of women, or women's societies meeting on ritual occasions, may have occurred at one time in Scotland among other places. In the great glen of Glenlyon among the mountains of Perthshire there is a small stone shrine, still containing cult objects, which continued to be thatched and unthatched at intervals of two years down to the present century.[6] As with the bull sacrifices of the Highlands, it is likely that the ritual and the worship of the cult continued at least to the sixteenth or seventeenth century.

Pomponius Mela, writing in the first century A.D., tells of another island of women off the coast of Brittany:

Sena in the Britannic sea, off the Osismic shore [Pont du Roz] is the oracle of a Gaulish divinity whose priestesses, nine in number are said to be sacred on account of their perpetual virginity. They are called Gallicenae and people think them endowed with extraordinary powers, able to arouse storms of wind and sea by chanting spells, and to be able to change themselves into animals at will, to be able to heal diseases which are elsewhere considered incurable and to know and foretell things to come. But they do not use these powers for any except those who have sailed on purpose to consult them.[7]

One is reminded of the virgin priestesses of Alba and Rome who guarded a sacred fire annually renewed for the goddess Vesta, originally perhaps a women's cult since at their festival on 9 June the Roman matrons brought their offerings to the 'store-house' in the temple. The Vestals were intimately connected with the security and prosperity of the Roman state. One is also reminded of Geoffrey of Monmouth's account of Morgain and her sisters, nine in number, who dwell on an island of extraordinary fertility in the ocean:

> There is no cultivation at all except that which nature provides; in abundance she produces the fertile corn and grapes and apples springing in her woods from self-sown seed. . . Life there lasts a century or more. There nine sisters rule with kindly sway those who come to them from our parts of the world. She who is first among them is the more learned in the art of healing and excels her sisters in superlative beauty; Morgen is her name and she teaches the virtues of all herbs useful in restoring enfeebled bodies. To her also is known the art of changing shape and of cleaving through the air like Daedalus with newly-formed wings.[8]

Geoffrey, writing in the twelfth century, attributes the account to Telgesinus, a bard who is probably the poet Taliesin. According to Nennius he was a great poet of the North Britons in the sixth century.[9] At any rate, the resemblance to Pomponius Mela's account is so striking that Geoffrey's is most likely to rest on ancient tradition of similar islands, as well as on Celtic mythology. Groagez off the Breton coast and Eigg in the Hebrides, according to J. A. Mac-Culloch, are still called 'the island of women'. In earlier times Eigg was called Eillan nan Banmore, 'island of the great women'.[10] It is an interesting fact that in the early seventh century Eigg was ruled by a woman who is called 'queen' in one account, 'a certain rich woman' in others. She ordered the massacre of St Donnan and his companions who had tried to establish a religious community on the island and her command was carried out by pirates or 'sea-robbers'. No reason for the massacre is given in the various versions of the story, but if Eigg was at the time a sacred island of women on which men were not allowed to live, the desecration of the site and the threat to the cult would be sufficient reason. The employment of pirates to carry out the killing suggests that the queen or chief priestess had no male subjects to call on for the purpose. One account says that earlier St Columcille had refused to hear St Donnan's confession since he was sure to suffer violent martyrdom. Two of the accounts say that the foolhardly monks established their monastery on a site where the queen used to pasture her sheep. If these were fields sacred to the goddess like the sacred fields of St Brigid at Kildare, the threat to the magical fertility of the island may have been an added reason for killing the desecrators.[11] Another women's island off the coast of Iona, the holy island, is recorded by Sir Donald Munro who was High Dean of the Western Isles in the sixteenth century:

> NABAN. On the southeist syde of the yland of Columkill, ther layes ane ile, callit in Erishe Ellan Naban, that is Woemens ile. It is full of heddir guid for store and fishing.[12]

Martin Martin's explanation that it was so called because St Columba banished all the wives and daughters of the 'tradesmen' who worked on Iona to this island, though he allowed the nuns to remain, sounds like a rationalisation to account for the name, though it was apparently a local tradition in the seventeenth century.[13] But Iona itself or this neighbouring isle may well have been a sacred island of women before the saint succeeded, unlike his colleague St Donnan, in banishing them and Christianising the site. Another such island may have been Taransay where Martin Martin records a superstition in his day that a man might not be buried there, 'because otherwise the corpse would be found above the ground the day after it is interred.'[14] Other islands with names that suggest similar sites are Lady Isle off the coast a few miles north of Ayr and now a bird sanctuary, the Maiden island near Oban in Argyll, Innishail, 'the isle of rest', site of a famous Cistercian nunnery, in Loch Awe, and Inchcailloch in Loch Lomond, also the site of a former nunnery. Both these last may owe their names purely to Christian associations, but, as at Kildare, the nunnery may well have been founded on a cult site. Innishail is just across the outlet of the Awe from Innis Fraoch, associated with the pagan legend of Fraoch and the dragon-guarded tree. Inchcailloch may mean the island of nuns or old women, but may equally mean the island of the goddess or the Cailleach. A large oak wood flourishing there in the eighteenth century suggests a sacred grove in former times.

But the sort of community that we can see dimly in these hints and fragments from the past is perhaps best exemplified by the great convent of St Brigid at Kildare which is generally agreed to have taken over a cult site and some of the customs and traditions of the worship of the goddess Brigid. Between 1183 and 1186 Giraldus Cambrensis visited Ireland several times and spent a good deal of his time there. He set out to inform himself about the island, its inhabitants, customs, and history and in 1188 he produced a book on the subject in which he had a good deal to say about this remarkable nunnery. It consisted, he said, of nineteen nuns, St Brigid herself always being counted as bringing the number up to twenty. As in other places St Brigid usually has nine attendants we may suspect a mistake, either that a simple misreading has changed nine into nineteen or that the original number was eighteen (two nines) with the saint making the nineteenth. The nuns tended a perpetual fire, each taking turn to watch it for a single night:

> on the evening before the twentieth night the last nun, having heaped wood upon the fire, says, 'Brigit, take charge of your own fire, for this night belongs to you.' She then leaves the fire, and in the morning it is found that the fire has not gone out and that the usual quantity of fuel has been used. This fire is surrounded by a hedge made of stakes and brushwood, and having a circle within which no male can enter; and if anyone should presume to enter, which has sometimes been attempted by rash men, he will not escape the divine vengeance. Moreover it is only lawful for women to blow the fire, fanning it or using bellows only, not their breath . . . in this neighbourhood there are some very beautiful meadows called St. Brigit's pastures in which no plough is ever suffered to turn a furrow. Respecting these meadows, it is held as a miracle that although the cattle in the province should graze the herbage from morning till night, the next day the grass is as luxuriant as ever.[15]

Giraldus mentions a bird called 'Brigid's bird', a falcon which was accustomed to perch on the great round tower at Kildare, was reputed to be many centuries old, and was held in great veneration till it was killed by an ignorant rustic.[16] He also recounts the dreadful fates of two English soldiers who tried to enter the sacred enclosure and approach the fire:

> At Kildare, an archer belonging to the household of Earl Richard leapt the hedge of St. Brigit and blew the fire with his mouth. On leaping back over the hedge he began to lose his senses, and blew into everyone's mouth he met, exclaiming, 'See how I blew St. Brigit's fire.' In the same way running from house to house through the city, wherever he found a fire he began to blow it using the same words. At last, having been seized by his comrades, and bound, he entreated to be taken to the nearest water. Being conducted there, and parched with thirst he took such deep draughts that he burst in the midst of them and died in their hands. Another who attempted to enter the circle round the fire . . . had already planted one of his legs across the hedge, though he was dragged back and held by his companions, had his leg and foot instantly withered; where afterwards, as long as he lived he was lame and an idiot.[17]

The historical accounts of communities and cult groups peculiar to women have so much in common with mythological accounts of islands or nations of women and with literary works based on mythology, that it seems probable that the fables reflect reality and sometimes preserve details obscured by confusion and degeneration of actual cults in later times. Putting all the accounts together some general characteristics appear and form a shadowy picture of the nature of such communities and the way they survived.

In the first place they nearly all worship a goddess, though in later practice a god, son or consort of the goddess, may displace her. At Thebes Semele; on the Aventine Stimula, about whom very little is known, though from what Ovid says about her in the *Fasti* and St Augustine in his *City of God*, the common equation of her with Semele is probably not justified. As she is also called Simila, it may have been merely a matter of like-sounding names.[18] Her cult appears to have been absorbed by that of Semele and Dionysus, as, according to Ovid's account that of the Roman goddess of Dawn, Matuta, was by that of the Greek Ino Leucothea.[19] The Vestal Virgins worshipped Vesta, goddess of the hearth, the island off the Loire estuary reported by Strabo worshipped Dionysus, but this is probably a name from classical 'equivalents' indicating a Celtic god of similar attributes. As was often the case with Celtic gods his female partner may well have been the more powerful element in the cult. Pomponius Mela's priestess-magicians worshipped a divinity who may have been either male or female:

> Sena in Britannico mari, Osismicis adversa littoribus, gallici numinis oraculo est.[20]

The precedessors of the nuns at Kildare worshipped the triple goddess Brigid. In the mythical stories Circe is, of course, the goddess of the island herself, a position similar to that of Morgain in the *Vita Merlini*. The Sirens and the Hesperides are likewise divine women but an archaic vase-painting from Corinth shows the Sirens singing to Odysseus and his shipmates in the presence of a great goddess who may be Persephone.[21] Hypsipyle and the Lemnian women appear likewise to have worshipped Persephone, though the madness that caused them to massacre all the males on the island was said to have been the vengeance of Aphrodite because they had neglected her rites.[22] The Amazons of Libya, according to Diodorus Siculus, worshipped Cybele, the Mother of the Gods.[23]

The rites of the goddess must be performed in secret, observed only by those who have been properly initiated into the cult. Men in particular must be excluded and for this purpose an island, a grove, a secluded valley or mountain top or a precinct within high walls is naturally chosen. Semele at Thebes had such a precinct and the word used for it is that used for the precinct of a hero-tomb. It was apparently an enclosed site and was visited by tourists as late as the second century A.D.[24] The rites of Stimula at Rome were held in a sacred grove, those of Brigid at Kildare in a fenced enclosure. Other island precincts in history or mythology have already been mentioned. The Amazons of Libya, according to Diodorus, lived on an island called Hespera in the great marsh Tritonis.

A feature common to many of these cults seems to have been the tending and renewal of a sacred fire. That this was the case in Semele's precinct at Thebes can be inferred from the opening lines of the *Bacchae*. The Vestal Virgins had as their most important task the care of the holy fire in the temple of Vesta and its renewal at the beginning of each new year. In Greek communities a sacred fire was similarly kept burning in the Prytaneum or town hall for the goddess Hestia. Brigid's sacred fire at Kildare and the sanctions surrounding it appear clearly in the account of Giraldus Cambrensis. The island of the Libyan Amazons contained Mere, a sacred city, 'subject to great eruptions of fire'.[25] Strabo makes no mention of a sacred fire, but the annual re-roofing of the temple on the women's island suggests the annual re-kindling of the hearth of Vesta. The Roman matrons celebrating the rites of Semele in the grove on the Aventine carried flaming torches down to the Tiber and immersed them in the river without their being quenched 'because they contained live sulphur mixed with calcium'.[26] This trick was plainly meant to show that it was magic or divine fire.

The fire cult was obviously connected in the case of the altars of Vesta, Hestia, and Brigid with the prosperity of the nation, the city, the tribe, or the family concerned and was perhaps a special instance of a general fertility cult. It is thought that the goddess worshipped at Thebes under the name of Semele was originally an earth-goddess and her consort the sky-god, her offspring the god of general fertility.[27] The islands of Circe and the Hesperides, and Lemnos and the island of the Libyan Amazons are all noted for their extraordinary fertility; like the Celtic islands of women where the earth puts forth without need of cultivation. Indeed as in Brigid's sacred meadows, the plough was probably forbidden as a sacrilege on the virginity of the earth. The island of the Sirens was known as Anthemoessa, Rich in Flowers,[28] according to Hesiod. With magical fertility go longevity, restoration of youth and health. These are part of the wisdom or magical power of the priestesses and derive from the goddess. Calypso promised Odysseus immortal life if he would stay with her on her island. The priestesses of Pomponius Mela and the virgins of Avalon heal, prolong life, and possess natural and supernatural wisdom. The goddess Brigid had similar powers. The shedding of blood is also often part of the ritual, the tearing apart of the victim, animal or human, as in the case of the Maenads and the priestesses recorded by Strabo. The frenzy was induced by dance and wild cries, noise, and chants rather than by wine. The *oreibasia* or mountain dancing described in the *Bacchae* was a ritual practised by women's societies at Delphi down to the days of Plutarch. The rite occurred every two years on the summit of Mount Parnassus.[29] The women must indeed have been 'possessed', since the occasion was mid-winter and the summit is a little over eight thousand feet. On at least one occasion the sacred taboos had to be broken when the dancers were lost in a snow-storm and a party of men went to rescue them.

These taboos on the presence of men seem to have been partly to prevent sacrilege, partly to guarantee the virginity of the priestesses, but the exclusion of men from the rites and the holy sites would seem to have been the common feature. In some instances the women appear to have lived ordinary lives in the community but to have excluded men at the time of the religious ceremonies. In other cases they were virgin priestesses secluded from contact with men. In others the virgin state was a temporary condition of service as a priestess. The Vestal Virgins could retire after thirty years and could marry. The Libyan Amazon had to remain a virgin until she had finished her military service, but could then resort to the company of men on the island, who were ordinarily employed in domestic tasks. The priestesses reported by Pomponius Mela and perhaps those at Kildare were vowed to virginity. The priestesses off the mouth of the Loire, on the other hand, like the Amazons of Scythia, resorted to men at intervals for the procreation of children. The inhabitants of the mythical islands of women seem always to have welcomed the visits of men and would try to retain them as lovers. It has been suggested that this wide variety of practices is consonant with an older stage of a common type of fertility cult in which the priestesses, like the goddess herself, would successively have the character of virgin, mother, and old woman, a cult which in fact was not only that of life but of death, with recurring cycles of birth, fruition, death, and rebirth. But whether these practices recorded in history or mythology are relics of one original cult or of many cults with common characteristics, there seems reason to suppose that women's societies persisted in many parts of Europe well into the Christian era.

What happened to them in later times is perhaps suggested by St Brigid's cult at Kildare and that of the unnamed divinity off the coast of Brittany. In the first instance the cult-site becomes a nunnery which preserves some of the old ritual and beliefs in a Christian form. In the second the close similarity between Pomponius Mela's account and that of the *Vita Merlini* suggests that the goddess and her attendants became fays or fairies. But in either case communities of real women existed to continue the cult. The nuns at Kildare were real women serving an imaginary Brigid; the 'queen' of the island of Eigg was a real woman, who presumably had followers who were real women serving an imaginary goddess. The extraordinary popularity of the cult of St Brigid in Ireland and Scotland suggests that there may originally have been many such communities. Her cult sites are often associated with nine virgin companions. Various folklore practices suggest that the cult of a closed society of women associated with her continued till recent times. For example, at a Maiden's festival on St Bride's Eve in some parts of Scotland, the girls, after carrying a sheaf dressed as a woman from house to house and soliciting presents, would then retire to a house where they fastened all doors and windows. The young men then gathered outside and asked permission to view the 'Bride'. They were then admitted and dancing, singing, and merrymaking went on till dawn. We have come a long way from Lemnos and Avalon but the homely custom perhaps preserves a continuation of the ancient rites.[30] Martin Martin records a custom in the Hebrides on the day after St Bride's Day:

> The mistress and servants of each family take a sheaf of oats and dress it up in women's apparel, put it in a large basket and lay a wooden club by it, and this they call Briid's-bed; and then the mistress and the servants cry three times, Briid is come, Briid is welcome. This they do just before going to bed, and when they rise in the morning they look among the ashes expecting to see the impression of Briid's club there; which if they do, they reckon it a true presage of a good crop and prosperous year, and the contrary they take as an ill omen.[31]

This looks like a continuation of a pagan custom, preserving features similar to those of the fire-watching at Kildare, and carried out as

253

a cult-ceremony by the women of individual houses. Bride has no saintly title and her attribute, a club, hardly suggests a Christian saint.

The story of Edric the Wild, as we have already noticed, could be interpreted as an actual case of the survival of a women's community in a remote spot, perhaps the Forest of Dean, in which ancient ritual and belief was carried on in the eleventh century. The women preserve their cult by its reputation for supernatural sanctions like those which attended the attempts of impious men to enter the enclosure of the sacred fire at Kildare, and by their reputed power to foretell the future and to bestow or withhold prosperity. In the way in which, when surprised, they attempted to deal with the intruders on their ceremony, by surrounding them, dragging them down and tearing them with nails and teeth, we have an odd echo of the bacchantes in Euripides:

> bulls which one moment were savagely looking along their horns, the next were thrown bodily to the ground, dragged along by the soft hands of girls—thousands of them; and they stripped the flesh off their bodies faster than you could wink your . . . eyes.[32]

The methods are essentially the same, though the numbers and strength are less, as in the case of the death of Pentheus when he rashly intrudes on the women and is torn to pieces in the same way, appealing in vain to his mother:

> She would not listen to him. She gripped his right arm between wrist and elbow; she set her foot against his ribs; and she tore his arm off by the shoulder. It was no strength of hers that did it; the god was in her fingers and made it easy. Ino was at him on the other side, tearing at his flesh; and now Autonoe joined them, and the whole pack of raving women. There was a single continuous yell—Pentheus shrieking as long as life was left in him, the women howling in triumph. One of them was carrying an arm, another had a foot with the shoe still on it; the ribs were stripped—clawed clean. Every hand was thick red with blood, and they were tossing and catching, to and fro, like a ball, the flesh of Pentheus.[33]

Such behaviour, while foreign to the Athenians, may well have still been going on in Macedonia where Euripides wrote the play.[34] The tearing to pieces of the priestess by her companions, as described by Strabo, reminds us that it was still going on two centuries later in the barbarian north of Europe, and the unroofing and roofing of the temple in Perthshire down to modern times suggests that similar scenes may have been witnessed in the British Isles in the Middle Ages, and that if there had been more women at a later stage of orgiastic frenzy, Edric and his page might not have escaped the fate of King Pentheus.

This is little more than fantasy, perhaps, and it may be pressing things too far for the evidence to suggest that Dunbar's three ladies represent the survival of an actual women's cult with an unbroken tradition back to classical times. Yet here are all the essential elements: the meeting on the occasion of the great fire-festival of midsummer, in a remote spot, in a sacred grove, and with the exclusion of men. There is the suggestion of the healing and restorative nature of the site blessed with supernatural fertility, the feast with wine and dances, and the women who are women of the town returning there when their rites, in which they become temporarily supernatural beings, have been fulfilled. It is the merest and perhaps the most fantastic of suggestions and yet, with so much evidence of the survival of ancient beliefs and customs, even in a distorted form, can one entirely dismiss the possibility suggested?

15

Lineaments of Gratified Desire

THE voyage of discovery on which I set out has led me to a lot of strange islands. It may seem to the reader that I have simply drifted farther and farther away from the poem which was my point of departure. But the nature and purpose of this book will be misunderstood if it is taken as an attempt to *prove* anything about Dunbar's poem. It is rather to provide a setting, a number of possible contexts in which the poem can be viewed and from its nature can perhaps be conjectured more accurately than when it is viewed in isolation or in the context of later literary and social attitudes. The eighteenth, nineteenth, and twentieth centuries, for example, had substantially the same texts of the *Iliad* and the *Odyssey* before them, but to the twentieth the context provided by archaeology has set them in a new light and given a new resonance to their poetry. A modern reader of Dunbar's 'Tretis of the Tua Mariit Wemen and the Wedo' can be pardoned for finding the fairy setting incongruous beside the coarse and colloquial realism of the main conversation and this is because his notion of 'faery' is so different from what it probably was in Dunbar's day. I have attempted to restore those probabilities by assembling a scrap-book of references against which this incongruity is diminished and its artistic intention may become clearer. The same reader may think by modern analogies that the first wife's proposals to exercise complete sexual freedom and to haunt markets, fairs, courts, and assemblies of all kinds to recruit new lovers means that she proposes to become a prostitute. He would be quite wide of the mark. He may take the widow's description of one of her entertainments as a flight of obscene fancy, and even, as some critics have suggested, as a fantasy prompted by the repressed desires of a celibate poet. Little in his own society or in the usual run of Scottish historical writing would suggest to him that Dunbar is simply giving a realistic account of contemporary social behaviour and sexual *mores* and that he may, if anything, be giving his readers a 'polite' version of an even cruder reality. Against the background of the anecdotes, the pieces of evidence from documents, and the comments of contemporaries assembled in some of these chapters it becomes clear that Dunbar is at least not exaggerating and that he may not even be particularly aiming at moral satire in the sense, for example, that Juvenal's sixth satire aims at lashing and exposing female vice. He appears to be treating with detached amusement a mild instance of manners and attitudes in secular life, which could be surpassed even by the habits of women in religious life if we are to believe the reports of contemporaries.

> All nunneries of every kind of religious women, and especially those of the Cistercian order . . . have come to such a pass of boldness that they utterly contemn the safeguards of chastity. [For] not only do they wander outside the monastic enclosures in shameless fashion through the houses of seculars, but they even admit all sorts of worthless and wicked men within their convents and hold with them unchaste intercourse. [Thus] they defile the sacred precincts with the birth of children, and bring up their progeny about them, go forth abroad surrounded by their numerous sons, and give their daughters in marriage dowered with the ample revenues of the Church.[1]

This was written in 1556 and represents a state of laxity and corruption which must, in the nature of what it describes, go back at least to Dunbar's day. It was not written by a zealous reformer, anxious to exaggerate anything to the discredit of the Catholic Church, but by Cardinal Sermoneta reporting on the state of the church in Scotland to the reforming Pope Paul IV, as part of the desperate effort of Archbishop Hamilton and others to avert the ruin and collapse that then faced his religion. No doubt things had got worse in the preceding half century but the situation when Dunbar's poem was written was even then bad enough to make his merry wives and widow seem like amateurs beside many of their sisters in religion. John Major, Dunbar's contemporary, is as forthright on the subject as the cardinal a generation later:

> Wherever there is a foundation for religious women, these ought to be shut up in the building devoted to their common life, so that they should not have the power of going beyond its walls, or of associating with men. . . For that sex is more thoughtless than the other—has a greater proclivity to intemperance of conduct; wherefore, when they have an opportunity of association with men, they easily violate their vow of chastity, and only rarely and with the greatest difficulty observe it. So that they ought to be kept apart from men, as it were, by a red-hot flame.[2]

Most of Major's earlier life had been spent in Paris, but he was in his native land from 1515 to 1525 as Principal Regent of the College and Paedogogium of Glasgow and canon of the Chapel Royal at Stirling. His remarks are not merely the generalisations of a medieval churchman on the frailty of women, but a commentary on what he saw going on around him.

The normal way to take Dunbar's poem is to regard it as a spirited satire on women, represented, as so often in medieval literature, in the aspect of a deadly bait leading men to destruction in this world and damnation in the next. Beauty and charm combined with rapacious greed for possessions, insatiable sexual appetite, and inordinate and perverse ambition to dominate. There is no incongruity between the exquisite beauty and youthful grace that meet us in the opening of the poem and the naked lust, selfishness, cruelty, and vulgar spite and cunning of the characters concealed under these delightful appearances, because this is precisely the medieval moralist's view of the devil's greatest snare. It was a romantic idea, a piece of delightful neo-Platonic nonsense dredged up by the Renaissance, to hold that beauty of face and body could be a reflection or mirror of the beauty of the soul within. Medieval thinkers were apt to go to the other extreme and to judge it the more likely that the soul would be corrupted by lust, avarice, and pride, the more seductively beautiful the frail flesh might appear.

There is no reason to doubt that this view forms at least one element in the poem, but it is an element which is treated with a certain ironic detachment. The stock materials are there and presume a stock reaction on which the author builds a structure of humorous fantasy and sardonic joy, very much as he does in his 'The Dance of the Sevin Deidly Synnis'. The Deadly Sins appear there with all the conventional characteristics they possess in other medieval allegories, in ugliness and horror enough to satisfy any moralist. But to the expected elements Dunbar adds a phantasmagoria of enormous energy and hilarious travesty which has the effect of making a good-humoured parody of the whole notion of mortal sin. Sin becomes not deadly but ludicrous, to the rhythm of a Highland reel:

> Than Lichery, that lathly cors,
> Come berand lyk a bagit hors,
> And Ydilnes him leid;
> Thair wes with him ane ugly sort
> And mony a stynkand fowll tramort,
> That had in syn bene deid.
> Quhen thay wer entrit in the dance,
> Thay wer full strenge of countenance,
> Lyk turkas birnand reid;
> All led thay uthir by the tersis,
> Suppois thay fyllt with thair ersis,
> It mycht be na remeid.

In much the same way the poet adds to the ordinary material of a debate type of poem on the woes and inconveniences of marriage, and to a conventional satire on the faults and failings of women, other elements which entirely transform the usual effect of these topics. By the fairy setting with its overtones of literary romance he puts the debate on marriage into the context of the ancient religions and cults still surviving in Scotland. Behind the festival jollification appear the magic feasts in mounds and hills and forest sanctuaries. Behind the three women of Edinburgh stand the ancient triple goddesses brilliant in beauty and terrible in their power, and the royal grace and imperious will of the great fays of romance. Because of this the discussion of marriage in all its matter-of-fact realism is moved, as it were, into another dimension. It becomes not the plaint or the protest of erring and misguided natures against

259

the injustices of the established order and the restrictions imposed by religion and society: it becomes, on the contrary, a challenge and a defiance to the whole of that society, its attitudes and its *mores*, the defiance of a rival and more ancient society and of once universal and still powerful religious ideas, fostered and maintained more or less in secret by obscure but pervasive cults. The result is a root-and-branch revolt, not merely against the failures of the institution of marriage, not even against that institution of marriage, but against the male species itself and all its assertions and assumptions of superiority and command over the female.

The force and fury and the elemental beauty of this great poem reside not only in the energy and brilliance of its execution but also in the way it is intelligently founded on fundamental issues. Its argument rests on the ultimate question of the sources of power, and in its exposition of these sources and forces it has the beautiful and terrifying clarity of Machiavelli's exposition of the sources of power in an Italian state or of Marx's analysis of the economic basis of the institutions of a given society in nineteenth-century Europe. Starting from the proposition that the interests of men and of women are different but mutually dependent, it draws a picture, illustrated by limiting examples, of the subjection of the interests of the female species to that of the male in human society. The exercise of power that leads to this subjection is indicated clearly enough: the two most important instruments of restraint are the institution of Christian marriage with its rules of obedience and submission of the wife to the rule of her husband, and the institution of the clan or family backed by the law and the secular state which regards women as possessions or chattels at the disposal of their male relatives. The two young wives in the poem propose revolt and a change of system but the widow's sermon points out that this is impracticable. Although it is not stated—perhaps because it is obvious—the ultimate power to enforce masculine control resides in masculine muscles and weapons. Man prevails and will prevail because he is on the whole bigger and stronger than woman and is not handicapped by child-bearing and child-nurture. But woman has two advantages, which, as Lysistrata argued in Aristophanes' play, she has only to exploit as thoroughly as men exploit their physical advantages, to match and perhaps conquer the male. One is the strong, ultimately the irresistible magnet of her sexual attraction and attractiveness, the other is the simple physiological fact that she can continue 'in the lists of love' longer than he can and that if she presses her advantage she can in the end exhaust and defeat him. Lysistrata is content to exploit the first of these advantages. By persuading her fellow women to deny themselves to men until their demands are met, she brings the men to their knees. But it is for a limited end and even then is only achieved by seizing the Acropolis, which prevents the men prevailing by overriding force. Dunbar's ladies propose to use both advantages: to grant their favours, but always on terms which must be met beforehand, and to make the competition so keen that no man can continue to keep his position of favour for long without ruining himself sexually and financially. At least, this is the proposal of the first two. The widow points out that this ruthless policy defeats its own ends. The war must be a secret one for its end is power, and open treatment of men as the enemy nullifies the charm on which the exercise of power depends. But more than this the possession of power is in itself only a means to the chief end of life, the pursuit of pleasure. The argument is not simply that if she can have pleasure with one lover, she may expect to have twice as much with two, and so on: it is rather that the pleasure she can have with any one lover is raised to the pitch of which it is possible only by the consciousness of her power over all. It is almost the opposite position to that argued in Machiavelli's *Prince*, on whether it is better to rule by love or by fear, but the case is equally firmly based on a *Realpolitik*. Machiavelli argues that it is better for a prince to rule by fear, since men remember injuries but soon forget favours. However, once a prince's power is firmly established on this basis he can gain added advantage by appearing to rule by winning the love of his subjects. The widow's argument is that a woman must appear to rule by love until she is secure enough and then she can further establish her position by two forms of fear that bind her subjects to her, the fear of being denied her favours, and the fear of humiliation in the sexual rat-race. But once this position is assured she can, like a Renaissance tyrant, assume a universal benevolence.

Every great poem derives at least part of its greatness from its amplitude of reference to great issues in human life and human history. The imagination of the later Middle Ages had exalted the idea of woman. The worship of the Virgin Mary had become such a cult as almost to appear a distinct religion within the wider constitution of Christendom. The conventions of Courtly Love had by a convenient fiction made love and marriage separate and irreconcilable institutions. In the latter a woman was subject to her husband and her male relatives; in the former her lover was absolutely subject to her will and it was only at her discretion that he could obtain even the favour of a smile or a kindly word. But the ideal in either case was one of exalted and perfect love. The reward for man's devotion was an answering love and care which had in it something of the divine condescension of a goddess giving her heart to a mortal and the generous affection of an overlord for a faithful and worthy vassal. There is none of this in the ideal proposed by Dunbar's ladies. For them the male sex is their natural prey, the material of pleasure to be trapped, used, and used up like any other product of the chase. Dunbar, looking with an unromantic eye at the Scottish society of his day, shows us what he sees behind the literary fictions of courtly love. His image of the time was soon to be matched by another which has held the imagination of Europe down to our own day. In 1630 Tirso de Molina launched the tremendous shadow of *El Burlador de Sevilla*. Don Juan, to whom every woman is *his* natural prey, stands as the counterpart to Dunbar's heroines. It is a pity that sentimentality about the 'nobler' sex and the 'gentler' sex should have obscured the latter view. The two parties should confront each other as the counterparts they are, symbols of the naked morality of the satisfaction of sexual appetites raised to an aristocratic principle of rule.

Both parties belong to the realm of comedy, for both deny the human its full humanity and only what is fully human can be taken quite seriously. There is no room, not even any comprehension in the world of either party for real human love, that relation of the

sexes in which each seeks not itself to please but to find its fulfil-
ment in 'the lineaments of gratified desire' in its partner. To attempt
to solve a tragic human problem by substituting an animal gratifica-
tion is essentially a comic contrivance, because it is only too clear
that the contriver has fooled himself by his own ingenuity. It is in
this that Dunbar's genius is evident: the poem above everything else
is full of laughter. The three women in their exuberance and beauty
fill their world with mockery and derision of the male sex. But in the
last line of the poem their magnificent and triumphant laughter is
returned as a derisive echo, mocking them with the hollow parody
of the human love and genuine passion which their victory has lost
them. In this sense Dunbar's achievement perhaps goes beyond his
intention, which may have been no more than a satire on contem-
porary manners. It has a resonance beyond the localised amusement
of a lively genre painting.

Yet the success of the comic on this level of depiction must also
be granted and is in fact essential to the total effect. The little
vignettes of contemporary life, the comedy of manners, and the
shrewd caricatures are full of essential fun: the bedroom fiascos,
the husband-and-wife dialogues, the domestic life of the widow
with her two husbands and the details of her well-tempered petting
party are the very stuff of comedy, and the vigorous, colloquial
Scots in which it is presented catches the exact accent and colour
of everyday life.

But the comic is often closely allied to a sense of tears, and in
this poem the alliance, the identification even of exquisite and
ideal beauty with gross, callous, and repulsive temperament and
vulgarity of character is more than a satirist's cynicism. We are made
to feel and respond to beauty so strongly at the beginning of the
poem that we cannot forget it in the sordid details of the genre
picture that follows, and indeed we are constantly reminded all the
way of the 'strong toil of grace' which these beautiful creatures
exercise. At the moment when the widow is revealing her greed,
duplicity, and hypocrisy with the greatest gusto she compares herself
in her widow's weeds to the pale moon peeping through black clouds
at night; an exquisite image and a pure feat of imagination:

And, as the new mone all pale, oppressit with change,
Kythis quhilis her cleir face through cluddis of sable,
So keik I through my clokis and castis kynd lukis,
To knychtis, and to cleirkis, and cortly personis.

(ll. 432-5)

Such touches, and they run all through the poem, take it out of the realm of mere comedy or mere satire into a world where the tragic paradoxes of the human condition intermingle a profound sadness with the hearty laughter and the sardonic contemplation of human triviality. It is the world where La Belle Dame sans Merci weaves her fatal spells, where Catullus stands by the door of the infamous tavern in which his late mistress in her clear beauty entertains the dregs of the town, where in his despair and hopeless grief the Chevalier des Grieux sits for a day and a night by the corpse of the worthless and exquisite Manon Lescaut. There is nothing very attractive about Dunbar's ladies as persons, so that the hint of the tragic dilemma is well contained within the comedy, but it is there just the same and the sense of irresistible beauty permeates the whole poem and reverberates in the beauty of the poetry throughout.

Beyond beauty, there is mystery. The reader may be surprised that, after assembling so much mythology as a background to the poem, I should in the end do so little with it. But there is a discretion to be observed in this respect. The late C. S. Lewis in an essay presented to J. R. R. Tolkien on his seventieth birthday argued against what he called the anthropological approach, the excessive interpretation of literary texts in terms of the mythology and folklore from which they possibly grew. Of a passage in Malory's *Le Morte Darthur,* where Gawain in battle grows stronger as the sun rises in the sky, which has been traced to an original solar myth, he pointed out that while it explains the origin of an otherwise puzzling element in the story, it explains nothing about the story as it stands:

> That peculiarity remains, in Malory's book, a complete irrelevance. Nothing leads up to it; nothing of any importance depends on it. Apart from it there is nothing divine and nothing solar about Gawain.[3]

This is salutary advice and the irrelevance introduced into criticism by adding 'source material' to the original text is not confined to medieval folklorists. The study of Shakespeare has been bedevilled by its confusions for over a century. But the case is not always as clear-cut as in the instance Lewis quotes. In the finest of all medieval alliterative poems, *Sir Gawain and the Green Knight*, as Lewis points out, it adds nothing to our knowledge or our power to appreciate the role of Bercilak in the poem to be told that he represents or is descended from an *eniautos daimon*, an annually recurring demigod in an ancient fertility religion. The information may be true but it is irrelevant and has no bearing on the poem which tells us all we need to know about the Green Knight both in his magical and his everyday character. But in the same poem there appears, briefly it is true, but with a sinister implication, the figure of 'Morgne the goddes'. All the modern reader learns from the poem is that she is old and ugly, that she learned her magic arts from Merlin, that she is Arthur's half-sister and Gawain's aunt and that she is the real owner of the castle and the author of the plan which leads to Gawain's adventure. The medieval audience obviously knew much more about Morgain la Fée than this, and the author of the poem expected them to know it. Part of the peculiar mystery of the poem resides in what is left unexplained between what everybody knew in general about Morgain and what the poet tells or fails to tell them about her appearance in this poem. This is not a mystery in the sense of something missing in the explanation of the poem, but a mystery which is part of the poem, an intentional and essential element in its structure. There is a nice point at which a critic or a literary editor must decide where his account of the antecedents of Morgain puts his modern reader in possession of all the medieval reader could have been expected to know, and where, for example, in relating Morgain to the Irish goddess Morrigan, he is introducing matter quite irrelevant to criticism and interpretation. Indeed it is sometimes impossible to decide where this nice point comes. Are the enigmatic hints of a fairy scene in Dunbar's poem merely elements incidental to a conventional romantic setting? If so we drag in irrelevant matter in tracing them to originals which neither Dunbar nor his audience had in mind. Indeed we distort the poem from its original intention, like the medieval critics who interpreted Ovid's *Ars Amatoria* as a Christian allegory. But we cannot answer this question, not only because of the lack of positive evidence but because Dunbar himself seems to be being deliberately enigmatic. If, on the other hand, cults and beliefs and practices from older religions still persisted in Scotland in the fifteenth century and were incorporated in fairy lore associated with and influenced by literary sources like the romances of chivalry, then what we take for an enigmatic presentation may be no more than humorous reticence, a hint to a contemporary audience of things better left unsaid but presented the more effectively for this very reason. It is a question which cannot be decided one way or the other, and I have therefore been content to assemble material for a possible interpretation, or even for several possible interpretations of this great poem. The external mystery of the work is that no one perhaps will ever know what is relevant to its interpretation. This is surely not such a bad thing for it leaves us in that state of receptive and imaginative speculation which is perhaps the most valuable experience the human mind can draw from works of art.

The inner mystery of the poem is its union of beauty and power, with laughter as the catalyst. It presents a vision of woman which is much more than a satirical caricature. It has in it something heroic, portentous, and magnanimous. It has less of the medieval moralist than of the Renaissance humanist questioning accepted values and attitudes and aware of the extraordinary variety and the even more extraordinary possibilities of variety in human affairs and the organisation of human society. Like all great works it transcends the limitation of the contemporary world view, and there seems to be a strange prescience of Nietzsche's view of woman as essentially a creature of a different *nature* from man, dangerous and indomitable, amoral and intrinsically and instinctively bent on the satisfaction of her animal passions. It is the conventional view of woman as the gentler sex, the submissive and dependent nature, or the nobler, purer and loftier moral being which Nietzsche held to be the sentimental caricature imposed by education and social pressure. It is his ability to present the tigress nature, the *domina victrix*, in her own terms, without overtones of moral disapproval, but with a note of detached and admiring amusement that is Dunbar's chief achievement. That the picture is taken from life we may well believe and one could summon a gallery of Scottish women from all ages to support its essential truth. I will content myself with the admirable and heroic Mrs M'Kenzie of Tomintoul, Banffshire. Tomintoul, described as the highest village in the Highlands, is surrounded by almost unpopulated stretches of mountain and moorland. Owing partly to its isolated position and partly to the benevolent protection of the Dukes of Gordon, it seems to have preserved some of the character of medieval Scotland down to the end of the eighteenth century. The population remained predominantly Catholic and the Reformation failed completely to eradicate the old customs, amusements, and beliefs. The Reverend John Grant, a learned and not illiberal minister who wrote the account of the parish in which Tomintoul stands, for *The Statistical Account of Scotland*, described the life of the village:

> No monopolies are established here; no restraints upon the industry of the community. All of them sell whisky, and all of them drink it. When disengaged from this business, the women spin yarn, kiss their innamoratos or dance to the discordant sounds of an old fiddle. The men when not participating in the amusements of the women, sell small articles of merchandise or let themselves occasionally for day labour, and by these means earn a scanty subsistance for themselves and families. In moulding human nature the effects of habit are wonderful. This village, to them has more than the charms of Thessalian Tempe. Absent from it, they are seized with the mal de pais; and never did a Laplander long more ardently for his snow-clad mountains, than they sicken to revisit the barren moor of their turf-thatched hovels.[4]

When one thinks of the dour Calvinism that ruled in so many Scottish villages at the time one can hardly wonder at their affection for the place, especially when we learn that the Duke of Gordon would not allow sheep, which had ruined and depopulated the rest of the Highlands, into the happy parish. Over this island of ease and ancient pleasures ruled not Mr Grant, not the Catholic priest, but the magnificent person of Mrs M'Kenzie to whom Mr Grant pays the following sardonic but not unappreciative tribute:

In personal respect and fortune, at the head of the inhabitants, must be ranked, Mrs. M'Kenzie, of the best inn, at the sign of the horns. This heroine began her career of celebrity in the accommodating disposition of an easy virtue at the age of 14, in the year 1745. That year saw her in a regiment in Flanders, caressing and caressed. Superior to the little prejudices of her sex, she relinquished the first object of her affections and attached herself to a noble personage high in the military department. After a campaign or two spent in acquiring a knowledge of man and the world, Scotland saw her again; but wearied of the inactivity of rural retirement, she then married and made her husband enlist in the Royal Highlanders, at the commencement of the war in 1756. With him she navigated the Atlantic, and sallied forth on American ground in quest of adventures, equally prepared to meet her friends, or encounter her enemies, in the fields of Venus or Mars, as occasion offered. At the conclusion of that war, she revisited her native country. After a variety of vicissitudes in Germany, France, Holland, England, Ireland, Scotland, America and the West Indies, her anchor is now moored on dry land in the village of Tamimtoul. It might be imagined, that such extremes of climate, and such discordant modes of living, such ascents and declivities, so many rugged paths, and so many severe brushes, as she must have experienced in her progress through life, would have impaired her health, especially when it is considered, that she added 24 children to the aggregate of general births, beside some homunculi, that stopped short in their passage. Wonderful, however, as it may appear, at this moment [1794] she is as fit for her usual active life as ever, and except for 2 or 3 grey hairs vegetating from a mole upon one of her cheeks, that formerly set off a high ruddy complexion, she still retains all the apparent freshness and vigour of youth.[5]

With this worthy successor to Boudicca and Cartimandua, to Morgain la Fée and Queen Medb, we may leave Dunbar's three noble ladies, confident that they represent no more than the truth of nature and art and that there were plenty of Mrs M'Kenzies in fifteenth-century Scotland who could have sat for these portraits.

Appendix

THE TRETIS OF THE TUA MARIIT WEMEN
AND THE WEDO

Apon the Midsummer evin, mirriest of nichtis,
I muvit furth allane, neir as midnicht wes past,
Besyd ane gudlie grein garth, full of gay flouris,
Hegeit, of ane huge hicht, with hawthorne treis;
Quhairon ane bird, on ane bransche, so birst out hir notis   5
That never ane blythfullar bird was on the beuche harde:
Quhat throw the sugarat sound of hir sang glaid,
And throw the savour sanative of the sueit flouris,
I drew in derne to the dyk to dirkin efter mirthis;
The dew donkit the daill and dynnit the feulis.   10

    I hard, under ane holyn hevinlie grein hewit,
Ane hie speiche, at my hand, with hautand wourdis;
With that in haist to the hege so hard I inthrang
That I was heildit with hawthorne and with heynd leveis:
Throw pykis of the plet thorne I presandlie luikit,   15
Gif ony persoun wald approche within that plesand garding.

    I saw thre gay ladeis sit in ane grene arbeir,
Aīl grathit in to garlandis of fresche gudlie flouris;
So glitterit as the gold wer thair glorius gilt tressis,
Quhill all the gressis did gleme of the glaid hewis;   20
Kemmit was thair cleir hair, and curiouslie sched
Attour thair schulderis doun schyre, schyning full bricht;
With curches, cassin thair abone, of kirsp cleir and thin:
Thair mantillis grein war as the gress that grew in May sessoun,
Fetrit with thair quhyt fingaris about thair fair sydis: 25
Off ferliful fyne favour war thair faceis meik,
All full of flurist fairheid, as flouris in June;
Quhyt, seimlie, and soft, as the sweit lillies
New upspred upon spray, as new spynist rose;
Arrayit ryallie about with mony rich vardour,   30
That nature full nobillie annamalit with flouris
Off alkin hewis under hevin, that ony heynd knew,
Fragrant, all full of fresche odour fynest of smell.
Ane cumlie tabil coverit wes befoir tha cleir ladeis,
With ryalle cowpis apon rawis full of ryche wynis.   35

THE TREATISE OF THE TWO MARRIED WOMEN
AND THE WIDOW

Upon a Midsummer's Eve, the merriest of nights, || I
went out alone, just after midnight, || beside a goodly
green enclosure full of gay flowers || and hedged to a
great height with hawthorn trees. || A bird on a branch   5
there burst into song || such that no more joyous bird
was ever heard upon bough. || What with the sweet sound
of her glad song || and what with the healing scent of the
pleasant flowers, || I secretly approached the bank* to lie
hid and overhear merrymaking. || The dew was moistening   10
the dale and the birds were singing loudly. ||

Close at hand, under a holly tree of heavenly green
colour, || I heard loud conversation in elevated language, ||
and thereupon I quickly thrust my way into the hedge
with such force || that I was covered by the hawthorn with
its sheltering leaves. || Presently I looked out through   15
the spikes of the tangled thorn || to see if any person
would draw near in that pleasant garden.||

I saw three gay ladies sitting in a green arbour, || all
adorned with garlands of choice fresh flowers; || their
glorious golden tresses were shining like gold itself ||
while all the grasses were glittering with the cheerful   20
colours; || their brilliant hair was combed out and elegantly
disposed || clear down over their shoulders and shining
very brightly, || with head-dresses of delicate and
transparent fabric arranged above. || Their mantles were
as green as the grass that grew in the May time || and   25
were held close with their white fingers about their
lovely bodies; || their gentle faces were of exquisite
complexion, || full of burgeoning beauty like flowers in
June; || they were as white, as soft and as well-favoured
as sweet lilies || newly opened upon their stalks, or as
the fresh-blown rose, || royally arrayed round about with   30
rich greenery || which Nature nobly enamelled with
flowers || of every known hue under heaven, || fragrant,
filled full of fresh odour, finest of smell. ||

A comely table was spread before those fair ladies ||
with royal cups in rows full of rich wines; || and two of   35

* or Fence.

And of thir fair wlonkes, tua weddit war with lordis,
Ane wes ane wedow, I wis, wantoun of laitis.
And, as thai talk at the tabill of many taill sindry,
Thay wauchtit at the wicht wyne and waris out wourdis;
And syne thai spak more spedelie, and sparit no matiris.   40

Bewrie, said the Wedo, ye woddit wemen ying,
Quhat mirth ye fand in maryage, sen ye war menis wyffis;
Reveill gif ye rewit that rakles conditioun?
Or gif that ever ye luffit leyd upone lyf mair
Nor thame that ye your fayth hes festinit for ever?   45
Or gif ye think, had ye chois, that ye wald cheis better?
Think ye it nocht ane blist band that bindis so fast,
That none undo it a deill may Бot the deith ane?

Than spake ane lusty belyf with lustie effeiris;
It, that ye call the blist band that bindis so fast,   50
Is bair of blis, and bailfull, and greit barrat wirkis.
Ye speir, had I fre chois, gif I wald cheis better?
Chenyeis ay ar to eschew; and changeis ar sueit:
Sic cursit chance till eschew, had I my chois anis,
Out of the chenyeis of ane churle I chaip suld for evir.   55
God gif matrimony were made to mell for ane yeir!
It war bot merrens to be mair, bot gif our myndis pleisit:
It is agane the law of luf, of kynd, and of nature,
Togiddir hairtis to strene, that stryveis with uther:
Birdis hes ane better law na bernis be meikill,   60
That ilk yeir, with new joy, joyis ane maik,
And fangis thame ane fresche feyr, unfulyeit, and constant,
And lattis thair fulyeit feiris flie quhair thai pleis.
Cryst gif sic ane consuetude war in this kith haldin!
Than weill war us wemen that evir we war fre;   65
We suld have feiris as fresche to fang quhen us likit,
And gif all larbaris thair leveis, quhen thai lak curage.
My self suld be full semlie in silkis arrayit,
Gymp, jolie, and gent, richt joyus, and gent[ryce].
I suld at fairis be found new faceis to se;   70
At playis, and at preichingis, and pilgrimages greit,
To schaw my renone, royaly, quhair preis was of folk,
To manifest my makdome to multitude of pepill,

these lovely creatures were wedded to lords, || and one was a widow of wanton habits. || And, as they talked at the table on a number of subjects, || they quaffed at the strong wine and let their tongues run on; || but afterwards they spoke more to the purpose and there were no holds barred. ||

'Disclose,' said the Widow, 'you young married women, || what enjoyment you have found in marriage since you became men's wives; || reveal whether you have ever repented that reckless contract, || or if ever you loved a living man more || than those to whom you have irrevocably fastened your allegiance; || or, if you had the choice, whether you think you would make a better one? || Do you consider that a blest bond which binds so fast || that no one can loosen it in the least except Death himself?'|| Then at once one gay creature spoke with spirit: || 'That which you call the blest bond that binds so fast || is empty of happiness and harmful and stirs up much trouble. || You ask whether, if I had free choice, I would choose better? || Chains are always to be avoided and changes are sweet. || If once I had my choice to avoid so cursed a lot, || I should escape for ever from the bondage of a boor. || Would to God that matrimony were made to engage in for one year! || It would only have claim to be longer, if it won our approval. || It is against the law of love, of humanity and of Nature, || to constrain hearts together which are at strife with each other. || Birds have a better law by far than mankind, || who each year with new joy, enjoy a mate || and take to themselves a fresh companion, constant and clean, || and let their out-worn companions fly where they please. || Christ! if such a custom were observed in this society, || then it would be a good thing for us women. For we should always be free. || We should be able to take fresh mates when and as it pleases us || and to dismiss the impotent ones when their vigour failed them. || For myself, I should be dressed most becomingly in silks, || graceful, attractive and beautiful, most cheerful and ladylike. || I should be found at fairs in order to see new faces; || at plays and preachings and at important pilgrimages, || in order to display my renown in royal style where there were gatherings of people; || in order to manifest my comely form

40

45

50

55

60

65

70

And blaw my bewtie on breid, quhair bernis war mony;
That I micht cheis, and be chosin, and change quhen me lykit.   75
Than suld I waill ane full weill, our all the wyd realme,
That suld my womanheid weild the lang winter nicht;
And when I gottin had ane grome, ganest of uther,
Yaip, and ying, in the yok ane yeir for to draw;
Fra I had preveit his pitht the first plesand moneth,   80
Than suld I cast me to keik in kirk, and in markat,
And all the cuntre about, kyngis court, and uther,
Quhair I ane galland micht get aganis the nixt yeir,
For to perfurneis furth the werk quhen failyeit the tother;
A forky fure, ay furthwart, and forsy in draucht,   85
Nother febill, nor fant, nor fulyeit in labour,
But als fresche of his forme as flouris in May;
For all the fruit suld I fang, thocht he the flour burgeoun.

I have ane wallidrag, ane worme, ane auld wobat carle,
A waistit wolroun, na worth bot wourdis to clatter;   90
Ane bumbart, ane dron bee, ane bag full of flewme,
Ane skabbit skarth, ane scorpioun, ane scutarde behind;
To see him scart his awin skyn grit scunner I think.
Quhen kissis me that carybald, than kyndillis all my sorow;
As birs of ane brym bair, his berd is als stif,   95
Bot soft and soupill as the silk is his sary lume;
He may weill to the syn assent, bot sakles is his deidis.
With goreis his tua grym ene ar gladderrit all about,
And gorgeit lyk twa gutaris that war with glar stoppit;
Bot quhen that glowrand gaist grippis me about,   100
Than think I hiddowus Mahowne hes me in armes;
Thair ma na sanyne me save fra that auld Sathane;
For, thocht I croce me all cleine, fra the croun doun,
He wil my corse all beclip, and clap me to his breist.
Quhen schaiffyne is that ald schalk with a scharp rasour,   105
He schowis one me his schevill mouth and schedis my lippis;
And with his hard hurcheone skyn sa heklis he my chekis,
That as a glemand gleyd glowis my chaftis;
I schrenk for the scharp stound, bot schout dar I nought,
For schore of that auld schrew, schame him betide!   110

to the crowds || and to advertise my beauty in places
where there were numbers of men, || so that I might choose   75
and be chosen and change when it pleased me. || Then
from the whole extent of the realm I should make the
very best choice || of one who should possess my woman-
hood through the long winter nights. || And when I had
got me a man, the most suitable of all others, || active and
young, to pull in the yoke for a year, || then after I had   80
tested his vigour for the first pleasant month, || I should
set about looking in church and in market-place, || and all
the country around, in the King's court and in others ||
where I might get me a gallant for the year to come || who
would keep the work going when the other one failed; ||
someone always eager and oncoming and straining to the   85
task, || neither feeble nor faint nor listless in labour, ||
but as fresh in his appearance as flowers in May. || For
I should take all the fruit, even though he put forth the
flower buds! ||

'I have a slack sloven, a worm, an old crawly cater-
pillar, || a worn-out boar good for nothing but clap-trap; || 90
a bumbler, a drone bee, a bag full of phlegm; || a scabby
scrag, a scorpion, a poop-bum. || To see him scratching
his own skin really fills me with disgust || [but] when
he kisses me, that cannibal, then all my misery flares
up. || His beard is as stiff as the bristles of a fierce   95
boar, || but his wretched tool is soft and supple like
silk; || well may he give assent to the sin but his acts
are innocent. || His two grim eyes are ringed with horrid
matter || and encrusted like a pair of gutters choked with
filth. || But when that glowering spectre takes me in   100
his grip, || then I think the hideous [devil] Mahound
has his arms about me. || Making the sign of the cross
will not save me from that old Satan, || for though I
cross myself completely from the top of the head down-
wards, || he will embrace my whole body and hug me
to his breast. || When the old churl is shaved with a   105
sharp razor, || he shoves his crooked mouth on mine and
scratches my lips; || and with his rough hedgehog skin
he scarifies my cheeks || so that my jaws glow like a
red-hot coal. || I shrink from the sharp scrape but I dare
not cry out || because of the threat of that bad-tempered   110
old wretch, shame befall him! || But the love leers of that

The luf blenkis of that bogill, fra his blerde ene,
As Belzebub had on me blent, abaist my spreit;
And quhen the smy one me smyrkis with his smake smolet,
He fepillis like a farcy aver that flyrit one a gillot.
Quhen that the sound of his saw sinkis in my eris,   115
Than ay renewis my noy, or he be neir cumand:
Quhen I heir nemmyt his name, than mak I nyne crocis,
To keip me fra the cummerans of that carll mangit,
That full of eldnyng is and anger and all evil thewis.
I dar nought luke to my luf for that lene gib,   120
He is sa full of jelusy and engyne fals;
Ever ymagynyng in mynd materis of evill,
Compasand and castand casis a thousand
How he sall tak me, with a trawe, at trist of ane othir:
I dar nought keik to the knaip that the cop fillis,   125
For eldnyng of that ald schrew that ever one evill thynkis;
For he is waistit and worne fra Venus werkis,
And may nought beit worth a bene in bed of my mystirs.
He trowis that young folk I yerne yeild, for he gane is,
Bot I may yuke all this yer, or his yerd help.   130
Ay quhen that caribald carll wald clyme one my wambe,
Than am I dangerus and daine and dour of my will;
Yit leit I never that larbar my leggis ga betueene,
To fyle my flesche, na fumyll me, without a fee gret;
And thoght his pene purly me payis in bed,   135
His purse pays richely in recompense efter:
For, or he clym on my corse, that carybald forlane,
I have conditioun of a curche of kersp allther fynest,
A goun of engranyt claith, right gaily furrit,
A ring with a ryall stane, or other riche jowell,   140
Or rest of his rousty raid, thoght he wer rede wod:
For all the buddis of Johne Blunt, quhen he abone clymis,
Me think the baid deir aboucht, sa bawch ar his werkis;
And thus I sell him solace, thoght I it sour think:
Fra sic a syre, God yow saif, my sueit sisteris deir!   145
Quhen that the semely had said her sentence to end,
Than all thai leuch apon loft with latis full mery,

bogle, from his bleary eyes, || make my spirits sink as if
Beelzebub had given me a look. || And when the snivel-
ling creature smirks at me with his nasty mug, || he
dribbles like a glandered cart-horse when it leers at a
mare. ||

'When the sound of his voice sinks into my ears, || 115
even before he comes near me, my repulsion always rises
afresh. || When I hear his name mentioned, I cross myself
nine times, || to protect me from the encumbrance of that
broken-down fool || who is full of jealousy and anger and
every evil habit. || I dare not glance at my sweetheart 120
because of that scrawny tomcat, || he is so filled with
jealousy and ill nature, || always thinking up malicious
designs, || compassing and imagining situations by the
thousand || in which by a trick he may catch me keeping
tryst with another man. || I dare not cast a glance at the 125
lad who fills my cup || for the jealousy of that old shrew
whose mind is always on evil. || Because he is wasted
and worn-out by the work of Venus, || what he can
provide for my needs in bed is not worth a bean. || He
believes I would like young folk to pay me, because he
is impotent, || but I may itch for it the year long before 130
his rod helps. ||

'Every time that cannibal wretch wants to climb on to
my belly, || I am disdainful and haughty and difficult to
persuade; || yet I never let that feeble creature get between
my legs || to soil my flesh, nor to fumble me except at a
high price; || and though his prick pays me poorly in 135
bed, || his purse pays richly in compensation afterwards. ||
For before he climbs on my body, that useless monster, ||
I make contract for a head-dress of the very finest
material, || a gown of dyed stuff, charmingly trimmed
with fur, || a ring with a royal stone, or some other rich 140
jewel; || otherwise his rusty rod may stay idle, no matter
if he flies into a blind rage for it. || Yet for all the
bribes of John Blunt, when he clambers on top, || it seems
an interval dearly bought, so feeble is his performance. ||
And thus I sell him comfort, though it is cold comfort
as far as I am concerned. || From such a master, God 145
save you, my dear sweet sisters!'

When that fair one had quite finished giving her
opinion || they all laughed loudly with the merriest

277

And raucht the cop round about full of riche wynis,
And ralyeit lang, or thai wald rest, with ryatus speche.

The wedo to the tothir wlonk warpit ther wordis;   150
Now, fair sister, fallis yow but fenyeing to tell,
Sen man ferst with matrimony yow menskit in kirk,
How haif ye farne be your faith? confese us the treuth:
That band to blise, or to ban, quhilk yow best thinkis?
Or how ye like lif to leid in to leill spousage?   155
And syne my self ye exeme one the samyn wise,
And I sall say furth the south, dissymyland no word.

The plesand said, I protest, the treuth gif I schaw,
That of your toungis ye be traist. The tothir twa grantit;
With that sprang up hir spreit be a span hechar.   160
To speik, quoth scho, I sall nought spar; ther is no spy neir:
I sall a ragment reveil fra rute of my hert,
A roust that is sa rankild quhill risis my stomok;
Now sall the byle all out brist, that beild has so lang;
For it to beir one my brist wes berdin our hevy: 165
I sall the venome devoid with a vent large,
And me assuage of the swalme, that suellit wes gret.
My husband wes a hur maister, the hugeast in erd,
Tharfor I hait him with my hert, sa help me our Lord!
He is a young man ryght yaip, bot nought in youth flouris;   170
For he is fadit full far and feblit of strenth:
He wes as flurising fresche within this few yeris,
Bot he is falyeid full far and fulyeid in labour;
He has bene lychour so lang quhill lost is his natur,
His lume is waxit larbar, and lyis in to swonne: 175
Wes never sugeorne wer set na one that snaill tyrit,
For efter vii oulkis rest, it will nought rap anys;
He has bene waistit apone wemen, or he me wif chesit,
And in adultre, in my tyme, I haif him tane oft:
And yit he is als brankand with bonet one syde,   180
And blenkand to the brichtest that in the burgh duellis,
Alse curtly of his clething and kemmyng of his hair,
As he that is mare valyeand in Venus chalmer;
He semys to be sumthing worth, that syphyr in bour,
He lukis as he wald luffit be, thocht he be litill of valour;   185

278

behaviour, || and passed the cup round and round, full of rich wines, || and for a long time they went on jesting with a riot of conversation. ||

The widow [then] to the second charmer addressed   150
these words: || 'Now, fair sister, it is your turn without pretence to tell us: || by your faith, how have you fared, since you first || received the honour of matrimony in church? Confess us the truth: || To bless or to curse that bond, which seems to you best? || How do you like leading   155
your life as a faithful spouse? || And afterwards you shall examine me in the same way || and I shall tell forth the truth, without a word of a lie.' ||

'I declare,' she said amiably, 'that if I avow the truth, || you are to bridle your tongues.' The other two agreed || and thereupon her spirits rose higher by a span. || 'I shall   160
not withhold what I have to say,' said she. 'There is no spy near. || I shall reveal a discourse that comes from the bottom of my heart, || a disturbance that rankles so that my gorge rises. || Now shall all the bile burst forth that has been swelling up for so long; || for it was too   165
heavy a burden to bear in my breast. || I shall give wide vent to the poison || and ease myself of a swelling which has so much increased. ||

'My husband was the greatest whore-master upon earth, || therefore I hate him from my heart, so help me God! || He is a young man, eager enough, but not in the flower of   170
youth, || for he has quite faded away and his strength is enfeebled. || A few years ago he was fresh and flourishing, || but now he has quite gone off and is decayed by his efforts; || he has been a lecher so long that he has lost his virility. || His tool has grown weak and lies in a swoon; || 175
nor is it any use to give that tired snail a period of repose, || for after seven weeks' rest it will not knock once. || He had exhausted himself upon women before he chose me as a wife, || and, in my time, I have often caught him in adultery. || And yet he swaggers about with his   180
bonnet at a rakish tilt || and making eyes at the prettiest girls that live in the town; || he is as courtier-like in his dress and the combing of his hair || as he that is more valiant in the chamber of Venus. || He gives the appearance of being worth something, that cipher in a lady's chamber. || His looks invite love; though he can scarcely   185

279

He dois as dotit dog that damys on all bussis,
And liftis his leg apone loft, thoght he nought list pische;
He has a luke without lust and lif without curage;
He has a forme without force and fessoun but vertu,
And fair wordis but effect, all fruster of dedis;   190
He is for ladyis in luf a right lusty schadow,
Bot in to derne, at the deid, he salbe drup fundin;
He ralis, and makis repet with ryatus wordis,
Ay rusing him of his radis and rageing in chalmer;
Bot God wait quhat I think quhen he so thra spekis,   195
And how it settis him so syde to sege of sic materis.
Bot gif him self, of sum evin, myght ane say amang thaim,
Bot he nought ane is, bot nane of naturis possessoris.
    Scho that has ane auld man nought all is begylit;
He is at Venus werkis na war na he semys: 200
I wend I josit a gem, and I haif geit gottin;
He had the glemyng of gold, and wes bot glase fundin.
Thought men be ferse, wele I fynd, fra falye ther curage,
Thar is bot eldnyng or anger ther hertis within.
Ye speik of berdis one bewch: of blise may thai sing,   205
That, one Sanct Valentynis day, ar vacandis ilk yer;
Hed I that plesand prevelege to part quhen me likit,
To change, and ay to cheise agane, than, chastite, adew!
Than suld I haif a fresch feir to fang in myn armes:
To hald a freke, quhill he faynt, may foly be calit.   210
    Apone sic materis I mus, at mydnyght, full oft,
And murnys so in my mynd I murdris my selfin;
Than ly I walkand for wa, and walteris about,
Wariand oft my wekit kyn, that me away cast
To sic a craudoune but curage, that knyt my cler bewte,   215
And ther so mony kene knyghtis this kenrik within:
Than think I on a semelyar, the suth for to tell,
Na is our syre be sic sevin; with that I sych oft:
Than he ful tenderly dois turne to me his tume person,
And with a yoldin yerd dois yolk me in armys,   220
And sais, "My soverane sueit thing, quhy sleip ye no betir?
Me think ther haldis yow a hete, as ye sum harme alyt."

stay the course; || he behaves like a fool of a dog making water on every bush || and lifting up his leg though he has no urge to piss. || He has a glance without desire and life without manly vigour; || form without force and the motions without the means; || fair words without effects, quite impotent in action. || In the matter of love he is for ladies a fine lusty shadow, || but in private, when it comes to the deed he is bound to be caught drooping; || he is for ever boasting in extravagant language, || praising himself for his bedroom feats and his randy behaviour, || but God knows what I think when he talks so big || and how it becomes him so to pronounce at large on such subjects, || unless one evening he should at least make some attempt at them; || but he is not such a one, not one of those in possession of their natural powers. ||

'She who has an old man is not completely defrauded: || he is no worse than he appears to be at the work of Venus. || I thought I had chosen a jewel, and I have got jet; || he had the glitter of gold and he turns out to be nothing but glass. || Men, though they be fierce, I find, when their manhood fails, || have nothing but jealousy and rage in their hearts. ||

'You speak of birds on the bough: they may well sing of their bliss, || who are vacant each year on St Valentine's day. || Had I that delightful privilege, to part when it pleased me, || to change and always to be able to choose again, then farewell Chastity! || Then I should [always] have a fresh companion to take in my arms: || To keep a fellow until he grows feeble may well be called folly. || I very often meditate at midnight upon such things || and grow so miserable and depressed that I could kill myself. || Then I lie sleepless for grief and toss to and fro || and often curse my wicked kinsmen who cast me away || on so spiritless and emasculate a creature as wedded my fresh beauty || when there were so many bold knights within this kingdom. || Then I think about some-one, to tell the truth, || a good seven times as attractive as his lordship and with that I frequently sigh. || Whereupon he turns his empty person towards me very tenderly || and, with a limp member, he yokes me in his arms || and says: "My sovereign sweet thing why do you sleep so badly? || It seems to me that you have a touch of fever as

190

195

200

205

210

215

220

Quoth I, "My hony, hald abak, and handill me nought sair;
A hache is happinit hastely at my hert rut."
With that I seme for to swoune, thought I na swerf tak;   225
And thus beswik I that swane with my sueit wordis:
I cast on him a crabit E, quhen cleir day is cummyn,
And lettis it is a luf blenk, quhen he about glemys,
I turne it in a tender luke, that I in tene warit,
And him behaldis hamely with hertly smyling.   230
     I wald a tender peronall, that myght na put thole,
That hatit men with hard geir for hurting of flesch,
Had my gud man to hir gest; for I dar God suer,
Scho suld not stert for his straik a stray breid of erd.
And syne, I wald that ilk band, that ye so blist call,   235
Had bund him so to that bryght, quhill his bak werkit;
And I wer in a beid broght with berne that me likit,
I trow that bird of my blis suld a bourd want.

     Onone, quhen this amyable had endit hir speche,
Loudly lauchand the laif allowit hir mekle: 240
Thir gay Wiffis maid game amang the grene leiffis;
Thai drank and did away dule under derne bewis;
Thai swapit of the sueit wyne, thai swanquhit of hewis,
Bot all the pertlyar in plane thai put out ther vocis.

     Than said the Weido, I wis ther is no way othir;   245
Now tydis me for to talk; my taill it is nixt:
God my spreit now inspir and my speche quykkin,
And send me sentence to say, substantious and noble;
Sa that my preching may pers your perverst hertis,
And mak yow mekar to men in maneris and conditiounis.   250
     I schaw yow, sisteris in schrift, I wes a schrew evir,
Bot I wes schene in my schrowd, and schew me innocent;
And thought I dour wes, and dane, dispitous, and bald,
I wes dissymblit suttelly in a sanctis liknes:
I semyt sober, and sueit, and sempill without fraud,   255
Bot I couth sexty dissaif that suttillar wer haldin.
     Unto my lesson ye lyth, and leir at me wit,
Gif you nought list be forleit with losingeris untrew:
Be constant in your governance, and counterfeit gud maneris,

though you were ailing for something." || "My honey,"
say I, "hold back and don't handle me roughly; || I have
had a sudden pain deep in my heart." || With that I appear   225
to swoon, though I am not subject to fainting. || In this
way I deceive the fellow with my sweet words: || when
daylight comes I give him a dirty look || and pretend it is
a love glance; when he glances back, || I put on a look of
tenderness which began as one of cursed rage || and gaze   230
at him like a good wife with a cheerful smile. ||

'I wish a tender delicate little piece || who hated men
with hard gear because they hurt || could have my good-
man in bed with her, for, I take God as my witness, || she
would not flinch a hair's-breadth on account of his
stroke. || And after that I would wish that the same   235
bond you call so blessed || should bind him to that fair
one until he recovered his manhood || and that I were
brought to bed with a man who pleased me. || I am sure
that that girl would have no occasion to mock at my
pleasure.' ||

As soon as this charming creature had stopped
speaking, || the others, laughing loudly, praised her   240
highly. || Those merry wives made sport among the green
leaves; || they drank and they drowned their sorrows
under the sheltering branches; || they drank heartily of
the sweet wine, those swan-white beauties; || but all the
livelier they voiced their grievances without restraint. ||

Then said the Widow: 'I suppose there is no other   245
way: || it is now my turn to talk, my story comes next: ||

'May God inspire my spirit, enliven my speech || and
send me noble and worthwhile ideas to express || so that
my preaching may pierce your obstinate hearts || and
make you meeker to men in your behaviour and in your   250
demands. || I reveal to you, my sisters in confession, that
I have always been a shrew, || but I hid this, by my
beautiful appearance and guileless looks. || But though I
was dour, haughty, despiteful and bold, || I dissembled so
well that I looked like a saint. || I seemed restrained   255
and sweet and simple without fraud, || though I could
deceive sixty who were supposed to be more subtle than I. ||

'Now listen to my lesson and learn sense from me: || if
you don't want to become the prey of faithless flatterers, ||
be steady in your control and keep up an appearance of

Thought ye be kene, inconstant, and cruell of mynd; 260
Thought ye as tygris be terne, be tretable in luf,
And be as turtoris in your talk, thought ye haif talis brukill;
Be dragonis baith and dowis ay in double forme,
And quhen it nedis yow, onone, note baith ther strenthis;
Be amyable with humble face, as angellis apperand, 265
And with a terrebill tail be stangand as edderis;
Be of your luke like innocentis, thoght ye haif evill myndis;
Be courtly ay in clething and costly arrayit,
That hurtis yow nought worth a hen; yowr husband pays for all.
   Twa husbandis haif I had, thai held me baith deir, 270
Thought I dispytit thaim agane, thai spyit it na thing:
Ane wes ane hair hogeart, that hostit out flewme;
I hatit him like a hund, thought I it hid preve:
With kissing and with clapping I gert the carll fone;
Weil couth I keyth his cruke bak, and kemm his cowit noddill, 275
And with a bukky in my cheik bo on him behind,
And with a bek gang about and bler his ald E,
And with a kynd contynance kys his crynd chekis;
In to my mynd makand mokis at that mad fader,
Trowand me with trew lufe to treit him so fair. 280
This cought I do without dule and na dises tak,
Bot ay be mery in my mynd and myrth full of cher.
   I had a lufsummar leid my lust for to slokyn,
That couth be secrete and sure and ay saif my honour,
And sew bot at certayne tymes and in sicir placis; 285
Ay when the ald did me anger, with akword wordis,
Apon the galland for to goif it gladit me agane.
I had sic wit that for wo weipit I litill,
Bot leit the sueit ay the sour to gud sesone bring.
Quhen that the chuf wald me chid, with girnand chaftis, 290
I wald him chuk, cheik and chyn, and cheris him so mekill,
That his cheif chymys he had chevist to my sone,
Suppos the churll wes gane chaist, or the child wes gottin:
As wis woman ay I wrought and not as wod fule,
For mar with wylis I wan na wichtnes of handis. 295

approved behaviour, || although you are [actually] sharp, 260
inconstant and bloody-minded. || Though you are as fierce
as tigers, be tractable in love || and be like turtle-doves
in your talk, though your hinder-parts be wanton; ||
always take on a double nature both of the dove and
dragon || and use the strength of either when at any time
you have need of it; || be amiable and look meek; seem like 265
angels, || and sting like adders with their fearsome tails; ||
be guileless in your appearance, though your minds be
full of mischief; || always wear the most fashionable and
costly clothes— || it is no skin off your nose since your
husband pays for everything. ||

I have had two husbands who both loved me dearly; || 270
although I detested them in return, they did not suspect
it in the least. || One was a hoary pig, always coughing
up phlegm. || I hated him like a dog, though I hid that
from him || and with kissing and petting I made a fool of
the man. || Well did I know how to ease his bent back 275
and comb his cropped noddle, || while I puffed out my
cheeks and pulled faces behind him, || and with a bow
came round and pulled the wool over his old eyes, || and
with a kindly expression kissed his shrivelled cheeks. || In
my mind I made mock of that mad father || who trusted 280
me to treat him so fair from true affection. || I could
manage this without trouble and no discomfort || but was
always able to be cheerful in spirit and full of gaiety. ||

'I had a more lovable man to slake my desire || who
knew how to be secret and reliable and always to protect
my reputation, || and to approach me only at certain times 285
and in secure places. || Every time the old man angered me
with his ill-natured talk, || it restored my cheerfulness to
gaze on my lover. || I was cunning enough to weep little
for actual grief || but I let the sweet always bring the sour
to a favourable moment. || When the brute wanted to 290
scold me, grimacing with his jaws, || I would chuck him
under the chin, pat his cheeks and make such a fuss of
him || that he was ready to assign his chief mansions to
my son, || even though the churl had become chaste before
that child was begotten. || I always managed things as a
wise woman and not as a poor fool, || for I gained more 295
by my wiles than by strength of my hands. ||

Syne maryit I a marchand, myghti of gudis:
He was a man of myd eld and of mene statur;
Bot we na fallowis wer in frendschip or blud,
In fredome, na furth bering, na fairnes of persoune,
Quhilk ay the fule did foryhet, for febilnes of knawlege,   300
Bot I sa oft thoght him on, quhill angrit his hert,
And quhilum I put furth my voce and Pedder him callit:
I wald ryght tuichandly talk be I wes tuyse maryit,
For endit wes my innocence with my ald husband:
I wes apperand to be pert within perfit eild;   305
Sa sais the curat of our kirk, that knew me full ying:
He is our famous to be fals, that fair worthy prelot;
I salbe laith to lat him le, quhill I may luke furth.
I gert the buthman obey, ther wes no bute ellis;
He maid me ryght hie reverens, fra he my rycht knew;   310
For, thocht I say it my self, the severance wes mekle
Betuix his bastard blude and my birth noble.
That page wes never of sic price for to presome anys
Unto my persone to be peir, had pete nought grantit.
Bot mercy in to womanheid is a mekle vertu,   315
For never bot in a gentill hert is generit ony ruth.
I held ay grene in to his mynd that I of grace tuk him,
And for he couth ken him self I curtasly him lerit:
He durst not sit anys my summondis, for, or the secund charge,
He wes ay redy for to ryn, so rad he wes for blame.   320
Bot ay my will wes the war of womanly natur;
The mair he loutit for my luf, the les of him I rakit;
And eik, this is a ferly thing, or I him faith gaif,
I had sic favour to that freke, and feid syne for ever,

    Quhen I the cure had all clene and him ourcummyn haill,   325
I crew abone that craudone, as cok that wer victour;
Quhen I him saw subject and sett at myn bydding,
Than I him lichtlyit as a lowne and lathit his maneris.
Than woxe I sa unmerciable to martir him I thought,
For as a best I broddit him to all boyis laubour: 330
I wald haif ridden him to Rome with raip in his heid,
Wer not ruffill of my renoune and rumour of pepill.

'Afterwards I married a merchant, well-provided with goods. || He was a middle-aged man and of low stature. || But we were not a match either in kinship or class, || in liberality, presence, or handsome appearance, || which the fool always forgot because of lack of breeding. || But I so often reminded him that his heart grew angry || and from time to time I would loose my tongue and call him Pedlar. || I used to talk irritatingly about my being twice married, || and how my innocence had ended with my old husband. || I was bold-looking even before I was grown up, || so says the curate of our church who knew me when I was quite young— || he is notorious for his falsehoods that fair worthy prelate || [and] I shall be loath to let him lie [about me] as long as I can get about— || Well, I made that huckster obey me: he had no other recourse; || he treated me with most profound respect once he knew what was due to me, || for though I say it myself, there was a great gap || between his bastard blood and my noble birth. || That menial would never have been worthy to presume even once || to be an equal of mine, had my pity not allowed it, || but mercy is a great virtue in womankind, || for compassion never springs from any but noble hearts. || I kept it always fresh in his mind that I took him only as an act of grace || and so that he should realise his position I courteously taught him. || He dared not sit down unless I told him to, for he was always ready to run || before I repeated an order, so terrified was he of my reproach. || But my will was always being worsted by my womanly nature; || the more he abased himself for my love the less I thought of him. || And also—this is an extraordinary thing—before I engaged myself to him || I had quite a favorable opinion of the fellow, and afterwards everlasting hostility. ||

'When I had the management of everything and he was completely under my thumb, || I crowed over that coward like a cock when it is victorious; || when I saw him abject and obedient to my commands, || then I despised him for a loon and loathed his habits. || Then I grew so merciless as to think of making him suffer martyrdom. || For I goaded him like a beast to every kind of puerile task. || I would have ridden him to Rome with halter on his head, || had it not been for the slur on my reputation

300

305

310

315

320

325

330

And yit hatrent I hid within my hert all;
Bot quihilis it hepit so huge, quhill it behud out:
Yit tuk I nevir the wosp clene out of my wyde throte,   335
Quhill I oucht wantit of my will or quhat I wald desir.
Bot quhen I severit had that syre of substance in erd,
And gottin his biggingis to my barne, and hie burrow landis,
Than with a stew stert out the stoppell of my hals,
That he all stunyst throu the stound, as of a stele wappin.   340
Than wald I, efter lang, first sa fane haif bene wrokin,
That I to flyte wes als fers as a fell dragoun.
I had for flattering of that fule fenyeit so lang,
Mi evidentis of heritagis or thai wer all selit,
My breist, that wes gret beild, bowdyn wes sa huge,   345
That neir my baret out brist or the band makin.
Bot quhen my billis and my bauchles wes all braid selit,
I wald na langar beir on bridill, bot braid up my heid;
Thar myght na molet mak me moy, na hald my mouth in:
I gert the renyeis rak and rif into sondir;   350
I maid that wif carll to werk all womenis werkis,
And laid all manly materis and mensk in this eird.
Than said I to my cumaris in counsall about,
"Se how I cabeld yone cout with a kene brydill!
The cappill, that the crelis kest in the caf mydding,   355
Sa curtasly the cart drawis, and kennis na plungeing,
He is nought skeich, na yit sker, na scippis nought one syd:"
And thus the scorne and the scaith scapit he nothir.
    He wes no glaidsum gest for a gay lady,
Tharfor I gat him a game that ganyt him bettir;   360
He wes a gret goldit man and of gudis riche;
I leit him be my lumbart to lous me all misteris,
And he wes fane for to fang fra me that fair office,
And thoght my favoris to fynd through his feill giftis.
He grathit me in a gay silk and gudly arrayis,   365
In gownis of engranyt claith and gret goldin chenyeis,
In ringis ryally set with riche ruby stonis,
Quhill hely raise my renoune amang the rude peple.
Bot I full craftely did keip thai courtly wedis,
Quhill eftir dede of that drupe, that dotht nought in chalmir: 370
Thought he of all my clathis maid cost and expense,
Ane other sall the worschip haif, that weildis me eftir;

and the way people gossip. || And yet I hid all my hatred in my heart, || though at times it heaped up so much that it was hard to restrain. || Yet I never quite took the stopper out of my throat || as long as I lacked anything I had set my mind to or anything I desired. || But when I had separated that man from his worldly goods || and got his buildings and his tall city tenements for my child, || the stopper flew out of my throat with a vengeance || so that he was quite stunned with the impact as if with a weapon of steel. || Then, after so long, I was so eager to be avenged || that I was as fierce in quarrel as a terrible dragon. || I had been pretending so long in order to flatter the fool, || until my documents of ownership were all sealed; || my breast was so crammed and so swollen with it, || that my rage very nearly burst forth before the conveyance was completed. || But when my bills and documents were all well sealed, || I would no longer answer to the bridle but reared up my head; || no bit could make me tame nor control my mouth. || I made the reins stretch and snap asunder. || I put that ninny to work only at women's tasks || and made him give up all masculine business and all earthly signs of manhood. || Then I would say to my gossips round about when we were chatting: || "Look how I haltered that colt with a tight bridle; || the nag that bucked off his paniers on the chaff dunghill, || now pulls the cart mannerly and would not dream of rearing, || neither shies nor takes fright, nor skips to one side." || And this way he escaped neither scorn nor injury. ||

'He was no pleasant companion for a gay lady; || therefore I found him a game that repaid him better. || He was a man with much money and rich in goods || [so] I let him be my broker to discharge all my business || and he was glad to accept that fine position from me || and expected to win my favours by his frequent gifts. || He clothed me in gay silk and choice raiment, || in gowns of dyed cloth and great golden chains, || in rings royally set with rich rubies || until my reputation rose high among the common people. || But I very cunningly put aside that courtly clothing || until the death of that drone who was useless in the bedchamber. || Though he bore all the cost and expense of my clothes, || some other who enjoys

335

340

345

350

355

360

365

370

289

And thoght I likit him bot litill, yit for luf of otheris,
I wald me prunya plesandly in precius wedis,
That luffaris myght apone me luke and ying lusty gallandis,   375
That I held more in daynte and derer be ful mekill
Ne him that dressit me so dink; full dotis wes his heyd.
Quhen he wes heryit out of hand to hie up my honoris,
And payntit me as pako, proudest of fedderis,
I him miskennyt, be Crist, and cukkald him maid;   380
I him forleit as a lad and lathlyit him mekle:
I thoght my self a papingay and him a plukit herle;
All thus enforsit he his fa and fortifyit in strenth,
And maid a stalwart staff to strik him selfe doune.

    Bot of ane bowrd in to bed I sall yow breif yit: 385
Quhen he ane hail year was hanyt, and him behuffit rage,
And I wes laith to be loppin with sic a lob avoir,
Alse lang as he wes on loft, I lukit on him never,
Na leit never enter in my thoght that he my thing persit,
Bot ay in mynd ane other man ymagynit that I haid;   390
Or ellis had I never mery bene at that myrthles raid.
Quhen I that grome geldit had of gudis and of natur,
Me thought him gracelese one to goif, sa me God help:
Quhen he had warit all one me his welth and his substance,
Me thoght his wit wes all went away with the laif;   395
And so I did him despise, I spittit quhen I saw
That super spendit evill spreit, spulyeit of all vertu.
For, weill ye wait, wiffis, that he that wantis riches
And valyeandnes in Venus play, is ful vile haldin:
Full fruster is his fresch array and fairnes of persoune,   400
All is bot frutlese his effeir and falyeis at the up with.

    I buskit up my barnis like baronis sonnis,
And maid bot fulis of the fry of his first wif.
I banyst fra my boundis his brethir ilkane;
His frendis as my fais I held at feid evir;   405
Be this, ye belief may, I luffit nought him self,
For never I likit a leid that langit till his blude:
And yit thir wisemen, thai wait that all wiffis evill
Ar kend with ther conditionis and knawin with the samin.

me hereafter shall have the credit of it. || And though I had little liking for him, yet for love of other men, || I would titivate myself charmingly in expensive clothes || so that lovers should gaze at me and lusty young gallants, || whom I find more attractive and dearer by far || than him who dressed me so smartly. He was quite senile. || When he had been plundered out of hand to increase my honours || and I was painted like a peacock in the proudest of feathers, || I despised him, by Christ, and I made him of feathers, || I left him as if he were a boy and held him in great loathing. || I thought myself a popinjay and him a plucked heron. || And this was the way he reinforced his enemy and built up her power, || and made a sturdy stick to strike himself down. ||

'But next I must tell you a joke about bed: || when, after a whole year of restraint he suddenly felt the urge, || I was loath to be leaped by such a clumsy cart-horse. || All the time he was on top, I never once looked at him || nor would I let myself think that he was piercing my thing, || but always I would imagine [that it was] another man I had there, || otherwise I should have had no pleasure from that cheerless assault. || When I had gelded that fellow of his goods and his manly vigour, || so God help me, I found him repulsive to look at; || when he had squandered on me all his wealth and his property, || it seemed to me that his spirit had all gone the way of the rest. || And so I despised him, I spat when I saw || that over-exhausted evil spirit, despoiled of all strength. || For well you know, you women, that he who lacks riches || and valour in the sport of Venus is considered absolutely contemptible; || quite in vain are his fresh array and his handsome person || and all his efforts are fruitless if he fails at the upping. ||

'I brought up my children like noblemen's sons || and made the fry of his first wife creatures of no account; || I banished from my bounds all his brothers || and his relations I always held in hatred as my enemies, || by which you may believe I had no love for the man himself, || for I never liked any person who belonged to his blood. || And yet there are wise men who believe all women || are known to be bad managers and can be recognised by this. ||

Deid is now that dyvour and dollin in erd: 410
With him deit all my dule and my drery thoghtis;
Now done is my dolly nyght, my day is upsprungin,
Adew dolour, adew! my daynte now begynis:
Now am I a wedow, I wise and weill am at ese;
I weip as I were woful, but wel is me for ever;   415
I busk as I wer bailfull, bot blith is my hert;
My mouth it makis murnyng, and my mynd lauchis;
My clokis thai ar caerfull in colour of sabill,
Bot courtly and ryght curyus my corse is ther undir:
I drup with a ded luke in my dule habit,   420
As with manis daill [I] had done for dayis of my lif.
    Quhen that I go to the kirk, cled in cair weid,
As foxe in a lambis fleise fenye I my cheir;
Than lay I furght my bright buke one breid one my kne,
With mony lusty letter ellummynit with gold;   425
And drawis my clok forthwart our my face quhit,
That I may spy, unaspyit, a space me beside:
Full oft I blenk by my buke, and blynis of devotioun,
To se quhat berne is best brand or bredest in schulderis,
Or forgeit is maist forcely to furnyse a bancat   430
In Venus chalmer, valyeandly, withoutin vane ruse:
And, as the new mone all pale, oppressit with change,
Kythis quhilis her cleir face through cluddis of sable,
So keik I through my clokis, and castis kynd lukis
To knychtis, and to cleirkis, and cortly personis.   435
    Quhen frendis of my husbandis behaldis me one fer,
I haif a watter spunge for wa, within my wyde clokis,
Than wring I it full wylely and wetis my chekis,
With that watteris myn ene and welteris doune teris.
Than say thai all, that sittis about, "Se ye nought, allace!   440
Yone lustlese led so lelely scho luffit hir husband:
Yone is a pete to enprent in a princis hert,
That sic a perle of plesance suld yone pane dre!"
I sane me as I war ane sanct, and semys ane angell;
At langage of lichory I leit as I war crabit: 445
I sich, without sair hert or seiknes in body;
According to my sable weid I mon haif sad maneris,
Or thai will se all the suth; for certis, we wemen

'That bankrupt is now dead and buried in the ground; || 410
with him died all my grief and my depression; || my
dismal nights are ended, my dayspring is at hand. || Fare-
well, sorrow, farewell! Now my voluptuous joy begins. ||
Now I am a widow, I am aware of it and am well at
ease. || I weep as though I grieved, but I am happy   415
henceforth. || I dress as though I were in mourning, but
my heart is blithe, || my mouth expresses grief and my
mind is laughing; || my cloaks express misery with their
sable colour, || but my body beneath is courtly and adorned
with great care. || I droop with a deathly look in my   420
mourning weeds || as though I had done with men for all
the days of my life. ||

When I go to church, clad in mourning, || I dissemble
my expression, like a fox in a lamb's fleece; || then I
lay my beautiful book spread open on my knee || with
many a splendid letter illuminated in gold || and draw the   425
hood of my cloak forward over my white face || so that
I may peep unespied at my surroundings. || I often glance
past my book, and break off my devotions || to see who is
the best set-up man with the broadest shoulders, || or
built the most powerfully to furnish a banquet, || valiantly   430
and without empty tricks, in the chamber of Venus. || And
as the new moon all pale, with change oppressed, || shows
her bright face at times through sable clouds, || so I peep
out through my cloak and cast encouraging glances ||
at knights and clerics and courtiers. || 435

'When relatives of my husband's see me at a distance, ||
I have a water sponge for grief inside my roomy cloak ||
and at these times I squeeze it cunningly and wet my
cheeks, || so that my eyes may water and the tears roll
down. || Then all those sitting around say: "Alas, do you   440
not see, || yonder unhappy creature, who loved her
husband so faithfully. || It is enough to impress pity in a
prince's heart, || that such a pearl of delight should have
to endure such suffering as that." || I cross myself like a
saint and look like an angel; || I behave as though   445
offended if I hear bawdy talk. || I sigh, though my heart is
not sad or my body sick. || I have to keep up sober
behaviour to go with my black weeds || otherwise they will
see the truth; for truly we women || set ourselves to

We set us all fra the syght to syle men of treuth:
We dule for na evill deid, sa it be derne haldin.   450
   Wise wemen has wayis and wonderfull gydingis
With gret engyne to bejaip ther jolyus husbandis;
And quyetly, with sic craft, convoyis our materis
That, under Crist, no creatur kennis of our doingis.
Bot folk a cury may miscuke, that knawledge wantis,   455
And has na colouris for to cover thair awne kindly fautis;
As dois thir damysellis, for derne dotit lufe,
That dogonis haldis in dainte and delis with thaim so lang,
Quhill all the cuntre knaw ther kyndnes and faith:
Faith has a fair name, bot falsheid faris bettir: 460
Fy one hir that can nought feyne her fame for to saif!
Yit am I wise in sic werk and wes all my tyme;
Thoght I want wit in warldlynes, I wylis haif in luf,
As ony happy woman has that is of hie blude:
Hutit be the halok las a hunder yeir of eild!   465
   I have ane secrete servand, rycht sobir of his toung,
That me supportis of sic nedis, quhen I a syne mak:
Thoght he be sympill to the sicht, he has a tong sickir;
Full mony semelyar sege wer service dois mak:
Thought I haif cair, under cloke, the cleir day quhill nyght,   470
Yit haif I solace, under serk, quhill the sone ryse.
   Yit am I haldin a haly wif our all the haill schyre,
I am sa peteouse to the pur, quhen ther is personis mony.
In passing of pilgrymage I pride me full mekle,
Mair for the prese of peple na ony perdoun wynyng.   475
   Bot yit me think the best bourd, quhen baronis and knychtis,
And othir bachilleris, blith blumyng in youth,
And all my luffaris lele, my lugeing persewis,
And fyllis me wyne wantonly with weilfair and joy:
Sum rownis; and sum ralyeis; and sum redis ballatis;   480
Sum raiffis furght rudly with riatus speche;
Sum plenis, and sum prayis; sum prasis mi bewte,
Sum kissis me; sum clappis me; sum kyndnes me proferis;
Sum kerffis to me curtasli; sum me the cop giffis;

blind men to the sight of truth; || we mourn for no evil   450
deed as long as it is kept concealed. ||

'Wise women have ways and wonderful traditions ||
for hoodwinking their jealous husbands with great
ingenuity; || and so quietly and so craftily do we manage
our affairs || that none of Christ's creatures knows of
what we do. || But folk may spoil a dish in the cooking   455
if they lack knowledge || and have no specious devices to
cover their defects of nature. || Such is the practice of
those damsels who, for foolishly concealed love, || hold
worthless fellows in estimation and have to do with them
so long || that the whole countryside knows of their
kindness and faithfulness. || Faith has a fair name, but   460
falsehood fares better. || Fie on her who cannot pretend
in order to save her good name! || But I am wise at such
work and have always been so. || Though I may lack grasp
in worldly matters, I have wiles in love || such as any
fortunate woman of good family [or of wanton disposi-
tion] has. || May the foolish virgin of a hundred years   465
old ever be an object of hate! ||

'I have a discreet servant whose tongue is perfectly
reliable || and who provides for me in such needs when
I give him a sign; || though he may be simple to look at he
has a sure tongue. || Many a more likely looking fellow
performs his service worse. || Though I suffer trouble in   470
my cloak all the bright day till nightfall, || yet have I
solace in my nightgown till the rising of the sun. ||

'Yet I am considered a pious woman throughout the whole
shire, || I am so piteous to the poor when there is a crowd
present. || I give myself credit for going on pilgrimages ||
though it be more because of the throngs of people than   475
in order to achieve any pardon.||

'And yet the best joke of all seems to me when barons
and knights || and other bachelors, blithe and in the bloom
of youth, || and all my faithful lovers throng to my house
and with abandon, || with jollity and merriment they pour
wine for me. || Some whisper, some jest, and some recite   480
love-poems; || some rattle on loudly in riotous talk; ||
some make their plaints of love and some plead for
favour; some praise my beauty; || some kiss me, some
pet me; some offer to do things for me; || one carves for
me with due ceremony; one hands me my cup; || and

Sum stalwardly steppis ben, with a stout curage,   485
And a stif standand thing staffis in my neiff;
And mony blenkis ben our, that but full fer sittis,
That mai, for the thik thrang, nought thrif as thai wald.
Bot, with my fair calling, I comfort thaim all:
For he that sittis me nixt, I nip on his finger;   490
I serf him on the tothir syde on the samin fasson;
And he that behind me sittis, I hard on him lene;
And him befor, with my fut fast on his I stramp;
And to the bernis far but sueit blenkis I cast:
To every man in speciall speke I sum wordis   495
So wisly and so womanly, quhill warmys ther hertis.
    Thar is no liffand leid so law of degre
That sall me luf unluffit, I am so loik hertit;
And gif his lust so be lent into my lyre quhit,
That he be lost or with me lig, his lif sall nocht danger.   500
I am so mercifull in mynd, and menys all wichtis,
My sely saull salbe saif, quhen sa bot all jugis.
Ladyis leir thir lessonis and be no lassis fundin:
This is the legeand of my lif, thought Latyne it be nane.
    Quhen endit had her ornat speche, this eloquent wedow,   505
Lowd thai lewch all the laif, and loffit hir mekle;
And said thai suld exampill tak of her soverane teching,
And wirk efter hir wordis, that woman wes so prudent.
Than culit thai thair mouthis with confortable drinkis;
And carpit full cummerlik with cop going round.   510

    Thus draif thai our that deir nyght with danceis full noble,
Quhill that the day did up daw, and dew donkit flouris;
The morow myld wes and meik, the mavis did sing,
And all remuffit the myst, and the meid smellit;
Silver schouris doune schuke as the schene cristall,   515
And berdis schoutit in schaw with thair schill notis;
The goldin glitterand gleme so gladit ther hertis,
Thai maid a glorius gle amang the grene bewis.
The soft sowch of the swyr and soune of the stremys,
The sueit savour of the sward and singing of foulis,   520
Myght confort ony creatur of the kyn of Adam,

another, inflamed with desire, comes stoutly forward || 485
and thrusts a stiff, standing thing into my fist. || And the
many who sit too far away, and cannot prosper as well as
they could wish || because of the crowd, cast glances of
love towards me. || But by speaking them fair [or, by my
charming practice] I comfort all of them. || For he that sits 490
beside me, I give his finger a nip || and serve him on the
other side in the same way; || and he who sits behind me
I lean hard on him || and he that sits in front of me I
press his foot firmly with mine || and to those who sit afar
in the outer room, I send winning looks. || And to each 495
man I speak a few words personally, || so wisely and so
womanly as warms their hearts. ||

'There is no man living of such low degree || that he
shall love me and not be loved in return, so tender-
hearted am I. || And if his desire be so set on my fair
face || that he would perish if he failed to lie with me, his 500
life shall be in no danger. || My heart is so merciful and I
so pity all men || that my simple soul shall be safe when
the Lord judges all. ||

'Ladies, learn these lessons and don't be taken for
[mere] girls. || This is the legend of my life, even though
it is not in Latin.' ||

When this eloquent widow had finished her elegant 505
discourse, || the others broke into gales of laughter,
praised her highly, || and said they would follow the
example of her sovereign teaching || and act as she had
advised, so prudent a woman was she. || Then they cooled
their mouths with comforting draughts || and gossiped 510
cosily as the cup went round. ||

So they finished out the agreeable night with the
noblest of dances || until the day dawned and the dew
bathed the flowers. || The morning was mild and bland
and the mavis was singing; || the mist had quite cleared
and the meadow was fragrant; || silver showers were 515
shaking down like clear crystal || and birds shouted in the
copse with their piercing notes; || so much did the golden,
glittering sunshine gladden their hearts || that they made
glorious entertainment among the green boughs. || The
soft sough of the breeze in the corrie and the sound of the
streams, || the sweet smell of the sward and the singing of 520
birds || might have brought comfort to any creature of the

And kindill agane his curage, thocht it wer cald sloknyt.
   Than rais thir ryall roisis, in ther riche wedis,
And rakit hame to ther rest through the rise blumys;
And I all prevely past to a plesand arber,   525
And with my pen did report thair pastance most mery.

   Ye auditoris most honorable, that eris has gevin
Oneto this uncouth aventur, quhilk airly me happinnit;
Of thir thre wantoun wiffis, that I haif writtin heir,
Quhilk wald ye waill to your wif, gif ye suld wed one?   530

(*The Poems of William Dunbar*, edited by W. Mackay Mackenzie,
                London, Faber & Faber, 1932, pp. 83-97)

kin of Adam ‖ and have rekindled his virility even though it had been quite extinguished. ‖

Then those royal roses got up in their rich clothes ‖ and set off home to their rest through the flowering sprays. ‖ And I furtively made my way to a pleasant arbour ‖ and with my pen recorded their merry pastime. ‖   525

You most distinguished auditors, who have given ear ‖ to this extraordinary adventure of the three wanton women ‖ I here have written down and that happened to me early one morning, ‖ which of them would you choose as your wife, if you had to wed one?   530

References

1. Introduction

1 H. Grierson and J. C. Smith, *A Critical History of English Poetry* (London, 1944), p. 59.

2 A. J. G. MacKay, *Memoir* (Vol. I, *The Poems of William Dunbar*) (Scottish Text Society [S.T.S.], Edinburgh, 1884-9), p. lxxxvii.

3 Tom Scott, *Dunbar: A Critical Exposition of the Poems* (Edinburgh, 1966), p. 202.

2. The Setting of the Poem

1 P. Hume Brown, *Early Travellers in Scotland* (Edinburgh, 1891), p. 47.

2 Philip Stubbes, *The Anatomy of the Abuses in England in Shakespeare's Youth, A.D. 1583*, ed. F. J. Furnivall (London, 1882), Pt I, p. 88.

3 James MacKinnon, *The Social and Industrial History of Scotland from the Earliest Times to the Union* (London, 1920), pp. 106-9.

4 Hume Brown, *Early Travellers in Scotland*, p. 140.

5 W. A. Craigie (ed.), *Maitland Folio Manuscript* (S.T.S., Edinburgh, 1919), Vol. I, p. 244.

6 John Major, *Expositio in Matthaeum* (Paris, 1518).

7 Sir John Sinclair, *The Statistical Account of Scotland* [*S.A.S.*] (Edinburgh, 1793), Vol. XII, p. 462n.

8 *S.A.S.*, Vol. VIII, p. 156.

9 Robert Kirk, *The Secret Commonwealth, 1691*, ed. R. B. Cunninghame Grahame (Stirling, 1933), p. 86.

10 Thomas Keightley, *The Fairy Mythology* (London, 1850), p. 355.

11 E. Estyn Evans, *Irish Heritage: The Landscape, the People and their Work* (Dundalk, 1945), p. 168; see also W. G. Wood Martin, *Traces of the Elder Faiths in Ireland* (London, 1902), Vol. II, p. 156.

12 'Dodona's Grove' (1664), quoted in Alexander Porteous, *Forest Folk-lore, Mythology and Romance* (London, 1928), p. 225.

13 *S.A.S.*, Vol. III, pp. 609-10.

14 John Graham Dalyell, *The Darker Superstitions of Scotland* (Edinburgh, 1834), p. 400.

15 Martin Martin, *A Description of the Western Islands of Scotland (c. 1695)*, 1703, ed. Donald Macleod (Stirling, 1934), p. 197.

[16] Giraldus Cambrensis, *The Topography of Ireland*, trans. Thomas Forester (London, 1905), p. 109.

[17] Keightley, *The Fairy Mythology*, p. 352.

[18] F. J. Child, *The English and Scottish Popular Ballads* (1957 reprint), Vol. II, pp. 56ff.

[19] *The Voiage and Travaile of Sir John Mandevile, Kt.*, reprinted from 1725 ed., ed. J. O. Haliwell (London, 1889), p. 13.

[20] Lady Jane Francesca Wilde, *Ancient Legends, Mystic Charms and Superstitions of Ireland* (London, 1888), pp. 243, 246.

[21] Barnabe Googe, *The Popish Kingdome or Reigne of Antichrist*, written in Latin verse by Thomas Neogeorgus (London, 1570).

[22] Porteous, *Forest Folklore, Mythology and Romance*, p. 104.

[23] Lucy Allen Paton, *Studies in the Fairy Mythology of Arthurian Romance*, 2nd ed., enlarged by R. S. Loomis (New York, 1960), pp. 211n., 4, 29; see also J. A. MacCulloch in Vol. III of *Mythology of All Races*, ed. L. H. Grey (New York, 1964), p. 121.

[24] *S.A.S.*, Vol. XV, p. 199.

3. GODDESSES AND FAIRIES

[1] In *The Discarded Image* (Cambridge, 1964), pp. 122-38.

[2] Nora K. Chadwick, *Celtic Britain* (London, 1963), p. 20, and Stuart Piggott, *The Prehistoric Peoples of Scotland* (London, 1962), p. 151.

[3] Peter Salway, *The Frontier People of Roman Britain* (Cambridge, 1965), p. 192.

[4] Isabel Henderson, *The Picts* (London, 1967), pp. 67, 117, 154, 218.

[5] Marie-Louise Sjoestedt, *Gods and Heroes of the Celts*, trans. Myles Dillon (London, 1949), pp. 18-21, 24-37.

[6] J. M. C. Toynbee, *Art in Britain under the Romans* (Oxford, 1964), p. 171.

[7] J. A. MacCulloch, *The Religion of the Ancient Celts* (Edinburgh, 1911), pp. 44-6.

[8] Sjoestedt, *Gods and Heroes of the Celts*, pp. 20ff.

[9] *S.A.S.*, Vol. XI, p. 181.

[10] Miss Dempster, 'Folk Lore of Sutherlandshire', *Folklore Journal*, Vol. VI (London, 1888), pp. 162-3. For another version see Sir Walter Scott, *Minstrelsy of the Scottish Border* (London, 1869), p. 432.

[11] *County Folklore* (Folk-Lore Society, London, 1914), Vol. VII, *Fife*, p. 309.

[12] K. H. Jackson, *A Celtic Miscellany* (London, 1951), pp. 176-7.

[13] Sir James George Frazer, *The Golden Bough*, 3rd ed. (London, 1936), Pt V, Vol. I, pp. 131-70.

[14] R. E. M. Wheeler, *Maiden Castle, Dorset* (Reports of the Research Committee of the Society of Antiquaries of London, No. XII, Oxford, 1943), pp. 8-9. See also Kenneth Cameron, *English Place-Names* (London, 1961), p. 156.

[15] *S.A.S.*, Vol. IX, p. 129.

[16] Whitley Stokes (ed.), *Tripartite Life of St. Patrick* (Rolls Series, London, 1887), p. 233.

[17] Nora Chadwick, *Celtic Britain*; see plate 13 and p. 222.

[18] *S.A.S.*, Vol. XIV, p. 550, Vol. IX, p. 581, Vol. XVIII, p. 295; Gilbert Skeyne, *Ane Brief description of the qualities and effectis of the well of the woman hill besyde Abirdene* (Bannatyne Club, Edinburgh, pub. 1580).

[19] Wheeler, *Maiden Castle, Dorset*, pp. 8-9.

[20] *S.A.S.*, Vol. XII, pp. 498-9.

[21] Ibid., Vol. XIII, pp. 99-100, and J. Romilly Allen, *Early Christian Monuments of Scotland* (Edinburgh, 1903), p. 209.

[22] MacCulloch, *Mythology of All Races*, Vol. III, pp. 187-9.

[23] M. Macleod Banks (ed.), *British Calendar Customs: Scotland* (London, 1939), Vol. II, pp. 146-50.

[24] Geoffrey of Monmouth, *The History of the Kings of Britain, c. 1136*, trans. Lewis Thorpe (London, 1966), Vol. II, Pt 7, p. 79.

[25] *Les Mabinogion*, trans. J. Loth (Paris, 1913), Vol. II, pp. 89-103 and 91n.

[26] *S.A.S.*, Vol. VIII, p. 347.

[27] MacCulloch, *Mythology of All Races*, Vol. III, pp. 130-1.

[28] *S.A.S.*, Vol. XII, pp. 182, 173-4.

[29] *The Chronicle of Perth* (Maitland Club, Edinburgh, 1831), p. 52, and *S.A.S.*, Vol. XVIII, p. 560.

[30] Lina Eckenstein, *Woman under Monasticism* (1896, reissued New York, 1963), pp. 1-44.

[31] Dalyell, *The Darker Superstitions of Scotland*, pp. 75-6.

[32] Jhone Leslie, *The Historie of Scotland*, trans. James Dalrymple, 1596 (S.T.S., Edinburgh, 1888), Vol. I, pp. 251-2, and *County Folklore*, Vol. VII, p. 13.

[33] Máire MacNeill, *The Festival of Lughnasa* (Oxford, 1962), p. 268, also following pages and p. 413.

[34] Ibid., pp. 274, 169.

[35] Leslie, *The Historie of Scotland*, Vol. I, p. 229.

[36] A. O. Anderson, *Early Sources of Scottish History* (Edinburgh, 1922), Vol. I, pp. cxx-cxxi.

[37] John of Fordun, *The Chronicle of the Scottish Nation*, trans. J. F. H. Skene, ed. W. Skene (Edinburgh, 1872), Vol. II, p. 407.

[38] *British Calendar Customs: Scotland*, Vol. II, p. 150.

[39] A. and J. Nicoll, *Holinshed's Chronicle as used in Shakespeare's Plays* (London, 1927), p. 210.

[40] Hector Boece, *The Chronicles of Scotland*, trans. J. Bellenden, 1531 (S.T.S., Edinburgh, 1941), Vol. II, p. 150. See also the Mar Lodge translation (S.T.S., Edinburgh, 1946), Vol. II.

[41] The Metrical Version of Boece, *The Buik of the Cronicles of Scotland*, ed. W. Stewart (Rolls Series, London, 1858), Vol. II, p. 635.

[42] Andrew of Wyntoun, *The Original Chronicle*, ed. F. J. Amours (S.T.S., Edinburgh, 1906), Vol. IV, pp. 272-5.

[43] *The Poems of Alexander Montgomerie*, ed. J. Cranstoun (S.T.S., Edinburgh, 1885-6), Vol. I, pp. 68-77.

[44] Ibid., Vol. II, p. 313. The text of the poem reads Pomathorne, a place a few miles from Edinburgh; but variations in the text of different versions make it probable that this is a corruption of an original Powarthorne, since Powarth or Polwarth was the birthplace and seat of Patrick Hume, the subject of the lampoon.

[45] Ernest Tonnelet, 'La Religion des Germains', in *Les Religions de l'Europe Ancienne* (Paris, 1948), Vol. III, p. 363.

[46] 'Matrib. Parc. Pro Salut./Sanctiae. Geminae.' See Salway, *The Frontier People of Roman Britain*, p. 215.

[47] MacCulloch, *Religion of the Ancient Celts*, pp. 44-5.

4. FAYS AND GODDESSES

[1] R. S. Loomis, 'A Survey of Scholarship in the Fairy Mythology of Arthurian Romance since 1903', appendix to Paton, *Studies in The Fairy Mythology*, p. 289.

[2] K. H. Jackson, 'The Sources for the Life of St. Kentigern' in Nora K. Chadwick and others, *Studies in the Early British Church* (Cambridge, 1958), pp. 335-6.

[3] N. K. Chadwick, 'Early Culture and Learning in North Wales' in ibid., pp. 58ff. and p. 23.

[4] R. H. Fletcher, *The Arthurian Material in the Chronicles* (New York, 1958), pp. 241-9.

[5] J. S. Stuart Glennie, 'Arthurian Localities' in *Merlin . . . A Prose Romance*, ed. H. B. Wheatley (Early English Text Society [E.E.T.S.] O.S. 36, London, 1899), Vol. I, p. lxxxix; I. and P. Opie, *The Oxford Dictionary of Nursery Rhymes* (Oxford, 1952), pp. 56-7.

[6] Andrew of Wyntoun, *The Original Chronicle*, Vol. IV, pp. 22-5.

[7] Boece, *The Chronicles of Scotland*, Bellenden translation, Vol. I, p. 380.

[8] *S.A.S.*, Vol. I, p. 506.

[9] Glennie, 'Arthurian Localities', pp. lxxvii-lxxviii, and E. K. Chambers, *Arthur of Britain* (London, 1927), p. 192.

10 Rachel Bromwich, *Trioedd Ynys Prydein* (Cardiff, 1961), pp. 154-6.

11 Loomis, 'Survey of Scholarship', pp. 280-91.

12 Translated by Archibald Constable (London, 1892), p. 82.

13 *The Works of Robert Fergusson*, ed. A.B.G. (Edinburgh, 1851), p. 44.

14 J. M. McPherson, *Primitive Beliefs in the North East of Scotland* (London, 1929), p. 79.

15 *S.A.S.*, Vol. XVI, p. 57.

16 *History of the Kings of Britain*, pp. 208-21.

17 Paton, *Studies in the Fairy Mythology*, pp. 137-41.

18 Child, *The English and Scottish Popular Ballads*, Vol. I, pp. 319-20.

19 James A. H. Murray (ed.), *The Romance and Prophecies of Thomas of Erceldoune* (E.E.T.S. O.S. 61, London, 1875), pp. 2-4.

20 Paton, *Studies in the Fairy Mythology*, pp. 228-9.

21 Ibid., pp. 49, 51, 56, 94, 191, 186, 76.

22 *Thomas of Erceldoune*, p. 6.

23 J. R. R. Tolkien and E. V. Gordon (eds.), *Sir Gawain and the Green Knight* (Oxford, 1925), p. 116.

24 Paton, *Studies in the Fairy Mythology*, ch. 8.

25 Ibid., chs. 4, 10, and 11; Loomis, 'Survey of Scholarship', pp. 280-91.

26 Paton, *Studies in the Fairy Mythology*, pp. 38, 30, and 76.

27 Henry B. Wheatley (ed.), *Merlin, or the Early History of King Arthur* (E.E.T.S. O.S. 10, 21, 36, London, 1869), pp. 418, 634, 681.

28 Thomas F. O'Rahilly, *Early Irish History and Mythology* (Dublin, 1964), pp. 286-94.

29 Quoted in Myles Dillon, *The Cycles of the Kings* (London, 1946), pp. 16-17.

30 MacNeill, *The Festival of Lughnasa*, p. 567.

31 David Fitzgerald, 'Popular Tales of Ireland', *Revue Celtique*, IV, pp. 189ff.

32 MacNeill, *The Festival of Lughnasa*, p. 408.

5. THE FAIRY CULT

1 *S.A.S.*, Vol. II, p. 556.

2 Ibid., Vol. XIX, p. 48.

3 Ibid., Vol. VI, p. 195.

4 Ibid., Vol. XI, p. 621.

5 Frazer, *The Golden Bough*, Pt X, p. 152.

6 Ibid., pp. 148, 153.

7 Pliny, *Natural History*, XVI.95.

8 Anne Ross, *Pagan Celtic Britain* (London, 1967), pp. 303, 304-5; Myles Dillon and Nora Chadwick, *The Celtic Realms* (London, 1967), plate 4.

9 Henderson, *The Picts*, pp. 141, 143, 220, and plate 45.

[10] William Mackay (ed.), *Records of The Presbyteries of Inverness and Dingwall, 1643-1688* (Scottish History Society, Edinburgh, 1896), p. 280.

[11] Ibid., p. 338.

[12] Frazer, *The Golden Bough*, Pt X, pp. 289-90.

[13] Ibid., Pt XI, p. 82.

[14] Pliny, *Natural History*, XVI.95.

[15] Ibid.

[16] *The Golden Bough*, Pt XI, pp. 85, 301.

[17] *The Chronicle of Lanercost*, trans. Sir Herbert Maxwell (Glasgow, 1913), p. 29.

[18] Martin, *A Description of the Western Islands of Scotland*, p. 107. Shony may be a Norse name, but the cult and the god are possibly Celtic. A similar libation was made to a sea-god in Iona; see W. Y. Evans Wentz, *The Fairy Faith in Celtic Countries* (London, 1911), p. 93.

[19] Kirk, *The Secret Commonwealth*, p. 67.

[20] Ibid., p. 79. See also H. C. Lea, *Materials toward a History of Witchcraft*, ed. A. C. Howland (New York, 1957), Vol. I, pp. 11-70.

[21] Gualteri Mapes, *De Nugis Curialium*, ed. Thomas Wright (London, 1850), pp. 154-8.

[22] Ibid., p. 157n.

[23] Child, *The English and Scottish Popular Ballads*, Vol. I, pp. 335-58.

[24] *Thomas of Erceldoune*, pp. 8-12.

[25] *S.A.S.*, Vol. XIII, p. 537; Vol. VI, p. 374.

[26] Ibid., Vol. III, pp. 335-6.

[27] Ibid., Vol. II, pp. 463-4; see also Vol. IV, p. 378 (Loggie Easter).

[28] The story occurs in Ailred of Rievaulx, *Epistola de Genealogia Regum Anglorum*, and was taken over from him by John of Fordun in *The Chronicle of the Scottish Nation*, Vol. II, pp. 195ff., though Fordun says he got it from Turgot. Rather different and less coherent versions occur in Andrew of Wyntoun's *Original Chronicle*, etc., and are followed by John Major and others.

[29] Major, *A History of Greater Britain*, pp. 124-5.

[30] John of Fordun, *The Chronicle of the Scottish Nation*, Vol. II, pp. 195ff.

[31] Ailred of Rievaulx, *Epistola de Genealogia Regum Anglorum* in A. O. Anderson, *Scottish Annals from the English Chronicles* (London, 1908), pp. 113-14.

[32] W. C. Hazlitt, *Faiths and Folklore of the British Isles* (reprinted New York, 1965), Vol. I, p. 210.

[33] *County Folklore*, Vol. VII, *Fife*, p. 199.

[34] *S.A.S.*, Vol. XIX, p. 472.

[35] Ibid., Vol. XIII, p. 453.

[36] Ibid., Vol. XXI, pp 121, 124.

37 *County Folklore, Fife*, p. 201.

38 *S.A.S.*, Vol. XII, p. 182.

39 Ibid., Vol. VII, p. 303; Vol. VI, pp. 136-7.

40 Alexander Nicholson, *History of Skye* (Glasgow, 1930), p. 73.

41 Kirk, *The Secret Commonwealth*, pp. 69, 73-4.

42 Scott, *The Minstrelsy of the Scottish Border*, pp. 464-5, quoting Richard Bovet, *Pandemonium, or The Devil's Cloister* (London, 1684).

43 Dalyell, *The Darker Superstitions of Scotland*, p. 538; Scott, *The Minstrelsy of the Scottish Border*, pp. 466-8.

44 Pitcairn, *Ancient Criminal Trials in Scotland*, Vol. I, Pt II, p. 57.

45 G. L. Burr in his introduction to Lea, *Materials toward a History of Witchcraft*, pp. xxxviii-xli.

46 Pitcairn, *Ancient Criminal Trials in Scotland*, Vol. I, Pt II, pp. 52ff., Pt III, pp. 161ff.; Vol. II, Pt I, p. 25, Pt II, pp. 537ff.; Vol. III, Pt II, pp. 602ff.

47 *Spalding Club Miscellany*, Vol. I, pp. 119ff.

48 D. A. McManus, *The Middle Kingdom* (London, 1959), p. 25.

49 Sir Walter Scott, *Letters on Demonology and Witchcraft, 1830* (London, 1884), p. 134.

50 Lewis Spence, *The Magic Arts in Celtic Britain* (London, 1945), p. 90.

51 *S.A.S.*, Vol. XIII, p. 245; Vol. XVI, p. 531.

52 *The Chronicle of Perth*, p. 52. See also McPherson, *Primitive Beliefs in the North East of Scotland*, p. 84.

53 *S.A.S.*, Vol. XVII, pp. 287-8; Vol. XIV, p. 187.

54 Ibid., Vol. XIX, p. 316.

6. LOVE AND CEREMONY

1 Lea, *Materials toward a History of Witchcraft*, Vol. II, p. 1325.

2 Pitcairn, *Ancient Criminal Trials in Scotland*, Vol. I, Pt II, pp. 49-58.

3 Ibid., Pt II, pp. 52ff.

4 Ibid., Pt III, pp. 161ff.

5 Ibid., Vol. III, Pt II, pp. 552ff.

6 *Spalding Club Miscellany*, Vol. I, pp. 119ff.

7 Pitcairn, *Ancient Criminal Trials in Scotland*, Vol. III, Pt II, pp. 603ff.

8 *Letters on Demonology and Witchcraft*, pp. 100, 182-3.

9 G. B. Harrison (ed.), *King James I, Daemonologie, 1597* (New York, 1966), p. 74.

10 *S.A.S.*, Vol. XII, p. 465.

11 J. A. MacCulloch, 'The Mingling of Fairy and Witch Beliefs in 16th and 17th Century Scotland', *Folklore*, Vol. XXXII, No. 4 (London, 1921), p. 238.

12 James I, *Daemonologie*, pp. 74-5.

[13] G. B. Harrison (ed.), *Newes from Scotland, 1591* (New York, 1966), frontispiece and p. 20.

[14] Joseph Stevenson, 'The History of William of Newburgh' in *Church Historians of England*, Vol. IV, Pt II (London, 1856), pp. 438-9.

[15] Scott, *Minstrelsy of the Scottish Border*, p. 448.

[16] 'The History of William of Newburgh', pp. 436-7.

[17] McPherson, *Primitive Beliefs in the North East of Scotland*, p. 97.

[18] A. G. Reid (ed.), *The Diary of Andrew Hay of Craignethan, 1659-1660* (Scottish History Society, Edinburgh), p. 158.

[19] *S.A.S.*, Vol. XII, pp. 552, 498-9.

[20] Scott, *Minstrelsy of the Scottish Border*, quoting a manuscript on heraldry in the Advocates Library, Edinburgh, p. 443.

[21] Mapes, *De Nugis Curialium*, pp. 79-81.

[22] Ibid., p. 79n.

[23] Thomas Forester (ed.), *The Chronicle of Florence of Worcester* (London, 1854), pp. 171, 175, and 177.

[24] Scott, *Minstrelsy of the Scottish Border*, p. 465.

[25] Mapes, *De Nugis Curialium*, p. 171.

[26] Walter W. Skeat (ed.), *The Romans of Partenay of Lusignan* (E.E.T.S., London, 1866), p. 19.

[27] Ibid., pp. v-vii.

[28] MacManus, *The Middle Kingdom*, p. 25.

[29] *Spalding Club Miscellany*, Vol. I, p. 119.

[30] Kirk, *The Secret Commonwealth*, p. 105.

[31] Evans Wentz, *The Fairy Faith in Celtic Countries*, p. 86.

[32] McPherson, *Primitive Beliefs in the North East of Scotland*, p. 106.

[33] Evans Wentz, *The Fairy Faith in Celtic Countries*, p. 112.

[34] Mapes, *De Nugis Curialium*, p. 171.

7. THE FAIRY CULT IN EDINBURGH

[1] Quoted in Scott, *Minstrelsy of the Scottish Border*, pp. 464-5.

[2] Kirk, *The Secret Commonwealth*, p. 68.

[3] Ibid., p. 69.

[4] Martin, *A Description of the Western Islands of Scotland*, p. 322.

[5] Ibid., pp. 321-4.

[6] Ibid., p. 330.

[7] D. A. Mackenzie, *Scottish Folk-Lore and Folk Life* (London, 1935), p. 225.

[8] Fergusson, *Works*, p. 138.

[9] *S.A.S.*, Vol. XXI, p. 148.

[10] Mackenzie, *Scottish Folk-Lore and Folk Life*, pp. 271-2.

[11] Sir J. Balfour Paul, 'Edinburgh in 1544 and Hertford's Invasion', *Scottish Historical Review*, Vol. XVIII (Edinburgh, 1911), p. 116.

[12] Royal Commission on the Ancient Monuments of Scotland, *An Inventory of the Ancient and Historical Monuments of the City of Edinburgh* (Edinburgh, 1951), p. 217.

[13] Fergusson, 'Caller Water' in *Works*, pp. 43-4.

[14] Robert Chambers, *The Book of Days* (London, 1864), Vol. I, p. 574.

[15] *The Journals of Dorothy Wordsworth*, ed. E. de Selincourt (London, 1953), Vol. I, p. 388.

8. THE BLEST BOND

[1] David Patrick (ed.), *The Statutes of the Scottish Church, 1225-1559* (Scottish History Society, Edinburgh, 1907), p. 39; see also pp. 67, 71, 72, 142, and 268.

[2] Caesar, *De Bello Gallico*, V.14.

[3] Henri Hubert, *The Greatness and Decline of the Celts* (London, 1934), p. 212; Strabo, *The Geography*, IV.v.4.

[4] See T. G. E. Powell, *The Celts* (London, 1958), p. 177; Henderson, *The Picts*, p. 19.

[5] Dio Cassius, *Roman History*, ed. Ernest Carey (Loeb ed., 1955), LXXVII.IX, p. 263.

[6] Ibid., LXII.VIII, p. 93.

[7] St Jerome, *Libri duo adversus Jovinianum*, Migne, *Patrologia Latina*, 23 (Paris, 1845), p. 295.

[8] Nora K. Chadwick, 'Intellectual Contacts between Britain and Gaul in the Fifth Century' in *Studies in Early British History* (Cambridge, 1954), pp. 205-6.

[9] Sjoestedt, *Gods and Heroes of the Celts*, pp. 58ff., p. 89.

[10] See MacNeill, *The Festival of Lughnasa*, p. 240; *The Tripartite Life of St. Patrick*, pp. 83, 87.

[11] Giraldus Cambrensis, *Expugnatio Hibernica* in *Giraldi Cambrensis Opera*, ed. J. F. Dimock, Vol. V (Rolls series, London, 1867), p. 282.

[12] Giraldus Cambrensis, *Topographia Hibernica* (Rolls series, Vol. V), pp. 164-5.

[13] Nennius, *Historia Brittonum* in *Six Old English Chronicles*, ed. J. A. Giles (London, 1866), pp. 400-1.

[14] Jackson, 'Sources for the Life of St. Kentigern', p. 275.

[15] In *Studies in Early British History*, pp. 254-63.

[16] F. M. Stenton, *Anglo-Saxon England*, 2nd ed. (Oxford, 1943), p. 4.

[17] Gildas, *Liber Querulus de Excidio Britanniae* in *Six Old English Chronicles*, pp. 314-21.

[18] Aileen Fox, *South West England* (London, 1964), pp. 165ff.

[19] H. M. Chadwick, 'Foundations of the Early British Kingdoms' and Rachel Bromwich, 'The Character of the Early Welsh Tradition' in *Studies in Early British History*, pp. 55, 122.

[20] *The History of the Kings of Britain*, p. 257.

[21] Fletcher, *The Arthurian Material in the Chronicles*, pp. 141, 119, and 198.

[22] Giraldus Cambrensis, *Descriptio Cambriae*, ed. W. Llewelyn Williams (London, 1908), p. 195.

[23] Jackson, 'Sources for the Life of St. Kentigern', pp. 273ff.

[24] Anderson, *Early Sources of Scottish History*, Vol. I, p. 132, Vol. II, p. 73.

[25] *S.A.S.*, Vol. XIII, p. 451.

[26] Richard of Hexham, *De Gestis Stephani* in Anderson, *Scottish Annals from the English Chronicles*, p. 187.

[27] Duncan Mactavish (ed.), *Minutes of the Synod of Argyll, 1639-1651* (Scottish History Society, Edinburgh, 1943), Vol. I, pp. 68 and 74, Vol. II, *passim*.

[28] *S.A.S.*, Vol. XII, p. 442.

[29] Sir John Edward Lloyd, *A History of Wales from the Earliest Times to the Edwardian Conquest*, 3rd ed. (London, 1948), Vol. I, p. 289.

[30] *S.A.S.*, Vol. VI, pp. 292-3.

9. St Valentine's Day

[1] *British Calendar Customs: Scotland*, Vol. II, p. 171.

[2] *Hamlet*, Act IV, Sc. v.

[3] *British Calendar Customs: Scotland*, Vol. II, p. 172.

[4] A. R. Wright and T. E. Jones (eds.), *British Calendar Customs: England* (London, 1939), Vol. II, p. 156.

[5] MacNeill, *The Festival of Lughnasa*, p. 316.

[6] Ibid., p. 317.

[7] Ibid.

[8] Giraldus Cambrensis, *Descriptio Cambriae*, p. 195.

[9] Lloyd, *A History of Wales from the Earliest Times*, p. 290.

[10] MacNeill, *The Festival of Lughnasa*, pp. 325-8.

[11] *S.A.S.*, Vol. X, pp. 537-8.

[12] *County Folklore, Fife*, p. 199.

[13] Ibid., p. 205.

[14] *S.A.S.*, Vol. XII, pp. 614-15.

[15] Martin, *A Description of the Western Islands of Scotland*, p. 175.

[16] Ibid., p. 23.

[17] Nicholson, *History of Skye*, p. 104.

[18] William F. Skene, *The Highlanders of Scotland* (London, 1902), pp. 108-9.

[19] 'Handfasting in Scotland', *Scottish Historical Review*, Vol. XXXVII, No. 124 (Edinburgh, Oct. 1958), p. 99.

[20] Ibid.

[21] *The Register of the Privy Council of Scotland*, ed. David Masson (Edinburgh, 1889), Vol. IX, p. 27.

[22] Ibid.

[23] Anton, 'Handfasting in Scotland', p. 99, quoting Ecclesiastical Records of Aberdeen. See also Robert Chambers, *Domestic Annals of Scotland* (Edinburgh, 1858), Vol. I, pp. 334-5.

[24] Anderson, *Early Sources of Scottish History*, Vol. II, p. 74n.

[25] *Register of the Kirk Session of Humbie* in *Maitland Club Miscellany* (Edinburgh, 1840), Vol. I, Pt II, pp. 434-5, 475.

[26] Alexander Maxwell, *Old Dundee prior to the Reformation* (Edinburgh, 1891), p. 286.

10. WAE WORTH MARYAGE!

[1] Procopius, *The Secret History*, trans. and ed. G. A. Williamson (London, 1966), p. 84.

[2] Stubbes, *Anatomy of the Abuses in England*, p. 149.

[3] *Statutes of the Scottish Church*, pp. cii-ciii.

[4] Archibald Campbell (ed.), *Chronicon de Lanercost* (Maitland Club, Edinburgh, 1839), p. 109.

[5] *S.A.S.*, Vol. X, pp. 501ff.

[6] *British Calendar Customs: Scotland*, Vol. II, p. 212.

[7] Ibid., p. 208.

[8] Ibid.

[9] *S.A.S.*, Vol. XIV, p. 526.

[10] *Maitland Folio Manuscript*, Vol. I, p. 176.

[11] *S.A.S.*, Vol. XII, p. 6.

[12] 'Of May' in *The Poems of Alexander Scott*, ed. A. K. Donald (E.E.T.S., E.385, London, 1902), p. 17.

[13] Robert Burns, *The Merry Muses of Caledonia*, ed. James Barke and Sidney Goodsir Smith (London, 1965), p. 101.

[14] Wilson, *Memorials of Edinburgh in the Olden Time*, Vol. II, p. 181.

[15] William Hore, *The Every-Day Book, 1826-1827*, quoted in *British Calendar Customs: Scotland*, Vol. II, pp. 223-4; also plate 7.

[16] *Maitland Folio Manuscript*, Vol. I, pp. 243-4.

[17] *The Poetical Works of Sir David Lyndsay of the Mount*, ed. David Laing (Edinburgh, 1879), Vol. III, pp. 40-2.

[18] Joseph Strutt, *The Sports and Pastimes of the English People* (London, 1876), Bk IV, p. 464.

[19] *The Chronicle of Perth*, p. 67.

[20] R. L. Greene, *The Early English Carols* (Oxford, 1935), p. 448n; E. Estyn Evans, *Irish Folk-Ways* (London, 1957), pp. 264-5.

[21] MacNeill, *The Festival of Lughnasa*, p. 602.

[22] Greene, *The Early English Carols*, p. 307.

11. THE BALL O' KIRRIEMUIR

[1] *S.A.S.*, Vol. II, p. 365.

[2] Ibid., Vol. XVII, p. 519.

[3] *County Folklore, Fife*, p. 202.

[4] *S.A.S.*, Vol. XI, p. 114.

[5] *The Poetical Works of Robert Burns*, ed. J. Logie Robertson (Oxford, 1948), p. 164.

[6] T. Crawford, *Burns, A Study of the Poems and Songs* (Edinburgh, 1960), pp. 67-9.

[7] Henry Grey Graham, *Social Life in Scotland in the Eighteenth Century* (Edinburgh, 1937), Vol. II, p. 46.

[8] Ibid., Vol. I, pp. 186-7.

[9] *Maitland Club Miscellany*, Vol. I, Pt II, pp. 435-6.

[10] *S.A.S.*, Vol. XXI, p. 146.

[11] Ibid., Vol. XV, p. 636.

[12] Brown, *Early Travellers in Scotland*, p. 285.

[13] *The Merry Muses of Caledonia*, p. 157.

[14] *S.A.S.*, Vol. XVII, p. 95.

[15] Allan Ramsay, *The Tea Table Miscellany* (Glasgow, 1876), Vol. I, p. 67.

[16] McPherson, *Primitive Beliefs in the North East of Scotland*, pp. 125-6.

[17] Frazer, *The Golden Bough*, Pt V, Vol. I, pp. 225-7.

[18] *County Folklore, Fife*, p. 210.

[19] Ibid., p. 211, and Frazer, *The Golden Bough*, Pt V, Vol. I, pp. 155-61.

[20] *The Merry Muses of Caledonia*, p. 31.

[21] *Chronicon de Lanercost*, pp. 99-100.

[22] *Statutes of the Scottish Church*, p. 40.

[23] R. J. Mitchell, *The Laurels and the Tiara: Pope Pius II* (London, 1962), p. 69.

[24] Ibid., p. 70.

[25] *The Commentaries of Pius II*, trans. F. A. Gregg (abridged, Capricorn Books, 1959), pp. 19-20.

[26] James Cranstoun (ed.), *Satirical Poems of the Time of the Reformation* (S.T.S., Edinburgh), Pt I, p. 201.

[27] S. L. Gardiner, *History of the Commonwealth and Protectorate* (London, 1903), Vol. I, pp. 340-1.

[28] John Mackintosh, *History of Civilisation in Scotland* (London, 1893), pp. 229, 233.

[29] *Burgh Records of Edinburgh*, Vol. III, pp. 82-3.

[30] Ibid., pp. 85-6, 129, 135, 152, 154.

[31] Duncan Mactavish (ed.), *Minutes of the Synod of Argyll* (Scottish Historical Society, Edinburgh, 1943), 3rd series, Vol. 37.

[32] Edward Burt, *Letters from a Gentleman in the North of Scotland*, ed. R. A. Jamieson (Edinburgh, 1876), Vol. I, pp. 194-5.

[33] Major, *History of Greater Britain*, p. 151.

[34] Boece, *The Chronicles of Scotland*, Bellenden translation, Vol. II, p. 391.

[35] *Statutes of the Scottish Church*, pp. 44 and 18.

[36] *The Poems of Alexander Scott*, p. 5.

[37] *S.A.S.*, Vol. IV, p. 229.

[38] James Boswell, *A Journal of a Tour to the Hebrides with Samuel Johnson, LL.D.*, ed. T. Ratcliffe Barrett (London, 1928), pp. 174-5.

12. THE THING THAT WOMEN MOST DESIRE

[1] John Knox, *History of the Reformation in Scotland*, ed. W. C. Dickinson (London, 1949), Vol. I, p. xliv.

[2] Ibid., Vol. II, pp. 14-15.

[3] Brown, *Early Travellers in Scotland*, p. 39.

[4] *Maitland Folio Manuscript*, Vol. I, pp. 390-1, also p. 193.

[5] Dillon and Chadwick, *The Celtic Realms*, p. 153.

[6] Tacitus, *De Vita Agricolae*, 16.2, ed. H. Furneaux and J. G. C. Anderson (Oxford, 1922), p. 13, and *The Annals*, 14.35.1, ed. H. Furneaux, H. F. Pelham, and C. D. Fisher (Oxford, 1907), Vol. II, p. 278.

[7] Dio Cassius, *Roman History*, Bk LXII, Vol. VIII, p. 85.

[8] Ammianus Marcellinus, *Historium Rerum Gestarum*, XV.12.1, ed. J. C. Rolfe (Loeb ed., 1956), Vol. I, p. 195.

[9] Dio Cassius, *Roman History*, Bk LXII, Vol. VIII, p. 93.

[10] Tacitus, *The Annals*, 14.35-7.

[11] Dillon and Chadwick, *The Celtic Realms*, p. 153.

[12] *The Cattle Raid of Cualnge* [Tain Bo Cuailnge], ed. L. W. Faraday (London, 1904), pp. 16, 71, 108-12.

[13] Ibid., p. 2.

[14] Tacitus, *The Annals*, 14.30.

[15] Dio Cassius, *Roman History*, Bk LXII, Vol. VIII, pp. 91-3.

[16] Ibid., p. 95.

[17] Dillon and Chadwick, *The Celtic Realms*, pp. 35-6.

[18] Tacitus, *The Annals*, 12.40.

[19] *The Cattle Raid of Cualnge*, pp. 7, 74-5, 77, 81-2, and 139.

[20] Nancy Pomer, 'Classes of Women described in the Senchas Mor', Pt II of Thurneysen and others, *Studies in Early Irish Law*, p. 139 (see note 22).

[21] *The Cattle Raid of Cualnge*, pp. 60-1.

[22] R. Thurneysen and others, *Studies in Early Irish Law* (Dublin, 1936), p. 87.

[23] Anderson, *Early Sources of Scottish History*, Vol. I, p. 204.

[24] Thurneysen and others, *Studies in Early Irish Law*, pp. 271-3.

[25] Anderson, *Early Sources of Scottish History*, Vol. I, pp. 203-4.

[26] Otta F. Swire, *The Highlands and their Legends* (Edinburgh, 1963), p. 117.

[27] William F. Skene (ed.), *Chronicles of the Picts, Chronicles of the Scots*, etc. (Edinburgh, 1967), pp. 3, 393.

[28] Martin Martin, *A Voyage to St. Kilda . . .*, ed. Donald J. Macleod (Stirling, 1934), pp. 412ff.

[29] Boece, *The Chronicles of Scotland*, Bellenden translation, Vol. I, pp. 20, 21.

[30] O. F. Swire, *Skye, the Island and its Legends* (Oxford, 1952), p. 197, and *S.A.S.*, Vol. XVI, p. 538.

[31] Andrew of Wyntoun, *The Original Chronicle*, Vol. VI, p. 90.

[32] Robert Lindsay of Pitscottie, *Historie and Cronicles of Scotland* (S.T.S., Edinburgh, 1899), Vol. I, p. 63.

[33] Pitcairn, *Ancient Criminal Trials in Scotland*, Vol. I, p. 162; Vol. II, pp. 346, 347.

[34] Ibid., Vol. II, pp. 381-2.

[35] *S.A.S.*, Vol. XIX, p. 294.

[36] Alexander Campbell, *A Manuscript History of Craignish*, ed. Herbert Campbell. *Miscellany of the Scottish History Society*, Vol. IV, 3rd series, No. 9 (Edinburgh, 1926), pp. 248-9.

[37] Pitscottie, *Historie and Cronicles of Scotland*, Vol. I, pp. 146-7.

[38] *The Chronicle of Perth*, p. 6.

[39] J. G. Fyfe and R. S. Rait, *Scottish Diaries and Memoirs, 1550-1740* (Stirling, 1928), pp. 155-6.

[40] *A Brief and True Relation of What Fell Out on the Lord's Day, the 23rd of July 1637*, quoted in Janet Lane, *The Reign of King Covenant* (London, 1956), p. 37.

[41] *S.A.S.*, Vol. XI, pp. 28-9.

[42] Fyfe and Rait, *Scottish Diaries and Memoirs*, p. 253.

[43] M. E. M. Donaldson, *Scotland's Suppressed History* (London, 1935), p. 102.

[44] 'Of Wemenkynd', *The Poems of Alexander Scott*, p. 59.

13. Mother to Daughter

[1] H. M. Chadwick, *Early Scotland* (Cambridge, 1949), pp. 92-4.

[2] Sjoestedt, *Gods and Heroes of the Celts*, pp. 60-1.

[3] *The Mabinogion*, trans. Gwyn and Thomas Jones (London, 1949), pp. 55-67.

[4] Dillon and Chadwick, *The Celtic Realms*, pp. 117-18.

[5] Ibid., pp. 94, 154.

[6] Tacitus, *The Annals*, 12.40.

[7] Nora Chadwick, *Celtic Britain*, p. 20.

[8] Ibid., p. 21.

[9] Tacitus, *The Annals*, 14.31.

[10] Dio Cassius, *Roman History*, Bk XII, Vol. VIII.

[11] Powell, *The Celts*, pp. 284-5; Fox, *South West England*, p. 111.

[12] Dio Cassius, *Roman History*, Bk LXXVII, Vol. IX.

[13] Ibid.

[14] Sir John Rhys, *The Welsh People* (London, 1902), p. 45.

[15] Bede, *A History of the English Church and People*, trans. Leo Shelley-Price (London, 1955), Bk I, pp. 38-9.

[16] Anderson, *Early Sources of Scottish History*, Vol. I, pp. cxiii-clviii; H. M. Chadwick, *Early Scotland*, pp. 89ff.

[17] Ibid., p. 91.

[18] Anderson, *Early Sources of Scottish History*, Vol. I, p. 122n.

[19] Henderson, *The Picts*, pp. 68-71.

[20] Anderson, *Early Sources of Scottish History*, Vol. I, pp. 7-8.

[21] Ibid., p. 7n.

[22] Ibid., pp. 127-9.

[23] Chadwick and others, *Studies in the Early British Church*, pp. 273-357.

[24] *S.A.S.*, Vol. X, p. 146.

[25] Henderson, *The Picts*, pp. 94-6.

[26] Boece, *The Chronicles of Scotland*, Vol. II, p. 33.

[27] H. M. Chadwick, *Early Scotland*, pp. 95ff.

[28] Andrew of Wyntoun, *The Original Chronicle*, Vol. IV, pp. 272ff.

[29] John of Fordun, *The Chronicle of the Scottish Nation*, Vol. II, pp. 299-300.

[30] *S.A.S.*, Vol. XV, pp. 134-5.

[31] Quoted in Brown, *Early Travellers in Scotland*, p. 276.

[32] Ibn Battuta, *Travels in Asia and Africa*, trans. H. A. R. Gibb (London, 1957), pp. 320-1.

[33] Ibid., pp. 337 and 335.

[34] Francis Rennell Rodd, *People of the Veil* (London, 1926), pp. 148-9. 151-2.

[35] Ibid., pp. 167-9.

[36] Ibid., pp. 170, 265, and 294.

[37] Lloyd Cabot Briggs, *Tribes of the Sahara* (Harvard, 1960), pp. 123-5.

[38] Ibid., p. 128.

[39] Ibid., p. 133.

[40] Ibid., pp. 131-2.

[41] Rodd, *People of the Veil*, pp. 173-5.

[42] Henri Lhote, *The Search for the Tassili Frescoes*, trans. A. H. Broderick (London, 1960), pp. 111-12.

14. ISLANDS OF WOMEN

[1] Euripides, *The Bacchae and Other Plays*, trans. Philip Vellacott (London, 1954), p. 188.

[2] Livy, *History of Rome*, XXXIX.8, Vol. XI, pp. 240-3.

[3] Ibid., XXXIX.13, Vol. XI, p. 253.

[4] Tacitus, *Germania*, 40, 43.

[5] Strabo, *Geography*, IV.4, Vol. II, p. 429.

[6] Ross, *Pagan Celtic Britain*, p. 40 and plates 12a and b.

[7] Pomponius Mela, *Chorographia*, III.6.

[8] Geoffrey of Monmouth, *Vita Merlini*, ll. 901-23.

[9] *Historia Brittonum*, p. 414.

[10] MacCulloch, *The Religion of the Ancient Celts*, p. 385, and *S.A.S.*, Vol. XVII, p. 283.

[11] Anderson, *Early Sources of Scottish History*, Vol. I, pp. 143-4.

[12] Sir Donald Munro, *A Description of the Western Islands of Scotland called Hybrides*, ed. D. J. Macleod (Stirling, 1934), p. 500.

[13] Martin, *A Description of the Western Islands of Scotland*, p. 292.

[14] Ibid., p. 123.

[15] Giraldus Cambrensis, *The Topography of Ireland*, pp. 96-7.

[16] Ibid., p. 98.

[17] Ibid., p. 106.

[18] P. Ovidius Naso, *Die Fasten*, ed. Franz Bömer (Heidelberg, 1958), Vol. II, p. 374.

[19] Ibid., Vol. I, pp. 280-5.

[20] Pomponius Mela, *Chorographia*, III.6.

[21] C. Kerényi, *The Gods of the Greeks* (London, 1951), pp. 58-9.

[22] Apollonius Rhodius, *Argonautica*, ll. 583-662.

[23] Diodorus Siculus, *Bibliotheke Historike*, III.54, 55.

[24] E. R. Dodds (ed.), *Bacchae* of Euripides (Oxford, 1960), commentary, pp. 62-3.

[25] Diodorus Siculus, *Bibliotheke Historike*, III.53.

[26] Livy, *History of Rome*, XXXIX.13.

[27] Euripides, *Bacchae*, ed. Dodds, pp. xi-xii, 62-5.

[28] Kerényi, *The Gods of the Greeks*, p. 60.

[29] Euripides, *Bacchae*, ed. Dodds, pp. xii-xiv.

[30] *British Calendar Customs: Scotland*, Vol. II, p. 150.

[31] Martin, *A Description of the Western Islands of Scotland*, p. 179.

[32] Euripides, *Bacchae*, trans. Vellacott, p. 204.

[33] Ibid., pp. 216-17.

[34] J. G. Frazer (ed.), *Pausonius's Description of Greece* (London, 1913), Vol. I, p. 548; Vol. V, p. 542.

15. LINEAMENTS OF GRATIFIED DESIRE

[1] J. H. Pollen, *Papal Negotiations with Queen Mary* (Scottish Historical Society, Edinburgh), pp. 528-9.

[2] Major, *History of Greater Britain*, p. 177.

[3] C. S. Lewis, 'The Anthropological Approach' in *English and Medieval Studies presented to J. R. R. Tolkien* (London, 1962), p. 219.

[4] *S.A.S.*, Vol. XII, p. 440.

[5] Ibid.

Glossary

abone: above
aboucht: bought
alkin: of every sort
alyt: ailed, hurt
ane: one, only, alone
anis, anys: one
annamalit: enamelled, variegated
anteris: adventures
apon(e) loft: loudly, aloft
armeit: hermit
assay: test, make trial of
attour: over, above
aver, avoir: cart-horse, old nag
awin: own

badie: bawdy
bagit hors: stallion
baid: waiting
bair: boar
bancot: banquet
band: bond
bardus: sports, amusements
baret, barrat: trouble, deception, strife, vexation
barne, bairne: bairn, child, man
bask: bitter, distasteful
bauchles: documents
bawch: feeble
be: by, about
behud: behoved, had to
behuffit: behoved, had to
beild(1): suppurated, swollen
beild(2): shielded, sheltered, refuge
beit: supply, amend, avail
bejaip: beguile

bek: sign, gesture with head or fingers
belyf: swiftly, at once
ben: in the inner room or part of a house; *but*: opposite of *ben*
berand: neighing, roaring
berne: man; *bernis*: men
beswick: trick, deceive
beuche(s), bewis: bough(s)
bewrie: reveal
biggingis: buildings
billeis, billies: companions, close friends
bird, see byrde
birline: a kind of boat
birs: bristles
blatter: blether, boast
blenk: to glance
blenkis: blinks, looks
blent: glanced, blinked
blew: downcast, dejected
blynis: cease, leave off
bo: to cry bo! or boo!
bogane: bogle, evil spirit
bogill: bogle, spectre, goblin
borit: pierced, bored
bourd, bourding, bowrd: sport, entertainment, jesting
boure, bowre: bower
bowdyn: swollen
bowit: bowed, bent
bownis: get ready, prepare; *bun*: prepared
brade, braid, breid, brod: broad
braid: start, spring, toss
brand: brawned, muscled

brankand: swaggering
brim: fierce
brist: burst
broddit: spurred
brukill: brittle, frail, lascivious
buclair: buckler, shield, (fig.) protection, modesty
buddis: bribes
bukis, buikis: books
bukky: whelk-shell, tongue-in-cheek
bumbart: drone
bun, see bownis
burrow: borough, burgh; *hie burrow landis*: houses in a high or principal burgh
buskit: dress, deck out
bussis: bushes
but, see ben
but, bot: without, except
bute: remedy
buthman: shopkeeper
byrde: bride, maiden

cabeld: haltered, tethered
caf: chaff
cailleach: old woman, nun, hag, goddess
caller: fresh, newly gathered
cappill: horse
carle, carll: man
carping: complaint
carpit: chatted, discoursed
carybald, caribald: cannibal, monster
cassin: cast
causey: causeway, paved street
cerne: circle
chaftis: jaws, chops
chaip: escape
chalmer, chalmir: chamber, bedroom
chalonis: blankets
cheide: chide, reproach
cheis: choose

chenyeis: chains
cheris: cherish
chesit: chose, chosen
cheson: cause, occasion, reason
chevist: assigned by deed
chuf: churl
chymis: mansion
claggit: clotted, clogged, filthy
clapping: fondling
clappis: pats, fondles
cleikit: start (to sing)
coist: cost, expense
compositouris: those empowered to settle cases in the king's exchequer
conable: knowledgeable
contienance, contynance: countenance
coppud: bad-tempered
cors: corpse, body
cought: could
cout: colt
cowit: cropped
crabit: offended
crack: converse, chat
crapotee: toadstone
craudoune, craudone: coward
crelis: creels, paniers
cruke: bent, crooked
crynd: wasted, shrivelled
cumaris: gossips
cummerans: encumbrance
cummerlik: like gossips, friendly
curage: virility, vigour, courage
curch: a woman's head-dress, kerchief
cure: care, management
curiouslie: with care, carefully, artfully
curtly: courtly
cury: dish of food

daine, dane: haughty
dainte, daynte: esteem, honour
dammis: dames, matrons

dammosalis: damsels, maids

damys: makes water

dangerous: haughty, difficult to deal with

daw: dawn

deasil: sunwise, in the same direction as the sun moves

deboshrie: debauchery

dede: death

delle, dele: deal, contend; *dalt*: dealt, engaged in

dere: injure

derne: secret, dark, darkness

detressit: hanging in tresses, combed out

devoid: get rid of, void

dink: neat, trim

dirkin: eavesdrop, listen in secret, lurk

dirrie dantoun: fanciful name of a dance

dispone: dispose

dogonis: worthless fellows

dollin: buried

dolly: doleful, dismal

donkit: make dank, moisten

dorty: pettish, unwilling, finicking, supercilious

dotit: foolish, 'dotty'

dow: does, are able

draucht: draught, pulling

dre: endure

drup(e): drooping, slack

drwry: love

dule: sorrow

dupped: opened

dyk: ditch, bank

dyvour: bankrupt

e: eye

edderis: adders

effeiris: behaviour, bearing, gestures

eild: age

eik: also

eldnyng: jealousy

Elfhame: fairyland

ellumynit: illuminated

elrich, elrege, elritche: elvish, fairy

eme(z): uncle(s)

ene: eyes

engranyt: dyed

engyne: disposition, talent

erd, eird: earth

Erishe: Irish, Erse

ersis: arses

evudens: evidence

ewin: even

ewin faw: evenfall

ewynnis: evenings

exeme: examine

expremit: expressed

fairheid: fairness, beauty

fa'll dae it: who'll do it

falwes: fallow ground

falyeid: failed, fallen off or away, perished

fangis: takes

fant: weak, listless

farcy: a disease of horses akin to glanders

fassones, fassoun, fessoun: fashions, customs, behaviour

faut: fault

fayerye, pharie, phairie: fairyland, the fairy people

feid: enmity

feill(1): many

feill(2): perception, knowledge

fenyeit, feynit: feigned

fepillis: fidgets, dribbles

ferliful, ferly: wonderful

fessoun, see fassones

fetrit: fettered, held close

feyr, fair, fere: comparison
fitraces: foot races
flessly: carnally
flewne: phlegm
flone: arrow
flouris: flowers
flycherit: flittered, fluttered
flyngand: flinging, prancing
flyrit: look lustfully
flyte: quarrel, scold
fonde, fand: found, came upon
fone: foolish
forgeit: forged
forky: vigorous, strong (?)
forlane: useless
forleit: lost, abandoned
forsy, forcy: vigorous, strong, full of force
fourtht: forth
fowk, foks: folk
fra: after
freiris: friars
freke, freik: fellow, man
fruster: frustrate, empty
fulyeit: defiled, exhausted
fumyll: fumble
fure(1): fared, went
fure(2): person, man, fellow (?)
furnyse: furnish
furth bering: bearing, carriage
fyllt: defiled

ga: go
galwes: gallows
gane(*st*): (most) suitable
garray: commotion, disturbance, uproar
gatis: ways; thus *gatis*: in these ways
geir: gear, substance, property
geit: jet
gent: beautiful
gentryce: ladylike, nobly born

gert: made, caused to
gib: tom-cat
gif: if
gillot: mare
girnand: grinning, grimacing
gladderit: besmeared
glar: mud, slime
glemys: glances
glew: glee, merriment
gleyd: a live coal
glore: glory
goif: gaze
gois: goes
gonne: began
goreis: filth, matter
gorgeit: gorged, encrusted
graythhit, grathit: adorned, dressed, made ready
gressis, gress: grasses, grass
grit(*e*), *grete, grett*: great
grome: groom, man
gutaris: gutters, channels
gymp: neat, graceful

hache: ache
haill: whole
hair: grey, hoary
haith: faith
halok: foolish
hals(*e*): neck, throat
halwes: saints
haly: holy
hanyt: spared, unspent
harde: heard
hatz: has
hautand: haughty, proud, elevated
hechar: higher
heddir: heather
heildit: concealed, covered
hekill: hackle, flax-comb
heklis: hackles, combs
herle: heron

heryit: harried, pillaged
hething: mockery, scorn
heved: head
heynd(1): pleasant, sheltering
heynd(2): person
hiddis: hides, skins
hing: hang
ho: she
hogeart: term of abuse, meaning uncertain
holyn: holly
hostit: coughed
houghmagandie: fornication
huirdom: whoredom
hur, hure: whore
hurcheone: hedgehog
hutit: hooted, despised (?)

ilk: each
ilkane: each one
inthrang: pushed or thrust in

jolie, joly, iolly: pretty, handsome, spirited, amorous, jolly
jolyus: jealous
josit: chosen

keik: peep, look
keipet: kept
kekill: cackle
kell: coif, woman's head-dress
kemm, kemmit: comb, combed
kend: known
kenrik: kingdom
kep: care to, wish to
keyth: show, make known, recognise
kirsp: a delicate fabric like lawn
klerk: clerk, sage
knaip: boy, lad
know(e): mound
kythis: makes known, shows

ladd(e): led
laif: rest, remainder
laitis: manners, behaviour, habits
lap: leaped
larbar(is): weak or impotent person(s)
lat, late: let
latis: behaviour
lave: rest, remainder
le: lie
led, leid, leyd: man, person of either sex
leif, lyff(e): line
leir: learn
leit: behave
lele: leal, loyal
lettis: pretend
leuch, lewch: laughed
lichory: lechery, lewdness
lechtlyit: despised, slighted
lig: lie
lige: liege, overlord
list: desires
lob: clumsy
loffit: praised
loik: warm
loppin: leaped
losingaris: deceivers
lous: discharge
loutit: bowed down, abased himself
lown(e): worthless person, boor
luff, luif, lufe: love
luffairis: lovers
lugeing: lodging
lumbart: lombard, banker
lume: tool, penis
lust: pleasure, desire
lychour: fornicator
lyll: little
lynne: leave off, stop
lyre: face
lyth: listen

maik: mate

makdome: form, figure, elegant appearance

mangit: bewildered, rendered stupid or helpless (?)

marrowis: companions

maystres: arts, skills

mekle: great, large

mell: mingle, meddle, to have intercourse with, to copulate

mensk: manliness, dignity

menskit: honoured

menys: take pity on

merrens: (obscure) perhaps deserving (Lat. *merens*), or corrupt for merrenes: merriness, pleasure

merrys: to make merry, to pleasure

meth: met

meynis: means, management, measures

mirriest, murgust: merriest

misteris: business

mo, mae: more

molet: bit (of a bridle)

moy: mild, tame, demure

mydding: midden, dung-heap

mynt: offer, attempt

mynyonis: minions, lovers

mystirs: needs

na(1): no, not

na(2): than, nor

ne: nor

neiff: neave, fist

nicht, nyt: night

nocht, noch, nout: not, nought

note: use, employ

noy: irritation, annoyance

ocht: ought, anything

on breid: abroad

onkend: unknown

onone: anon, presently

on steid of: instead of

ony: any

or: before

oulkis: weeks

our: over

pako: peacock

papingay: parrot

pappis, paps: breasts

parochynis: parishes

pastance: pastime

peddar: pedlar, huckster

peist: beast, monster

percace: perchance

perfurneis: accomplish

peronall: wanton young woman, concubine

pert: pretty, lively

Peychtes: Picts

pik: pitch

pillie: post, stake, penis

pische: piss

pitht: pith, strength, vigour

plack: a trifle or a trifling sum

plane: complaint

plantit: established, settled in a place

plenis: complain, make a plaint

plet: intertwined

ploddeill: a band of threshers, a gang armed with cudgels

preis: press, crowd

presandlie: at once, presently

preve: privately, secretly

preve: prove; *preveit*: proved, tested

prime: early morning, sunrise

prunya: preen, dress, adorn

pykis: prickles, thorns

quha: who

quhair: where

quhairfoir: wherefore

quhairoff: whereof
quhame, *quhome*: whom
quhen: when
quhilis: at times
quhilk(e): which
quhill: while, until, till
quhilum: at times, from time to time
quhite, *quhyt*: white
quhow: how
quhyt: quite, white

raches: a type of hunting dogs
rad: afraid
ragment: list, discourse, evidence
raid, *rade*: rode
raid: rod
raiffis: raves, talks nonsense
rak, *rakit*: reck, care, recked, cared
rak: stretch, crack
rakit: went
ralyeis, *ralyeit*: rallies, jests, rallied, jested
ratton: rat
raucht: reached, passed around
reaggeth: shaggy
rede wod: furious
reilling: railing, raillery
remeid: remedy, remedied
rennes: runs, is reputed
renone: renown
rewit: rued, repented
rid: advise
rif: rive, split
rise: brushwood, bushes
roche: rock
roelle bone: ivory
ron: thorn, hawthorn
rone: ran
roust: disturbance
rousty: rusty
rowndis: whisper
rownis: whisper

ruch, *ruf*: rough
ruit: root
rusing: boasting

Sabot: God
sad: sober, demure, serious
saghe, *saugh*: saw
sair: sore
sakles: innocent, blameless
sal: shall
salwes: willows
samyn: same
sane: make the sign of the cross, cross oneself
sanyne: blessing, making the sign of the cross
sarie: sorry, wretched
saw: utterance, saying
say: essay, make trial of, attempt
scart: scratch
schaiffyne: shaven
schalk: churl
schawis: shows
sched: divided, parted, disposed
schedis: injures, hurts, damages (or divides)
schene: bright, beautiful
schetus: sheets
schevill: wry, twisted
schill: piercing, shrill
scho, *shue*: she
schore: threat
schowis: shoves
schyre: clear, shining, sheer
scunner: disgust
scutarde: incontinent
sege: man
seignorie: authority, impressive bearing or appearance
selis: seals
selit: sealed
selle: saddle, seat

semblit: assembled
sen: since
sentence: opinion, speech
serk: sark, shirt, nightgown
sew: sue, plead
sich, sicht, sych: sigh
sicir, sickir: sure, safe
side: the fairy people
siller: silver
sindry: sundry, various
skabbit: scabbed, shabby
skarth: cormorant
skeich: shy
sker: scared, timid
slaps: gaps or breaches
sloknyt: slaked, extinguished
slokyn: slake, satisfy
smake: wretched
smolt: soft, mild
smy: wretch
solist: solicit
solistaris: solicitors
soune: sound
south, sooth, suth: truth
sowch: sough, sighing
spedelie: successfully, to the purpose
speir: ask, question
spreit: spirit
spulyeit: spoiled, despoiled
spynist: opened, blown
staiffis: stuffs
staig: stag
stangand: stinging
stekill: bolt, pin
stoppell: stopper
stound: sharp pain, sting, stunning
　blow
straide: strode, bestrode
stramp: press down
stunyst: astonished, bewildered
sugeorne: delay, sojourn
sulde: should

surquidré: arrogance, presumption
swalme: swelling
swanquhit: swan-white
swapit: tossed off, quaffed
swerf: faint, swoon
swonne, swoune: swoon
swylke, soche: such
swyr: neck, declivity, corrie
sych, see sich
syde: at large, expansively
syle: mislead
synd: wash
syndrie: sundry, several
syne: then, after, afterwards
syphyr: cipher, of no account
sythis: times

tane: taken
taste: handle, feel, test
tene: anger, misery
ter: tar
terne: fierce
tersis: tarses, penises
therk: dark
thewis: habits, customs
thirlit: bound, enslaved
tho: then
thocht: thought
thole: bear, endure
thra: bold, boldly
thrang: thronged, crowded
tiend, teynd: tithe
tothir: the other, the second
traist: true, trusty, trustworthy
tramort: dead body, corpse
trattles: foolish talk
trawe: device, trick
tretable: tractable, compliant
trow: believe
tuichandly: touchingly
tume: empty, vacant
turkas: tongs, pincers

turtoris: turtledoves
twined: deprived
tydis me: it betides me, it is time for me
tyrit: tired
tysed: enticed

uncouth: strange, unknown
unfulyeit: unexhausted

vardour: verdure
vertu: virtue, force, effect

waill: choose
wait: know
walkand: waking, awake
wallidrag: sloven
walteris: welter, toss
war: worse
warieand, wariand: cursing
waris, warit: spend, lay out; expended, sent out
warpit: cast, uttered
wauchtit: quaffed
wedis: clothes
weet: wet

wene: expect, think
wer: worse
wicht(is): wight (s), person(s)
wichtnes: strength
wlonk(es): fair ones
wobat: caterpillar
wod, wode: mad, furious
woddit: wedded, married
wolroun: wild boar, beast, brute
wosp: stopple, wisp of straw
wourth, worth: be, become
wrokin: avenged
wthyr: other
wychtis, see wicht

yaip: eager, active
yait: gate
Yc, Y, *J*: I
yeild: impotent
yerd: yard, penis
ygo: gone
yie: yea, yes
ying: young
ympe: sapling, young tree
yok, yolk: clasp, embrace
yoldin: yielded, yielding, limp
yuke: itch

Index

Aberdeen Breviary, The, 44

Aeneas Silvius (Pius II), 191-2; *The Commentaries of Pius II*, 191-2

Ailred of Rievaulx, 103-4; *Epistola de Genealogia Regum Anglorum*, 86-7

Aine, 43, 66-9, 71

Ancient Criminal Trials in Scotland, see Pitcairn, Robert

Andrew of Wyntoun, *The Original Chronicle*, 46, 51-2, 213, 229, 230-1

Anglo-Saxon Chronicle, 144

Annales Cambriae, 51

Anton, A. E., 160-2

Arden of Faversham, 153

Aristophanes, *Lysistrata*, 260-1

Arthur, King, 29, 39, 50, 51-3, 60-1, 141-2, 240, 265

'Ball o' Kirriemuir, The', 187-9

Barke, James, *The Merry Muses of Caledonia* (ed. with S. G. Smith), 187-8, 189

Bataille Loquifer, 58, 60

Battuta, Ibn, 233-4, 237, 238

Bede, *A History of the English Church and People*, 141, 219, 225

Boadicea (Buduica, Budicca), 136, 204-6, 207-8, 209, 217, 222, 223, 236, 268

Boece, Hector, *The Chronicles of Scotland*, 46, 51, 52, 195, 212, 229

Book of Leinster, 66, 227

Boswell, James, 197

Bovet, Richard, *Pandemonium, or the Devil's Cloister*, 90, 105, 111, 118-19, 120, 121, 122

Briggs, Lloyd Cabot, 236-7, 238

Brigit (Brigid), 43, 44, 45, 46, 208, 248, 250, 251, 253-4

Brown, P. Hume, 183

Burgh Records of Edinburgh, 193

Burns, Robert, 181; 'Blyth Will an' Bessie's Wedding', 184; 'Epistle to J. Lapraik', 181; 'Here's his Health in Water', 173; 'The Holy Fair', 181-2

Burt, Edward, 194

Caesar, Julius, *De Bello Gallico*, 134-5, 137

Campbell, Alexander, 214

Cartimandua, Queen, 204-5, 208, 209, 222, 223, 224, 268

Cassius Dio, see Dio Cassius

Chadwick, H. M., 220, 225-6, 229

Chadwick, Nora K., 51, 139, 204, 208, 221

Chaucer, Geoffrey: 'Against Women Inconstant' attrib., 15; *Parlement of Foules*, 150; 'The Parson's Tale', 199; 'The Wife of Bath's Tale', 13, 14, 132, 175, 198

Child, F. J., 56

Chronicle of Lanercost, The, 78, 117, 167-8, 169-70, 171, 190-1,

Chronicle of Perth, The, 41, 177

Chronicle of the Kings of the Picts, 44-5, 219, 225

Chronicle of the Picts, Chronicle of the Scots, 212

Chronicon de Lanercost, see Chronicle of Lanercost, The

Clapperton, —, 'Wa wourth maryage', 10-11, 174-5

Claris and Laris, 58

Dalyell, John Graham, 19, 42

Dean of Lismore's Book, 41

Dio Cassius, 135, 223-4; *Roman History*, 135-6, 142, 190, 205, 206, 207-8, 223-4, 226

Diodorus Siculus, 250

Dunbar, William: 'Lament for the Makaris', 50; 'Of a Dance in the Quenis Chalmer', 173; 'Of Ane Blak-Moir', 7; 'Of the Ladyis Solistaris at Court', 202-3; 'The Dance of the Sevin Deidly Synnis', 259; 'The Golden Targe', 7, 11-12, 13; 'To Aberdein', 12

Euripides, *Bacchae*, 241-2, 250-1, 252, 254

Evans, E. Estyn, 18

Evans Wentz, W. Y., 114

Fergusson, Robert, 54 ,125, 127

Festival of Lughnasa, The, see Mac-Neill, Máire

Floriant et Florete, 58

Frazer, Sir James George, *The Golden Bough*, 35, 77

Fyfe, J. G., and Rait, R. S., 215-16

Gardiner, S. R., *History of the Commonwealth and the Protectorate*, 192-3

Geoffrey of Monmouth: *The History of the Kings of Britain*, 38, 39-40, 50, 51, 52, 55, 141; *Vita Merlini* attrib., 54, 61, 240, 246, 250, 253

Gildas, *Liber Querulus de Excidio Britanniae*, 139-40, 141, 221, 225

Giraldus Cambrensis, 142, 248; *Descriptio Cambriae*, 142, 146, 155, 156, 221; *Topographia Hibernica*, 20, 138, 248-9, 251

Googe, Barnabe, *The Popish Kingdome or Reigne of Antichrist*, 22

Graham, Henry Grey, 182

Guenevere (Guanora, Gaynor, etc.), 51, 52-3, 55, 60-1, 141

Hay, Andrew, 106

Henderson, Isabel, 74

Holinshed, *Chronicles*, 46

Homer: *Iliad*, 256; *Odyssey*, 256

Howell, James, 19

Huth Merlin, 56

Jackson, K. H., 51, 228

James I, King of England, *Daemonologie*, 98, 99, 100

James I, King of Scotland, 'Peblis to the Play' attrib., 170-2

John of Fordun, *The Chronicle of the Scottish Nation*, 45, 86-7, 232-3

Keightley, Thomas, 20

Kennedy, William, *Annals of Aberdeen*, 169

Kirk, Robert, *The Secret Commonwealth*, 17, 79, 80, 90, 114, 121, 122

Kirke, Thomas, *A Modern Account of Scotland by an English Gentleman*, 183, 184

Knox, John: *History of the Reformation in Scotland*, 199-200; *The First Blast of the Trumpet against the Monstrous Regiment of Women*, 199-200

Lancelot, 58
Layamon, *Brut*, 55
Leborna-h'Uidre, 25, 62
Leslie, Bishop Jhone, *The Historie of Scotland*, 42, 44
'Lewd Ballet', 192
Lewis, C. S., 28, 264
Liber Hymnorum, 226
Life of St. Kentigern, 142-3, 227-8
Linklater, Eric, 218
Livy, *History of Rome*, 220, 242-4
Lloyd, Sir John Edward, 146
Loomis, R. S., 50, 53-4, 61
Lyndsay, Sir David, of the Mount, 106, 196; *Ane Satyre of the Thrie Estatis*, 194; 'Dialog Betuix Experience and ane Courteour', 176

Mabinogion, The, 25, 39, 40
Macbeth, King, 85, 229-32
MacCulloch, J. A., 32, 246
Machiavelli, N., *The Prince*, 260, 261
MacNeill, Máire, *The Festival of Lughnasa*, 43, 67, 153-5, 156
McPherson, J. M., 114
Maidens, the, 35-46 *passim*, 48, 54, 71, 73-4, 106, 125, 126, 186-7, 253
Major, John, 258; *Expositio in Matthaeum*, 13; *History of Greater Britain*, 54, 86, 194-5, 258
Malcolm Canmore, King (Malcolm III), 86-7, 143, 212, 230
Malory, Thomas, *Le Morte Darthur*, 54, 141, 264-5
Mandevile, Sir John, *see Voiage and Travaile . . .*
Mapes, Walter, 82, 109-10; *De Nugis Curialium*, 81-2, 107-12, 113, 115, 116, 117
Marcellinus, Ammianus, 206; *Historium Rerum Gestarum*, 205-6

Martin, Martin, 122; *A Description of the Western Islands of Scotland*, 19, 72, 78, 121-2, 123, 159-60, 161, 247, 253; *A Voyage to St. Kilda*, 212
Matres, Matronae, 31-2, 39, 43, 48, 54, 71, 225
Medb, Queen, 40-1, 207, 209-10, 221, 222, 223, 268
Mela, Pomponius, *Chorographia*, 245, 246, 250, 251, 252, 253
Merlin, 54, 62-5, 265
Merlin, or The Early History of King Arthur, 62-4
Merry Muses of Caledonia, The, see Barke, James
Minutes of the Synod of Argyll, 1639-1651, 144-5, 193-4
Montgomerie, Alexander, 46-7, 48, 49, 184, 185
Morer, Thomas, 233
Morgain la Fée, 53-64 *passim*, 240-1, 244, 250, 265, 268
Morrigan, 43, 53-4, 55, 210, 265
Munro, Sir Donald, 247

Nennius, *Historia Brittonum*, 138-9, 141, 246
Newes from Scotland, 1591, 99-100, 121
Niniane (Viviane), 56-7, 62-5

O'Rahilly, Thomas F., 66
Ovid: *Fasti*, 249; *Ars Amatoria*, 266
Owl and the Nightingale, The, 26

Papal Negotiations with Queen Mary, see Pollen, J. H.
Paton, Lucy Allen, 55, 56, 61
Pennant, *A Tour in Scotland*, 73, 158-9, 161
Pitcairn, Robert, *Ancient Criminal*

Trials in Scotland, 90-2, 94, 96-8, 213

Pitscottie, see Robert Lindsay of Pitscottie

Pliny, Natural History, 74, 76-7

Pollen, J. H., Papal Negotiations with Queen Mary, 257

Porteous, Alexander, 25

Procopius, The Secret History, 166

Prophecies of Merlin, The, 59

Queen of Elphame (Elfin, Fairy Queen, etc.), 47, 48, 53, 56, 57, 58, 59, 62, 83-4, 90, 92, 96, 98, 106-7

Ramsay, Allan, 'Polwart on the Green', 184-5

Records of Elgin, The, 170

Records of the Parish of Auchterhouse, Angus, The, 170

Records of the Presbyteries of Inverness and Dingwall, 1643-1688, 75

Register of the Bishopric of Moray, 164

Register of the Kirk Session of Humbie, 164

Registrum de Neubolte, 38

Richard of Hexham, De Gestis Stephani, 143-4

Robert Lindsay of Pitscottie, Historie and Cronicles of Scotland, 213, 214-15

Rodd, Francis Rennell, 235-6, 238

Romans of Partenay, The, or Lusignan (The Tale of Melusine), 112-13

St Adamnan, 211-12

St Augustine, City of God, 249

St Brigid (St Bridget, St Bride), 33, 39, 44, 45, 155, 227, 247, 248-9, 253

St Ciaran (St Kieran), 156-8

St David I, King, 50, 55, 86-7, 102, 103, 144, 168

St Jerome, 137; Libri duo adversus Jovinianum, 136, 137, 190, 214

St Kentigern (St Mungo), 51, 142-3, 221, 227-8, 232

St Margaret, 87, 143, 221, 231

St Patrick, 45, 138, 156

Scott, Alexander: 'Of May', 173, 175; 'Of Wemenkynd', 196, 218

Scott, Sir Walter: Letters on Demonology and Witchcraft, 98; The Heart of Midlothian, 127; The Minstrelsy of the Scottish Border, 104, 106

Secret Commonwealth, The, see Kirk, Robert

Shakespeare, William: Hamlet, 152; Macbeth, 46, 225

Sinclair, Sir John, The Statistical Account of Scotland, 14, 18, 72, 85, 157-8, 161, 180, 267-8

'Sir Cawline', 21

Sir Gawain and the Green Knight, 23, 60-1, 64, 265

Sir Orfeo, 12, 16-17

Skene, William F., 160

Statistical Account of Scotland, The, see Sinclair, Sir John

Statutes of Iona, The, 161-2

Statutes of the Scottish Church, 134, 167, 191, 195

Stenton, F. M., 139

Strabo, Geography, 135, 244-5, 249, 251, 255

Stubbes, Philip, The Anatomy of the Abuses in England . . . , 9, 167

Tacitus, Cornelius: De Vita Agricolae, 205; Germania, 244; The Annals, 206, 209, 222

Tain Bo Cualnge, 207-10, 221
Tain Bo Fraich, 40-1
Tale of Bricriu, The, 35
'Tam Lin', 83
'The vse of court so weill I knaw', 203
Thomas of Erceldoune, The Romance and Prophecies of (Thomas the Rhymer), 56, 57, 59, 83-4
Tirso de Molina, *El Burlador de Sevilla*, 262
Tripartite Life of St. Patrick, 37, 138
Turgot, Bishop, 87; *Life of Queen Margaret*, 143

Voiage and Travaile of Sir John Mandevile, Kt., The, 21

Wace, *Brut*, 141
Weird Sisters, 46-8, 71
Wheeler, R. E. M., 36
William of Newburgh, 102-4, 107, 109; *History*, 101-5, 112, 117
Wordsworth, Dorothy, 127
Wulfstan, Archbishop, *Sermon of Wulfstan to the English*, 139

Yellow Book of Lecan, 226